Goals of Civil Justice and Civil Procedure in Contemporary Judicial Systems

IUS GENTIUM

COMPARATIVE PERSPECTIVES ON LAW AND JUSTICE

VOLUME 34

For further volumes:
http://www.springer.com/series/7888

Alan Uzelac
Editor

Goals of Civil Justice and Civil Procedure in Contemporary Judicial Systems

Springer

Editor
Alan Uzelac
Department for Civil Procedure
Faculty of Law
University of Zagreb
Croatia

ISSN 1534-6781 ISSN 2214-9902 (electronic)
ISBN 978-3-319-03442-3 ISBN 978-3-319-03443-0 (eBook)
DOI 10.1007/978-3-319-03443-0
Springer Cham Heidelberg New York Dordrecht London

Library of Congress Control Number: 2014930010

Printed on acid-free paper

Springer is part of Springer Science+Business Media (www.springer.com)

Preface

Comparative research on civil procedure usually starts with the presupposition that the key notions of the discipline such as 'procedure', 'court' and 'civil justice' are generally similar and comparable. What is different, and what can be compared, are the technical elements, such as the rights and duties of the main actors in the process, the effects of their procedural activities and the legal institutions which define them. In a globalising world, one can expect convergence and harmonisation, simply because of the more intense communications and general effects of the globalisation of the economy. But contemporary development of national systems of civil justice demonstrates that simple explanations and solutions do not work. The reason why national judiciaries continue to show persistence in opposing the harmonisation and unification processes, so that even the fundamental notions of procedure like *res iudicata* or 'fair trial' are understood and accepted in a dramatically different way, lies beneath the surface: it is in the different fundamental attitudes regarding the goals and aims of civil procedure and the civil justice system in general.

Recognising the importance of the topic, the International Association of Procedural Law (IAPL) decided to devote a part of the 2012 Moscow Conference to the topic Goals of Civil Justice. Two main questions that had to be addressed were How do the goals of civil procedure differ from country to country? and What is the role of civil justice in the contemporary world? The following chapters are mainly derived from the reports presented at this conference. For the purpose of publication in this book they have been thoroughly revised, extended and updated to reflect the situation in September 2013. The ten conference contributions are expanded by an additional text, which fitted neatly the profile of this book and was based on a report from a separate conference held in Vilnius.

I hope that the readers will find that this book is much more than a mechanical collection of national reports which were summarised in one general paper. The intention of the editor was not to cover all jurisdictions, but to find excellent writers who are at the same time knowledgeable experts in comparative law, and motivate them to produce inspired papers that, when read together, cover a representative selection of all major legal traditions and systems. A journey through the chapters of this book reveals a great number of fundamental dilemmas that determine contemporary development of civil justice systems and shed a different light on the judicial reforms that happen around the globe. In the mosaic of contrasts and oppositions, special place is devoted to the continuing battle between the individualistic/liberal approach, and the collectivist/paternalistic approach (the battle in which, seemingly, paternalistic tendencies regain momentum in a number of justice systems). But other topical issues are discussed as well, like the attempts to ensure effective but still fair and accurate adjudication, differences between 'bureaucratic' judiciaries that process large numbers of routine cases, and 'policy-making' judiciaries that shape important decisions in representative or collective litigations that affect social and economic policies, as well as the pressures to reduce the expenses of justice systems, and demands to make them chiefly responsible to their users.

My gratitude goes to all contributors to this volume who showed a remarkable patience when dealing with my continuing requests to improve, update and clarify their contributions. I am in particular debt to Randolph W. Davidson who – once again – did a remarkable job improving and fine-tuning the language of this book, and to my research assistant Marko Bratković who provided valuable technical assistance in revising and formatting the contributions.

Zagreb, Croatia
September 2013

Alan Uzelac

Contents

Contributors

Inge Lorange Backer Department of Public and International Law, University of Oslo, Oslo, Norway

David Chan Barrister-at-law, Hong Kong, Hong Kong, China

Peter C.H. Chan School of Law, City University of Hong Kong, Hong Kong, China

Gergely Czoboly Faculty of Law, University of Pécs, Pécs, Hungary

Fu Yulin School of Law, Peking University, Haidian District, Beijing, China

Aleš Galič Department of Civil Procedure, Faculty of Law, University of Ljubljana, Ljubljana, Slovenia

Miklós Kengyel Faculty of Law, University of Pécs, Pécs, Hungary

Christian Koller Department of Civil Procedure, Faculty of Law, University of Vienna, Vienna, Austria

Richard Marcus Hastings College of Law, San Francisco, CA, USA

Dmitry Heroldovich Nokhrin The Constitutional Court of the Russian Federation, Saint Petersburg, Russia

Elisabetta Silvestri Dipartimento di Giurisprudenza, Università degli Studi di Pavia, Pavia, Italy

Alan Uzelac Faculty of Law, Zagreb University, Zagreb, Croatia

C.H. (Remco) van Rhee Faculty of Law, Maastricht University, Maastricht, The Netherlands

Teresa Arruda Alvim Wambier Catholic University of São Paulo, São Paulo, Brazil

Part I
General Synthesis

Chapter 1
Goals of Civil Justice and Civil Procedure in the Contemporary World

Global Developments – Towards Harmonisation (and Back)

Alan Uzelac

Abstract Some of the most thrilling topics of civil procedure are those that revisit its very roots. What are the goals of civil justice? This question seems to be simple only on the surface, viewed from the closed perspective of national law and jurisprudence. However, the moment when we embark on a comparative journey, the adventure starts. How do the goals of civil justice differ from country to country? Are they compatible? Is it possible at all to speak of the universal tasks of civil justice in the contemporary world? And, if not, are we making a mistake when we consider that 'judges' and 'courts' have the same meaning and same importance in all cultures? In this chapter, the author presents a synthetic study on these issues, based on the reports that present a particular approach to the goals of civil justice and civil procedure from the angle of a representative set of different contemporary legal traditions and systems.

1.1 Introduction

What is the goal of courts and judges in civil matters in the contemporary world? It would be easy to state the obvious and repeat that in all justice systems of the world the role of civil justice is to apply the applicable substantive law to the established facts in an impartial manner, and pronounce fair and accurate judgments. The devil is, as always, in the details. What is the perception of an American judge about his or her social role and function, and does it correspond to the perception of the judge in the People's Republic of China? What are the prevailing opinions on the goals of civil justice in doctrine and case law of Russia and Brazil? Do courts in

A. Uzelac (✉)
Faculty of Law, Zagreb University, Trg m. Tita 14, HR-10000 Zagreb, Croatia
e-mail: auzelac@pravo.hr

A. Uzelac (ed.), *Goals of Civil Justice and Civil Procedure in Contemporary Judicial Systems*, Ius Gentium: Comparative Perspectives on Law and Justice 34,
DOI 10.1007/978-3-319-03443-0_1, © Springer International Publishing Switzerland 2014

Hong Kong and in Hungary understand in the same way the need to balance accuracy and speed of court procedures, or to take into account public interests when adjudicating civil disputes?

The research presented in this book addresses the same set of these and other fundamental questions from the angle of various legal traditions in the contemporary world. It presents insights of reputed and knowledgeable authors who were able to bring profound insights from almost all corners of the globe. Indeed, in a small book it is difficult to claim that all globally relevant national systems of civil justice are covered. Instead, we tried to collect some typical and representative insights from major legal traditions, respecting at the same time geographical, cultural, political and historic diversity. In addition to contributions from Europe, Asia and North and South America, this book contains views from both the common law countries and the civil law countries. The contributions also cover the span of ideologically very different viewpoints (e.g. from the USA and mainland China), but also contain material regarding the countries that may be generally categorised as countries in a (post-) transition (Hungary, Russia, Slovenia, Croatia). The jurisdictions covered also display various levels of trust in their civil justice, which often correspond to the rather diverse levels of the overall effectiveness of their civil justice; it suffices to note the contrast between generally well-functioning systems, as in Norway or the Netherlands, and those burdened with systemic deficiencies, as in Italy or Croatia.

Through the prism of the main question about the goals of civil justice, the papers collected in this book touch upon some of the most topical issues of contemporary legal and judicial reforms. What matters are regarded as being typical, important matters that deserve judicial attention, and what is the collateral task that may and should be outsourced to other state agencies or private professionals? Should civil courts deal with registers, enforcement and collection of uncontested debt, or should they stick to dispute resolution in contested matters? Do all civil disputes deserve equal attention and thorough deliberation of all factual and legal aspects, or should they be awarded only that level of attention that is proportionate to their social importance? When dealing with cases, should the principal task of civil judges be to resolve 'hard cases' that raise difficult new issues of law and facts, or should they instead focus on steady and fast mass processing of routine cases? All these and other issues have a profound impact on the social image and perception of the judiciary, and define expectations that citizens have from the courts in their country. On the other hand, the state authorities also give rather different assignments to their judicial bodies. Dispensing justice may be only one of them – contemporary trends demonstrate that civil courts face increasing pressure to focus on costs, and even provide their services on a quasi-commercial basis. On the other side of the spectrum are the expectations to implement high social goals and public policies while making decisions in private disputes, such as the need to achieve social harmony or objective truth. Civil justice today has many faces. This book should help the interested reader from any given legal tradition to recognise and understand them.

The purpose of this introductory chapter is to summarise the main ideas presented in the 11 chapters that follow. They were motivated by the questionnaire which was distributed to the authors (see Annex A below). In spite of the fact that the approach to the flagged issues and questions was rather diverse, this chapter basically follows the structure of the questionnaire. It will start with the section on the general attitude and doctrinal opinions on the goals of civil justice. However, as ideology often differs from reality, in the following sections some particular topics which can help explain these goals will be discussed:

- The matters regarded as being within the scope of civil justice (in particular, whether the goal of civil justice is confined to litigation, or also includes other, non-contested matters);
- The balance between the protection of individual rights and the public interest;
- The balance between the desire to reach accurate results ('material truth') and the need to ensure trial within a reasonable time;
- The level to which the civil justice system sees its goal in the handling of 'hard cases', as opposed to the routine mass processing of a large number of cases;
- (Non-) recognition of the principle of proportionality;
- The level to which civil justice sees its task as the resolution of complex, multi-party matters;
- The balance between strict formalism and the wish to reach equitable and fair results;
- The precedence of approaches to civil justice: problem solving v. case processing;
- The level to which civil justice is understood as a freely available public service – as opposed to a quasi-commercial source of revenue for the public budget; and
- Self-understanding of the goals of civil justice – user-orientation (satisfying the wishes of the public), or self-centred goals (satisfying the criteria set by 'insiders' – judges, higher courts, lawyers, etc.).

1.2 The Two Main Goals of Civil Justice

For some, the topic of the goals of civil justice may seem to be an old, exhausted subject. The standard textbooks of civil procedure pay lip-service to this issue. It is usually part of an obligatory introduction, repeating outworn formulas, a more or less attempt to exercise the private style or originality of the author. Defining the general goals of civil justice at least in some of the national legal systems does not stir much interest among the legal community, and the focus is rather on pragmatic and practical solutions, on the micro-management of affairs (Silvestri: 4.1).[1]

Yet, as the following chapters will demonstrate, the topic of the goals of civil justice is at present tending to be revived. A thorough discussion or even a full reconceptualisation of the goals of civil justice may be a precondition for successful procedural reforms – especially if it is desired that such reforms be deep, far-reaching

[1] The papers collected in this book will be cited by the name of the author and the number of the section.

and effective. The most successful procedural reforms of the past, from Franz Klein's reforms in the 1890s to the Lord Woolf reforms in the 1990s, were rooted in the profound perception of the procedural goals – social function (Klein), or overriding objective (Woolf) – of civil justice. Today, the goals of civil justice are being discussed and used as arguments and counter-arguments in the context of many jurisdictions. Among those, the conceptual discussion contrasting the various perceptions of the goals of civil justice is on-going, for example in the Netherlands (Van Rhee: 3.1), and it was also behind the 2009 reform of the CJR in Hong Kong (Chan and Chan: 7.2). Even in the common law countries, such as the United States, where civil justice evolved organically and its founding principles were traditionally not a subject of scholarly work, the goals of the process became an interesting topic, as demonstrated by the works of Damaška, Scott and others (Marcus: 6.3). The oscillating balance between the opposed goals is behind many important changes in procedural law and practice, which can best be illustrated in the examples of the countries that are undergoing dynamic social changes, such as mainland China, and transitioning countries in Europe, such as Russia. As pointedly put forward by Professor Silvestri, some justice systems require radical reforms, 'and no radical reforms can be devised unless they are prepared by a thorough process aimed at identifying which goals must or can be reached' (Silvestri: 3.1).

Several authors in this book mention that there is no general consensus about the goals (functions, purposes, aims) of civil procedure. Indeed, there may be many forms of expressing the ideas upon which civil justice is founded. But, it is striking that, in the end, all collected papers speak of the goals of civil justice in surprisingly similar terms. The words may be different, but all authors present the goals as a contrast between two main approaches, whereby any given system of civil justice may be defined by the balance (or imbalance) reached between them.

The two main goals of civil justice may be in the broadest sense defined as:

- resolution of individual disputes by the system of state courts; and
- implementation of social goals, functions and policies.

In various doctrinal works, these goals have different names. For the first, the conflict-resolution (dispute-resolution, conflict-solving) goal is often spoken of. The second, the policy-implementation goal, is more difficult to denote uniformly, as the social policies and functions that civil justice should have may be rather diverse and serve different political or social ideologies or paradigms.[2]

The two goals of civil justice are almost never fully separated. But, the balance between them may be very different, and may shift over time. The relative weight and importance attributed to the interests of the individuals in the dispute, and the level and scope to which others (including the state and its officials) may or should intervene in order to protect trans-individual (collective, social, political, national, state, etc.) interests may be quite different. The tasks of civil justice or matters regarded as being within its scope may also be influenced by the one or the other

[2] On the general level, the conflict-resolution and policy-implementation goals are elaborated in the still topical book by Mirjan Damaška (1986).

goal – e.g. while the conflict-resolution goal would use civil justice only for the settlement of contested matters, the policy-implementation goal may have an impact on the transfer of jurisdiction to civil justice for a number of other purposes (from the holding of public registers to decision making in non-contested matters; see more at Sect. 1.3 below). Moreover, the implementation of social goals may also play a role at the level of system design, as the state may encourage or discourage the use of civil justice (or its use in a particular way) for reaching the other, external goals (i.e. private enforcement of public law rights, as is the case in the USA; correcting inappropriate government activity, as is the case in Brazil; or achieving social harmony, as is the case in China).[3] In order to explain the opposition of the two goals, it may be useful to briefly present the extremes, which may serve as the ideal type models or reference points for the presentation of the current situation.

The exclusive focus of civil justice on the conflict-resolution goal was historically associated with the liberal states of the nineteenth century. In its purest form, this goal concentrates only on the enforcement of the challenged rights of individuals, and sees the function of civil justice in providing a neutral forum which is put at the disposal of the litigants in order to evade resorting to self-help. As an instrument of the reactive liberal state, civil justice had to provide its services in the way that would ensure a minimum of intervention. Just as the *laissez-faire* economy refrains from intervening in the business transactions between private parties, the liberal system of civil justice refrains from intervening in the legal transactions of private law, by giving the maximum powers to the litigants. In the same way as the owners in a classic liberal state possess an absolute freedom to dispose of their property, the litigants in a civil litigation have an absolute freedom to dispose with their claims and with the process as a whole – they are *domini litis,* the masters of civil litigation. Under the principle of minimum intervention, the role of the state and its officials – judges – is limited to the role of a referee, who passively observes the interplay of the parties, maintains the observance of the rules of the game, and only in the end (if ultimately necessary) intervenes and makes a decision. The end result, in the interest of putting an end to the conflict, must therefore be final – *res iudicata* – but it affects only the parties (*facit ius inter partes*), and is none of anybody else's business. From the state's perspective, the only systemic interest is to keep its conflict-resolution services running at the minimum cost, while at the same time still fulfilling the main task – diverting the private parties from resorting to forcible self-help (Marcus: 6.2, citing Posner).

The other extreme as regards the balance between the individual and collective interests may be found in the Marxist critique of the (private) law. In fact, the most radical approach argues that the conflict-resolution machinery of the state is, by its focus on the interests of private individuals (private property, private entrepreneurs), in its essence bourgeois and anti-social, and that it should be abandoned or at least radically restructured. As Lenin argued, the comfortable illusion about the neutrality and the objectivity of the liberal justice system was wrong. He stated that 'all bourgeois law is private law', and as such reflects a capitalistic, imperialistic,

[3] See Chaps. 6, 12 and 8 written by Marcus; Wambier; Fu.

exploitative system of government (Lenin 1918; Merryman and Pérez-Perdomo 2007: 95). In reversing this submission, all law, on the contrary, should become public law, meaning that civil justice (to the extent that it temporarily remained indispensable) should also become an instrument of the economic and social policy of the socialist state (Vyshinsky 1950: §1). To that extent, the conflict-resolution function in civil procedure would in principle have no particular value in itself – it should be viewed only within the broader context of the implementation of desired social and political goals. The individualistic element should be controlled and put in the function of social(ist) aims and targets. Even more so because it was also, as an expression of *a priori* negative remnants of private rights and private property, ideologically suspect. Therefore, in a system of civil justice founded exclusively on policy-implementation goals, we may encounter an interesting mix of two features – the general marginalisation of civil justice, and the paternalistic state control of individual litigants (Uzelac 2010: 382–387). The weak powers of the parties in the process could be in theory contrasted with the strong powers of the judge. But in fact, the state intervention needed to control private actions of the parties, and steer them towards the benefit of the society, could happen on multiple levels (from local to national, from the lowest to the highest courts and judges), by a multitude of officials (most prominently, by state prosecutors) and at any point in time (irrespective whether the decision has become formally final or not). To that extent, the passive parties in such an activist state did not stand in contrast to active judges. The judges were rather passive – bound to follow political instructions (either directly or through the concept of 'socialist legality') and controlled and scrutinised at many levels (including the political control at the time of their appointment and periodical re-election). To that extent, the concept of civil justice rooted in an extreme policy-implementation goal leads more to the general passivisation and marginalisation of civil procedure, rather than to (as sometimes incorrectly interpreted) civil procedure characterised by an omnipotent judge and passive parties.[4]

All papers collected in this book depict civil justice systems that see their role and social task somewhere between these two extremes. None of them is pure, in the sense that none of them denies completely either the conflict-resolution or the policy-implementation goal of civil justice. Several authors speak of the multitude of goals (e.g. Chan and Chan, in Chap. 7), but in my opinion all of them could fall either under the first or the second main goal.

The systemic position and relative importance of the first or the second goal are, of course, different. The first apparent contrast may be between the jurisdictions that generally shy away from resolving disputes by court judgments, like mainland China, and those that, on the contrary, tend to use the courts and court judgments in private matters in a large number of areas, also in cases that would in other places be handled by other means, like the USA. However, this contrast may be softened upon closer examination. While Professor Fu clearly states that the 'the courts [in China] are often viewed as a tool to promote policies and serve political needs'

[4]A very good portrait of such practice of civil procedure is given by Aleš Galič in respect to civil justice of socialist Yugoslavia (below: 11.6). See also Dika and Uzelac (1990).

(Fu: 8.1), the analysis by Professor Marcus may also imply, although in a somewhat different sense, that civil justice in America has the clear political purpose[5] of serving as a substitute for administrative modes of enforcement of legal rules. The widespread use of class actions and the use of punitive damages as methods of influencing or altering behaviour at the larger scale may also serve as examples that American civil justice has advanced far beyond the pure conflict-resolution model of the liberal state.[6]

In the civil law countries, the 'dualist conception' of the goals of civil procedure (Kengyel and Czoboly: 10.1) – the one that recognises both conflict resolution and the implementation of trans-individual policies – is expressed in other terms. While the conflict-resolution goal is often phrased similarly (as enforcement of substantive rights and obligations, authoritative determination of rights by provision of enforceable judgments, or resolution of disputes between individuals and businesses in accordance with the law), the expression of the policy-implementation goals is less uniform. In some countries depicted in this book, the trans-individual function of civil justice is expressed in terms of legal order: 'civil justice protects legal order as a whole' (Hungary), 'the goal is to maintain social order' (China), 'legal order proves itself through civil proceedings' (Austria) or 'the aim of civil procedure is to strengthen legality and law and order' (Russia). Some other formulas reveal more precisely the content of this goal and the way in which it transcends the individual interests of the litigants. Professor van Rhee speaks below (3.1) of two such particular goals – demonstrating the effectiveness of private law, and development and uniform application of private law. These two aspects include the elements of general prevention (based on the assumption that the citizens will be more likely to act in accordance with the law if they see that it works in practice) and the elements of general recognition and acceptance of civil justice (based on the assumption that the citizens will be more likely to respect their obligations if they have a clear horizon of expectations, and see that the law is uniformly and reasonably interpreted by the courts, in the light of the social changes and the new requirements of the society).[7] It is safe to argue that these two aspects are among the most generally accepted and the least controversial aspects of the policies that are viewed as the goal of civil procedure.[8] In a narrow sense, both goals may even be compatible with the liberal, conflict-resolution concept of the goals of civil justice (if they are viewed exclusively from the perspective of effectiveness and costs).

[5] A good illustration of the opposition to the conflict-resolution approach is the quote from Fiss, who argued that the social function of the lawsuit should not be trivialised to only resolving private disputes (Marcus: 6.3).

[6] At least due to the relative infancy of collective litigation schemes, the civil justice systems of continental Europe and Latin America may be categorised closer to the classical liberal concept than to the USA.

[7] The preventive function is also noted with respect to Russia as one of the 'auxiliary aims' of civil procedure. For Germany, *Rechtsfortbildung* (development of law) is recognised as one of the important functions of civil procedure.

[8] However, new debates in some countries may show its relevance in a new light; see Sect. 1.10 below.

As a supplement to the preventive function of civil justice, some authors in this book speak of the educational goal and purpose of civil procedure. This purpose is, for example, noted in Article 2 of the Code of Civil Procedure of the Russian Federation (Nokhrin: 9.1). It is also noted with respect to China, though with the note that it is generally not achieved due to the easy and frequent challenges to final judgments (Fu: 8.12). The educational function was also frequently cited in the former socialist states, where it was put in the context of demonstration of political ideology. For that reason, this function is today rarely cited in the other states, especially the (post-) transition states.

Another indication of the policy-implementation goal of civil justice may be found in the concept of the socialisation of civil justice, understood in the sense that civil justice should promote social justice, and bring justice closer to the needs of the society at large. Although this concept was only conveyed in one chapter of this book, with a note that it was influential in the 1970s and early 1980s, and that it has today a 'retro flavour' (Silvestri: 4.2), the ideas of the access to justice movement should not be completely disregarded. It seems that, at least in continental Europe, it is often considered that civil courts should promote the equal opportunities of both parties to protect their rights and represent their interests in the process, which may require some forms of proactive behaviour on the part of the judges in order to secure the equal chances of the weaker party in the proceedings.

In the same direction, but a little bit further, goes the demand that civil procedure be in the service of achieving the overarching social goal of social harmony. This concept is, after the brief period of the strengthening of the conflict-resolution goal, since the 2000s again gaining momentum in China (Fu: 8.1, 8.4). In the Chinese context, the emphasis on the harmonious development of society is combined with the channelling of the civil cases towards judicial mediation. The 'broader aim of social harmonisation' is also noted among the goals of civil justice in Russia (Nokhrin: 9.1). In Russia, but also in the former socialist states of Central Europe such as Hungary, Slovenia or Croatia, another value that is or was listed among the goals of civil procedure is the pursuit, assertion and revelation of material/objective/substantive truth.[9] This goal, so Kengyel and Czoboly (below: 10.1), was at the centre of the concept of a civil action according to socialist procedural law. From the national reports, it seems that this goal plays, to the extent that it is still recognised in some countries, a much less prominent role today. However, establishing the truth in the proceedings is ranked among the goals of civil procedure also in Austria, as consistently recognised by decisions of its highest court.[10] In German procedural theory, the finding of substantive truth in civil procedure is also noted, but has an instrumental value, serving as a means to achieve the parties' acceptance of the decision, as well as the aim of legal certainty.[11] Whether the goal of civil proceedings is

[9] See Kengyel and Czoboly (below: 10.1); Nokhrin (below: 9.1, 9.4 – mentioning also as a general aim the search for 'social truth'); Galič (below: 11.6).

[10] Koller (2.1). However, the same court (OGH) balances this goal with the other goals, such as finality of judgments, or suppressing the use of illegally obtained evidence.

[11] Koller, ibid. (citing Brehm).

to establish substantive truth or not may be relevant for the concept of an active or passive judicial role in the proceedings, but can also have an effect on their overall effectiveness (or the lack thereof).

The discussion about the role of substantive truth (and substantive justice) is also connected to the general evaluation of the role of procedural formalism in the achievement of the goals of civil justice. Under a liberal conflict-resolution model, the procedural forms have a purpose in themselves. They are nothing but the rules of the game that have to be meticulously observed to guarantee the fairness of the outcome. But, it seems that the times when procedural formalism was a goal in itself are long gone. Even in Germany, which is often regarded as the fortress of formalism, there is a well-established line of case law originating from the *Reichsgericht* decision which held that procedure must not impede the enforcement of rights, and argued that even *res iudicata* must give way to the 'paramount goal of civil justice, which is, to reach justice in the individual case'.[12] The instrumental function of civil justice (or, as Bentham called it, the 'adjective function' of procedural law)[13] rejects the inherent values of the procedure, or at least trades them off against the external goals that have to be reached through the administration of justice. But, although 'excessive formalism' is today rejected even at the constitutional level (through the case law of the European Court of Human Rights),[14] it can hardly be argued that all procedural forms are *a priori* harmful, and that they should be gradually eliminated (as was the ideology in Soviet times). The formalism contributes to legal certainty and predictability, and to that extent can be compatible with moderate policy-implementation concepts.

The bare effectiveness – the ability to produce, in as many cases as possible, any sort of decision on civil rights and obligations within a reasonable time – also appears in the context of the discussion about the goals of civil justice. Although a functional and capable system of civil justice should be among the preconditions, and not the goals of civil justice, the grave problems in dealing with caseload and securing appropriate and predictable time for handling the matters entrusted to civil justice led to focusing on only one goal – to keep the system from falling apart, hoping to reduce caseload and shorten the length of the proceedings (Silvestri: 4.1). The Italian case may be one of the most dramatic ones, but many other civil justice systems, in particular in south-eastern Europe, suffer from systemic deficiencies that sublimate all procedural goals and their employment in only one direction – fighting against the tide of new cases and handling the overcrowded dockets of long-overdue matters. Whether this may be categorised as a goal in itself, or just a symptom and the reason for the absence of any (other) goals, may be a topic for discussion.

Partly for reasons described in the preceding paragraph, but also for several different reasons, a rather prominent and influential trend in the reconceptualisation of

---

[12] Decision of the highest German court, BGH, from 1951, cited in Koller, ibid.

[13] See Marcus (below: 6.2); similarly the German *Reichtsgericht* spoke of the instrumental function (*dienende Funktion*) of procedural law; see Koller (below: 2.1.2).

[14] See more at Sect. 1.10 below.

procedural goals has emerged. It is the trend which seeks to improve the cost effectiveness of civil litigation, to reduce the expenses for civil justice paid from the taxpayers' purse, or even to require the civil justice system to produce revenues for the state budget. One of the forms of this trend is advancing the goal of proportionality, or, as reported by Peter and David Chan for Hong Kong, towards the concept of justice under which 'efficiency and expedition are as important as the correctness of the outcome' (quoting Zuckerman).[15] Such efficiency requires that the limited public resources for the justice system be distributed fairly and appropriately, *inter alia* by saving costs and time by active judicial case management and a continuing effort to streamline procedures (Chan and Chan: 7.2). According to Zuckerman's 'three-dimensional concept of justice', a contemporary civil justice should not focus on accurate and lawful decisions only, but should also take into the same equation the time and costs needed to deal with the case (Zuckerman 2009: 49, 69–71).

But, while the 'three-dimensional concept' in theory needs careful balancing of several factors (the social and individual importance of the court case, the expectations and needs of the society and the litigants, and the available resources), the cost awareness may be in some countries driven less by conscious attempts to improve the effectiveness, fairness and quality of the proceedings, and more by external factors, e.g. by the general policy of cutting public funds and expenses for public services. Such a situation, according to Professor van Rhee, may be found in the Netherlands, where the governmental policy to reduce expenses for civil justice has produced controversial plans to increase court fees and to mandate mediation. This is all happening under the same policy – the policy of discouraging litigation, which has to be only the *ultimum remedium,* the last resort if all other attempts by private parties to resolve the dispute fail. These plans led to a 'clash between the government on one side and lawyers and legal scholars on the other as regards the goals of civil justice', whereby the government advocated, more or less, a conflict-resolution model, while the other side opposed the reforms with references to the beneficial public effect (so-called positive externalities) of litigation on public order (Van Rhee: 3.1).

The transposition of general concepts of the goals of civil justice in concrete procedural designs may be better illustrated by analysing how the perception of procedural goals affects various topical issues of contemporary procedural law.

1.3 What Should Be the Object of Civil Justice? Various Matters Within the Jurisdiction of Civil Courts

The goals of civil justice may be closely connected with the scope of its work. As described above, the conflict-resolution goal is in many legal systems seen as the very core of the goals of civil justice. However, it is interesting to note that dealing

---

[15] Chan and Chan (below: 7.1.1); also see Zuckerman (2009: 49 and 71).

with dispute resolution, i.e. with disputed matters, for many national systems of civil justice constitutes only a minor part of their overall caseload.[16] Obviously, in most uncontested (or extra-contentious) cases[17] the policy goals and reasons are in the forefront. It is also noted that, in essence, the tasks of the courts in such proceedings are 'more or less administrative in nature'.[18] In fact, while the public and cultural image of judicial work is associated with adjudication, in cases such as issuing excerpts from land registers, appointment of guardians or stamping of payment orders while collecting uncontested debt, there is very little adjudication indeed. The use of courts for essentially non-judicial, administrative purposes is also the reason for the significant divergence among national justice systems: all civil courts deal with adjudication, but it depends on the political choice of each state as to how many other tasks will be transferred to the judiciary. Evaluated by the universal standards of due process, as expressed in Article 10 of the UN Universal Declaration of Human Rights or Article 6 of the European Convention for the Protection of Human Rights and Fundamental Freedoms (ECHR), the residual right to have a contested case dealt with by the *courts* cannot be outsourced; but, all other matters and tasks are subject to the discretionary and changeable choice of state authorities. As modern societies become more complex, one can rarely encounter pure and logical distribution or functions, i.e. courts that only deal with dispute resolution, and the state or local administration that deals with the rest. Entrusting the judiciary with other duties, based on different motives and different reasons, seems to be popular in many parts of the world. In many countries, more and more 'externalities' are being transferred to the courts, from the regulation of family relations to the control of local elections.[19]

The national reports confirm this description. None of the reported jurisdictions confine their civil justice systems to dealing with 'proper court cases', i.e. with contested matters only. But, the relative share of the uncontested matters in the overall work of the civil courts differs from country to country. Professor van Rhee points to the fact that, though Dutch civil courts deal with diverse types of uncontested matters, the more administrative (i.e. uncontested) matters 'do not play such

[16] For example, the contested matters in Croatia constitute in all courts only about 25 % of the annual caseload, while the rest is composed of enforcement, public register cases and other non-contentious matters. At the level of the first instance courts of general jurisdiction, this percentage is even lower. In 2012, among all civil matters received by municipal courts, there were 154,466 litigations, 476,543 land register cases, 176,713 enforcement cases, 11,039 inheritance cases and 112,112 other extra-contentious cases (i.e. litigations constituted only 16.6 % of their annual caseload). See *Statistički pregled za 2012.* (Statistical survey for 2012) of the Croatian Ministry of Justice, http://www.mprh.hr/lgs.axd?t=16&id=3851 (last visited in September 2013).

[17] Their names are different, what reflects the lack of uniformity: *ex parte* or voluntary jurisdiction; *jurisdiction gracieuse* (French); *Freiwillige Gerichtsbarkeit, Ausserstreitverfahren* (German), etc.

[18] See Van Rhee (below: 3.2); Silvestri (below: 4.3); Koller (below: 2.2 – speaking of 'administrative activity' in the area of civil justice – *Verwaltungstätigkeit im Bereich der Privatrechtsordnung*).

[19] For Austria, it is noted that 'the legislator decided to submit more and more matters to non-contentious jurisdiction which do not share the same characteristics as those matters forming traditionally the core of non-contentious jurisdiction'. Koller (below: 2.2).

a preponderant role [in the Netherlands] as in some other jurisdictions' (Van Rhee: 3.2). Compared to the Netherlands, the share of non-contentious matters is apparently larger in Austria and Germany. Christian Koller notes 'numerous non-contentious matters' and lists several categories of cases: matters which 'traditionally encompass areas of civil law which require an active intervention by the judge in the interest of parties not in a position to adequately protect their interests'; administration of land and commercial registers, guardianship, estates, cartel matters, bankruptcy, forcible execution of judgments and other titles, etc. (below: 2.2). Even more non-contentious matters may be within the scope of the Italian judiciary which has a 'vast array of proceedings dealing with non-contested cases' regulated in an entire book of the Italian Code of Civil Procedure and in a number of special statutes (Silvestri: 4.3).

Whether the judiciary is the best forum to resolve non-contentious matters is another topical question. Professor Wambier notes the concerns regarding the quality that the judicial branch of government may provide in non-contentious matters ('voluntary judicial proceedings') where the 'judge plays a chiefly administrative role'. Based on such considerations, some procedures in Brazil are being reformed so that they will no longer require the intervention of a judge. These reforms include the transfer of jurisdiction in matters such as amicable divorce or the execution of wills to other legal professionals, such as public notaries or registrars (Wambier: 12.3).

Does the involvement of the courts in a smaller or larger number of non-contested matters change the overall assessment of the goals of civil justice? Or, does it only complicate and multiply the goals? Professor Silvestri states that the intensive involvement of the courts in non-contested matters is open to dispute, and that it creates a 'multifaceted puzzle' of *giurisdizione volontaria* (Silvestri: 4.3). User-friendliness, clarity and efficiency may be only some of the values jeopardised by a too colourful mix of diverse tasks 'pushed' by the legislator onto the courts.[20]

But, there may be even worse consequences than confusion for those who use the services of the state's justice system. The judges, as those who are bound to enforce the procedural rules, may confuse their roles and the goals of particular types of proceedings. It is considered that the proceedings in non-contested matters should be simpler, faster and less formal than the 'regular' proceedings in disputed matters. Is this really the case? And whether or not there is an overspill of unnecessary formality and complexity from the default model of proceedings in contested matters is a topic that deserves attention. The overspill in the opposite direction may be even more disastrous: if the large number of cases encountered by judges in the practice of their judicial work is pure administration, the same attitude may reflect on their method of acting in 'proper' court cases which require a prudent, reasonable and professional adjudication.

While the scope of the matters may influence the perception of the goals of civil procedure, the overarching goal of the procedure may influence the matters within

[20] The engagement of judges in the supervision of parliamentary and local elections exists, e.g., in Belgium and Croatia (see Van Rhee – quoting B. Allemeersch (below: 3.2)).

the scope of the proceedings and the method of dealing with them. The most apparent example is China, where the goal of social harmony imposes obligations on all courts to see to it that, irrespective whether the case is contested or uncontested, it is primarily settled in an amicable way, and only very exceptionally by a decision that would not be voluntarily subscribed to by all of the participants in the proceedings. In such a manner, the specific goal of civil justice in China leads to an interesting contrast with the European judiciaries. Whereas in Europe the chief product of civil justice is still adjudication (the production of enforceable titles), the chief products of civil justice in China are conciliation and mediated settlements (Fu: 8.3).[21] Some convergence, however, may be observed in more recent developments both in Europe and in China. While mediation has become more desirable and prominent at the European level, civil procedure reforms in China since the 1990s have introduced more space for classic adjudication, although the 'transplanted' Western procedures are still perceived as legal irritants.[22]

1.4 Individual Rights v. Public Interest in Civil Procedure: From Pure Liberalism to Full State Paternalism

The general aspects of the underlying tension between the two approaches to civil justice – that is, civil justice focused on the protection of individual rights as opposed to civil justice which is a part of the mechanisms for the implementation of policies aimed at the promotion of the public interest – were already discussed in Sect. 1.2 above. The issues that will be elaborated here deal with the fine-tuning between the two opposing targets, as well as with the particular forms in which their pursuit takes place.

The first issue may be observed as a link between the scope of matters entrusted to civil justice, and the objectives of the process. The pronounced inclination of American civil justice is a good example of a justice system which has extended the target of protection of individual rights to a more overarching target of public interest goals. As reported by Professor Marcus, the aims of American civil justice frequently go beyond the context of bipartisan dispute resolution. American civil justice does not merely take on some essentially administrative tasks – it replaces state administration: 'The very heart of the common law system contemplates that

[21] As Professor Fu notes, the goal of social harmony is even emphasised in the enforcement proceedings, where reaching a settlement through court mediation (usually by forcing the creditor to waive partially his right) has become almost a norm.

[22] A good example is the introduction of the system of collection of uncontested debt by payment (dunning) orders, for which the goal of protection of the creditor's rights is failing in practice due to ample opportunities to file frivolous objections. The inclination to mediated solutions also leads to ample opportunities to evade the payment, which results in the fact that payment orders are issued in an ineffective procedure that currently 'accounts for no more than 1 % of the first instance civil cases in China' – Fu Yulin (ibid.). For the notions of 'legal transplants' and 'legal irritants' see Watson 1974, Kahn-Freund 1974, Ewald 1995, and Teubner 1998.

the courts themselves will develop and enforce – via private litigation – the sorts of legal protections that are ordinarily adopted by legislative or administrative actions in other legal systems' (Marcus: 6.4). The resemblance to the European fashion of entrusting the courts with many essentially administrative tasks and obligations exists, but is superficial. Namely, while in Europe it is legitimate to view this process as the bureaucratisation of the state judiciary, in the USA one may speak of the judicialisation of the matters otherwise dealt with by the state bureaucracies. Not only that private litigation is a good substitute for governmental law enforcement, the essentially judicial, adjudicative manner in which the American courts deal with mass claims, collective actions and class litigation provides conclusive proof of this submission (see more in Sect. 1.7 below).

The (North) American situation may be in some respects exceptional, but in its general attitude it is not entirely alone. Professor Wambier notes the 'judicialisation of politics' in Brazil, and explains how the Brazilian judiciary is being given more powers to interfere with the activities of the government, and exert control over public administration (below: 12.4).

In cases where legislation entrusts the courts with the implementation of statutory provisions that express certain public policies, the courts would, in theory, have to follow faithfully such public policies and protect the public interests at stake. The element of public interest is particularly expressed in some fields, e.g. in family law. Still, as some issues in those fields are a matter of public controversy, the judicial implementation of the public policies may take its own course. As Professor Silvestri notes, in Italy it sometimes happened that the 'courts … opposed the very policy they were expected to implement' (Silvestri: 4.4).

Something like that would hardly be imaginable in China, where, 'in the context of a "socialist" society based on public ownership, the ideas of protection of public interest permeate civil justice' (Fu: 8.4). Accordingly, Chinese judges have wide discretion to intervene for reasons of public interest in the parties' disposition of their private rights. The courts have the duty to control whether the parties' actions in civil cases violate the 'interests of the state, social/public interests, or third party interests'. At least in theory, the courts have vast powers: if, in their view, the public interest is disregarded, they may deny the claimant the right to withdraw the claim; control the court judgments irrespective of the parties appeals; refuse to enforce the arbitral awards; etc.[23] The extra-judicial influences motivated by local interests or the views of the ruling elites occur more often through unofficial rather than official channels, examples being the telephone calls of government officials to the court, 'the masses filing administrative petitions against the court or staging sieges on the internet', etc. The courts have special closed committees which discuss the cases, and whose records cannot be accessed by the parties or the public, but only by those who have the power to supervise the courts (ibid.).

The Russian approach to the role of public interest in civil proceedings is, at least in its own self-understanding, closer to the balance of private and public rights and interests (Nokhrin: 9.3). Still, some recent cases demonstrate dynamic development,

[23] Ibid. Fu Yulin notes, however, that in practice those measures are rarely applied.

as well as some tensions between the two goals – the protection of individual rights and the public interest. In some cases, the public interest played a role in the form of protection of the proprietary interests of the state; in others, it was referred to when various Russian courts prohibited (for 'reasons of public morals') Gay Pride marches. As noted by D. Nokhrin, this was due to the Russian doctrinal position according to which 'homosexuals in Russia aren't exposed to any real discrimination, because Russian legislation does not recognize sexual orientation as a circumstance in any way significant'.[24]

European and American systems of civil justice generally deny that in core matters processed by the courts such extra-judicial influences or political considerations play an important role.[25] In Western systems of civil justice, to the extent that it exists, the involvement of public interest in the operations of civil justice is proportional to the share of matters of a non-judicial (administrative) nature entrusted to them (see Sect. 1.3 above). The non-contentious matters are often motivated by public interest. For instance, the court administration of public registers has as its motivation the safeguarding of legal certainty regarding real estate and land transfers (Koller: 2.3). On the contrary, in conventional, bi-party civil law disputes, the doctrine of judicial independence dictates the detachment of court decisions and actions from policy-related considerations. The courts 'must apply the relevant norms to the facts established in the proceedings ... [and] not [be] bound by any overriding policy or national interest that would necessarily affect their decision'.[26] The public interest plays a role in conventional disputes only in the matters that transcend the interests of the individual litigants, e.g. in cases where the interests of children or people with mental disabilities are concerned. In the same category are also labour and housing cases, cases regarding environmental or consumer protection, antitrust cases, etc. In the latter two cases, the trans-individual and supra-individual interests are often combined with special types of proceedings, such as collective or representative actions (see more in Sect. 1.7 below).

In spite of the Western ideological rejection of the idea that the civil courts should in their dealing with private law matters directly serve societal, national or governmental goals, there is a trend in many European and non-European countries that the courts exert a more active role in the process and engage in a number of matters on their own initiative, even against the dispositions of the parties. For instance, in France, Austria, Germany, the Netherlands and in many other jurisdictions on the European continent, the courts have to apply the applicable

---

[24] Below, 9.2.3. The decisions in those cases led to the finding of the violation of the human right of peaceful assembly, together with violations of the right to an effective remedy and of the prohibition against discrimination (Arts. 11, 13 and 14 of the ECHR). See *Alekseyev v. Russia*, ECtHR app. nos. 4916/07, 25924/08 and 14599/09, judgment of 21 October 2010.

[25] However, some features of the US system, such as the possibility to award punitive damages, show a higher level of inclination to use the individual case for the general goal of changing behaviour in a larger segment of the society.

[26] Koller, ibid. See also Van Rhee (below: 3.3).

procedural and substantive law *ex officio* when administering justice.[27] A number of countries give courts also right (and obligation) to explore facts *ex officio* – see more in Sect. 1.5 below.

One goal related to the protection of public interests plays, however, an important role in almost all contemporary systems of civil justice. It is a goal that, though policy-based, may be defined as the *intrinsic* goal of civil justice – the goal of the efficient and fair administration of justice. In England and in Hong Kong, this goal is expressed in terms of the overriding/underlying objective which lies at the centre of recent civil justice reforms (Chan and Chan: 7.1.2, 7.2, 7.4.3, 7.5.1, etc.). Civil justice as another important public service should be 'effective, efficient and fair' (Zuckerman 2009: 54). Active case management and, where necessary, *ex officio* actions by the court should function in the service of swift, streamlined and inexpensive proceedings, the predictable timing of the procedure, and the prevention of abusive and delaying behaviour of the parties. An interesting new development in this direction can be observed in the recent reforms and the subsequent case law in Hong Kong, where the courts now may (and will) strike out the claimant's case for inordinate delay (provided that the decision to strike out must be founded on the abuse of the process of the court, namely that the delay causes a substantial risk that a fair trial is not possible).[28] In stark contrast, the civil justice systems of the European socialist and post-socialist countries, while formally adhering to an active role of the judge and the high level of importance of the (external) public interest, in the areas of intrinsic procedural values usually show their rather weak, passive face. Poor case management and time management and the resulting inefficiency are often confirmed by the findings of systemic deficiencies and the violations of the right to a trial within a reasonable time before the European Court of Human Rights.[29]

In the cases in which public interest elements are recognised, one may inquire whose role it is to enforce them. Is it the task of judges (only), or of some other participants or the internal/external stakeholders? In about half of the reported legal systems, an important side-body that may participate or intervene in the civil proceedings is the state prosecutor (public prosecutor, public minister, procurator). The names of the office may be different, but the main function of intervention is always the same – it is the intervention on the side of trans-individual interests. Though, the scope and reach of the prosecutorial intervention varies. In China, it is a continuing power to supervise the courts and challenge their judgments – even those that have already become effective.[30] In Russia, the intervention takes a twofold form: the prosecutor can either initiate public interest litigation as a claimant; or, he can

[27] See, *inter alia* Van Rhee (also supported with comments by Frédérique Ferrand regarding France).

[28] See in particular the leading case of *Nanjing Iron* cited in Chan and Chan, 7.2 below.

[29] See for examples from Croatia Grgić (2007); Uzelac (2004, 2006). On common socialist roots for inordinate delay and inefficiency in post-Yugoslav countries see Galič (below: 11.6).

[30] Fu (below: 8.4). The powers of the Chinese prosecutors to intervene in civil proceedings were recently reinforced and augmented.

appear as a quasi-neutral evaluator of legality that provides 'impartial' opinions to the court.[31] A similar regime also exists in France and in the Netherlands, where the members of the office of the Public Ministry may initiate various proceedings (e.g. for annulment of marriage) and issue advisory opinions (*conclusions*). At the highest court level, the advisory opinions are issued by the Procurator General and the Advocates General (*avocats généraux*) at the Supreme Court (Cour de cassation/Hoge Raad).[32] The procurator at the highest court may also challenge final and binding judgments in the interest of the law, but – in the French and Dutch cases – the decision has only an exemplary effect and does not affect the rights and duties of the applicant.[33] The German and Austrian systems, on the other hand, do not have comparable bodies with broad powers, although some modest forms of prosecutorial intervention exist there as well. For example, the public prosecutor in Austria has the right to commence proceedings for annulment of marriage; the chief financial state attorney, *Finanzprokurator*, may intervene in order to protect the public interest.[34] In Germany, all powers of the public prosecutors to intervene in civil proceedings were abandoned, and the direction of development in several post-socialist countries is the same (e.g. in Hungary, in successor countries of the former Yugoslavia).[35]

1.5 Establishing the Facts of the Case Correctly v. the Need to Provide Effective Protection of Rights Within an Appropriate Time

Contemporary systems of civil justice vary considerably in their attitude towards substantive truth as the goal of civil procedure. Naturally, accurate fact-finding is always recognised as an important target in the proceedings. At the end of the nineteenth century Franz Klein wanted to shape a model of civil procedure in which establishing substantive truth, and engaging in efficient case management, would be two mutually non-exclusive goals. Yet, in the course of history it was proved that, in

[31] The two colliding functions of the prosecutor in Russia caused issues with the fairness of the proceedings – see Nokhrin (below: 9.2.5); similar considerations in some transition countries led to reform and/or abandonment of the prosecutorial intervention in civil cases.

[32] See Van Rhee (below: 3.3).

[33] On the contrary, in the socialist countries that knew the prosecutorial challenge to final judgments, the effect of the successful challenge was the reversal of the decision, with full effects on the parties to the proceedings.

[34] Koller (below: 2.3). The apparently broader powers of the State Financial Procurator were in practice limited through the case law of the OGH.

[35] See Kengyel and Czoboly (below: 10.3). For instance, in Croatia the powers of the public prosecutor to challenge final judgments (the so-called *request for the protection of legality*) were dismantled in 2003, just as the third-party intervention by the public prosecutor. The only remaining role of the public prosecutor is to initiate certain public interest litigation. This happens in practice infrequently and has only marginal importance.

extreme cases, the ideological demand for objective (or even absolute) truth could overshadow all other goals of procedure. Soviet doctrine thought that the principle of material truth was embedded in the principle of (socialist) legality. The need to establish 'material truth' was the ideological justification for paternalistic supervision through the reports by the highest courts and the Office of the Public Prosecutor.[36] With the same background, in Hungary during the socialist period truth-finding was also placed at the pinnacle of all procedural values. The pursuit of truth was the duty of the judge, who had to actively control the parties and their dispositions. The spirit of paternalistic inquisitorialism was motivated by distrust in individual freedom and the suspicious attitude towards private initiative (Uzelac 1992).

In the 1990s, as a counter-reaction, a new approach to the role of truth in civil proceedings occurred in many former socialist countries. In Hungary, for instance, the pursuit of truth was deleted from the procedural principles contained in the code. This was supported by the Constitutional Court's decision that 'there was no constitutional guarantee relating to the revelation of the material truth'.[37] Consequently, in the new Hungarian Code of Civil Procedure, the fairness of the proceedings (impartial decision making based on the principle of party representation and the right to be heard) replaced the revelation of truth as the principal procedural goal. In more recent times, though, the exclusive focus on the acceleration of proceedings raised criticisms that speed was placed above the accuracy of the results. These critiques may lead to the (moderate) rehabilitation of the value of truth-seeking in adjudication (Kengyel and Czoboly: 10.3). The 'change of paradigm' also happened in Russia, where many scholars today advocate the concept of 'formal truth' (Nokhrin: 9.4).

While the debates over the place of objective/absolute truth in civil procedure often had a highly ideological context and background, the more important set of issues today is linked to the rights and obligations of trial judges to investigate factual issues on their own motion. One issue is whether judges may order the taking of evidence *ex officio*. Another issue is whether judges have the duty to actively stimulate the parties to state the facts and produce evidence. If there is an obligation of the judge to give instructions to the parties, advise them and encourage them to put forward all their procedural material in a truthful and comprehensive manner, we may ask about the consequences of eventual failures to do so. The description of the systems in Austria and Germany may indicate that speedy and accurate civil procedure is not incompatible with active judicial involvement in the evidence-taking process.[38] On the other side, in some post-socialist jurisdictions, such as in Slovenia and Croatia,[39] the pronounced expectations that the court (and not the parties)

[36] Nokhrin (below: 9.4). Under Art. 14 of the Russian Code of Civil Procedure of 1964, the judge had to 'take all measures … for full and objective investigation of the real circumstances of the case' irrespective of the parties' disposition.

[37] See Kengyel and Czoboly (below: 10.3).

[38] See Koller (below: 2.4) on the situation in Austria and Germany.

[39] For Slovenia and Croatia see Galič (below: 11.6), Uzelac (2004, 2006).

actively investigate facts and supply evidence led to several systemic anomalies: to passive and abusive behaviour of the parties, to a protracted and de-concentrated style of the proceedings ('the piecemeal trial') and to the practice of successive remittals of the judgments based on the argument that the court has to 'try harder' and continue to investigate what really happened (even if the parties have not actively contributed to the clarification of disputed facts).[40]

The problem of such imposed judicial 'pursuit' for truth disappears in common law systems that are concerned, so Chan and Chan (below: 7.5.1), 'with legal truth and not material truth'. The clarification of all disputed facts is in common law systems regularly seen as the more or less exclusive obligation of the parties. Since the Woolf reforms, the trend is not only to burden the parties with the gathering of facts, but also to compel the parties to collect, present and verify their procedural material at the earliest possible stage of the proceedings ('the front-loading of facts-gathering exercise before the action is commenced').

1.6 One Size Does Not Fit All: Proportionality Between Case and Procedure

The axiology of civil procedure gets its flavour from cases that may be considered typical for the national civil justice system. But, the spectrum of cases is rarely uniform: most national judiciaries handle 'small' and 'big' cases; complex and routine cases; unique cases and repetitive/cloned cases. Two issues arise in this context: first, whether some types of cases are for one or the other system more 'typical'; and, second, whether or not the goals and modalities of their implementation are in each given system adjusted to the different nature of the case at hand. The authors of this book were invited to comment on the extent to which the goals of civil justice are viewed from the perspective of resolving the 'hard cases' (difficult legal matters that raise new issues of law and fact) and on the extent to which they are viewed from the perspective of the mass processing of routine, repetitive matters. They were also asked to comment on the proportionality between the methods of treatment of cases, and their social importance. The issues that occur here are also related to the application of filtering mechanisms and various summary proceedings adjusted to the processing of small claims. The specific procedures regarding the courts' processing of collective, diffuse and group interests are dealt with separately in Sect. 1.7 below.

A very clear reply on the question of 'hard cases' and their treatment in China was given by Fu Yulin: 'Hard cases are not welcomed by courts and frequently get

[40] One foreign observer of the practice of Croatian courts argued that the usual approach of the appeals courts in civil trials was 'no stone should be left unturned'. The practice of successive remittals was repeatedly found to be among the 'systemic deficiencies' of civil procedure in Croatia, Slovenia, Poland, Hungary, Bulgaria, Ukraine, Romania and Russia. See Grgić (2007: 158).

refused at the beginning of the proceedings' (below: 8.6). This is, seemingly, not only a feature of Chinese exceptionalism. A straightforward answer to the question about the goals of adjudication is also given by Elisabetta Silvestri: 'At present, Italian civil justice is more about processing a huge number of ordinary cases than handling "hard cases"' (below: 4.8). She also points to the relative nature of the 'hard case' notion, namely, in a dysfunctional legal system, poorly drafted legislation and systemic inability to deal with the everyday caseload may cause cases that would otherwise be regular and simple to look like irresolvable puzzles. But, also for most other civil law systems it can be stated that they have an inclination to focus on the resolution of a large number of average and small cases, rather than on dealing with socially significant individual cases.

Not only for Italy can one say that the goal of the system is first to survive the influx of matters, and only second to produce high-quality justice. In such a situation, it is not surprising that separate mechanisms, developed outside of the state's justice system, are gaining momentum. Today, arbitration, for instance, is becoming pre-eminent in dispute resolution in complex and valuable international commercial cases. The new trend in some countries is to discourage litigation and to keep the cases that do not belong in the courts away from the courts. Efforts by the new Dutch government to suppress litigation, fostering early settlements and out-of-court mediation, may serve as an example of this trend.[41]

Bureaucratic excellence in dealing with a large number of repetitive cases is a feature that has become a hallmark of Austrian and German civil justice. The Austrian example of automated, IT-supported order for payment proceedings (*Mahnverfahren*) may serve as a model example of a system that corresponds to the goal of fast and cost-effective, mass processing of cases and fast filtering of uncontested claims (Koller: 2.6).

The processing of small claims poses bigger challenges for many legal systems. While common law countries generally have a policy of keeping the small cases off judicial dockets by various means (including the high costs of litigation), the civil law world is more sympathetic to small claims. The principle that judges should not waste their time on irrelevant, small matters (*de minimis non curat praetor*) is generally rejected by the European systems of civil justice. In extreme cases, e.g. in Italy or in Croatia, 'it is inconceivable that courts refuse to take into consideration cases which are deemed trivial or inappropriate'. After a long and exhausting process, 'frivolous and groundless claims will end up being rejected, but not to entertain them would amount to a denial of the fundamental right of access to justice' (Silvestri: 4.9). In Hungary, up until 2009, there was no special procedure in small cases, and the same procedural rules applied for all cases, irrespective of their value (Kengyel and Czoboly: 10.6).

[41] See Van Rhee (below: 3.1, 3.6). On the other hand, the intention of the Dutch reforms may be mixed, and attributed more to a policy of the saving of public funds than to a well-considered plan to secure optimal, proportionate court procedures (below: 3.10).

In most countries, however, some proportionality is achieved by channelling small claims to special courts or special summary proceedings.[42] It is also achieved by the availability of early provisional relief, e.g. by conditional judgments (*Vorbehaltsurteil*) in Germany. In spite of the introduction of the European Small Claims Procedure in the EU (which has only added to the maze), the papers presented below show that the approaches to small claims are dissimilar and varied even if we focus only on European territory. While Italy has justices of the peace (*giudice di pace*), the Netherlands and France use *référé* proceedings (*Kort Geding*) and Austria and Germany channel small claims to the jurisdiction of special courts (*Bezirksgerichte, Amtsgerichte*). The procedure before such courts is also a special one: 'formalities are kept to a minimum, emphasis is put on the oral part of the proceedings, and admissibility of appeals is restricted'. Koller goes on to note that 'it would be incorrect to conclude that [small] cases are considered less important based on their amount in dispute' and pointed to the constitutional limitations to simplification and streamlining (Koller: 2.6).

The procedure in small cases may be less formal, but it is still regulated. An exception is German law, which leaves the procedure in cases where the amount in dispute does not exceed €600 entirely to the discretion of the court (but only if it is in conformity with constitutional guarantees). The relationship between proportionality and specialisation reveals interesting problems and paradoxes. Legislative division into cases and courts that have to deal with matters in special proceedings with a differing level of formality may be more formal and less flexible than a regime which would give courts full discretion to deal with cases in the way they deserve. Bureaucratic inertia may, however, prevent the courts from using such discretion in the way that would be appropriate. But, excessive specialisation accompanied by the multiplication of courts of different types and procedures with special features may be confusing, ineffective and contrary to the wish to secure predictable and appropriate standards for all cases. It can also contribute to the blurring and fuzziness of the goals of civil justice.

1.7 Multi-party Litigation and Collective Actions

All replies given by the authors of this book regarding the role of class litigation end up in a simple division – 'only in America' on one side, and all other jurisdictions on the other side. A case such as *Daar v. Yellow Cab Co*,[43] in which the court ordered the taxi company to charge unduly low fares to future customers because unidentifiable customers were overcharged in the past, cannot happen in

[42] See texts in this book that deal with the situation in Austria, Brazil, Hong Kong, Italy and Hungary.

[43] *Daar v. Yellow Cab Co*, 433 P.2d 732 (Cal. 1967). See Marcus (below: 6.3). He argues that this case is an example of the 'behavior modification view' which 'favor[s] creative use of the class action'.

any other place, not even today when many systems are flirting with some forms of collective proceedings (and the cited Californian case has a history of over four decades in the USA).

The replies from all other jurisdictions are diverse, but reflect the same basic attitude: in all other countries civil justice is still predominantly focused on 'one-on-one' resolution of individual disputes. As to the multi-party and aggregate proceedings, it is stated that 'multi-party litigation is still in its infancy' (the Netherlands); that the reception of it is 'far from stellar' (Italy); that 'the handling of complex multi-party matters cannot … be considered as a major goal of civil justice' (Austria); that 'judges are reluctant to process multi-party cases' (China); etc. A notable exception only is Brazil, for which it is stated that it has 'a very well-developed class action system' within which 'complex matters are frequently handled' (Wambier: 12.2).

In spite of low use and poor reception in practice, legislators of many countries show a continuing interest for regulation in this field, from Hong Kong[44] to Germany.[45] But, the scepticism and critical attitudes are also strong.[46]

The ambition to include the resolution of complex multi-party matters in the goals of civil procedure is certainly present in many systems of civil justice. Many legal scholars share the view that in complex contemporary societies the courts should be equipped to address complex social matters. Some types of proceedings which provide the right to conduct representative litigation to certain associations or independent public bodies (e.g. *Verbandsklage*) exist in several jurisdictions, but have all gained more theoretical interest than practical relevance. In reality, very few civil justice systems are ripe for the adequate processing of multi-party claims even by means of conventional methods of case and court administration (merger of cases, strategic litigation, etc.). This will, obviously, remain the challenge to be addressed in the future.

1.8 Equitable Results v. Strict Formalism

Is the goal of civil procedure substantive justice, or should it be the correct application of legal provisions, irrespective of the outcome? There are many ways to attack this question as a false dilemma. Indeed, in an ideal case the two should converge. However, it is undeniable that the inclination towards substantive justice vs. formal legality varies considerably.

The preference for substantive justice may be diagnosed in systems as different as China and the United States. As explained by Fu Yulin, 'in the Chinese legal

[44] New initiative pending since 2009; see Chan and Chan (below: 7.7).

[45] Koller presents the 'experimental law' on pilot cases of investors in the capital markets (*Kapitalanleger-Musterverfahrensgesetz*), which combines the elements of a collective action and a test-case procedure (below: 2.7).

[46] According to Koller, such criticisms had the result that the Civil Justice Reform Act of 2007 could not be passed in Austria.

culture and judicial customs, achieving an equitable result and substantive justice has always been the priority, and less emphasis is placed on strict formal compliance of formalism or entrenchment of the principle of legality'. In the 1990s, more emphasis was placed on the principle of legality, but in the 2000s a contrary trend under the concept of 'active justice' emerged (Fu: 8.9). On the other side, the active use of civil justice for policy implementation in the United States[47] and the American reliance on civil litigation for the purpose of public law enforcement can hardly be manageable on the basis of strict legal formalism.

Stronger loyalty to strict legalism may be diagnosed in the civil law environment. Civil law judges are in most cases predominantly 'concerned with finding the correct legal solution to resolve a dispute'.[48] The principle of legality is, as expressed by Christian Koller, 'enshrined' in the Austrian and German constitutions, while the principles of equity and observance of the basic principles of justice, though present incidentally in statutory law, are far lower in the hierarchy of values (infra: 2.8). Moving to Eastern Europe, it seems that the adherence to formalistic behaviour is even more pronounced there. At least, that may be the inference from the jurisprudence of the European Court of Human Rights which often found violations of fair trial rights on the basis of excessive formalism in several countries of eastern and southern Europe.[49]

In some countries, a movement away from 'unnecessary formalism' may be diagnosed. Remco van Rhee states that since the 1970s 'the keyword in Dutch civil procedure has been "deformalisation"' (below: 3.8). The motivation for loosening strict formal requirements is at least in part to bring nearer the attainment of the goal of substantive and equitable results, as the intention of the reforms is to prevent the parties from using the rules of civil procedure to twist the result in their favour on formal grounds. The traditional sympathy for solutions based on equitable results and substantive justice is also attributed to Norway (Backer: 5.9).

1.9 Problem Solving v. Case Processing

The contrast between the goal of substantive justice and the goal of strict legalism is mirrored in another opposition of values. The authors of this book were invited to comment on how their national civil justice systems and their main actors predominantly view their purpose and aim – whether they regard the administration of justice as an activity that should focus on finding adequate solutions to the problems underlying the disputes or whether, on the contrary, the main systemic goal is to efficiently process the cases within their jurisdiction, engaging the least amount of effort and expense.

In the comments given, it was sometimes suggested that the balance between those two objectives would be the best solution. However, evaluated on the content

[47] See Marcus, ss. 6.4 and 6.5.

[48] Alvim Wambier (below: 12.6).

[49] E.g. Croatia, Russia, Greece, Ukraine, Czech Republic, etc. See Fernhout (2008).

of their replies, it may be concluded that the balance has decisively shifted towards case processing. As noted by Kengyel and Czoboly, in times of economic crisis, the pressure on courts increases and everything is directed 'at solutions requiring the least effort and expense' (below: 10.9). Where the justice system is not working, the 'idea of courts as problem solvers is met with a good measure of scepticism' (Silvestri: 4.11). Sometimes the idea of problem solving is rejected on doctrinal grounds. Van Rhee states that 'problem solving is not, according to the majority of Dutch authors, a primary goal of the civil justice system', although it may be its by-product (below: 3.9). The recent trend in Norway also places stronger emphasis on the efficient management of cases (Backer: 5.10). For Austria, in spite of Franz Klein's legacy that requires civil justice to resolve social conflicts and fulfil welfare tasks, 'the need to solve the parties' problem does not prevail over the goal of civil procedure to swiftly decide the case' (Koller: 2.9). Finally, even for China, which cherishes court settlements the most, the short time limitations of 3–6 months within which the courts have to dispose of civil matters 'strongly compel the courts and judges to focus on case processing' (Fu: 8.10). Mediation is, of course, supported in many jurisdictions, but it seems, unfortunately, that this support rests today more on the ideas of case processing (how to dispose of the case quickly; how to keep cases away from the courts) than on the ideas of finding adequate solutions for the problems of the individuals and the society.

1.10 Freely Available Public Service v. Quasi-commercial Source of Revenue for the Public Budget

Should civil justice be a free and accessible service open to everyone, or should it be run as a business always aware of costs and hence concerned with cost efficiency? Should civil justice be funded by taxpayers, or should its operations be funded by the concrete users of its services via court fees? Should civil justice be an expense, or a source of revenue for the state budget? All these issues may also be viewed as 'goals', or at least as targets closely connected with the more general understanding of the goals of civil justice.

In the light of comments from different sides of the globe, it seems that we cannot avoid the conclusion that civil justice is increasingly being commercialised. Only in a very few countries do the parties to civil litigation still not pay any court fees due to the adherence to the principle of free access to the courts.[50] But, even in the countries which are traditionally model examples of the social state, such as

[50] In the 2012 report of the European Commission for the Efficiency of Justice (CEPEJ) it is noted that 'only 2 member states provided for a free access to all courts: France and Luxembourg'. As the report deals with the data for 2010, it could only note that, since October 2011, also in France a contribution to legal aid of €35 is paid. See European Judicial Systems (2012: 74). Two years before, the CEPEJ reported that five members of the Council of Europe did not have receipts from court fees as they apply the principle of free access to court (EJS 2010: 63).

Norway, trends are changing. While 'civil justice was originally largely perceived as a freely available public service … nowadays, court fees as well as lawyers' salaries have risen to such an extent as to make civil litigation an expensive exercise for the ordinary citizen' (Backer: 5.11). It may get even worse: in the Netherlands, the government proposed legislation that intended to dramatically increase court fees, seeking to raise the level of self-financing of the civil justice system.[51] In Austria, civil justice is already covering its costs by 110.9 %, effectively subsidising other branches of the justice system.[52] Interestingly, ever since the courts started to operate as dispute-resolution providers in China in the 1980s and early 1990s, they have 'operated like commercial institutions' and are expected to 'cover budgetary deficiencies'. As even at present local governments still plan their expenditures for the courts in relation to the courts' contribution to the local treasury, Fu Yulin concludes that 'given such background, … Chinese civil justice remains a quasi-commercial source of revenue for the public budget' (below: 8.11).

In the jurisdictions that are raising court fees, the intention of introducing higher court tariffs is not always focused exclusively on increasing contributions to the budgets of the state or local administration. Another reason, as testified by Silvestri, is to reduce the caseload of the courts (below: 4.12). This reason may have a pragmatic background; it can also have a systemic justification, in the context of the proportionality principle. However, for all countries that consider it, the increase in the court fees raises the issue of access to justice, in particular if – as stated for Italy – the citizens cannot count on a modern and adequately funded system of legal aid (Silvestri: ibid.).

1.11 User Orientation?

The ultimate goal of civil justice may be captured in the question regarding the ultimate purpose and aim of the civil justice system. One of the possible phrasings of this question is – Does civil justice have to serve the interests of its ultimate users, or do citizens and other members of the society have to serve the interests of civil justice? This may be seen as a mean and apparently unscientific question. However, many of the reports confirm directly or indirectly that a lot can be done to establish and improve a user-friendly attitude on the part of national civil justice systems. The ecosphere of civil justice is all too often polluted by an eco-centric – or even *ego*-centric – attitude, and the 'insider's' values often prevail over the values that serve the interests of users as 'one-shotters' and 'outsiders'.[53]

[51] Van Rhee (below: 3.10). The target was to cover approximately 64 % of the costs through court fees. Due to the change in government, this project is currently on hold, but similar projects are underway in Germany (Koller: 2.10).

[52] The high revenue of the civil justice system in Austria can, though, be connected with its engagement in some non-contested matters, such as land and company registers, as well as with the fees collected from automated payment order processing (*Mahnverfahren*).

[53] See more in Uzelac (2008: 413–427).

A direct example comes again from the admirably sincere article written by Fu Yulin. The politicians, she says, in principle plan legislation keeping in mind the interests of the users. But, as the 'participants of the legislative process are mainly senior judges and top-notched professors, procuratorate, and only a small number of lawyers', the initial intentions often become diluted (Fu: 8.12). Backer also suggests that 'it is probably not unfair to say that the goals of civil justice used to be somewhat self-centred'. The concept of judicial independence also feeds the view that this is rightly so, and only in recent years are the needs and wishes of the court users being explored independently of judges and lawyers (Backer: 5.12).

Currently, a fashionable method of proving (rightly or wrongly) the level to which civil justice systems cater to the needs of the users is to conduct user satisfaction surveys. In the Netherlands, such surveys have been conducted on a regular basis since the start of the new millennium. The results of the surveys are relatively favourable – e.g. 84 % of the users are generally satisfied, but the users are less happy with the length of proceedings, the empathy displayed by the judge and with some other special issues (Van Rhee: 3.11). The results of similar user satisfaction surveys are more ambiguous in Austria, where seemingly different polls organised by different organisations have resulted in significant differences in results. For example, contrary to the usual view of the Austrian judiciary as fast and efficient, a poll organised by the Bar Association of Lower Austria showed that 86 % of participants thought that judicial proceedings lasted too long or 'much too long' (Koller: 2.11). Most surveys in Austria and in Germany still display at least an average level of satisfaction (in Germany 60 % of the population has fair or considerable trust in German courts). In general, the civil justice systems of the nations of northern and western Europe still seem to do a fairly good job in relation to their users. But improvements are possible even there, and the self-centred goals (e.g. judicial independence, good financial status and job security) are still better protected than the wishes and the needs of the users.

The situation in some other countries is much worse. In the dysfunctional systems of civil justice even the weak and unreliable results of user satisfaction surveys are missing. There is, however, a strong feeling of dissatisfaction: some systems do not work, and all users are unhappy – even the professional ones (Silvestri: 4.13). Crisis is usually a good motivator for change, but change may require a long time, and meanwhile the society may suffer from the *status quo*.

1.12 Conclusion

The goals of civil justice are a topic that needs rethinking. Civil justice should serve the interests of the society of the twenty-first century, and the new social context imposes the need for significant changes. These changes require clear starting points. Without clearly stated goals, it is hard to make solid and consistent plans, produce indicators of their success and maintain the momentum of the reforms. The study of diverging goals in different justice systems helps us to compare and understand the differences in procedures and legal institutions. Maybe, if we realise that some of our goals are the same, it will also help us to reduce comparative differences, and improve our judiciaries even where everybody believes that any reform is doomed to fail.

Annex A: The Questionnaire

IAPL – INTERNATIONAL ASSOCIATION OF PROCEDURAL LAW
MOSCOW CONFERENCE
September 2012

TOPIC: **GOALS OF CIVIL JUSTICE**
Questionnaire for National Reporters

General framework: The main questions indicated are:

- How do the goals of civil justice differ from country to country?
- What is the role of civil justice in the contemporary world?

The National Reporters are invited to present their views and the current state of affairs in their jurisdictions (and, if so agreed, in other similar jurisdictions), and comment (however briefly) on all or any of these issues:

1. *Prevailing opinions on goals of civil justice.* Please state doctrinal sources and relevant case law.
2. *Matters regarded to be within the scope of the goals of civil justice:* Are the goals of civil justice limited to litigation (decision making in contested matters), or do they also encompass non-contested matters? What is the portion of the work of civil justice in matters such as enforcement, holding of registers (land, company registers), collection of non-contested debt, regulation of future relationships between the parties, etc.? To what extent are the goals of civil justice viewed from the perspective of such tasks of the civil courts?
3. *Protection of individual rights v. protection of the public interest* (conflict resolution v. policy implementation). Please comment:

   - to what extent is it considered that the system of civil justice should pay attention to matters of public interest (public policy, morals, infringement of the rights of third parties);
   - to what extent should civil procedures reach results that are in line with certain policies (national interest, views of ruling elites or classes, governmental programmes, suppression of illegal activities, reasons of national security, confidentiality obligations, professional privileges, etc.);
   - what are the issues that the court should (in the context of the goals of civil procedure) determine *ex officio*;
   - which other actors or bodies (except the court and the parties) have an obligation to ensure that the goals of civil justice are being reached; which actors or bodies have the right to intervene in the judicial process on that account?

4. *'Material truth' v. fair trial within a reasonable time.* Please comment on the attitude in your jurisdiction with regard to the desirable balance between the wish to establish the facts correctly and the need to provide effective protection of rights in an appropriate time. What has precedence: the accuracy of adjudication, or the need to afford parties legal security and effective remedy in due time?
5. *'Hard cases' v. mass processing of routine matters.* Please comment to what extent the goals of civil justice are viewed from the perspective of resolving difficult legal matters which raise new issues of law and fact, and to what extent they are connected with the need to ensure the steady and routine handling of the courts' workload, coping with backlogs and the administrative requirements of efficiency.
6. *Principle of proportionality (de minimis non curat praetor) or same standards and processes to everyone, irrespective of the importance of the case.* To what extent is it considered that the goal of civil justice is to afford as much attention to the cases as they deserve, discarding all the matters that do not belong there? What filtering mechanisms are available? Or, is it considered that refusal to deal with a case in the same manner would be denial of justice? What are the real differences in the way and style of handling 'small claims' and 'proper court cases'?
7. *Bi-party proceedings v. resolution of complex, multi-party matters.* To what extent are the goals of civil justice limited to handling simple matters in which only rarely the cases involve more than two parties? Or, is the handling of complex, multi-party matters, where the courts have to exercise complex functions of social regulation, also considered to be the core goal of the civil justice system?
8. *Equitable results and substantive justice v. strict formalism and the principle of legality.* Is the goal of civil justice to reach an equitable result, or to find a correct legal solution by the strict application of the law?
9. *Problem solving or case processing.* Is it the dominant view that the civil justice system needs to approach the cases by trying to find an adequate solution to the underlying problems? Or, that cases have to be efficiently resolved by means requiring the least effort and expense by the competent authorities?
10. *Civil justice as freely available public service, or as a quasi-commercial source of revenue for the public budget.* Is the goal of the civil justice system (in particular: courts) to be available at no expense to everyone who needs legal protection, or is it just another social service that has to be paid by those who use it? What is the level of the court fees and is their rationale to cover the costs of the functioning of civil justice?
11. *Orientation towards the users, or self-centred goals?* Are the goals of civil justice defined to cater to the needs and wishes of the users? How is the perception of users regarding the fulfilment of the goals of civil justice established; who represents it? Or, are the goals defined mainly from the perspective of the civil justice system itself – by its professional actors (courts, judges, lawyers) and not by those whose rights are at stake?

References

Damaška M (1986) The faces of justice and state authority. Yale University Press, New Haven

Dika M, Uzelac A (1990) Zum Problem des richterlichen Aktivismus in Jugoslawien. Zbornik Pravnog fakulteta u Zagrebu 40(4):391–416

European Judicial Systems. Facts and Figures. 2012 (2010 Data). Strasbourg: Council of Europe (CEPEJ Report, http://www.coe.int/cepej)

Ewald W (1995) Comparative jurisprudence (II): the logic of legal transplants. Am J Comp Law 43:489

Fernhout F (2008) Formal rules in civil procedure and access to justice: striking a balance between excessive formalism and "anything goes". In: van Rhee CH, Uzelac A (eds) Civil justice between efficiency and quality: from ius commune to the CEPEJ. Intersentia, Antwerp, pp 207–216

Grgić A (2007) The length of civil proceedings in Croatia – main causes of delay. In: van Rhee CH, Uzelac A (eds) Public and private justice. Dispute resolution in modern societies. Intersentia, Antwerpen, pp 153–173

Kahn-Freund O (1974) On uses and misuses of comparative law. Mod Law Rev 37(1):1–27

Lenin VI (1918) The state and revolution. Collected Works 25:381–492

Merryman JH, Pérez-Perdomo R (2007) The civil law tradition, 3rd edn. Stanford University Press (first published 1969)

Teubner G (1998) Legal irritants: good faith in British law or how unifying law ends up in new divergences. Mod Law Rev 61(12):11–32

Uzelac A (1992) Istina u sudskom postupku [The concept of truth in judicial proceedings]. Pravni fakultet, Zagreb

Uzelac A (2004) Accelerating civil proceedings in Croatia – a history of attempts to improve the efficiency of civil litigation. In: van Rhee CH (ed) History of delays in civil procedure, Maastricht. Intersentia, Antwerpen, Groningen, pp 283–313

Uzelac A (2006) The rule of law and the Croatian judicial system: court delays as a barrier on the road to European accession. In: Frosini JO, Lupoi MA, Marchesiello M (eds) A European space of justice. Longo, Ravenna, pp 87–108

Uzelac A (2008) Turning civil procedure upside down: from judges' law to users' law. In: Tweehonderd jaar/Bicentenaire Code de Procédure civile. Kluwer uitgevers, Mechelen, pp 413–427

Uzelac A (2010) Survival of the third legal tradition? In: Walker J, Chase O (eds) Common law, civil law and the future of categories. Lexis Nexis, Markham, pp 377–396

Vyshinsky AJ (1950) Теория судебных доказательств в советском праве [Theory of judicial proof in Soviet law]. Gos. izd. iur. lit, Moscow

Watson A (1974) Legal transplants. Scottish Academic Press, Edinburgh

Zuckerman A (2009) The challenge of civil justice reform: effective court management of litigation. City Univ Hong Kong Law Rev 1(1):49–71

Part II
National Perspectives

Chapter 2
Civil Justice in Austrian-German Tradition

The Franz Klein Heritage and Beyond

Christian Koller

Abstract The first part of this chapter focuses on the goals of civil justice from an Austrian perspective including references to German law. The goals discussed include (a) the enforcement of individual rights; (b) the implementation of the legal order (*Bewährung der Rechtsordnung*); (c) the fulfilment of a 'social function' (*Sozialfunktion*), i.e. by providing an instrument for the resolution of 'social conflicts'; (d) legal certainty; (e) the development of the law itself (*Rechtsfortbildung*); and (f) the protection of public interests. Subsequently the following issues are discussed with regard to Austria (including references to German law): (1) matters within the scope of civil justice, (2) civil procedure as a tool to protect private rights and public interests, (3) the tension between procedural efficiency and the 'search for the truth' in civil proceedings, (4) access to the supreme court and its role in the system of civil justice, (5) proportionality between case and procedure, (6) complex and multi-party litigation, (7) substantive justice and the principle of legality, (8) case processing and problem solving as co-existing goals of civil justice, (9) the costs of litigation and (10) the user's perception.

C. Koller (✉)
Department of Civil Procedure, Faculty of Law, University of Vienna,
Schenkenstraße 8-10, A-1010 Vienna, Austria
e-mail: christian.koller@univie.ac.at

A. Uzelac (ed.), *Goals of Civil Justice and Civil Procedure in Contemporary Judicial Systems*, Ius Gentium: Comparative Perspectives on Law and Justice 34,
DOI 10.1007/978-3-319-03443-0_2, © Springer International Publishing Switzerland 2014

2.1 Goals of Civil Justice from an Austrian-German Perspective

2.1.1 Legal Doctrine

Theories on the goals of civil justice are numerous and have triggered a vast amount of scholarly writings.[1] Most commentaries or textbooks on civil procedure start by discussing and/or listing the 'goals', 'function' or 'purpose' of such procedure.[2] However, no general consensus has emerged.

It is often stated that civil justice provides a means for the citizens to enforce and determine their substantive rights and obligations (Fasching in Fasching and Konecny 2000: Einl para. 11; Brehm in Stein and Jonas 2003: vor Sec. 1 para. 5; Murray and Stürner 2004: 4; Rauscher in Rauscher et al. 2008: Einl para. 8). Consequently, enforcement of individual rights forms one of the main goals of civil justice. At the same time, the existence of an effective enforcement mechanism affects the level of compliance with legal norms in society at large. It might, therefore, also be argued that the legal order proves itself through civil proceedings (*Bewährung der Rechtsordnung*) and is implemented thereby (Brehm in Stein and Jonas 2003: vor Sec. 1 para. 6; Fasching in Fasching and Konecny 2000: Einl para. 11). It is, however, doubtful whether the implementation of the legal order amounts to a goal of civil justice in its own right. Rather, protection (and enforcement) of individual rights and implementation of the legal order (in general) form two sides of the same coin (Brehm in Stein and Jonas 2003: vor Sec. 1 para. 12; Rosenberg et al. 2010: Sec. 1 para. 9).

In Austria, the procedural ideology of Franz Klein (who, in 1893, prepared the draft on which the Austrian Code of Civil Procedure[3] was based) has strongly influenced theories on the goals of civil justice. According to Klein's procedural thinking, each legal dispute qualifies as an 'evil in society' (or a 'social conflict') negatively affecting the functioning of today's economy.[4] Following this ideology, civil procedure serves as a remedy to cure such deficiencies in an expedient and efficient way (Oberhammer and Domej 2005a: 121; Ballon 1983: 427). In other words, it was Klein's understanding that civil procedure fulfils a 'social function' (*Sozialfunktion*). Settling specific disputes is, therefore, not the sole purpose of civil

---

[1] This is particularly true for Germany, see, e.g., Gaul (1968: 27 et seqq.); Henckel (1970: 41 et seqq.); F. von Hippel (1939: 170 et seqq.); F. von Hippel (1952: 431 et seqq.); Meyer (2004: 1); Pawlowski (1967: 345); Stürner (1990: 545); the issue has been less controversial in Austria, for an overview see Fasching in Fasching and Konecny (2000: Einl para. 11 et seqq.); for a more detailed analysis see Böhm (1986: 211); Klein (1927: 117 et seq.); Klein and Engel (1927: 190); Novak (1961: 64); Kuderna (1986: 182); Schoibl (1990: 3); Sprung (1977: 393).

[2] As already aptly noted by Gaul (1968: 27).

[3] Hereinafter referred to as 'ZPO'; RGBl. No. 113/1895 as last amended by BGBl. I No. 21/2011.

[4] See Klein and Engel (1927: 190 and 280); cf. Oberhammer and Domej (2010: 257) with further references.

procedure, rather, it also serves (and fosters) welfare (*Wohlfahrtsfunktion*). Klein's procedural thinking is reflected in the opinion prevailing in Austria according to which civil justice not merely serves the enforcement of individual rights but also has the goal to provide an instrument for the resolution of 'social conflicts'. Consequently, it fulfils public welfare tasks.[5]

Moreover, civil procedure has the goal to provide legal certainty (*Rechtssicherheit* and *Rechtsgewißheit*) for the parties by putting their dispute to an end (*Rechtsfriedensfunktion*).[6] The significance of the latter function is evidenced by the provisions on *res judicata* (see, e.g., Sec. 411 Austrian Code of Civil Procedure and Sec. 322 German Code of Civil Procedure)[7] which ensure that a (final) decision cannot be re-litigated in subsequent proceedings but is binding for the parties (and courts). Establishing the substantive truth in civil procedure enhances the parties' acceptance of the decision and thereby fosters legal security. It follows that discovery and determination of the substantive truth do not as such form goals of civil justice but rather serve as a means to achieving other goals, most notably legal certainty and security (Brehm in Stein and Jonas 2003: para. 25; Zeuner 2003: 1790; Böhm 1986: 227).

In German legal literature it is argued that the further development of the law itself (*Rechtsfortbildung*) and its uniform application rank among the functions of civil procedure (Brehm 2001: 57; Böhm 1986: 230). Such submission is, *inter alia*, based on Sec. 132 para. 4 GVG (Judicature Act) according to which an adjudicating panel of the Supreme Court may submit an issue of fundamental importance to the Grand Panel[8] for a decision if it deems such submission necessary for the development of the law or for its uniform application.[9] Although case law is not legally binding (*stricto sensu*) it does have an influence on courts exercising their discretionary power in subsequent cases. It is, therefore, legitimate to assume that civil procedure contributes to the further development of the law by the adoption of certain court practices (Brehm in Stein and Jonas 2003: vor Sec. 1 para. 23).

In special areas of law, such as consumer protection law, unfair competition law, environmental law and labour law, certain (representative) bodies are granted the right to file an action on behalf of collective interests (*Verbandsklage*) (Koch 2001: 358; Rechberger 2010: 156). The control mechanism implemented by this instrument primarily serves the protection of public or collective (non-individual) interests.[10]

[5] See, e.g., Fasching in Fasching and Konecny (2000: Einl para. 12); Ballon (2009: para. 7); Holzhammer (1976: 2).

[6] Fasching in Fasching and Konecny (2000: Einl para. 13); Brehm in Stein and Jonas (2003: vor Sec. 1 para. 7); for a different opinion see Rosenberg et al. (2010: Sec. 1 para. 10).

[7] Hereinafter referred to as 'dZPO', BGBl I, p. 533 as last amended by BGBl. I, p. 3044 of 22 December 2011.

[8] According to Sec. 132 para. 5 GVG the Grand Panel for civil matters shall be composed of the president of the Supreme Court and one member from each of the (12) civil panels.

[9] F. Brehm in Stein and Jonas (2003: vor Sec. 1 para. 7); Rauscher in Rauscher et al. (2008: Einl para. 10); but see Murray and Stürner (2004: 4), referring to the improvement of the law itself as a 'by-product' of civil justice.

[10] It also enhances legal protection; see Schoibl (1990: 3 et seqq.).

Consequently, the protection of public interests ranks, at least within the scope of application of such actions, among the goals of civil justice (Fasching in Fasching and Konecny 2000: Einl para. 17; Murray and Stürner 2004: 4).

The question of whether one goal of civil justice takes priority over another has led to some controversy in legal doctrine (Böhm 1986: 219). In the author's view, the best approach would be to individually analyse the interplay between different goals of civil justice in each case when interpreting procedural norms instead of applying a strict hierarchy that is unable to comprise the civil justice system as a whole.

2.1.2 Case Law

Not surprisingly, the general question of what goals underlie civil justice is not addressed in case law. However, reference to the goals of civil justice has been repeatedly made when interpreting procedural provisions (Henckel 1970: 47). The German *Reichsgericht*, for instance, already held that the aim of the provisions of the code of civil procedure is not to impede the enforcement of rights, but rather to provide a functional and swift procedure for deciding a dispute.[11] This is sometimes referred to as the 'auxiliary function' (*dienende Funktion*) of procedural law, which is, however, an overly simplistic expression. The enforcement of individual rights is, occasionally, invoked as a goal of civil justice in order to overcome formalistic results. By contrast, the need to comply with formal requirements stipulated in the code of civil procedure is in some cases justified by reference to legal certainty and security as goals of civil procedure.[12] This discrepancy shows that the goals of civil justice may serve as interpretative tools to reach a certain outcome in a particular case.[13] A similar line of reasoning is applied in German case law that permits *res judicata* to be overturned on the basis of an action in tort (i.e. Sec. 826 BGB).[14] The German Supreme Court[15] argues that the principle of *res judicata*, which aims to establish legal certainty, must give way to the 'paramount goal of civil justice, which is, to reach justice in the individual case'.[16] The question is therefore framed as one of 'justice vs. legal certainty' (*Gerichtigkeit vs. Rechtssicherheit*). While justice was

[11] See RG III 120/22, 8 December 1922, RGZ 105, 421 (427); cf. BGH III ZR 310/51, 8 October 1953, NJW 1953, 1826.

[12] See, e.g., BGH V ZB 31/54, 14 December 1954, NJW 1955, 546, justifying the requirement for certain written submissions to be personally signed by an attorney by relying on the (procedural) goal of achieving legal certainty and security; cf. BGH VIII ZR 154/86, 3 June 1987, NJW 1987, 2588.

[13] Cf. Gaul (1968: 39 et seqq.), who critically comments on the developments in case law.

[14] For the reversal of judgments on the basis of Sec. 826 BGB just see Hess (1999: 172); cf. Wagner in Säcker and Rixecker (2013: Sec. 826 para. 179 et seqq.).

[15] Hereinafter referred to as 'BGH'.

[16] BGH III ZR 210/50, 21 June 1951, NJW 1951, 759 ('In allen diesen Fällen muß der Grundsatz der Rechtskraft, der dem Rechtsfrieden und der Rechtssicherheit dient, dem höchsten Zweck der

given priority in the case law overturning *res judicata* according to Sec. 826 BGB, the BGH, most interestingly, based a narrow reading of the grounds upon which a re-opening of the proceedings may be granted (see Sec. 580 dZPO et seqq.), which also allows for a setting aside of *res judicata*, on the principle of legal certainty. The inconsistency underlying the varying reliance on different goals of justice regarding the interpretation of Sec. 826 BGB, on the one hand, and Sec. 580 dZPO et seqq., on the other, has attracted criticism.[17]

Specific references to goals of civil justice in Austrian case law are rare. However, the Austrian Supreme Court[18] has in a number of decisions stated that the goals of civil procedure need to be taken into account when interpreting procedural acts of the parties.[19] Similar to the BGH, the OGH has consistently held that the provisions that allow for proceedings to be re-opened (Sec. 530 ZPO et seqq.) need to be interpreted restrictively since they interfere with the *res judicata* effect of a decision and thereby with legal certainty.[20] Additionally, the OGH acknowledged that establishing the truth ranks among the goals of civil procedure.[21] According to the OGH this goal does not, however, as such render the taking of illegally obtained evidence admissible.[22]

2.2 Matters Within the Scope of Civil Justice: From Settling of Private Disputes to Legal Welfare and Enforcement Proceedings

Under Austrian and German law matters falling within the scope of civil justice are not limited to contested matters.[23] Matters dealt with by civil courts in non-contentious proceedings are numerous and traditionally encompass areas of civil

Rechtspflege, Gerechtigkeit zu wirken, weichen.'); cf. BGH VI ZR 160/97, 30 June 1988, NJW 1998, 2818 with further references.

[17] See Gaul (1968: 41) with further references.

[18] Hereinafter referred to as 'OGH'.

[19] See, e.g., OGH 7 Ob 604/92, 15 October 1992, EvBl 1993/44 = RZ 1994/30; OGH 3 Ob 146/93, 24 November 1993; for further references see RIS-Justiz RS0017881 and RS0037416 (available online at: www.ris.bka.gv.at).

[20] See, e.g., OGH 17 Ob 31/08w, 23 September 2008; OGH 3 Ob 72/08x, 11 June 2008 ('... die Wiederaufnahmsklagemöglichkeit [ist] als außerordentlicher Eingriff in die Rechtskraft und damit in die Rechtssicherheit und den Rechtsfrieden einschränkend auszulegen.')

[21] See OGH 2 Ob 708/54, 3 December 1954; OGH 2 Ob 590/56, 17 October 1956 ('Ziel des modernen Zivilprozesses ist die Erforschung der Wahrheit; der Richter hat sich daher nicht passiv zu verhalten, sondern sich von Amts wegen im Sinne des Prozeßzweckes zu verhalten.')

[22] OGH 6 Ob 190/01m, 27 September 2001, RdW 2002/289.

[23] See, e.g., Rosenberg et al. (2010: Sec. 1 para. 16 et seqq.). In Austria and Germany, as in many other jurisdictions, a distinction is made between contentious and non-contentious jurisdiction. In Austria the latter is governed by the Non-contentious Proceedings Act of 2003 (*Außerstreitgesetz*), which entered into force in 2005; cf. Klicka et al. (2006: para. 2), in Germany by the Law on the

law which require an active intervention by the judge in the interest of parties not in a position to adequately protect their own interests (Klicka et al. 2006: para. 10; Murray and Stürner 2004: 443). Moreover, in matters such as the administration of (land and commercial) registers, guardianship, estates and the like, non-contentious proceedings serve the protection of public interest. It has, however, become increasingly difficult to draw a clear distinction between contentious and non-contentious jurisdiction since the legislator decided to submit to non-contentious jurisdiction more and more matters which do not share the same characteristics as those matters traditionally forming the core of non-contentious jurisdiction (Rosenberg et al. 2010: Sec. 11 para. 1; Klicka et al. 2006: para. 9 and 17). Therefore, the goals of civil justice viewed from the perspective of contentious proceedings cannot be clearly distinguished from the goals pursued by non-contentious proceedings; they are as diverse as the matters falling within the scope of non-contentious jurisdiction.[24] However, the characteristics underlying non-contentious proceedings in certain areas of law and the specific functions of such proceedings add (the following) additional goals of civil justice to the list enumerated above (see Sect. 2.1).

According to the Official Comment on the (new) Austrian Non-contentious Proceedings Act the major focus of non-contentious proceedings is not so much the settlement of individual disputes but rather the regulation of long term legal relationships between parties that are dependent on one another; such relationships may, for instance, be rooted in marriage law, family law, inheritance law or joint-ownership.[25] Moreover, non-contentious proceedings sometimes serve the formation of legal relationships or legal rights (*Rechtsgestaltung*). This is, for instance, the case in certification proceedings (*Beurkundungsverfahren*), registration procedures, e.g. based on applications for entries in the land or company register provided they have constitutive effect, and proceedings involving matters of personal status (e.g. guardianship) (Rosenberg et al. 2010: Sec. 11 para. 4). At the same time, these proceedings form part of the so-called preventive administration of justice by providing legal security for the parties in certain transactions (Brehm 1993: Sec. 1 para. 12 et seq.). It has, however, correctly been pointed out that court decisions having the effect of changing legal relationships or rights (*Gestaltungswirkung*) are rendered not only in non-contentious proceedings (Pabst in Rauscher et al. 2010: Sec. 1 FamFG para. 12).

Traditionally, matters of legal welfare (*Rechtsfürsorgematerien*) are dealt with in non-contentious proceedings. It follows that the principles of party control over the subject matter (*Dispositionsgrundsatz*) is restricted, i.e. the so-called *Offizialmaxime*

Procedure in Family Matters and in Matters of Non-Contentious Jurisdiction (*Gesetz über das Verfahren in Familiensachen und in den Angelegenheiten der freiwilligen Gerichtsbarkeit* or *FamFG*).

[24] Including, e.g., appointment of a guardian (Sec. 117 et seqq. AußStrG), adoption (Sec. 86 et seqq. AußStrG), divorce by consent (Sec. 55a EheG), probate proceedings (Sec. 143 et seqq. AußStrG), proceedings for a declaration of death (Sec. 14 TEG), administration of the company register (Sec. 75 para. 2 GBG) and the land register (Sec. 15 et seqq. FBG), joint ownership disputes (Sec. 838a ABGB), certain tenancy law matters (Sec. 37 MRG); for a detailed list see Mayr and Fucik (2006: para. 37 et seqq.).

[25] See the Official Comment (ErläutRV) 224 BlgNR 22. GP at p. 7 (AußStrG).

applies instead of the *Dispositionsgrundsatz*. Moreover, the court has, at least in principle, the power to establish the facts of the case *ex officio*, following the so-called *Untersuchungsgrundsatz* as opposed to the *Verhandlungsgrundsatz* (Klicka et al. 2006: para. 10; Mayr and Fucik 2006: para. 17; cf. for German law Murray and Stürner 2004: 443). In general, the procedure is more flexible and less formal (Mayr and Fucik 2006: para. 17; Rosenberg et al. 2010: Sec. 11 para. 7). This is particularly important for multi-party proceedings in which the parties involved cannot be divided in two groups, i.e. claimants' and respondents' sides, such as probate proceedings or proceedings concerning certain condominium and tenancy law matters (Klicka et al. 2006: para. 12). It is often noted, both with regard to German and Austrian law, that non-contentious proceedings are more administrative in nature or qualify as 'administrative activities in the area of private law' (*Verwaltungstätigkeit im Bereich der Privatrechtsordnung*) (Borth and Grandel in Musielak and Borth 2011: Sec. 1 para. 2; cf. Koch and Diedrich 1998: 11; Murray and Stürner 2004: 443; Klicka et al. 2006: para. 13). This is particularly true for adoption proceedings under Austrian law (see Sec. 88 et seqq. AußStrG) and the supervisory functions Austrian courts have with regard to the administration of assets of people placed under guardianship (see Sec. 132 et seqq. AußStrG). By the same token, proceedings concerning the appointment of a guardian for minors (see Sec. 1773 et seqq. BGB) or the invalidation of documents (see Sec. 466 et seqq. FamFG) under German law are administrative in nature (Brehm in Stein and Jonas 2003: Sec. 1 para. 12).

In Austria, civil courts also serve as competition authorities, namely the Viennese court of appeal as cartel court and the OGH as cartel court of appeal. The AußStrG also applies to proceedings before cartel courts.

In addition, Austrian and German courts are involved in the forced execution of judgments (and other titles) (Murray and Stürner 2004: 445). It goes without saying that enforcement proceedings have the goal to enforce the creditors' rights by using coercive power (if necessary) (Rechberger and Oberhammer 2009: para. 1). By contrast, the purpose of insolvency proceedings, which also fall within the jurisdiction of civil courts, is twofold: on the one hand, insolvency proceedings aim at the liquidation of the debtor's assets in order to (jointly) satisfy the creditors' claims on the basis of the *par conditio creditorum* principle; on the other hand, more and more emphasis is placed on the debtor's reorganization as a major goal of insolvency proceedings (Pape in Uhlenbruck 2010: Sec. 1 para. 1 et seqq.).

2.3 Courts in the Service of Public Interest or *Sozialfunktion* Revisited (Land Registers, Consumer Protection and Verbandsklagen)

On the basis of Franz Klein's procedural ideology, it might be argued that civil procedure as such serves the protection of public interest by fulfilling a 'social function' (*Sozialfunktion*) (Klein and Engel 1927: 190 et seqq.). According to his understanding, settling specific disputes is not the sole purpose of civil procedure, rather it also serves (and fosters) welfare (*Wohlfahrtsfunktion*) (see Sect. 2.1.1; Schoibl 1990: 3). Additionally, the administrative activities assigned to civil courts in non-contentious proceedings (see Sect. 2.2. and n. 25 above.) often serve public interest and/or the interest of third parties. The administration of land registers, for instance, guarantees legal security as regards land tenure and land transfers. Such positive externality also serves public interest. Apart from that, cases in which the Austrian and German civil justice systems aim to vindicate public interest are rather limited.

A notable exception are those provisions of Austrian and German law that grant certain associations or independent public bodies the right to bring representative actions for injunctive or declaratory relief in specific areas of law (so-called *Verbandsklagen*), most importantly consumer protection law and competition law (see, e.g., Koch 2011: 442; Murray and Stürner 2004: 4; Rosenberg et al. 2010: Sec. 47 para. 2 et seqq.; Rechberger 2010: 156). The *Verbandsklage* also serves public (or supra-individual) interest by providing an effective law enforcement mechanism in those cases in which traditional instruments of control and law enforcement fail (Koch 2001: 360; Schoibl 1990: 3). In Austria, the *Verbandsklage* (cf. Rechberger 2010: 156 et seqq.) is enshrined in the following provisions : Sec. 14 of the Act against Unfair Commercial Practices[26] empowers certain bodies[27] to bring an action to enjoin parties from violating specific competition law rules; Sec. 28 of the Consumer Protection Act[28] provides the basis for a *Verbandsklage* against unfair and illegal clauses in general contract terms; and under Sec. 28a KSchG a representative claim against noncompliance with consumer protection standards can be raised.[29] Section 29 KSchG assigns the right of action to certain associations and chambers,[30] most notably the Consumer Information Association. By the same token, a number of German laws (Baetge 2007: 4; Rosenberg et al. 2010: Sec. 47 para. 2 et seqq.) provide for actions by certain qualified associations or interest groups: according to Sec. 1 of the Act on Injunctive Relief[31] qualified consumer associations and commercial interest groups have the right to ask for injunctive relief against the use of unfair standard terms of contract. Section 2 UKlaG provides for such action with regard to violations of all provisions protecting consumer rights.[32] Moreover, under

[26] Hereinafter referred to as UWG (*Gesetz gegen den unlauteren Wettbewerb*).

[27] I.e. the Austrian Federal Economic Chamber, the Austrian Federal Chamber of Workers and Employees, the Board of Directors of the Austrian Chamber of Agriculture, the Austrian Trade Union Federation and the Consumer Information Association.

[28] Hereinafter referred to as KSchG (*Konsumentenschutzgesetz*).

[29] For a detailed analysis see Kühnberg (2006).

[30] Such as the Austrian Federal Economic Chamber, the Federal Chamber of Labour, the Council of Austrian Chambers of Agricultural Labour, the Presidential Conference of Austrian Chambers of Agriculture, the Austrian Trade Union Federation, the Consumer Information Association and the Austrian Council of Senior Citizens.

[31] Hereinafter referred to as UKlaG (*Unterlassungsklagengesetz*).

[32] Sec. 28 et seq. KSchG as well as the provisions of the UKlaG that serve consumer protection constitute an implementation of the EU Directive on Injunctions for the Protection of Consumers' Interests, European Parliament and Council Directive No. 98/27, 1998 OJ (L 166) 51; see Baetge 2007: 5.

Sec. 8 of the Law Against Unfair Competition[33] associations having the purpose of promoting commercial interests are granted the right to bring a claim for injunction in case of certain violations of competition law (Halfmeier 2006: 89 et seqq.). Another instrument that needs to be mentioned in this context is the so-called *Gewinnabschöpfungsklage*, i.e. an action for the recovery of ill-gotten gains according to Sec. 10 of the German UWG. This provision empowers certain organizations and so-called 'qualified entities' to bring an action for the recovery of gains obtained by intentionally violating competition law to the detriment of a large number of customers. The action seeks the payment of the recovered sum to the public purse. In addition, the German Competition Act[34] authorizes organizations for the promotion of commercial or independent professional interests to file a complaint in case of a violation of the GWB or of (ex-) Articles 81 and 82 EC (now Articles 101 and 102 TFEU). In general, the private enforcement of competition law through state courts serves the protection of both public and individual interest.

It follows from the foregoing that, unlike in the United States, in Austria and Germany civil litigation does not serve as a prime tool for vindicating public interest.[35] This is also evidenced by the fact that instruments similar to punitive damages are not part of the Austrian and German legal systems.

Austrian and German courts must apply the relevant legal norms to the facts established in the proceedings.[36] In doing so they are not bound by any overriding policy or national interest that would necessarily affect their decision. Even if the court is of the opinion that a certain provision is unreasonable, it cannot simply 'correct' national legislation by interpreting the relevant provision against its wording, the legislator's clear intention and its underlying rationale.[37] However, traditional interpretative methods require the courts to take into account policies, societal values, goals and interests underlying the provisions applicable to the specific case. All of these elements might have changed in the period between the enactment of certain legislation and its application (Haas 2011: 94). In other words, the policy enshrined in a certain provision is indirectly implemented by the courts in civil

[33] Hereinafter referred to as German UWG.

[34] Hereinafter referred to as German GWB.

[35] This seems to be generally the case for Europe; see Kötz (2003: 75).

[36] The rule-of-law principle is stipulated in Article 20 para. 2 of the German Constitution and in Article 18 para. 1 of the Austrian Constitution.

[37] See, e.g., BGH 16 August 2006, VIII ZR 200/05, NJW 2006, 3200. In this case it was disputed whether under German law the seller is entitled, in cases where goods not in conformity are replaced, to payment by way of compensation for the benefits derived by the purchaser from the use of those goods until their replacement with new goods. The BGH expressed doubts regarding the unilateral burden thus placed on the purchaser but stated that it saw no way of correcting national legislation by means of interpretation (*contra legem*); cf. *Wenzel*, Die Bindung des Richters an Gesetz und Recht, NJW 2008, p. 347. See also OGH 25 October 1972, 1 Ob 211/72, JBl 1974, 99, where it was held that the strict requirements for a divorce on the ground of irretrievable breakdown (in force at that time) could not be loosened by way of interpretation. According to the OGH it is not the judiciary's but rather the legislature's task to change unsatisfactory legal provisions.

procedure. Consequently, governmental programmes or 'views of ruling elites' only have an influence on the outcome of civil proceedings to the extent they are reflected in existing law.

Under Austrian and German law a number of persons are either excluded from giving testimony altogether or may invoke professional privileges to refuse to give testimony on a certain matter.[38] In these cases professional privileges might have an impact on the result of civil proceedings, be it because the court does not have the benefit of hearing the testimony or because a claim of privilege may, in some instances, give rise to common-sense inferences (Murray and Stürner 2004: 305). However, contractual confidentiality obligations generally do not grant the right to refuse to give evidence (Rosenberg et al. 2010: Sec. 120 para. 20). The broad scope of witness privileges in German and Austrian civil procedure can be seen as a protection against excessive intrusion by the state (represented by the court) into the private (or most personal) sphere (Murray and Stürner 2004: 303).

Under Austrian and German law the parties have control over the subject matter in contentious proceedings[39] according to the so-called *Dispositionsmaxime* (i.e. principle of party control) (Oberhammer and Domej 2005b: 295). However, within the framework of the subject matter of the dispute the court has the power, and in some cases even the duty, to raise a number of issues *ex officio* (which in turn casts light on the goals of civil justice in general): the judge has a duty to discuss relevant factual and legal aspects of the case with the parties, to ask appropriate questions, for instance in case of incomplete allegations, and to give necessary instructions.[40] This is particularly important for the goal of civil justice to provide an efficient mechanism for the enforcement and determination of individual rights and obligations since the duty to ask questions and give instructions is a crucial instrument in fostering procedural economy (Oberhammer 2004a: 91). At the same time, it protects the parties from being taken by surprise by the court's decision, which in turn guarantees the parties' right to be heard, and to some extent places the parties on a level playing field (Wagner in Rauscher et al. 2008: Sec. 139 para. 1). Overall, according to said duty the court bears responsibility for the proceedings to be conducted in a fair and non-arbitrary way, which, *inter alia*, aims at establishing the truth (Stadler in Musielak 2013: Sec. 139 para. 1) and prevents injustice in the individual case (Murray and Stürner (2004: 166). Moreover, it is the court's task to take care of the formal course of the proceedings on its own initiative (Oberhammer and Domej 2005b: 302), which (again) correlates with the civil justice goal of enforcing individual rights and obligations. Austrian and German law also follow the maxim *iura novit curia* according to which the court is assumed to know the law (including foreign law) and apply it *ex officio* (Oberhammer and Domej 2005b: 302;

---

[38] E.g. clergypersons, journalists and professional persons to whom confidential information is entrusted; cf. Murray and Stürner (2004: 298 et seqq.); Rosenberg et al. (2010: Sec. 120 para. 20 et seqq.).

[39] For the court's powers in non-contentious proceedings see Sect. 2.2.

[40] See Sec. 139 dZPO and Sec. 182 and 182a ZPO; cf. Oberhammer and Domej (2005b: 300); Murray and Stürner (2004: 166 et seqq.).

Haas 2011: 93; Rauscher in Rauscher et al. 2008: Einl para. 306). The *iura novit curia* principle not only serves the enforcement of rights but also the implementation of the legal order in general. Additionally, the court is, at least to a certain degree, entitled to take evidence *ex officio* (Oberhammer and Domej 2005b: 304; Haas 2011: 100). The judge may, for instance, take expert evidence or order the production of a certain document provided one of the parties has referred to it.[41] The court's power to take evidence *ex officio* can be considered, at least according to Franz Klein's procedural thinking, as a tool to advance the process of establishing the truth (Parker and Lewisch 1998: 206). On balance, the strong position afforded to the judge in German-speaking countries can, at least today,[42] best be characterized as a contribution to the goal of civil justice of providing a swift and efficient determination of the parties' rights and obligations which in turn establishes legal certainty by putting the parties' dispute to an end. Finally, the court has to decide *ex officio* on a number of procedural requirements (so-called *Prozessvoraussetzungen*) that need to be fulfilled for the court to take a decision on the merits of the case. These procedural requirements, *inter alia*, include questions of jurisdiction, procedural capacity of the parties, *res judicata*, *lis pendens* and so forth.

The responsibility for the goals of civil justice being reached is shared between the parties and the court. Other actors and bodies generally do not have the duty to secure the achievement of the goals of civil justice in the particular case. Bodies similar to the French *avocats généraux* or the admissibility of *amicus curiae* briefs, which form part of common law systems, are unknown to the Austrian and German legal systems. In Austria, the public prosecutor (*Staatsanwalt*) has the right (and duty) to file an action for annulment of a marriage, especially if the marriage was entered into for the sole or prevailing purpose of obtaining a certain name or Austrian citizenship.[43] In this context the public prosecutor acts as a representative of the state in order to protect the public interest by initiating civil proceedings (Kralik 1974: 66 et seqq.). Apart from that, Austrian law assigns the task to the State Financial Procurator (*Finanzprokuratur*) to intervene (in proceedings) in order to protect the public interest and to file all requests and legal remedies available if the urgency of the case requires such immediate intervention or no other administrative body considers itself to be competent.[44] However, the State Financial Procurator's function has never played a significant role in practice (Kralik 1974: 66). The OGH has repeatedly decided that the State Financial Procurator does not have the power

[41] See Sec. 182 ZPO and Sec. 142 dZPO. However, under Austrian law the hearing of a witness and the taking of documentary evidence (*ex officio*) is not permissible if both parties object to it.

[42] Historically the discussion on the judge's power in German-speaking doctrine was mainly influenced by ideological implications (i.e. the question of 'liberal vs. social view of civil procedure'); see, e.g., Oberhammer (2004a: 90); Oberhammer (2004b: 1040).

[43] See Sec. 28 para. 1 Austrian marriage law (hereinafter referred to as 'EheG'). Additionally, the public prosecutor has the right to intervene in proceedings for the declaration of death according to Sec. 20 et seqq. *Todeserklärungsgesetz-TEG*.

[44] See Sec. 3 para. 6 of the State Financial Procurator Act (*Finanzprokuraturgesetz*). Section 3 para. 6 explicitly mentions the State Financial Procurator's task to secure and collect charitable donations *mortis causa*.

to intervene in all civil proceedings but rather only in limited cases where the public interest is directly affected by the subject matter of the decision. Indirect ramifications on matters of public interest do not suffice for the State Financial Procurator's intervention.[45] Under German law, the public prosecutor no longer has any power to intervene in civil proceedings (Rosenberg et al. 2010: Sec. 27 para. 1). The competence of the public prosecutor to bring an action for annulment of a marriage based on certain grounds, i.e. legal incapacity (Sec. 1304 BGB), bigamy (Sec. 1306 BGB), intermarriage (Sec. 1307 BGB) and so forth,[46] was transferred to administrative bodies of the respective (German) state (Rosenberg et al. 2010: Sec. 27 para. 2).

2.4 The Search for the 'Material Truth' and the Right to a Fair Trial Within a Reasonable Time as Co-existing Goals

According to Franz Klein, the concept of the active judge had a dual function: on the one hand, it aimed to reach a correct and just decision by establishing the substantive truth *ex officio* (which was truly important for Klein) and, on the other hand, efficient case management by the judge provided an effective method for accelerating the proceedings without impairing their quality. Ensuring the quality of decisions and accelerating proceedings are, in Klein's view, not mutually exclusive goals. He (Klein 1900: 10; Oberhammer and Domej 2010: 260) emphasized that the courts should not strive for speedy proceedings at the cost of the quality of judgments. In the authors' opinion, differentiating strictly between substantive and formal truth seems rather naïve considering procedural practice. On the one hand, the 'battle' between the parties to enforce their rights and/or the court's fact-finding measures will always lead to a (more or less adequate) convergence of those facts on which the court's decision is based and reality. On the other hand, it would be illusory to assume that a system existed which guarantees the establishment of substantive truth within a reasonable time and with reasonable effort (Oberhammer 2004a: 90). However, an analysis of Austrian civil procedural law shows that it aims at a balanced approach, i.e. the accuracy of the decision does not overrule the need to ensure legal security and provide the parties with an effective remedy in due time (and vice versa). According to Sec. 178 ZPO each party is obliged to bring forward factual allegations supporting their requests *truthfully* and *comprehensively*. In other words, this provision enshrines a duty of truth (so-called *Wahrheitspflicht*). Equally, the judge is responsible for establishing the 'true' facts underlying the rights and claims brought forward by the parties by exercising his or her duty to ask questions and give instructions under Sec. 182 para. 1 ZPO (Parker and Lewisch 1998: 207). In general, the

[45] See, e.g., OGH 19 September 2002, NZ 2003/66; cf. RIS-Justiz RS0071582.

[46] For an exhaustive list see Hilbig in Rauscher et al. (2010: Sec. 129 FamFG para. 1).

judge's power to take evidence *ex officio* (see Sect. 2.3) serves as an instrument to establish the truth and render a judgment on that very basis. In the interest of procedural efficiency the 'search for the truth' in civil proceedings is, however, limited, which can be exemplified as follows. Firstly, according to Sec. 183 para. 2 ZPO the judge has no power to order the production of documents or hear a witness if both parties object. Secondly, it is settled case law that the court has to consider factual allegations made by one of the parties but not contested by the opposing party to be correct and base its decision on those facts without further examination.[47] Exceptions to this rule are only made where (i) it is generally known that the uncontested fact is incorrect, (ii) the factual statement in question contradicts generally acknowledged principles derived from experience (so-called *Erfahrungssätze*) or (iii) the judge found out about the incorrectness of the uncontested fact when exercising his or her official activities (Rechberger and Simotta 2010: para. 775). Thirdly, new factual submissions are, in most cases, not admissible at the appeal stage under the ZPO.[48] Finally, Sec. 179 ZPO empowers the judge to dismiss late allegations if they were not made earlier due to gross negligence and provided their admission would significantly delay the proceedings (Oberhammer and Domej 2010: 271; Oberhammer 2004c: 227).

The German approach corresponds, *cum grano salis*, to the Austrian. Consequently, it also tries to strike a balance between taking a decision on a solid factual basis while at the same time ensuring a speedy and efficient decision-making process. A number of provisions of the dZPO indicate that civil procedure aims at establishing the substantive truth.[49] Section 138 dZPO, for instance, enshrines the parties' duty to tell the truth.[50] Moreover, Sec. 286 dZPO provides that the court has the power to freely evaluate evidence in order to decide whether a factual allegation is to be deemed *true* or *untrue*. According to Sec. 395 para. 1 dZPO a witness shall be instructed to tell the truth prior to his or her examination.[51] Also under German law the judge has the power to take evidence *ex officio* (Haas 2011: 100). On the other side of the spectrum, the process of establishing the truth is limited by the admissions of one party of the facts submitted by the other party,[52] the restriction to plead new arguments before the Court of Appeal (Gottwald 2004: 128) and the judge's power to dismiss late submissions of means of attack or defences under Sec. 296 dZPO (Gottwald 2004: 126). On the basis that there is no equivalent to the civil law concept of limited legal capacity of minors in civil proceedings[53] it was submitted

[47] See Sect. 2.3. Decision of 21 November 1988, 5 Ob 631/89, JBl 1990, 590; OGH 16 September 2011, 2 Ob 89/11v; RIS-Justiz RS0039949, RS0040110; this view is, however, rejected by the prevailing view in legal doctrine, cf. Rechberger and Simotta (2010: para. 775).

[48] See Sec. 482 para. 2 ZPO; cf. Oberhammer and Domej (2010: 271).

[49] This seems to be widely accepted in legal doctrine, see Zeuner (2003: 1788 et seqq.) with further references.

[50] The exact limits of that duty are, however, disputed among scholars, see Haas (2011: 91).

[51] See also Sec. 451 dZPO.

[52] See Sec. 288 dZPO; cf. Prütting in Rauscher et al. (2008: Sec.288 para. 32 et seqq.).

[53] This is not, however, the case in non-contentious proceedings.

that the interest of securing efficient proceedings would, in this very case, prevail over the minor's individual personal interest to influence the truth-finding process (Zeuner 2003: 1792).[54]

2.5 'Hard Cases' v. Mass Processing of Routine Matters: The Leading Role of the Highest Courts

In Austria, access to the OGH has been gradually limited since the enactment of the ZPO. While originally all cases (except those where a very small amount was in dispute) could be brought before the OGH, today access to the OGH is, on the one hand, only admissible if the amount in dispute (in the second instance) exceeds €5,000, and, on the other hand, depends on the existence of a question of law of considerable importance to legal uniformity, legal certainty or the development of the law.[55] If the amount in dispute ranges between €5,000 and €30,000, the admissibility to file an appeal to the OGH depends on permission to appeal granted by the second instance.[56] According to Sec. 8 of the Supreme Court Act (OGHG) the OGH's decision has to be taken by an enlarged panel (*verstärkter Senat*) of 11 members if (i) the decision on a legal question of fundamental importance would lead to a deviation from the OGH's established case law or a decision of an enlarged panel, or (ii) the legal issue of fundamental importance in question has not yet been answered in a uniform manner by the OGH. It follows from the Austrian appeal system that different goals of civil justice are implemented at different stages of the appeal process. While the lower courts are, in principle, responsible for mass processing of routine matters, it is the OGH's task to provide guidance with regard to new matters of law and thereby to contribute to the development of the law. This is generally referred to as the OGH's leading role (*Leitfunktion*) (Rechberger and Simotta 2010: para. 1037). The problem of civil procedure becoming a mass phenomenon correlates with Franz Klein's procedural thinking that civil litigation has a social function, economic ramifications and serves public interest. Legislative measures taken in that respect, such as the adoption of small claims procedures (please see Sect. 2.6), can, therefore, be seen in the context of the just-mentioned civil justice goals.

The role and function the BGH has in the German civil justice system is very similar to that of the OGH in the Austrian system. In other words, access to the BGH depends on the significance of the legal issue in question to the system of

[54] This trend is, however, reversed in those proceedings where parties are granted procedural capacity irrespective of their legal capacity under civil law; cf., in detail, Zeuner (2003: 1796).

[55] See Sec. 502 ZPO which also stipulates some exceptions to the value limit, especially in family law, tenant law and labour law matters; cf. Rechberger and Simotta (2010: para. 1038 et seqq.).

[56] If the amount in dispute exceeds €30,000, the parties can file a so-called extraordinary *Revision* and bring the case before the OGH irrespective of whether the second instance denied permission to appeal.

justice as a whole (see Murray and Stürner 2004: 386). As a result of the civil procedure reforms in 2001 access to the BGH is limited to cases in which appeal has been granted either by the second instance or by the BGH itself (Rosenberg et al. 2010: Sec. 141 para. 1). According to Sec. 543 para. 2 dZPO an appeal to the BGH is admitted only if (i) the legal matter is of fundamental significance, or (ii) the further development of the law or the interests in ensuring uniform adjudication require a decision by the BGH. Moreover, Sec. 132 para. 4 GVG provides that an adjudicating panel of the BGH may submit an issue of fundamental importance to the Grand Panel for a decision if it deems this necessary for the development of the law or in order to ensure uniform application of the law (Jacobs in Stein and Jonas 2011: Sec. 132 GVG para. 2 et seqq.). It follows that mass processing of routine matters is handled by the lower courts while the BGH is responsible for rendering decisions on (new) legal issues or 'hard cases' having an impact on the entire civil justice system. Both the OGH and the BGH generally do not decide issues of fact.

Interestingly, the caseload of the OGH is quite similar to that of the BGH, even though Germany has about ten times as many inhabitants as Austria. In 2010, for instance, the OGH completed 2,050[57] cases (excluding labour and social law matters) and the BGH 3,530.[58] This might indicate that the OGH employs a more general understanding of the 'importance' of cases (Oberhammer and Domej 2010: 274).

2.6 Proportionality in Action: Small Claims Proceedings, Mahnverfahren and Conditional Judgments

Under both German and Austrian law small claims fall within the jurisdiction of special courts. In Austria, the *Bezirksgerichte* are competent for all cases where the amount in dispute is not more than €15,000[59] and for certain cases of landlord and tenant law and family law (with regard to these matters irrespective of the amount in dispute). Similarly, in Germany the *Amtsgerichte*, *inter alia*, have jurisdiction for cases involving a dispute of up to €5,000 (and irrespective of the amount in dispute – especially cases of landlord and tenant law and family law). In both countries, the general rules on ordinary proceedings also apply to these 'small claims proceedings'. In addition, however, a number of provisions (see, e.g., Sec. 495 to 510b dZPO) provide for detailed rules in order to simplify these proceedings. The procedure according to these rules provides many features of a typical small claims process, e.g. formalities are kept to a minimum, emphasis is put on the oral part of

[57] See http://www.statistik.at/web_de/services/stat_jahrbuch/index.html (item 35).

[58] See https://www.destatis.de/DE/ZahlenFakten/GesellschaftStaat/Rechtspflege/Gerichtsverfahren/Tabellen/Gerichtsverfahren.html;jsessionid=562303AE9E5BD0AEA4B848038EFB9BC5.cae2

[59] According to the most recent legislative changes this amount will gradually be raised to €25,000 until January 2016; see BGBl I 2012/35.

the proceedings and admissibility of appeals is restricted (Oberhammer and Domej 2010: 274). Additionally, in most cases, representation by attorneys is not required; as a consequence, the provisions mentioned afford the judge a stronger position especially with respect to his or her role in the fact-finding process.[60] The differentiation between small claims procedure and ordinary proceedings might be interpreted as an implementation of the proportionality principle. It would, however, be incorrect to conclude that these cases are considered less important on the basis of their amount in dispute. Rather, the simplified procedure aims at making the enforcement and determination of rights and obligations easier. At least in Austrian court practice the number of cases decided in small claims proceedings before the *Bezirksgericht* by far exceeds the number of cases dealt with in ordinary proceedings (Kodek and Mayr 2011: para. 835).

Unlike Austrian civil procedural law, the dZPO provides for (even more) simplified proceedings in cases where the amount in dispute does not exceed €600 (Rosenberg et al. 2010: Sec. 108 para. 17 et seqq.). According to Sec. 495a dZPO the procedure is entirely left to the court's discretion in such cases. However, oral proceedings are obligatory if one party requests an oral hearing. In addition, the party's fundamental rights granted by the German Constitution limit the court's discretion with respect to the procedure.[61]

The Austrian procedure for an order for payment (*Mahnverfahren*) does not really qualify as a special procedure but rather a specific form of commencing ordinary proceedings. All money claims up to and including an amount of €75,000 have to be filed in the form of a request for an order for payment (*Mahnklage*). Subsequently, the court issues an order for payment (*Zahlungsbefehl*) which is sent to the defendant and becomes binding and enforceable if the defendant fails to object within 4 weeks. If the defendant objects in due time, the proceedings are continued in the ordinary way. Consequently, it might be stated that ordinary procedure under Austrian law provides a 'multi-track' procedure, reserving a fast track for smaller claims (Oberhammer and Domej 2010: 274). The German procedure for an order for payment significantly differs from the Austrian one, most notably it provides for a two-step procedure and the claimant can choose between commencing ordinary proceedings and applying for an order for payment.

In addition, German civil procedural law provides for 'summary proceedings' in which only documents and party interrogation are admissible evidence (Rosenberg et al. 2010: Sec. 163 para. 2). These proceedings apply to cases where the claim is based upon a document or a promissory note. The procedure is divided in two parts: in the first part, the court issues a *Vorbehaltsurteil* (conditional judgment), which forms an executory title; however, the defendant has the right to present his case without any restrictions as to the means of evidence in a subsequent (i.e. second part) *Nachverfahren* leading to a definitive judgment. It is the goal of summary

[60] See, e.g., Sec. 432 ZPO.

[61] See Federal Constitutional Court (*Bundesverfassungsgericht*) 21 March 2006, 2 BvR 1104/05, NJW 2006, 2248.

proceedings under German law to offer creditors an efficient and fast mechanism to enforce their claims.

In cases where the amount in dispute does not exceed €2,700, Austrian law restricts the grounds that can be raised in an appeal against the court's decision. According to Sec. 501 ZPO an appeal (so-called *Bagatellberufung*) can only be based on nullity and incorrect legal evaluation. Under German law an appeal against a judgment of the court of first instance is only admissible if the amount in dispute exceeds €600.[62]

Moreover, the requirements for the admissibility of an appeal to the OGH and BGH (see Sect. 2.5) serve as a filtering mechanism. As a result, cases in which a certain amount in dispute is not exceeded are dealt with differently than disputes which do not raise significant issues of law. Such differentiation is not, however, considered a denial of justice.

2.7 Creeping Introduction of Group Litigation

Despite intense discussions in legal doctrine and recurring events leading to mass tort, in the wake of the financial crisis, in particular damages arising out of investments (Oberhammer 2010: 248), the Austrian legislator has not yet adopted specific provisions for class or group actions. Consequently, the handling of complex multi-party matters cannot, at least as regards matters falling within contentious jurisdiction,[63] be considered a major goal of civil justice. To overcome the legislative lacuna, a sort of group litigation based on traditional procedural tools was developed in practice (Kodek 2009: 87 et seqq.). Under the label of 'Austrian-style group action' (*Sammelklage österreichischer Prägung*) harmed individuals transfer their claims to an association (in most cases a consumer association). Subsequently, the association (or another legal entity) brings all collected claims in one action on its own behalf before the court on the basis of Sec. 227 para. 1 ZPO (*objektive Klagenhäufung*) (see, e.g., Rechberger 2010: 162 et seqq.). In 2007 a draft bill based on a text prepared by an expert working group set up by the Austrian Ministry of Justice was presented. It was later called Civil Justice Reform Act 2007 (*Zivilverfahrensnovelle* 2007). The draft provides for a new 'group litigation procedure' (*Gruppenverfahren*) and a 'test case procedure' (*Musterverfahren*) (Kodek 2009: 89 et seqq.; Rechberger 2010: 166 et seqq.). However, due to criticism the bill did not pass parliament and the adoption of a group litigation procedure, therefore, remains on the political agenda (Rechberger 2010: 166).

Like Austrian law, German civil procedural law does not provide for a class or group action, as it is known in other jurisdictions, most prominently the United States. As a consequence of the *Deutsche Telekom* case, in which thousands of individual securities claims were filed against Deutsche Telekom, the German legislator

[62] See Sec. 511 para. 2 dZPO.

[63] For non-contentious matters see Sect. 2.2.

adopted the Act on the Initiation of Model Case Proceedings in respect of investors in the capital markets.[64] In simplified terms the KapMuG provides for a (interlocutory) procedure in which factual and legal issues common to a group of similar actions are decided. The decision rendered has binding effect for the individual cases. The hybrid procedure combines elements of a test case procedure and a collective procedure (Lange 2011: 82 et seqq.). The KapMuG was originally adopted as 'experimental law' and its trial period of 5 years was extended until 31 October 2012. The German legislator has recently submitted a draft bill according to which the KapMuG is to be maintained and slightly modified. Consequently, the scope of application of the KapMuG remains limited to certain rights and claims of investors. The draft bill does not propose to incorporate the procedure in the code of civil procedure and enlarge its scope of application arguing that it has not yet been sufficiently tested.[65] It follows that the resolution of complex multi-party matters is only gradually considered as a goal of civil justice.

In addition, Austrian and German law grant certain associations or independent public bodies the right to bring a representative action for injunctive or declaratory relief in specific areas of law (so-called *Verbandsklage*).[66]

2.8 From Strict Formalism to 'Equitable Discretion' of the Court

The principle of legality is enshrined both in the Austrian[67] and in the German[68] Constitution. In general, courts, therefore, have to decide the case in accordance with the applicable legal norms. It is a yet more difficult question how far the court's decision needs to take into account basic principles of justice underlying the legal order as such if they conflict with applicable legal norms.[69]

In some cases reference to equity is made in the law itself. According to Sec. 904 Austrian Civil Code (ABGB), for instance, the court may be requested to fix an equitable time of performance if the parties agreed that the debtor might perform his or her personal and not inheritable duty at any time. Section 78 AußStrG might serve as an additional example. It empowers the judge in non-contentious proceedings to deviate from the general rule that costs are awarded to the successful party if equity so requires (Klicka et al. 2006: para. 148). In Germany, Sec. 81 FamFG even provides that the court has 'equitable discretion' in deciding which party shall bear

---

[64] *Kapitalanleger-Musterverfahrensgesetz*; hereinafter referred to as KapMuG; see, e.g., Baetge (2007: 7).

[65] See BT-Drucks 17/8799, p. 1.

[66] See Sect. 2.3.

[67] See Article 18 para. 1 of the Austrian Constitution.

[68] See Article 20 para. 2 of the German Constitution.

[69] This might be illustrated by reference to the case law mentioned above (point II. B.) in which the BGH permits *res judicata* to be overturned on the basis of an action in tort under Sec. 826 BGB.

the costs. On the basis of these isolated provisions it cannot, however, be established that reaching an equitable result would form part of the goals of civil justice.

By way of concluding an arbitration agreement and empowering the arbitrators to decide the case *ex aequo et bono*, Austrian and German law offer the parties a possibility to opt out of the strict application of the law. However, Sec. 603 para. 3 ZPO and Sec. 1051 para. 3 dZPO require that the parties expressly authorize the arbitral tribunal to decide *ex aequo et bono*.

As regards a party's failure to comply with formal requirements stipulated in the code of civil procedure neither Austrian nor German law apply a very strict approach. In general, parties are given the opportunity to correct formally incorrect submissions within a certain time limit.[70] If the error is corrected within the given time limit, the date of the submission will even remain the date of the initial filing under Austrian law (see, e.g., Rechberger and Simotta 2010: para. 708 et seqq.). In Germany, Sec. 295 dZPO stipulates that violations of non-mandatory procedural provisions, and in particular of rules governing the form of procedural acts, can no longer be raised if the party has waived the rule's application, or if the party has failed to object to the irregularity in a timely manner.

2.9 Problem Solving and Case Processing as Non-exclusive Goals

Under Austrian and German law these goals do not seem to be mutually exclusive. The goal of problem solving can, on the one hand, be viewed from the parties' perspective and, on the other hand, from the society's perspective. Regarding the latter, the prevailing view in Austria is that civil justice also serves the resolution of 'social conflicts' and thereby fulfils public welfare tasks.[71] Additionally, several provisions of the Austrian ZPO suggest that it is, at least to some extent, also a goal of civil justice to find an adequate solution for the parties' dispute without necessarily deciding the case by rendering a judgment. Section 258 para. 1 ZPO, for instance, requires the judge to undertake the attempt to settle the case. According to Sec. 204 para. 1 ZPO the judge can (*ex officio*) try to facilitate an amicable settlement of the dispute, or even of single issues in dispute, at any stage of the oral hearing. However, the need to solve the parties' problem does not prevail over the goal of civil procedure to swiftly decide the case. Again it seems the approach is a balanced one (see already Sect. 2.4).

German law generally takes a favourable stance towards voluntary settlement of legal disputes (Murray and Stürner 2004: 486 et seqq.). Section 278 para. 2 dZPO, for instance, lays down an obligatory conciliation hearing (*Güteverhandlung*) in all cases except those where the parties have unsuccessfully attempted to settle the case

[70] See, e.g., Sec. 84 ZPO et seqq.; with regard to the statement of claim see Rosenberg et al. 2010: Sec. 96 para. 47; Becker-Eberhard in Rauscher et al. 2008: Sec. 253 para. 154.

[71] See Sect. 2.1.1.

before an out-of-court settlement institution or in which there is obviously no hope that a successful settlement will be reached (see, e.g., Oberhammer and Domej 2005c: 220; Rosenberg et al. 2010: Sec. 104 para. 15 et seqq.). This provision already shows that problem solving should not be forced at the expense of case processing. Moreover, Sec. 278 para. 1 dZPO authorizes the judge to take an active role and encourage a settlement between the parties when appropriate (Murray and Stürner 2004: 487). Besides, following the enactment of the new Mediation Act (*Mediationsgesetz*, MediationsG) in 2011, the concept of conciliatory judges (*Güterichter*) has been extended.[72] This in-court conciliation replaces the so-called in-court or judicial mediation (*gerichtsinterne Mediation* or *Richtermediation*) that was introduced as a 'pilot project' at several courts and was included in a government bill. Today, Sec. 278 (5) dZPO authorizes the judge to refer the parties to a requested or commissioned judge not only for the purpose of the preliminary conciliation hearing but also for a further attempt at conciliation.[73] At the same time, however, the German civil justice system does not sacrifice procedural efficiency for voluntary dispute resolution (Murray and Stürner 2004: 488).

2.10 Civil Justice with Revenue?

Neither in Austria nor in Germany is access to the civil justice system free of charge. The level of court fees depends on the type of dispute. In most cases, however, court fees as well as attorneys' fees are calculated on the basis of the amount in dispute.[74] The claimant (or applicant as the case may be) has to pay all of the court fees in advance (Murray and Stürner 2004: 344). If the amount in dispute is €10,000, by way of example, the court fees (in the first instance) will amount to €673 in Austria[75] and €588[76] in Germany. For an appeal in the just-mentioned example the court fees in Austria amount to €1,036[77] and in Germany to €784.[78] For parties having insufficient financial means access to court is ensured by a developed legal aid system according to which a party is fully (or partially) exempt from paying fees (Murray and Stürner 2004: 116 et seqq.; Rechberger and Simotta 2010: para. 442 et seqq.). In addition, it is quite popular in Germany and Austria to purchase legal cost insurance offered by private insurance companies (Murray and Stürner 2004: 124).

According to the information published on the website of the Austrian Ministry of Justice, 73 % of the overall costs of the justice system, including civil and

[72] See BT-Drucks 17/8058, p. 17.

[73] BT-Drucks 17/8058, p. 21.

[74] For Austria see Court Fees Act (*Gerichtsgebührengesetz*, hereinafter GGG) and for Germany the Act on Court Costs (*Gerichtskostengesetz*, hereinafter GKG).

[75] See Sec. 2 para. 1 lit a GGG, tariff item 1 (*Tarifposten* 1).

[76] See Sec. 34 GKG, Attachment 1, No. 1210 and Attachment 2.

[77] See Sec. 2 para. 1 lit c GGG, tariff item 2 (*Tarifposten* 2).

[78] See Sec. 34 GKG, Attachment 1, No. 1220 and Attachment 2.

criminal justice, are covered.[79] Data limited to the civil justice system are only provided by the report of the European Commission for the Efficiency of Justice (CEPEJ) on 'Efficiency and quality of justice'.[80] According to this report (see p. 63) the court fees in Austria cover 110.9 % of the court's budget. The high level of court fees in Austria arguably results from the court's responsibility for land and business registers. Acquiring information from these registers or recording modifications, for instance, gives rise to court fees. At the same time a high degree of standardization and computerization of the judiciary, especially in the branches with large numbers of cases, enable courts to keep costs low and allow revenue to be generated.[81] However, since revenue derived from court fees is, arguably, used to cross-subsidize other parts of the justice system, most notably the costly area of criminal justice, it would be difficult to conclude that court fees qualify as a 'quasi-commercial source of revenue for the public budget'.

In Germany, court fees cover an average of 40 % of the costs of the justice system.[82] This percentage is considered too low and, *inter alia*, caused the Ministry of Justice in November 2011 to spring into action and prepare a draft for the second Act for the Modernization of the Law on Costs.[83]

2.11 User Orientation? Efficiency Despite Public Criticisms

At least in theory, many of the goals of civil justice, such as quick and efficient enforcement and determination of rights and obligations, legal certainty and the like, positively affect the users of the system. In practice, the Austrian judiciary works efficiently and effectively, which is evidenced by the fact that the majority of cases, at least in contentious proceedings, is resolved within a year or even a shorter period of time (see, e.g., Mayr 2009: 62). Interestingly, however, the user's perception does not correspond with the just-mentioned objective data. By contrast, recent opinion polls draw a different picture: according to the opinion poll organized by the Bar Association of Lower Austria, 86 % of the participants hold the view that proceedings take too long or even 'much too long'. Other polls show slightly more

[79] See http://www.justiz.gv.at/internet/html/default/8ab4a8a422985de30122a921079062e5.de.html;jsessionid=433D2829175BBD00521117745088034B

[80] See https://wcd.coe.int/ViewBlob.jsp?id=1700697&SourceFile=1&BlobId=1694098&DocId=1653000. Hereinafter referred to as CEPEJ-report.

[81] See CEPEJ-report, p. 63.

[82] See the final report of the 82nd conference of the ministers of justice held on 18 and 19 May 2011 in Halle; available online at http://www.justiz.bayern.de/imperia/md/content/stmj_internet/ministerium/ministerium/jumiko/2011/i_8_kostendeckunsgrad.pdf. The percentage, however, varies from federal state to federal state. At least in 1995 the court fees covered 100 % of the court's budget in Bavaria and Baden-Württemberg; see Blankenburg 2011: 19 et seq.

[83] 2. *Kostenrechtsmodernisierungsgesetz* - 2. *KostRMoG*, available online at http://www.bmj.de/SharedDocs/Downloads/DE/pdfs/RefE_Zweites_Gesetz_zur_Modernisierung_des_Kostenrechts.pdf?__blob=publicationFile

positive results: 75 % of respondents believe that the length of proceedings is inappropriate. The poll commissioned by the Ministry of Justice, however, reveals that only 10 % of respondents have an 'overall negative impression' of proceedings and characterize them as being slow, complicated, or long. Sixteen per cent of respondents to this poll voiced an 'overall positive impression' of the system and indicated that this was due to the 'fast handling' of cases. On balance, the level of user satisfaction ranks between high and average. This is not only confirmed by the poll commissioned by the bar association, according to which 79 % of respondents trust in the Austrian justice system, but also by the most recent poll.[84] The scientific value of such polls, however, remains doubtful since users usually do not differentiate between civil and criminal justice. Regarding the latter, cases involving public figures have led to highly negative media coverage in Austria and thereby negatively influenced the image of the justice system in general.[85]

At least as regards the use of modern means of communication and IT matters in general (so-called 'e-justice'), the Austrian civil justice system takes a very user-friendly stance. It provides not only for electronic filing of claims but also, for instance, for the online publication of court edicts, such as bankruptcy edicts, court auctions and publications from commercial registers.[86]

Equally, in Germany confidence in the civil justice system seems to be widespread (Murray and Stürner 2004: 631). This is confirmed by a recent poll indicating that 60 % of the German population place a lot of trust, or at least a fair amount of trust, in German courts (Roland Rechtsreport 2011: 12). According to said poll, however, the length of the proceedings seems to exceed the German users' demands. Seventy-six per cent of respondents having participated in court proceedings indicate that the process takes too long. Moreover, 67 % of the respondents share the view that those who can afford legal representation will be successful in the proceedings (Roland Rechtsreport 2011: 19, 20).

On balance, the goals of civil justice are defined, on the one hand, from the perspective of those whose rights and obligations are at stake and, on the other hand, from the perspective of society in general and its need for an effective civil justice system.

2.12 Conclusion

The traditions on which the Austrian and German civil justice systems are based have successfully stood the test of time. They are, however, facing new challenges due to recurring events leading to mass tort, in the wake of the financial crisis, in particular damages arising out of investments. At least in Austria, the implementation of more elaborate provisions on group litigation should be considered to guarantee the effective and efficient enforcement of individual rights in the future.

---

[84] This poll, however, indicates a slightly lower number of 65 %; see Karmasin (2012: 7 and 24).

[85] This is confirmed by the Karmasin (2012: 19).

[86] See www.edikte.justiz.gv.at

References

Baetge D (2007) Class actions, group litigation & other forms of collective litigation – Germany. Published online: http://globalclassactions.stanford.edu/sites/default/files/documents/Germany_National_Report.pdf

Ballon O (1983) Der Einfluß der Verfassung auf das Zivilprozeßrecht. Zeitschrift für Zivilprozess 96:409–486

Ballon O (2009) Einführung in das österreichische Zivilprozessrecht. Leykam, Graz

Blankenburg E (2011) Europäische Justizindikatoren: Budgets der Justiz, Richter und Rechtsanwälte. Betrifft: Die Justiz 105:18–32

Böhm P (1986) Bewegliches System und Prozesszwecke. In: Bydlinski F, Krejci H, Schilcher B, Steiniger V (eds) Das bewegliche System im geltenden und künftigen Recht. Springer, Wien/New York, pp 211–241

Brehm W (1993) Freiwillige Gerichtsbarkeit. Boorberg, Stuttgart

Brehm W (2001) Rechtsfortbildungszweck des Zivilprozesses. In: Gottwald P, Roth H (eds) Festschrift Schuhmann. Mohr Siebeck, Tübingen, pp 57–70

Fasching HW, Konecny A (2000) Kommentar zu den Zivilprozessgesetzen. Manz, Wien

Gaul F (1968) Zur Frage nach dem Zweck des Zivilprozesses. Archiv für die civilistische Praxis 168:27–62

Gottwald P (2004) Defeating delay in German civil procedure. In: van Rhee R (ed) The law's delay. Intersentia, Antwerpen/Oxford, pp 121–124

Haas U (2011) The relationship between the judge and the parties under German law. In: Lipp V, Fredriksen H (eds) Reforms of civil procedure in Germany and Norway. Mohr Siebeck, Tübingen, pp 87–112

Halfmeier A (2006) Popularklagen im Privatrecht. Mohr Siebeck, Tübingen

Henckel W (1970) Prozessrecht und materielles Recht. Schwartz, Göttingen

Hess B (1999) Abuse of procedure in Germany and Austria. In: Taruffo M (ed) Abuse of procedural rights. Kluwer International, The Hague, pp 149–177

Holzhammer R (1976) Zivilprozessrecht. Springer, Wien/New York

Karmasin (2012) Grundlagenstudie: 'Die neue Justiz: Stärkung des Vertrauens in die österreichische Justiz'. Available online: http://www.justiz.gv.at/internet/file/2c94848534e6045f01353d1854d30356.de.0/studie.pdf;jsessionid=C3AF8ED72D64755004594238139D3655

Klein F (1900) Vorlesungen über die Praxis des Civilprozesses. Manz, Wien

Klein F (1927) Reden, Aufsätze, Briefe I. Manz, Wien

Klein F, Engel F (1927) Der Zivilprozess Oesterreichs. Scientia Verlag, Aalen

Klicka T, Oberhammer P, Domej T (2006) Außerstreitverfahren. Manz, Wien

Koch H (2001) Non-class group litigation under EU and German law. Duke J Comp Int Law 11:355–367

Koch H (2011) Sammelklage und Justizstandorte im internationalen Wettbewerb. Juristenzeitung 9:438–445

Koch H, Diedrich F (1998) Civil procedure in Germany. C.H. Beck, München

Kodek G (2009) Collective redress in Austria. In: Hensler D, Hodges C, Tulibacka M (eds) The globalization of class actions, Annals of the American Academy of Political and Social Sciences. Sage, Thousand Oaks, 622(86)

Kodek G, Mayr P (2011) Zivilprozessrecht. Facultas WUV, Wien

Kötz H (2003) Civil justice systems in Europe and the United States. Duke J Comp Int Law 13:61–77

Kralik W (1974) Die Wahrung öffentlicher Interessen im österreichischen Zivilverfahren. Wiener Rechtswissenschaftliche Studien 13:65–75

Kuderna F (1986) Soziale Funktion und soziale Elemente des Zivilprozesses. Das Recht der Arbeit, pp 182–191

Kühnberg S (2006) Die konsumentenschutzrechtliche Verbandsklage. Verlag Österreich, Wien

Lange S (2011) Das begrenzte Gruppenverfahren. Mohr Siebeck, Tübingen

Mayr P (2009) Neue Rechtstatsachen aus der Zivilgerichtsbarkeit. Anwaltsblatt 2:54–66
Mayr P, Fucik R (2006) Das neue Verfahren außer Streitsachen. Facultas WUV, Wien
Meyer P (2004) Wandel des Prozessrechtsverständnisses – vom 'liberalen' zum 'sozialen' Zivilprozess? Juristische Rundschau 1:1–6
Murray P, Stürner R (2004) German civil justice. Carolina Academic Press, Durham
Musielak H-J (2013) Zivilprozessordnung. Franz Vahlen, München
Musielak H-J, Borth H (2011) Familiengerichtliches Verfahren. Franz Vahlen, München
Novak G (1961) Die Stellung des Zivilprozeßrechts in unserer Gesamtrechtsordnung. Juristische Blätter 64
Oberhammer P (2004a) Die Aufgabenverteilung zwischen Gericht und Parteien – Überlegungen à propos 'Een nieuwe balans' aus Sicht des deutschen Rechtskreises. In: Ingelse P (ed) Commentaren op fundamentele herbezinning. Ars Aequi Libri, Nijmegen, pp 81–97
Oberhammer P (2004b) Zivilprozessgesetzgebung: content follows method. In: Honsell H (ed) Festschrift Kramer. Helbing Lichtenhahn, Basel, pp 1025–1050
Oberhammer P (2004c) Speeding up civil litigation in Austria: past and present instruments. In: van Rhee R (ed) The law's delay. Intersentia, Antwerpen/Oxford, pp 217–232
Oberhammer P (2010) 'Österreichische Sammelklage' und Sec. 227 ZPO. In: Fucik R, Konecny A, Lovrek E, Oberhammer P (eds) Jahrbuch Zivilverfahrensrecht 2010. NWV Verlag, Wien, pp 247–274
Oberhammer P, Domej T (2005a) Germany, Switzerland, and Austria (CA. 1800–2005). In: van Rhee R (ed) European traditions in civil procedure. Intersentia, Antwerpen/Oxford, pp 103–122
Oberhammer P, Domej T (2005b) Powers of the judge – Germany, Austria, Switzerland. In: van Rhee R (ed) European traditions in civil procedure. Intersentia, Antwerpen/Oxford, pp 295–305
Oberhammer P, Domej T (2005c) Conciliation and other types of alternative dispute settlements – Germany, Austria, Switzerland. In: van Rhee R (ed) European traditions in civil procedure. Intersentia, Antwerpen/Oxford, pp 215–221
Oberhammer P, Domej T (2010) Delay in Austrian civil procedure. In: van Rhee R (ed) Within a reasonable time: the history of due and undue delay in civil litigation. Duncker & Humblot, Berlin, pp 255–277
Parker J, Lewisch P (1998) Materielle Wahrheitsfindung im Zivilprozeß. In: Bundesministerium für Justiz, Lewisch P, Rechberger W (eds) 100 Jahre ZPO – Ökonomische Analyse des Zivilprozesses. Manz, Wien, pp 203–224
Pawlowski H-M (1967) Aufgabe des Zivilprozesses. Zeitschrift für Zivilprozess 80:345–391
Rauscher T, Wax P, Wenzel JW (2008 and 2010) Münchner Kommentar zur Zivilprozessordnung. C.H. Beck, München
Rechberger W (2010) Class actions. In: Verschraegen B (ed) Austrian law – an international perspective. Selected issues. Jan Sramek, Wien, pp 151–185
Rechberger W, Oberhammer P (2009) Exekutionsrecht. Facultas WUV, Wien
Rechberger W, Simotta D-A (2010) Zivilprozessrecht. Manz, Wien
Roland Rechtsreport (2011) Available online: http://www.roland-konzern.de/media/downloads/roland_rechtsreport2011_kl.pdf
Rosenberg L, Schwab K-H, Gottwald P (2010) Zivilprozessrecht. C.H. Beck, München
Säcker F, Rixecker R (2013) Münchener Kommentar zum Bürgerlichen Gesetzbuch. C.H. Beck, München
Schoibl N (1990) Die Verbandsklage zur Wahrung öffentlicher oder "überindividueller" Interessen im österreichischen Zivilverfahrensrecht. Zeitschrift für Europarecht, internationales Privatrecht und Rechtsvergleichung 31:3–33
Sprung R (1977) Die Grundlagen des österreichischen Zivilprozeßrechts. Zeitschrift für Zivilprozess 90:380–394
Stein F, Jonas M (2003) Kommentar zur Zivilprozessordnung, vol 1. Mohr Siebeck, Tübingen
Stein F, Jonas M (2011) Kommentar zur Zivilprozessordnung, vol 10. Mohr Siebeck, Tübingen
Stürner R (1990) Prozesszweck und Verfassung. Festschrift für Baumgärtel, pp 545–552
Uhlenbruck W (2010) Insolvenzordnung Kommentar. Franz Vahlen, München

Von Hippel F (1939) Wahrheitspflicht und Aufklärungspflicht. V. Klostermann, Frankfurt am Main
Von Hippel F (1952) Zur modernen konstruktiven Epoche der 'deutschen Prozessrechtswissenschaft'. Zeitschrift für Zivilprozess 65:431–464
Zeuner A (2003) Rechtsvergewisserung und Wahrheitsermittlung als Funktionen des zivilgerichtlichen Verfahrens und ihre Beeinflussung unter persönlichkeitsrechtlichen Aspekten in der neuen Entwicklung des deutschen Rechts. In: Nakamura H et al (eds) Festschrift Kostas Beys. Athen Sakkoulas, Athens, pp 1787–1809

Chapter 3
Civil Justice in Pursuit of Efficiency

The Netherlands (with Some Reflections on France and Belgium)

C.H. (Remco) van Rhee

The information on Belgium and France was kindly provided, respectively, by Prof. Benoît Allemeersch (Catholic University of Leuven) and Prof. Frédérique Ferrand (Université Jean Molin, Lyon 3).

Abstract This chapter addresses first of all the goals of civil justice that are recognised in the Netherlands. These are (a) the authoritative determination of rights recognised by private law and the provision of enforceable titles; (b) demonstrating the effectiveness of private law; and (c) the development of private law and guaranteeing its uniform application. Subsequently the following issues are discussed with regard to the Netherlands: (1) matters within the scope of civil justice, (2) the emphasis on the protection of individual rights in civil litigation, (3) the quest for a certain balance between a decision based on a sound factual basis and speed and efficiency in reaching this decision, (4) access to court, (5) proportionality between case and procedure, (6) multi-party litigation, (7) the absence of strict formalism, (8) case processing instead of problem solving, (9) the costs of litigation and (10) user orientation.

C.H. (Remco) van Rhee (✉)
Faculty of Law, Maastricht University,
PO Box 6.6, 6200 MD Maastricht, The Netherlands
e-mail: remco.vanrhee@maastrichtuniversity.nl

A. Uzelac (ed.), *Goals of Civil Justice and Civil Procedure in Contemporary Judicial Systems*, Ius Gentium: Comparative Perspectives on Law and Justice 34,
DOI 10.1007/978-3-319-03443-0_3, © Springer International Publishing Switzerland 2014

3.1 Introduction: One Procedure, Various Goals

There is no general consensus on the goals of civil justice in the Netherlands. Within the circles of lawyers and legal scholars, however, usually at least three goals are distinguished:

1. The authoritative determination of rights recognised by private law and the provision of enforceable titles (judgments) (i.e. 'deciding disputes');
2. Demonstrating the effectiveness of private law;[1]
3. The development *of* private law and guaranteeing its uniform application.[2,3]

The authoritative determination of rights and the provision of an enforceable title where the opposing party is not willing to act in accordance with its obligations resulting from these rights voluntarily is the obvious aim of a civil action and usually the reason why litigation is commenced in the Netherlands (as elsewhere). According to the Dutch government,[4] it is the primary aim of civil litigation. In its opinion, civil litigation should be regarded as *ultimum remedium*, only to be commenced when all other means of obtaining what one is entitled to have been exhausted. According to lawyers and legal scholars,[5] this is however too narrow a view since, in their opinion, the other two aims mentioned above are as important. Since litigation is conducted in public, these lawyers and scholars claim it serves an important goal in demonstrating the consequences of not acting in conformity with one's obligations under private law (an issue in which the litigants involved in the lawsuit may not be interested; in that sense this goal may be considered a so-called positive externality according to economic theory).[6] When these consequences are the enforcement of the rights in dispute, this may serve as a strong impetus for the public at large to behave in the required manner, without the need for litigation, since it demonstrates the effectiveness of the law also for similar cases. Additionally, it may prevent parties from taking the law into their own hands, something which may occur in societies where it is not so clear that private rights can be adequately

[1] According to Benoît Allemeersch, in Belgium not only the effectiveness of private law is at stake here, but also the effectiveness of the court system as a whole. In each individual case, Belgian judges are at least implicitly trying to demonstrate that in the long run the system is an effective one. This also means that the length of the proceedings is not an issue to be determined by the parties. The judge may even disallow delays that are mutually requested by both of the parties.

[2] Asser et al. (2003: 33–46). See also Asser et al. (2006: 27–32).

[3] According to Frédérique Ferrand, the following goals of civil justice are usually distinguished in France within the circles of legal scholars: (1) the determination and enforcement of rights recognised by substantive private law and (2) demonstrating the effectiveness of private law and the realisation of 'social peace'. The development and uniform application of private law are not officially mentioned as goals of French civil justice. However, in practice, these goals are recognised where the *Cour de cassation* is concerned.

[4] See Contourennota (1998: 2 and 15ff.).

[5] See, e.g., n. 2 above.

[6] On externalities and civil procedural law, see, e.g. Visscher (2012: 65–92).

enforced. As a result, it is claimed that the individual lawsuit has a wider significance than only being a means to obtain a decision in individual cases.

The wider significance of civil lawsuits is also demonstrated by the third goal of civil justice that is distinguished in the Netherlands, the development of the law and guaranteeing its uniform application. Again, this may not be in the interest of the litigants involved in the particular lawsuit (it is also a positive externality, although this is different in test cases, e.g. cases brought by insurance companies), but this does not prevent Dutch scholars from defining it as an important goal. The existence of a large volume of periodicals and (more recently) internet sources aimed at publishing relevant case law and commenting on it is proof that this goal is taken seriously in the Netherlands.[7] This particular goal may also prevent further litigation since many of the issues regarding the interpretation of the Civil Code and related statutes may be answered on the basis of previous case law without the need of bringing a new case.

Unfortunately, outside the circles of lawyers and legal scholars, notably within government circles, views seem to be different (for the view of the government, see above). This appeared clearly when a group of three university professors presented their ideas on the future of the civil justice system in the Netherlands in their interim report in 2003.[8] They stated that civil litigation should not be seen as *ultimum remedium*, namely, as something one should only resort to if all other means of dealing with the dispute (including mediation and other means of ADR) have failed. After all, these other means do not generate what I have qualified as positive externalities here, that is, externalities by which the goals of the civil justice system under (2) and (3) are realised. Mediation, for example, cannot demonstrate the effectiveness of private law in situations where a party is unwilling to live up to its obligations (in that case usually an action needs to be brought at a state court in order to obtain an enforceable title, unless the mediation agreement itself has been sanctioned by the court), nor does it function as a vehicle for the development of that law and its uniform application since it is, by its very nature, conducted outside the public domain. Of course, this is less problematic if a representative sample of cases fail in mediation, allowing the state courts to deal with such matters (after failed mediation the state courts should always be available), but whether this will occur in practice is questionable. From the perspective of the second and third goals of civil justice distinguished in the Netherlands, therefore, looking at civil litigation as *ultimum remedium* is unjustified. Nevertheless, the Minister of Justice in his reaction to the 2006 final report of the three university professors[9] did adhere to the *ultimum remedium* view, most likely because mediation and other means of ADR are not paid

---

[7] The major collection of case law is the *Nederlandse Jurisprudentie* ('Dutch Case Law'), which also contains influential case annotations by leading lawyers.

[8] See n. 2 above.

[9] *Visie op het civiele proces: reactie fundamentele herbezinning burgerlijk procesrecht*, p. 8, available at http://www.rijksoverheid.nl/bestanden/documenten-en-publicaties/kamerstukken/2007/02/05/reactie-fundamentele-herbezinning-burgerlijk-procesrecht-7026/reactie-fundamentele-herbezinning-burgerlijk-procesrecht-7026.pdf (last consulted in September 2013).

from the public purse or at least are less costly for the government than litigation before a court of law.[10]

A recent example of a clash between the government on one side and lawyers and legal scholars on the other as regards the goals of civil justice appeared in a discussion on proposed legislation aimed at a substantial increase in court fees in the Netherlands[11] (it was the intention of the draft legislation that the total revenues would double) in order to make sure that from 2013 the civil justice system would be paid for by its users[12] (although the government claimed that the increase in fees would mean that 100 % of the costs of the civil justice system would be covered by court fees, in actual practice the suggested changes would have resulted in roughly 64 % coverage).[13] In the explanatory memorandum,[14] the government justified the sometimes dramatic increases in fees (occasionally, the increase would amount to a staggering 52 times the current fee)[15] by advancing (1) that litigation should be regarded as the personal responsibility of the parties involved (in other words as a kind of commodity), pointing out that only 5 % of all possible conflicts reach a court of law, meaning that 95 % of cases are handled in a different manner. When reading the explanatory memorandum, one gets the impression that the government felt that those who are 'stubborn' enough to bring their case before a court of law should pay for this. This should not, in the government's opinion, be the public in general, as it held that they do not benefit from litigation.

---

[10] According to Frédérique Ferrand, civil litigation is not seen as *ultimum remedium* in France. Even though ADR mechanisms (so-called *Modes alternatifs de règlement des litiges* or MARC) are being promoted by the State, mandatory preliminary mediation is only prescribed in rare cases (this last point is, as a matter of fact, also true in the Netherlands). For a proposal of mandatory preliminary mediation in family matters where a court order has been made with regard to the exercise of parental responsibilities, see Rapport Guinchard (2008: 24).

[11] Available at http://www.rijksoverheid.nl/bestanden/documenten-en-publicaties/regelingen/2011/04/04/memorie-van-toelichting-invoering-van-kostendekkende-griffierechten/mvt-griffie.pdf (last consulted in September 2013).

[12] Both plaintiffs and defendants traditionally pay court fees in the Netherlands. The defendant in small claims cases ('cantonal' cases up to €25,000) is exempt from this. Court fees can be recovered by the winning party from the losing party.

[13] See n. 11 above. The Dutch government was following the example of England & Wales, Scotland and Northern Ireland, where court fees are set at a level to cover the costs of the civil justice system. The Dutch proposal was of course opposite to the approach of France and some other European countries that have elevated the free administration of justice to a principle of civil procedure. It should be noted that in the Dutch proposal the costs of the administration of justice would not necessarily be covered completely at the level of individual cases but at a more general level since otherwise particular types of litigation would have become too costly.

[14] See p. 1–2; available at http://www.rijksoverheid.nl/bestanden/documenten-en-publicaties/regelingen/2011/04/04/memorie-van-toelichting-invoering-van-kostendekkende-griffierechten/mvt-griffie.pdf (last consulted in September 2013).

[15] See Council for the Judiciary (*Raad voor de Rechtspraak*) in its advisory opinion to the Minister of Safety and Justice, *Advies wetsvoorstel kostendekkende griffierechten* (21 June 2011), p. 7, available at http://www.rechtspraak.nl/Organisatie/Raad-Voor-De-Rechtspraak/Wetgevingsadvisering/Adviezen%202011/2011-24-Advies-wetsvoorstel-kostendekkende-griffierechten-21-6-2011.pdf (last consulted in September 2013).

Of course, in this approach the government completely disregarded the positive externalities generated by civil litigation (often being of a much higher economic value than the actual value of the particular lawsuit for the litigants) which may be considered as a justification for the public purse paying a considerable share of the costs of the civil justice system. The other two reasons advanced for the increase of court fees were that (2) the increase fitted well into the government's programme of improving the justice system (although it is hard to understand how this would have been achieved since the operation only resulted in transferring costs from the public purse to the litigants; courts would not obtain a larger budget as a result of the operation)[16] and that (3) higher fees were mandatory given the need for cuts in the state budget.

Various bodies and organisations were asked to comment on the draft. From these reactions, including those of the Dutch Council for the Judiciary[17] and the President and Procurator General at the Supreme Court of Cassation in the Netherlands (*Hoge Raad*),[18] it became clear that there was considerable opposition against the proposed legislation, especially because it was felt that in many cases access to justice would be severely threatened: large numbers of cases would no longer be brought before a court of law by economically calculating litigants or by litigants who did not have the means to pay the increased fees (this could occur even though according to the explanatory memorandum about 60 % of the population would have been entitled to a reduced fee rate, since even so the fees to be paid would increase dramatically also for this group). As a result, positive externalities such as the demonstration of the effectiveness of the law in these cases would be at risk, in the end resulting in high costs for society at large (calculating debtors of smaller claims, for example, would not be willing to pay voluntarily under the new system since the message imparted by it would no longer be that it is effective in these cases, but on the contrary that it is ineffective since creditors who have some doubts about whether they would be awarded costs or whether their opponent would be able to pay these costs would not go to court due to the high costs involved in litigation). In the end, therefore, it may be claimed that if the proposed legislation had become law, a comparatively small savings in the budget for the justice system (ca. €240 million per year; the Netherlands has a population of ca. 17,000,000) would have hurt the Dutch economy for an amount that would probably have been many times higher due to the disappearance of at least the positive externality mentioned under (2) above, but also since international businesses would have

[16] The government stated that higher court fees would stimulate 'innovation' since they would result in the parties' finding ways to resolve a larger number of disputes outside the court. The higher fees meant, in its opinion, also that litigants would have higher expectations of the administration of justice, which in the government's view would stimulate the courts to innovate, a somewhat curious line of reasoning indeed.

[17] See n. 15 above.

[18] Available at http://www.rijksoverheid.nl/documenten-en-publicaties/kamerstukken/2011/10/31/reactie-hoge-raad-der-nederlanden-op-wetsvoorstel-kostendekkende-griffierechten.html (last consulted in September 2013).

found the Dutch civil justice system less attractive as a result of it.[19] Due to a change in government, the suggested legislation has not been introduced and has been shelved by the present government.

3.2 Matters Within the Scope of Civil Justice

Matters within the scope of civil justice do not only encompass contested matters. This is reflected by the existence in the Netherlands of two ways of bringing a case to the notice of the court which – but this issue will not be explored here – also affect the type of procedure that will be followed afterwards. Originally, the ordinary civil action was to be initiated by a writ of summons (*dagvaarding*) served on the opposing party by a bailiff (*gerechtsdeurwaarder*; in French *huissier de justice*). Non-adversarial matters, on the contrary, were originally brought to the notice of the court by way of a petition (*verzoekschrift*). Although this strict division of starting litigation has become somewhat diluted, in the sense that currently also certain contested matters are initiated by way of a petition,[20] the origin of the distinction between the two ways of bringing cases to the attention of the court lies in the recognition of the fact that courts also deal with uncontested subject matter (i.e. 'voluntary jurisdiction' or jurisdiction ex parte; in French, *juridiction gracieuse*).[21] The present Dutch government has proposed abolishing the distinction between the two ways of bringing a civil lawsuit in court.

Uncontested matters brought before the Dutch civil courts are very diverse, but they have in common that they are more or less administrative in nature and that the measure that the petitioner wants to obtain can only be granted by a court of law since issues of public order are at stake: examples are adoption, the appointment of a guardian, making a person a ward and the emancipation of a minor.[22]

The 'administrative' tasks of the courts mentioned above are rather limited when compared to the administrative tasks of courts in some other jurisdictions. Dutch courts are usually not involved in enforcement proceedings (unless legal questions arise as a result of the enforcement proceedings, and in a limited number of other instances)[23] or in the holding of land or company registers.[24] Also, the existence of

---

[19] According to Benoît Allemeersch, in Belgium court fees only cover 10 % of the costs of the court system. An increase of court fees is not on the agenda and it is politically not acceptable.

[20] Examples are contested divorce proceedings and the contested dissolution of a labour contract.

[21] Hugenholtz and Heemskerk (2013: No. 34).

[22] Arts. 1:227, 1:295, 1:378 and 1:235 Dutch Civil Code, respectively.

[23] Enforcement is the domain of specialised enforcement officers who are appointed by the State and who function outside the court; they are known as *gerechtsdeurwaarders* (court bailiffs) and share their origin with the French *huissiers de justice*.

[24] The holding of such registers is the task of specialised agencies; the land or, more in general, real rights (real property) register is held by the Kadaster (see http://www.kadaster.nl/web/show; last consulted in September 2013), while the companies register is held by the Chambers of Commerce.

the Latin notariat in the Netherlands means that various other administrative tasks are performed by specialised and well-trained state-appointed officials outside the court. This means that in the definition of the goals of civil justice, the more administrative matters do not play such a preponderant role as in some other jurisdictions.[25,26]

3.3 Protection of Individual Rights v. Protection of the Public Interest

Apart from matters of a more administrative nature, where considerations of public order or public interest lie at the basis of entrusting the courts with these matters (see the examples given above; often the interests of a third party such as a minor are involved), it cannot be said that the Dutch system of civil justice puts a very strong emphasis on furthering matters of public interest or public policy by way of the civil justice system. The Dutch system does not, for example, know punitive damages or a comparable institute.[27] Of course, there are several issues which the court has to take into consideration *ex officio* when administering justice (e.g. the applicable law including foreign law: *ius curia novit*),[28,29] and the court also has

[25] According to Benoît Allemeersch, the administrative tasks of the courts in Belgium are comparable to those in the Netherlands. Different from the Netherlands, the Belgian judiciary is also involved in the supervision of the parliamentary elections.

[26] As in the Netherlands, the scope of civil justice in France does not only encompass contested matters (*juridiction contentieuse*). According to Frédérique Ferrand, non-contested matters (*matière gracieuse*) also belong to the jurisdiction of the French civil courts (see Art. 25 Code de procédure civile). Uncontested matters (such as adoption, emancipation of a minor and appointment of a guardian) are initiated by way of a petition (*requête*), while contested matters are usually initiated by *assignation* (writ of summons). It has been suggested to transfer some uncontested matters to other officials than the judge, for example to the clerk of the court (e.g. orders for payment). The aim of this suggestion is to allow the judge to concentrate on contested matters and to increase the efficiency of the courts. See especially Rapport Guinchard (2008: 21–22).

[27] France knows neither punitive damages nor a comparable institute. Frédérique Ferrand states, however, that a recent decision of the *Cour de cassation* determines that punitive damages ordered by a foreign court are not automatically contrary to the French *ordre public* (Cass. Civ. I, 1.12.2010, n°09-13303, *BICC* n°739 of 1.4.2011). Such punitive damages only violate this *ordre public* when the amount is disproportionate to the real damages and in violation of the contractual obligations of the party that has been ordered to pay these damages.

[28] Art. 25 Dutch Code of Civil Procedure.

[29] Frédérique Ferrand states that with regard to the application of legal rules *ex officio*, Art. 12(1) and (2) Code de procédure civile contains important powers and duties for the judge: Art. 12(1) 'The judge decides the case in accordance with the rules of law applicable thereto.' Art. 12(2) 'He must give or restore the proper legal definition to the disputed facts and deeds notwithstanding the definitions provided by the parties.' These provisions may be interpreted as encompassing the formulas 'Iura novit curia' and 'Da mihi factum, dabo tibi ius'. However, in a recent decision (Cass. ass. plénière, 21.12.2007, n°06-11343), the Plenary Assembly of the *Cour de cassation* provided a restrictive interpretation of them which has been criticised strongly by a majority of scholars.

certain powers to guarantee the proper and efficient administration of justice,[30] but outside these domains courts do not normally have the explicit task of furthering other societal or external goals.

In reaching the goals of civil justice, courts may be assisted by members of the Public Ministry, who function as part of the Executive. The Public Ministry may not only initiate proceedings in which an element of public order is at stake (e.g. asking the court to declare a marriage null and void, or requesting the dissolution of a legal person whose aims or activities are in contravention to public order), but may also render advice to the court known as the *conclusion* of the Public Ministry.[31] This is especially important at the Dutch Supreme Court of Cassation. There, the conclusions are, however, not taken by members of the Public Ministry but by the Procurator General and the Advocates General at the Supreme Court, who since 1999 officially function independently from the Executive.[32] These conclusions are often very influential and are published in collections of case law.[33]

3.4 Establishing the Facts of the Case Correctly v. the Need to Provide Effective Protection of Rights Within an Appropriate Amount of Time

Establishing the material or substantive truth is not necessarily the task of the Dutch civil judge; facts that are advanced by one party and that are not contested or not sufficiently contested by the other party do not have to be proven and may form the basis of the judge's decision. The judge does not have the powers to investigate these facts himself or herself.[34] Facts that are contested, however, may *ex officio* be subject to his or her scrutiny by way of, for example, a judicial viewing (such as the on-site inspection by the judge of premises which are the subject of a

[30] Art. 20 Dutch Code of Civil Procedure.

[31] Arts. 42–44 Dutch Code of Civil Procedure.

[32] Art. 111ff. Dutch Code of Judicial Organisation.

[33] According to Frédérqiue Ferrand, the French Public Ministry may initiate proceedings in which an element of public order is at stake. It can, for example, ask the court to declare a foreign adoption based on a contract with a surrogate mother null and void; the same applies to a marriage contracted only to obtain French citizenship. In such cases, the Public Ministry is a full party to the proceedings (*partie principale*). In other cases, the Public Ministry may act as *partie jointe* to the proceedings, which means that it can defend the public interest. At the French *Cour de cassation* there is a strong body of *avocats généraux* (unlike in the Netherlands, they are members of the Public Ministry), whose head is the *procureur général près la Cour de cassation*. In each civil case at the cassation court, the Public Ministry advises the court and suggests a solution by way of its conclusion. As in the Netherlands, the *procureur général près la Cour de cassation* can also bring an application in the interest of the law (*pourvoi dans l'intérêt de la loi*). In such cases, the sanction is only 'Platonic' and does not affect the original parties to the action.

[34] Art. 149 Dutch Code of Civil Procedure.

dispute), the hearing of experts or by way of an interrogation of the parties.[35] In addition, in its Article 21 the Dutch Code of Civil Procedure states that the parties have the duty to submit all facts that are relevant for their case in a truthful manner. If this duty is not complied with, the judge is allowed to draw the necessary inferences from this.[36,37]

This division of powers between the judge and the parties may be an indication that the Dutch civil justice system tries to seek a certain balance between a decision based on a sound factual basis, on the one hand, and speed and efficiency in reaching this decision, on the other.

3.5 Developing New Case Law v. Mass Processing of Routine Matters

Ordinary appeals before the ordinary appellate courts can only be brought if the value of the claim on which the court of first instance has ruled exceeds €1,750.[38] Obviously, this hardly functions as a serious selection mechanism.[39]

Just as the Dutch courts of first instance, the Supreme Court of Cassation in the Netherlands (which is the main source of case law) has no mechanism available to select cases, for example cases which it finds relevant for the development of new case law (however, see below as regards new legislation).[40] There is no system of permission to bring a case before the Supreme Court. In order to allow the cassation

[35] Hugenholtz and Heemskerk (2013: No. 78).

[36] According to Benoît Allemeersch, Belgian litigants are also subject to a duty to be truthful and exhaustive in their presentation of the case. If the litigants do not live up to this duty, the judge may draw the necessary inferences from this, just as his or her Dutch counterpart.

[37] According to Frédérique Ferrand, in France parties have control over the 'litigious matter' (*matière litigieuse*) and can even 'pursuant to an express agreement and in the exercise of rights that they may freely alienate, bind the judge as to the legal definitions and legal arguments to which they intend to restrict the action' (Art. 12(3) Code de procédure civile). This shows that establishing the substantive truth is not necessarily the task of the civil judge. In France the parties are not required to submit all facts in a truthful manner (unlike in Germany or in the Netherlands); they are responsible for the allegation and proof of the facts on which their claims or defences are based (Arts. 6 and 9 Code de procédure civile). They are, however, required to cooperate in good faith in all investigation measures the judge may order (Art. 11 Code de procédure civile). The judge has extended powers to order any legally admissible investigation measure (*mesure d'instruction*, Art. 10 Code de procédure civile) *ex officio*.

[38] Art. 332 Dutch Code of Civil Procedure.

[39] In France ordinary appeals may only be brought if the value of the claim exceeds €4,000. Frédérique Ferrand states that further appellate review is possible and widely available at the *Cour de cassation* (there is no direct selection mechanism as in Germany). However, at the *Cour de cassation* a 'procédure de non admission' was created in 2001 (Law of 25 June 2001): a *pourvoi en cassation* can receive a preliminary refusal (*déclaré non admis*) if it is not based on a serious cassation ground.

[40] The grounds for appeal in cassation are to be found in Art. 79 Dutch Code of Judicial Organisation.

court to concentrate on relevant matters, until recently it could only make use of the procedure of Article 81 of the Dutch Code of Judicial Organisation, which allows the court to give abbreviated reasons for its decision where the case can clearly not result in a ruling quashing the decision of the lower court.[41]

Recently, cassation proceedings have been under review. A Government Commission of Inquiry drafted a report (2008)[42] in which it was indicated that a considerable number of cases that reach the cassation court do not pose questions that are significant from the perspective of safeguarding the unity of the law, the development of the law or the legal protection of individual citizens. In the report, various options were considered to strengthen the role of the cassation court, allowing it to be involved only in cases that are relevant from the above perspectives. One option was allowing the court to declare cases that are not relevant inadmissible. At the same time, alternative ways for bringing relevant cases before the cassation court were being investigated, such as strengthening the procedure of cassation in the interest of the law, which allows the Procurator General at the court to start cassation proceedings even if the parties in the case do not choose to do so (consequently, the ruling of the cassation court will not influence the legal position of these parties, but will only be significant for the legal community at large),[43] and the possibility of allowing lower courts in civil cases to submit preliminary questions to the court of cassation in mass litigation. New legislation has been introduced. It allows the cassation court to declare the appeal in cassation inadmissible without giving grounds for its decision if on the basis of the statement of case containing the complaints of the claimant, and the statement of case containing the reply of the defendant, it comes to the conclusion that the complaint does not justify proceedings in cassation, either because the claimant does not have a reasonable interest in bringing cassation proceedings or because the complaint cannot result in the decision of the lower court being quashed.[44] According to one author, the legislation does not result in selection at the entrance of the court, but only just after the entrance has been passed.[45] However, indirectly it may allow the cassation court to select relevant cases from the above-mentioned perspectives. Additionally, legislation has been introduced which allows lower courts to submit preliminary questions to the cassation court in mass litigation and related matters.[46,47]

---

[41] According to Benoît Allemeersch, civil cases that reach the Belgian cassation court are informally filtered by the 20 specialised cassation attorneys in the country who have the monopoly on representing clients at this court. These lawyers see it as part of their deontology to determine whether cases are suitable for cassation proceedings. As a result, one out of two cassation proceedings in civil cases in Belgium is successful.

[42] *Versterking van de Cassatierechtspraak* (2008).

[43] See the still relevant PhD thesis of W.H.B. den Hartog Jager, *Cassatie in het belang der wet. Een buitengewoon rechtsmiddel*, Arnhem, Gouda Quint bv, 1994.

[44] Art. 80a Dutch Code of Judicial Organisation.

[45] H.J. Snijders (2011: 82).

[46] Arts. 392–394 Dutch Code of Civil Procedure.

[47] According to Frédérique Ferrand, in France during the course of civil proceedings the first instance or appellate court may suspend the hearing in order to ask the *Cour de cassation* a legal

3.6 Proportionality Between Case and Procedure[48]

The Netherlands does not know many specialised courts in civil matters – although there are various specialised divisions within the ordinary courts[49] – and only a few specialised procedures (such as the so-called *Kort Geding* (in French: *référé*), a quick and informal procedure to obtain provisional measures in urgent cases).[50] There is one standard model of procedure for adversarial litigation (the summons procedure),[51] which may be applied with a certain degree of flexibility by the judge based on the specific features of the case.[52] Consequently, there is no specific small claims procedure in domestic cases.[53] Claims of €25,000 or less and some specific subject matter belong to the domain of the cantonal section of the Court of First Instance (the cantonal section was created when the former Lower First Instance Court – the *Kantongerecht* – was merged with the general Court of First Instance), where parties may litigate in person without the assistance of an advocate (also there the uniform, flexible standard procedural model is followed). Higher value claims must be brought before the ordinary civil section of the general Court of First Instance, where the assistance of a lawyer is mandatory. There are no filtering mechanisms as regards the importance and relevance of the case, as long as the claimant brings an action concerning his own private rights and duties and not a case in the general interest (in the latter case, his claim will be declared inadmissible).[54] As stated above, new legislation has been introduced in the Netherlands introducing a filtering mechanism at the Supreme Court of Cassation.

---

question. This is often done when a new law which has not yet been interpreted by the *Cour de cassation* has to be applied. This mechanism is called *saisine pour avis de la Cour de cassation*. The cassation court only gives an 'avis' which does not bind the lower court. However, this court usually follows the 'avis'.

[48] I will not discuss the output-related manner of funding the Dutch court system here. This manner of funding is meant to be an incentive for courts and judges to deal with cases efficiently.

[49] Belgium also knows specialised divisions in the courts, although in that country there are various specialised courts, too.

[50] Arts. 254–259 Dutch Code of Civil Procedure.

[51] I will not discuss the procedure initiated by petition which is sometimes also applicable in adversarial cases – see above.

[52] According to Benoît Allemeersch, Belgium knows two procedural tracks in civil cases, the long track (ordinary track) and the fast track (*korte debatten*). In both tracks, a court hearing is scheduled immediately after the writ of summons has been served. At this hearing, parties may plead orally if they wish to do so and the judge may give a final judgment immediately afterwards. When subsequent procedural acts are necessary, which happens in the long track, the judge is in charge of fixing the time limits. As is widely known, France also knows various procedural tracks.

[53] At the EU level there is of course the small claims procedure (Regulation (EC) No. 861/2007 of the European Parliament and of the Council of 11 July 2007, establishing a European small claims procedure) which is, however, only applicable in case of cross-border litigation.

[54] Art. 3:303 Dutch Civil Code.

Proportionality between case and procedure may also be reached by an early settlement of the case. The ordinary first instance procedure in the Netherlands aims at such a settlement of the case. To this end, courts have the duty – unless the judge is of the opinion that this will be futile in the case at hand – to order a court appearance of the parties at an early moment in the litigation.[55] Additionally, in order to enable parties to settle their case at an early stage with minimal involvement of the judiciary, a special procedure (*deelgeschillenprocedure*) has been introduced by law (17 December 2009)[56] as regards claims for damages as a result of physical injury or death.[57] One or both of the parties in such cases may ask the judge, either before or during the proceedings in court, to decide about a sub-issue that is either directly relevant or related to part of the matter that is keeping the parties divided, but only if such a decision is likely to contribute to the parties' settling their case out of court by way of a settlement agreement (*vaststellingsovereenkomst*).

3.7 Multi-party Litigation

There are possibilities to bring multi-party litigation before Dutch courts, although these cannot be equalled to class or group actions as they are known in other jurisdictions.[58,59] The Dutch alternatives are discussed below.[60]

The Dutch Civil Code contains a set of articles on organisations litigating in the interest of their members or in the general interest. Originally, claims brought by such organisations would be declared inadmissible, since the rule is that a claim can only be brought when the claimant litigates in his own personal interest.[61] Later, such claims were sometimes allowed by the courts. In 1994, the Civil Code was modified with the introduction of Articles 3:305a and 3:305b, and in 2001 with the addition of Article 3:305c. In these articles, the right of foundations, associations with full legal personality and other legal persons to bring an action in the interest of a collectivity is, under certain conditions, recognised. Conditions are that the interests of those for whom the action is brought must be similar in nature and that the aim of representing their interests is expressed in the documents by

[55] Art. 131 Dutch Code of Civil Procedure. See also Arts. 87 and 88 of the same Code.

[56] Official Journal (Stbl.) 2010, 221; in force since 1 July 2010.

[57] Arts. 1019w–1019cc Dutch Code of Civil Procedure.

[58] Belgium does not know class actions or similar types of litigation either.

[59] In France there are no general provisions on group litigation. Frédérique Ferrand states that only an *action en représentation conjointe* by consumer associations is possible, which is designed as an opt-in procedure.

[60] See also Eliantonio et al. (2013: 425ff.).

[61] Art. 3:303 Dutch Civil Code.

which the legal person was created (*statuten*). Damages *cannot* be claimed in actions brought in this way.[62]

In 2005, Articles 7:907–910 were introduced in the Dutch Civil Code, and Articles 1013–1018 in the Code of Civil Procedure. These articles govern situations in which a large number of individuals suffer harm due to an act or related acts of one or more natural or legal persons (e.g. a tobacco company). The articles open the possibility for the natural or legal persons having caused the harm and a foundation or association representing the interests of those who have suffered harm to reach an agreement which can be submitted to the Court of Appeal in Amsterdam in order to have it sanctioned as an agreement applicable to all who have suffered harm in the context of the agreement. The decision is binding for everyone involved in the dispute, except for those who decide to opt out.

3.8 Equitable Results v. Strict Formalism

For a few decades now (especially since the 1970s), the keyword in Dutch civil procedure has been 'deformalisation', that is to say, the elimination of unnecessary formalism. The litigants should not be able to use the rules of civil procedure to win their case, but the action should concern the specific problem that keeps the parties divided. Furthermore, the infringement of procedural rules should only result in sanctions if the interest protected by the infringed norm has actually been harmed.[63]

Recent examples of 'deformalisation' are that the initiation of a particular action in the wrong manner, namely, by way of a petition where a summons is prescribed or vice versa, will not result in the inadmissibility of the claim but in an order to correct the wrong initiation of the action; and the date of commencement of the action will remain the original date of commencement even though it was commenced in the wrong manner.[64] Another example is that litigants who introduce an action themselves where legal representation is required will be given the opportunity by the court to correct their omission without the action being discontinued.[65] Also, all kinds of irregularities in the writ of summons

[62] According to Benoît Allemeersch, in Belgium the 'Eikendael doctrine' teaches that legal persons *cannot* represent the interests of others; they may only bring an action in their own interest. Currently, there is some debate about this issue, but it is unlikely that changes will be introduced in Belgian law in the near future. There are a few exceptions to the 'Eikendael doctrine', e.g. where it concerns civil litigation as regards racism or environmental issues.

[63] *Herziening van het procesrecht voor burgerlijke zaken, in het bijzonder de wijze van procederen in eerste aanleg* (effective from 2002), Explanatory memorandum, Kamerstukken *II* 1999/2000, 26 855, Nr. 3, p. 5, available at https://zoek.officielebekendmakingen.nl/dossier/26855/kst-26855-3?resultIndex=33&sorttype=1&sortorder=4 (last consulted in September 2013).

[64] Art. 69 Dutch Code of Civil Procedure; e.g. relevant in the light of the statute of limitations.

[65] Art. 123 Dutch Code of Civil Procedure.

will only result in the summons being declared void if it can be assumed that the interests of the addressee of the summons have been harmed in an unreasonable manner.[66]

3.9 Problem Solving v. Case Processing

Problem solving is not, according to the majority of Dutch authors,[67] a primary goal of the civil justice system, although it may be a by-product of it (in civil proceedings, Dutch courts will explore whether a friendly settlement of the case is possible). The primary goal of the civil justice system is to produce authoritative, enforceable decisions (judgments) within a reasonable amount of time. This is, according to the same authors, the main difference with, for example, mediation. Mediation is of a completely different nature than the administration of justice in a court of law since mediation is aimed at allowing the parties to find a solution to their conflict that is acceptable to both of them.

3.10 Freely Available Public Service v. Quasi-commercial Source of Revenue for the Public Budget

The Netherlands does not recognise the principle of the administration of civil justice free of charge. For various reasons, this is not an acceptable principle. Parties think more about the necessity of bringing an action when there are court fees than when court fees are not levied, while it may also be claimed that court fees are justified since it is in the end the parties that (also) profit from a court decision in their case. However, due to the positive externalities of civil litigation for society at large (see above), there are good reasons not to introduce a system of court fees that covers all the costs of the civil justice system; part of these costs should be borne by the public purse since society at large also profits from civil litigation. As stated above, the previous government proposed legislation aimed at introducing a system of court fees that would cover the costs of the justice system to a larger extent than at present. The new system would have meant that approximately 64 % of the costs would have been covered, partly due to the higher court fees and partly due to a lower number of cases. Even the new system would not, however, have meant that the civil justice system in the Netherlands could have been viewed as a 'quasi-commercial source of revenue for the public budget'; in the end, even under

[66] Art. 66 Dutch Code of Civil Procedure.

[67] E.g. Asser et al. (2003: 35ff. and Chapter 5).

that system the State would have borne part of the costs of the administration of civil justice. As mentioned, the plans of the previous government have been shelved by the present government.

3.11 User Orientation?

Over the last 10 years or so, the Dutch legislature and legal authors have begun to view the civil justice system also from the perspective of its users.[68] User satisfaction surveys have been conducted on a regular basis since the start of the new millennium, but until recently only a limited number of courts participated. In 2011, for the first time a nationwide survey was organised in which all courts of first instance and all courts of appeal, including some special administrative tribunals, were involved. The results of the survey were published in 2011.[69] From the survey it appears that Dutch litigants were satisfied with the administration of justice in general (81 % satisfied). When focusing on the civil division (excluding family litigation) of the general first instance court, 86 % of litigants were satisfied; at the civil division (excluding family litigation) of the court of appeal, 80 % of litigants were satisfied. For professional court users (advocates, court experts, etc.) the relevant percentage was 73 %. When focussing on the civil division (excluding family litigation) of the general first instance court, 70 % of professional court users were satisfied; at the civil division (excluding family litigation) of the court of appeal, 68 % of professional court users were satisfied.

Eighty-six per cent of the litigants were satisfied with the way the judges functioned. This percentage was 78 % for professional court users. More critical remarks were made as regards the length of the proceedings. Twenty-nine per cent of litigants and 27 % of professional court users were dissatisfied with respect to this issue. The satisfaction rate differed on the basis of whether or not litigants were successful in their case: 89 % of litigants who had received or who expected a favourable judgment were generally satisfied, whereas this percentage was only 55 % for those who received or who expected an unfavourable judgment.

[68] The same applies to France. The report of the Guinchard Commission (2008) is especially important. The Commission had to think about a new 'répartition des contentieux', i.e. a new distribution of cases over courts and other judicial bodies. The Guinchard Commission promoted different reforms aiming at placing the *justiciables* (i.e. those searching for the administration of justice) in the centre of the judicial system. This requires clearer, easier and more foreseeable access to justice (*accès plus facile, plus aisé et assurant une plus grande prévisibilité*). The Report has already been implemented on several issues. A new law was enacted at the end of 2011 in order to implement other proposals formulated by the Report.

[69] The report *Klantwaardering Rechtspraak 2011* is available at http://www.rechtspraak.nl/Organisatie/Raad-Voor-De-Rechtspraak/Nieuws/Documents/Landelijk%20Klantwaarderingsonderzoek%20Rechtspraak%202011.pdf (last consulted in September 2013).

Professionals considered three aspects of the administration of justice very favourably: the expertise of the judges, their impartiality and the comprehensibility of the judgments. They were less favourable as to the quality of the grounds expressed in the judgment. Litigants, on the contrary, were satisfied with the quality of these grounds.

Earlier results are those published in 2006 (data October–December 2005) (data published in 2008 are also available, but these are not discussed here).[70] Different from the 2011 results, however, a smaller number of courts was involved. The 2006 results showed that professional court users were of the opinion that the courts of first instance were better organised in 2005 than in 2001, and they were also more satisfied with the professional behaviour of the judges (ca. 84 % of the respondents were generally satisfied; this percentage is higher than in 2011). They shared their opinion about the professional conduct of the judges with the litigants (litigants were satisfied with the way in which the judge listened to their respective positions (85 % of the respondents were satisfied), with the room offered by the judge for the litigants to tell their story (86 % satisfied) and with the judge's expertise and his or her impartiality (79 % satisfied); fewer litigants were satisfied with the amount of empathy displayed by the judge (69 % satisfied)). Also according to the 2006 data, professional court users were *not* so satisfied with the manner in which grounds were expressed in the judgment: they stated that the manner of expressing grounds sometimes made it hard for them to establish whether similar cases were decided in a similar manner. Litigants were *not* so satisfied with the length of proceedings (the same dissatisfaction was expressed in 2011),[71] with the availability of information about the manner in which their case would be handled in court and with the facilities at the court buildings (availability of food too limited, separate rooms to discuss cases in private with their lawyer not available, etc.).

3.12 Conclusion

From the above it appears that – albeit after a long period of gestation – the Netherlands has introduced fundamental reforms in the civil justice system. These reforms are successful, at least from the perspective of court users such as advocates and litigants. The present financial crisis may, however, endanger the successes achieved by the reforms, although plans to increase court fees to such an extent that the court system as a whole could be financed from these fees have been shelved. These fees would most likely have proven detrimental to access to justice and were not justified given the various positive externalities that litigation by private litigants creates for

[70] See *De zaken meer op orde* (2006).

[71] Although, the record is not bad. Just before the survey was conducted in 2005, the median case processing time in defended cases for the courts of first instance in the Netherlands had dropped by 20 %, from 525 days in 1996 to 413 days in 2003. In the same period, the percentage of cases terminated within 1 year rose from 34 to 49 %.

society at large. However, new austerity measures cannot be excluded, and therefore the current Dutch successes in civil litigation cannot be considered to be secure. Also, new far-reaching reforms have been announced by the current Minister of Justice which include the abolition of the role of the *huisser de justice* in serving the writ of summons, an increase in the role of IT technology in litigation and a less complicated and more similar procedural model in civil and administrative cases.

References

Asser WDH, Groen HA, Vranken JBM (in cooperation with I.N. Tzankova) (2003) Een nieuwe balans. Interimrapport Fundamentele herbezinning Nederlands burgerlijk procesrecht. Boom Juridische uitgevers, The Hague

Asser WDH, Groen HA, Vranken JBM (in cooperation with I.N. Tzankova) (2006) Uitgebalanceerd. Eindrapport Fundamentele herbezinning Nederlands burgerlijk procesrecht. Boom Juridische uitgevers, The Hague. Also available at http://www.rijksoverheid.nl/documenten-en-publicaties/rapporten/2006/02/01/uitgebalanceerd-eindrapport-fundamentele-herbezinning-nederlands-burgerlijk-procesrecht.html. Last consulted in Sept 2013

Contourennota, Visie op het civiele proces: reactie fundamentele herbezinning burgerlijk procesrecht (1998) Available at http://www.rijksoverheid.nl./documenten-en-publicaties/kamerstukken/2007/02/05/reactie-fundamentele-herbezinning-burgerlijk-procesrecht-7026.html. Last consulted in Sept 2013

De zaken meer op orde. Klantwaarderingsonderzoek in tien rechtbanken (2006) Prisma. Available at: http://www.rechtspraak.nl/Organisatie/Publicaties-En-Brochures/rapporten-en-artikelen/Documents/dezakenmeeroporde.pdf. Last consulted in Sept 2013

Den Hartog Jager WHB (1994) Cassatie in het belang der wet. Een buitengewoon rechtsmiddel. Gouda Quint bv, Arnhem

Eliantonio M, Backes C, Van Rhee CH, Spronken T, Berlee A (2013) Standing up for your right(s) in Europe. A comparative study on legal standing (Locus Standi) before the EU and member States' Courts. Intersentia, Antwerp

Hugenholtz W, Heemskerk WH (2013) Hoofdlijnen van Nederlands Burgerlijk Procesrecht. Convoy, Dordrecht

Rapport Guinchard (2008) L'ambition raisonnée d'une justice apaisée. Doc. française, Paris

Snijders HJ (2011) Verandering van cassatierechtspraak. Tijdschrift voor Civiele Rechtspleging 3:81–88

Versterking van de Cassatierechtspraak. Rapport van de Commissie normstellende rol Hoge Raad (2008) Available at http://www.eerstekamer.nl/behandeling/20080327/versterking_van_de/f=/virxe1o18gc3.pdf. Last consulted in Sept 2013

Visscher L (2012) A law and economics view on harmonisation of procedural law. In: Kramer X, van Rhee CH (eds) Civil litigation in a globalising world. Asser Press, The Hague, pp 65–92

Chapter 4
Goals of Civil Justice When Nothing Works: The Case of Italy

Elisabetta Silvestri

Je voudrais pouvoir aimer mon pays tout en aimant la justice.

Albert Camus, *Lettres à un ami allemand*

Abstract This chapter addresses some critical aspects of Italian civil justice with the view to clarifying the reasons why the goals it is supposed or expected to reach are difficult to identify. For those who are in charge of a justice system faced with a longstanding 'identity crisis', known worldwide for the unbearable length of its judicial proceedings and constantly in a state of emergency, the search for 'exit strategies' seems to be an absolute priority, one that overshadows the importance of a clear vision of the goals civil justice is intended to pursue. But short of such a vision, no reforms will be able to reverse the present situation.

4.1 Introduction

To describe the goals assigned to civil justice in the legal system of present-day Italy is not an easy task. Truth be told, the topic does not seem to stir much interest either in scholarly debate or among the citizens at large. As far as the courts are concerned, only the Constitutional Court occasionally elaborates on the proper role of jurisdiction, in general by way of *obiter dicta*. All the actors involved in the performance of civil justice (users, lawyers and judges) appear to be concerned with the more mundane task of handling a system that has reached an unbearable level of inefficiency and slowness: when the situation is dramatically serious – as it is in Italy – it does

E. Silvestri (✉)
Dipartimento di Giurisprudenza, Università degli Studi di Pavia,
Strada Nuova 65, 27100 Pavia, Italy
e-mail: elisabetta.silvestri@unipv.it

A. Uzelac (ed.), *Goals of Civil Justice and Civil Procedure in Contemporary Judicial Systems*, Ius Gentium: Comparative Perspectives on Law and Justice 34,
DOI 10.1007/978-3-319-03443-0_4,

not seem useful to waste time in theoretical speculations, and there is a sort of natural tendency to look for practical solutions. Unfortunately, though, practical solutions may work, at best, only in the short run: to reverse the misfortunes of Italian civil justice would require radical reforms, and no radical reforms can be devised unless they are prepared by a thorough process aimed at identifying which goals must or can be reached by the courts as the main providers of civil justice.

4.2 The 'Identity Crisis' of Italian Civil Justice

As mentioned above, the issue concerning the goals civil justice should accomplish (or, at least, try to accomplish) does not fall within the 'hot topics' debated in Italy, in spite of the fact that the proper role played by the judicial system within a democratic State is a matter at the centre of heated discussions, due to the political aftermath of criminal trials involving members of the Parliament.

As far as legal scholars are concerned, with few exceptions[1] they have an exegetic approach to the law in force, and do not embark upon passing judgment on the quality of the rules or the soundness of their rationale. Obviously, every manual and treatise on civil procedure defines the goals of civil justice, but such definitions either have a touch of repetitiveness or, when they try to be original, call upon complex notions borrowed from jurisprudence and general theory of law. Therefore (and offering no more than a few examples), adjudication is described as the institutional method of dispute resolution (Comoglio et al. 2011: 15), or the method by which rights are made effective via resorting to the courts; more sophisticated analyses shift the focus from adjudication to jurisdiction, advancing different definitions of it, but arriving at a sort of tautological conclusion, and stating that jurisdiction is the function of the State performed by the judges (Verde 2010: 27).

Definitions aside, some hints of the different scholarly opinions about the goals of civil justice can be read between the lines of a lively debate that animated Italian academia a few years ago, that is, the debate revolving around the question whether the Code of Civil Procedure – adopted in 1940, entered into force in 1942 and still governing the pace of most civil and commercial proceedings – was a 'fascist' code, meaning an authoritarian code, providing for a pattern of civil justice centred on the strong and broad powers bestowed on the judge, with consequential limitations in the leeway for manoeuvring left to the parties.[2] Whatever the original intent of the Code's drafters was, one must keep in mind that the Code has gone through so many reforms that to investigate whether it had a fascist 'soul' seems a futile exercise; besides, a vast number of the diverse special proceedings conventionally covered by

[1] See in particular Taruffo (2009: 63).

[2] Foreign readers may be immune to the spell of such an all-Italian debate. In any event, for the benefit of those who would like to know more about it, here is a capsule bibliography: Cipriani (2003: 455); Cipriani (2002: 425); Cipriani (1997: 3, 103, 121, 157); Monteleone (2003: 575); Verde (2002: 676).

the umbrella term 'civil justice' are more recent than the Code and do not reflect the values embedded in it. Last but not least, the advent of the Republican Constitution in 1948 has had a strong impact on the Code, either because some of its rules have been repealed by the Constitutional Court, or because the same Court requires every legal rule (whether substantive or procedural), when applied by a judge, to be given an interpretation that is 'constitutionally oriented'.

Certainly, the constitutional dimension of jurisdiction has changed the meaning of the goals assigned to civil justice. Several constitutional guarantees affect civil justice directly. The main one is contained in Article 24, which provides as follows: '1. Anyone may bring cases before a court of law in order to protect their rights under civil and administrative law. 2. Defence is an inviolable right at every stage and instance of legal proceedings. 3. The poor are entitled by law to proper means for action or defence in all courts'.[3] Article 24 must be read in conjunction with another fundamental guarantee, namely, the principle of equality, according to which 'All citizens have equal social dignity and are equal before the law, without distinction of sex, race, language, religion, political opinion, personal and social conditions' (Article 3, sec. 1), to the extent that 'It is the duty of the Republic to remove those obstacles of an economic or social nature which constrain the freedom and equality of citizens, thereby impeding the full development of the human person and the effective participation of all workers in the political, economic and social organisation of the country' (Article 3, sec. 2). Articles 3 and 24 give constitutional status to a specific right, the right of action and defence, as this right is commonly referred to in Italy. The right of action and defence has become the pillar of access to justice and the basis on which the guarantee of due process has been built, even before a constitutional amendment enacted a rule specifically devoted to such a guarantee. According to this rule (Article 111, as amended in 1998), 'jurisdiction is implemented through due process regulated by law', and 'all court trials are conducted with adversary proceedings and the parties are entitled to equal conditions before an impartial judge in third party position'.

It is worth mentioning that the same rule goes on by stating that 'the law provides for the reasonable duration of trials', which may sound absurd in a country known worldwide for the inefficiency of its justice system and the excessive length of both criminal and civil cases. As a matter of fact, the amendment that elevated the reasonable length of judicial proceedings to a constitutional guarantee sounds precisely like an attempt to 'exorcise' the curse under which the Italian justice system has been living for so many years that it is impossible to remember whether there was ever a time when criminal trials, but most of all civil cases, had an acceptable length. For those who believe in the cathartic strength of religious rites, exorcisms are acceptable ways to release people or places from evils, but no reasonable person could think that simply stating in a legal rule (even a constitutional one) that judicial proceedings must have a 'reasonable duration' is enough to do the trick, and

[3] The English translation of the Italian Constitution quoted in the text is the official one available on the Italian Senate's website, at http://www.senato.it/documenti/repository/istituzione/costituzione_inglese.pdf (last accessed in August 2013).

magically reduce the delay of court cases. Apparently, though, Italian lawmakers do not subscribe to this point of view, since they also concocted another fanciful device that is supposed to perform wonders and shorten the length of judicial proceedings, that is, determining by law the maximum length deemed reasonable: 3 years for adjudications before courts of first instance; 2 years for appellate proceedings; 1 year for cases pending before the Court of Cassation (*Corte di cassazione*, i.e. the Italian Supreme Court); and, in any event, 6 years as the maximum lifespan of cases. One may puzzle over why some brilliant minds thought it necessary to set these time limits: the reason is quite simple, and has to do with the special procedure by which the parties to a case can claim damages against the Italian State for the unreasonable length of the case itself. This special procedure was established in 2001: its official goal was to advance the cause of those who claimed to have been harmed by the excessive length of judicial proceedings, by providing for a domestic form of redress, that is, a special proceeding to be instituted before appellate courts. In reality, the true goal pursued by the famous (or infamous, depending on the point of view) 'Pinto Act'[4] was to restrain the increasing flow of Italian cases reaching the European Court of Human Rights, claiming a violation of Article 6, § 1 of the European Convention on Human Rights (hereinafter, ECHR), since the new domestic remedy had to be experimented with before turning to the Strasbourg Court with the view to claiming the 'just satisfaction' provided for in Article 41 of the Convention.

Unfortunately, it did not take long to realise that the special procedure laid down by the Pinto Act was by itself a cause of further problems, due to the already congested caseloads of appellate courts; the damages awarded were often inadequate and, most of all, their payments were delayed, since the national budget lacked the funds necessary to cover them. A new wave of Italian cases began to reach the European Court, challenging the very remedy by which the infringement of the right to have one's case resolved within a reasonable time should have been compensated adequately at the national level.

In 2010 the Court issued an important judgment[5] finding Italy in violation of both Article 6, § 1 of the ECHR and Article 1 of Protocol No. 1 to the Convention

[4] Law no. 89 of 24 March 2001, known as 'Legge Pinto' ('Pinto Act') from the name of the Senator who drafted the text of the statute. The law was heavily amended in 2012: among the new features, it is worth mentioning the determination of the maximum length of proceedings (as mentioned in the text), as well as the provision of a threshold for the compensation that can be claimed, since the compensation is calculated on the basis of a sum (not less than €500.00 and not more than €1,500.00) for each year (or a fraction of a year longer than 6 months) exceeding the maximum length allowed by the statute itself. See Porcelli (2012: 3391–3408). The allegedly positive effects of the new rules governing the national remedy for unreasonable length of judicial proceedings are yet to be seen. It may be interesting to remark that as of July 2013, according to a note released by the Ministry of Justice, the debt of the Italian State for failure to compensate the victims of excessive delays of judicial proceedings amounted to the astronomical sum of €340 million: see Ministero della giustizia – Direzione generale del contenzioso e dei diritti umani, Nota 11 luglio 2013 – Legge 89/2001. Pagamento da parte del Ministero della giustizia degli indennizzi, available at http://www.giustizia.it/giustizia/it/mg_1_8_1.wp?previsiousPage=mg_1_8&contentId=SDC937574 (last accessed in August 2013).

[5] *Gaglione and others v. Italy* (application no. 45867/07), 21 December 2010.

(that is, the rule granting the right to peaceful enjoyment of property) on account of the fact that plaintiffs had not been able to recover the compensation they were entitled to receive within a reasonable time, which – according to the Court – cannot exceed 6 months running from the date the judgment awarding compensation became enforceable. With an extensive opinion, the Court performed a merciless analysis of the Italian situation, underlying that, as of December 2010, almost 4,000 cases were pending against Italy for alleged delays in the payment of the compensations granted under the Pinto Act, and therefore calling for a radical reform of the domestic remedy, on the one hand, and for the allocation of the funds required to comply with the State's obligations in the national budget, on the other. Most of all, though, the Court made a point of emphasising that the problem with Italy had escalated over the years into a real threat not only for the effectiveness of the very right to the 'just satisfaction' owed to the victims of violations of the rights granted under the ECHR, but also – in a wider perspective – for the proper functioning of the Court itself, and therefore for its ability to perform its role within the redress scheme established by the ECHR.

It seems pointless to list the numerous interim resolutions issued by the Committee of Ministers of the Council of Europe on both the excessive length of Italian judicial proceedings and the defective enforcement of the judgments rendered by the European Court of Human Rights against Italy for violation of Article 6, § 1 of the ECHR, but, in order to understand the extent of the problem, it is worth mentioning the report prepared by the Commissioner of Human Rights of the Council of Europe in September 2012, following a visit to Italy.[6] The Report expands on several aspects of the critical state of the Italian justice system, and analyses the most evident causes of its malfunctioning, such as the overwhelming caseload of the courts, the unusually high propensity of Italians to litigate, the maze of complex and formalistic procedures, the extremely high number of lawyers, the lack of managerial culture in the organisation of judicial work and – last but not least – an irrational distribution of the financial resources allocated to the administration of justice at large. The conclusions drawn by the Commissioner are lapidary: Italy needs 'nothing short of a holistic rethinking of the judicial and procedural system, as well as a radical shift in judicial culture'.[7]

But a 'holistic rethinking' of how to improve the quality of justice is exactly what is missing. After decades of constant and often contradictory reforms of the rules governing civil proceedings, no signs of improvement can be seen, as is displayed by the data offered by a few recently published surveys on the performance of the justice systems of several countries, such as the working paper on the relationship between economic growth and a well-functioning dispute resolution system

[6] Report by Nils Muižnieks, Commissioner for Human Rights of the Council of Europe, following his visit to Italy from 3 to 6 July 2012, CommDH (2012) 26, Strasbourg, 18 September 2012, paragraphs 6–60, available at https://wcd.coe.int/com.instranet.InstraServlet?command=com.instranet.CmdBlobGet&InstranetImage=2143096&SecMode=1&DocId=1926434&Usage=2 (last accessed in August 2013).

[7] Ibid., at paragraph 49.

prepared by the Organisation for Economic Co-operation and Development (OECD),[8] the EU Justice Scoreboard issued by the European Commission,[9] or the inescapable Doing Business 2013.[10] Also at the national level, a few institutional actors are aware that the strategy pursued until now by lawmakers through an endless inventory of piecemeal changes to the law of civil procedure has failed, and that the problems affecting Italian justice cannot be solved unless some difficult and certainly controversial policy choices involving the entire organisation of the State are made.[11] Policy choices, in their turn, must be supported by a clear vision of the goals pursued and, as far as justice is concerned, these goals do not seem clear, nor do they appear to be shared by all the stakeholders.

Stakeholders (ordinary citizens as well as legal professionals at large) do agree on the fact that the caseload of civil courts is too heavy and must be reduced, but there are different views on the ways by which this objectives can be attained. Lawmakers, too, seem at a loss to devise successful strategies aimed at allowing courts to regain control over their burgeoning dockets. Two examples seem in order which both come from a recent statute that was passed with the view to 're-launching' the national economy[12] but brought about a disparate variety of innovations in many sectors, not necessarily connected with economics, following a trend that has become quite common in the Italian legislative drafting process, that is, to draft a statute officially aimed at regulating a specific matter, and in the process 'sneak in' rules that have nothing to do with the main topic of the statute itself. The first example is the anticipated recruitment of 400 'auxiliary judges' who will be assigned to appellate courts with the view to accelerating the definition of cases on appeal so as to reduce the backlogs that are weighing down the courts. Retired lawyers, judges, notaries public and law professors will be able to apply; they will have the status of lay judges (or honorary judges, as they are called in Italy) and will be paid as 'pieceworkers', that is, based upon the number of cases they decide: €200 per judgment, for a maximum amount of €20,000 a year. The idea of confiding in the wisdom of a small army

[8] OECD (2013), 'What makes civil justice effective?', OECD Economics Department Policy Notes, No. 18, June 2013, available at http://www.oecd.org/eco/growth/Civil%20Justice%20Policy%20Note.pdf (last accessed in August 2013).

[9] Communication from the Commission to the European Parliament, the Council, the European Central Bank, the European Economic and Social Committee and the Committee of the Regions, The EU Justice Scoreboard – A Tool to Promote Effective Justice and Growth, COM (2013) 160 final, available at http://ec.europa.eu/justice/effective-justice/files/justice_scoreboard_communication_en.pdf (last accessed in August 2013).

[10] World Bank. 2013. Doing Business 2013: Smarter Regulations for Small and Medium-Size Enterprises. Economic Profile: Italy. Washington, DC: World Bank Group, available at http://www.doingbusiness.org/reports/global-reports/~/media/giawb/doing%20business/documents/profiles/country/ITA.pdf (last accessed in August 2013).

[11] See, e.g., Consiglio Nazionale dell'Economia e del Lavoro, Relazione annuale al Parlamento e al Governo sui livelli e la qualità dei servizi erogati dalle pubbliche amministrazioni centrali e locali alle imprese e ai cittadini, II, 13 dicembre 2012, 8–55, available at http://www.cnel.it/53?shadow_documenti=22678 (last accessed in August 2013).

[12] Statute no. 98 of 2013.

of pensioners or law graduates in search of employment for the improvement of the performance of the judicial system is not new, since it already inspired the recruitment of 'adjunct' judges in the 1990s. The results were not as positive as expected, but apparently the lesson has not been learned, and – which seems even more disheartening – those who conceived the idea of increasing the number of judges evidently ignored the array of studies showing that to inflate the size of the judiciary *per se* neither reduces court congestion nor speeds up the disposition of cases.[13]

The second example is mediation. In 2010, while implementing Directive 2008/52/EC on certain aspects of mediation in civil and commercial cases, the Italian government made mediation mandatory in almost all civil cases. The duty to attempt out-of-court mediation before turning to courts did not reduce in a significant way the number of incoming cases, since very often at least one party failed to appear in front of the mediator or, even if both parties participated in the mediation sessions, no agreements were reached. In any event, in December 2012 the Constitutional Court repealed the rules on mandatory mediation, holding them unconstitutional.[14] In spite of that, the new statute mentioned above has reinstated mandatory mediation, which seems to create the perfect scenario for yet another time-consuming round of institutional 'arm-wrestling'. That aside, lawmakers seem to ignore that according to widespread opinion making mediation mandatory and, in general, placing over-optimistic reliance on the virtues of ADR as a 'better' form of access to justice, can be seen 'as less about the positive qualities of mediation and more about diverting cases to mediation as an easier and cheaper option than attempting to fix or invest in dysfunctional systems of adjudication' (Genn 2010: 116): in short, it can be seen as the acknowledgment of a defeat. And, as regards Italy, it is a defeat on a grand scale.

The 'identity crisis' affecting Italian civil justice is a longstanding condition, but, not so far in the past, many nurtured great expectations on the role civil justice could play in changing Italian society for the better. At that time it was said that the Constitution had advanced the 'socialisation' of civil justice,[15] removing adjudication from the realm of technical matters and bringing it closer to the needs of the society at large. The idea of adjudication as an instrument to promote social justice had its heyday in the 1970s and in the early 1980s, when civil courts were more and more entrusted with the task of enforcing the diverse rights constituting what has been forcefully defined as 'the new property' (Reich 1964: 733–787). The essence of civil justice was not only the resolution of disputes between two individuals allegedly on equal footing, but also the settlement of social tensions and conflicts[16]: courts were expected to be proactive and to exercise an array of new powers with the view to making sure that both parties to a case shared an actual equality of arms, so

[13] See, among many others, Priest (1989: 527–559).

[14] On the vicissitudes of mandatory mediation in Italy, see Silvestri and Jagtenberg (2013: 29–45).

[15] See Comoglio (1970: 131); Andolina and Vignera (1997: 7).

[16] Among the scholars who vigorously supported the cause of civil justice as a powerful instrument for the achievement of social justice, see in particular Denti (1970: 56–74).

that the weaker party (for instance, the employee who had been unfairly dismissed, the worker whose rights as a member of a union had been infringed, or the victim of gender discrimination) would suffer no disadvantages in the conduct of adjudications.

Nowadays, to talk about the social function of civil justice has a retro flavour. The changes that have taken place in Italy in the political, economic, social and cultural landscape are too complex to be analysed here. Undeniably, they have all affected the way the goals of civil justice are perceived, even though – as noted at the very beginning of this essay – it is hard to understand exactly which ones are deemed to be desirable or attainable. One may object that more important than the goals theoretically and ideally ascribed to civil justice are the goals the system seems to pursue through the law governing civil justice. But these very goals are difficult to decipher. The most recent reforms in the field of civil procedure could persuade one to venture a guess, and say that they show a return on a grand scale of an old-style liberal concept of civil justice, that is, the concept according to which the parties are the absolute masters of adjudication, and the court is supposed to play a passive role, unless the parties request its intervention.[17] In reality, though, a more accurate analysis of the constant amendments to the rules governing adjudication shows that the lawmaker deliberately refrains from enforcing a specific concept of the goals civil justice is expected to attain. Does this mean that the lawmaker has yet to devise his own vision of civil justice? Maybe it is so, but another possible explanation is that the constant state of emergency within which Italian civil justice is struggling (Silvestri 2011) brings about the necessity of moving from one 'quick fix' to the next one, without reflecting on the big picture. Maybe in a distant future – if ever – the goals civil justice should fulfil will be identified, and the law of civil procedure will be changed accordingly; as of now, the only goal that matters is to reduce the caseload of the courts, hoping that will be enough to shorten the length of proceedings.

4.3 Matters Within the Scope of Civil Justice: An Abundance of 'Special Proceedings' Contrasted with a Scarcity of Resources

Traditionally, Italian civil justice covers not only litigation, that is, the resolution of disputes arising out of civil and commercial matters, but also a vast array of proceedings dealing with non-contested matters. Whether such proceedings are consistent with the proper goals of civil justice is questionable: the fact is that the Code of Civil Procedure includes an entire book regulating many 'special proceedings' in non-contested matters. Similar proceedings of the same nature are governed also by several special statutes: the result is a multifaceted conundrum that Italian scholars call

[17] That was the concept underlying the first Code of Civil Procedure enacted by the unified Kingdom of Italy in 1865: see Taruffo (1980: 107–149).

giurisdizione volontaria (non-contentious jurisdiction), an expression underscoring the absence of a dispute between parties.

As regards certain non-contested matters, courts are called upon to perform a role that borders on activities that are more administrative than judicial. It is said that the involvement of the courts in such matters is justified because they all touch upon public interest, even though to different extents, and therefore it is appropriate to entrust them to the courts in their capacity as the ultimate defenders of the rule of law. For other proceedings, the same rationale does not hold true, since the concept of public interest is sensitive to changes in the political and societal perception of what 'public interest' amounts to.

The Code of Civil Procedure makes no specific reference to non-contentious jurisdiction; the expression was included in a single article of the Code (Article 801, concerning the recognition of foreign judgments and orders) that was repealed in 1995 by the statute reforming the rules governing the Italian system of private international law. Non-contentious jurisdiction is mentioned, without any further specification, in one of the rules enacted for the implementation of the Civil Code: a rule of negligible relevance, since it applies to a family-related matter pre-empted by more recent statutes.

As mentioned above, even though the main source of Italian procedural law apparently seems to ignore non-contentious jurisdiction, one cannot overlook the fact that in reality a whole section of the Code of Civil Procedure (exactly, Book Four of the Code) provides for a variety of special proceedings that are conventionally ascribed to non-contentious jurisdiction. Just to mention a few, one may list the procedures for having a person declared incompetent, the procedures for the declaration of absence and presumed death of those who have disappeared from their last known residence for a certain number of years, the many procedures by which the interests of minors and incompetent persons are protected (e.g. the appointment of guardians), and the procedures to be followed for the administration and the settlement of decedents' estates. But quite a number of other non-contentious proceedings are governed by different legal sources, namely, the Civil Code or specific statutes, while Book Four of the Code of Civil Procedure also provides for many contentious proceedings, such as the summary *ex parte* proceeding leading to orders for payment, the eviction proceeding, a wide variety of provisional remedies, divorce proceedings and – last but not least – arbitration. In other words, Book Four of the Code of Civil Procedure is conceived as a legal 'department store',[18] in which one can find the judicial proceeding that fits one's needs: it is as if the legislators, after having abided by strict analytical accuracy in the preparation of the previous three Books of the Code, had given up and decided to toss into Book Four all the leftover proceedings, the ones that could not be properly located anywhere else.

An explanation for the reasons why non-contentious proceedings do not have an autonomous place in the Code of Civil Procedure and are not governed by a single group of uniform rules can be found in the explanatory report accompanying the

[18] This is the definition in Book Four of the Code given by a prominent Italian scholar, the late Virgilio Andrioli: see Andrioli (1979: 52).

original text of the Code. In the report, the Ministry of Justice at that time explained that the original idea of the drafters of the Code – that is, to concentrate in a single book all non-contentious proceedings so as to distinguish them from any other special proceedings provided for by the Code – had to be abandoned, due to the difficulty of drawing a clear-cut divide between contested matters (meaning, matters calling for the adjudication of substantive rights) and non-contested ones: it is up to scholars and not to legislators, the Ministry wrote, to elaborate further on the distinction.[19] In this regard, the rationale underlying the choice made by the drafters of the Code has its roots in the previous code, that is, the first Code of Civil Procedure of the unified Kingdom of Italy, enacted in 1865. Commenting on the rule stating that 'unless the law provides otherwise, non-contentious matters are assigned to proceedings in chambers' (my translation),[20] scholars acknowledged the vagueness surrounding the concept of non-contentious jurisdiction, emphasising that legislators could only take note of such vagueness and devise a procedural model adaptable to the matters that, from time to time, would be identified as non-contested.[21] Such a procedural model was the so-called proceedings in chambers.

Similar to the Code of Civil Procedure of 1865, the Code in force today too provides for a set of rules governing proceedings in chambers, rules to be applied unless the law dictates otherwise, but these rules make no explicit reference to matters falling within non-contentious jurisdiction. In spite of that, conventional wisdom tends to identify the procedure in chambers as the archetype of the procedural model according to which courts handle non-contested matters. In reality, there is more to this than meets the eye, since – as will be described shortly – on the one hand, for several non-contested matters judicial intervention follows a pattern that does not conform to the procedure in chambers and, on the other hand, for quite a number of contested matters special statutes provide for proceedings in chambers. Therefore it would be misleading to say that, according to the Italian law in force, an equivalence between non-contentious jurisdiction and the procedure in chambers can be established: a more accurate statement would picture the rules governing proceedings in chambers as 'default rules', that is, rules to be applied absent a specific regulation of the non-contested matter at stake.

These 'default rules' outline a procedure that is simpler than the ordinary one and, at least supposedly, much faster.[22] Among the noteworthy features of such a procedure, one can mention the fact that standing is often granted to every

---

[19] See Relazione alla Maestà del Re Imperatore del Ministro Guardasigilli Grandi, presentata nell'udienza del 28 ottobre 1940-XVIII per l'approvazione del testo del Codice di procedura civile. Available at http://www.academia.edu/210011/Relazione_al_re_per_l'approvazione_del_testo_del_codice_di_procedura_civile, at 15 (last accessed in August 2013).

[20] See Article 778 of the Code of Civil Procedure of 1865.

[21] See, for instance, Saredo (1874: 29–31).

[22] Reference is made to Articles 737–742 *bis* of the Code of Civil Procedure. The academic literature on proceedings in chambers and the rules governing them is extensive, but since this chapter is addressed to international readers, who may not be familiar with Italian, the author has chosen to avoid complex bibliographical information. For a general overview of the subject, see Laudisa (2002: 1–17); Arieta (1996: 435–459); Civinini (1994).

'interested person' and, in exceptional circumstances, to the Public Prosecutor as well. More frequently, though, the Public Prosecutor can or even must make an intervention in the proceeding once it has been instituted by a private party, as a rule when the matter involves aspects of public interest. In spite of that, generally speaking the role played by the Public Prosecutor is not a very active one, and it is limited to the filing of short, written opinions.

Another interesting feature of proceedings in chambers concerns the development of the procedure: as opposed to the typical allocation of powers between the parties and the court in ordinary proceedings, proceedings in chambers are marked by the extensive inquisitorial powers bestowed upon the judge in charge of the case. As a matter of fact, the judge can call for the production of any kind of evidence *ex officio*, since the wording of the relevant article of the Code is interpreted so as to grant the judge ample discretion as regards the evidence-taking phase of the procedure.

The orders issued by the court take the form of decrees. A special avenue of appeal, known as *reclamo*, is open to the applicant, any interested party and sometimes the Public Prosecutor. In principle, no further appeals are allowed.

Decrees issued in chambers in non-contentious matters have no *res judicata* effects. Upon application lodged by any interested party, a decree can be modified or revoked if the circumstances originally taken into account by the court have changed, provided that the rights acquired in good faith by third parties are safeguarded.

The 'default rules' just described are applied to non-contested matters only insofar as the law does not ordain otherwise. And, as a matter of fact, the law does ordain otherwise in a wide variety of non-contested matters: the deviation from the 'default rules' of non-contentious proceedings is not a rare exception, but the rule in Italian civil procedure. Often, the procedural model is a sort of hybrid that mixes together steps typical of ordinary proceedings and steps borrowed from the procedure in chambers, which is likely to cause practical problems, for instance as regards the appeal that can be brought against the court order, with reference to the form the appeal is supposed to take, as well as its latitude and effects: as an example, problems of this kind are common in the practice of separation and divorce proceedings, which quite a number of scholars still ascribe to non-contentious jurisdiction.[23]

It seems important to emphasise again the lack of consistency in the procedural treatment of matters that rightly or wrongly are deemed to be non-contested: a lack of consistency that in recent years has brought about a proliferation of multifaceted 'special proceedings' that have turned the administration of Italian civil justice into a maze, causing further problems for a system already in bad shape.

It has previously been mentioned that the 'default rules' of proceedings in chambers outline a procedural pattern that is simpler, less formal, and supposedly faster than the one to which ordinary proceedings conform. For these reasons, the legislators have increasingly turned to proceedings in chambers when they have decided to update the judicial treatment of a few contentious matters.

[23] For an extensive overview of separation and divorce proceedings, see Graziosi (2011).

In light of the excessive length of Italian civil cases it is not difficult to understand the appeal of proceedings in chambers. At the same time, it is undeniable that when the adjudication of substantive rights is in question, the fundamental guarantees of due process must be safeguarded to their full extent, which is not always the case in proceedings in chambers since they are conceived for cases in which, at least allegedly, there is no controversy between the opposing parties over substantive rights.

The trend followed by the legislators extending the procedure in chambers to contested matters has not been well received by scholars, who have emphasised the dangers this choice could bring about in the judicial enforcement of the right of action and its procedural applications, enshrined in the Constitution or implied by the constitutional rules on the guarantee of due process. In particular, it has been maintained that proceedings in chambers lack an adequate protection of the right to be heard, grant the court an excessive amount of discretion and, most of all, result in orders unable to become *res judicata*, since they can be modified or revoked at any time. The features that make proceedings in chambers valuable for a quick and efficient disposition of non-contested matters become serious flaws in the framework of contentious jurisdiction, since substantive rights, when disputed, have to be adjudicated with the full panoply of the guarantees offered by ordinary proceedings, leading to judgments able to acquire the irrefutable certainty and everlasting durability that only *res judicata* can assure.[24]

In spite of the concerns voiced by scholars, the Italian Supreme Court has repeatedly supported the policy upheld by the legislators in adopting the 'default rules' of proceedings in chambers also for contested matters, such as family matters concerning parental authority, adoption, as well as matters related to the management of companies and to bankruptcy, just to mention a few. According to the Court, proceedings in chambers are 'neutral containers', that is, they outline (by virtue of the 'default rules') a malleable procedural model suitable to being adopted as it is by the legislators, or to being enriched with the features that, according to the matter at stake, are necessary to comply with the constitutional mandate upholding the due process clause.[25] By the same token, the case law of the Constitutional Court supports the position that the choice of the procedural rules to be applied to contested or non-contested matters falls completely within the discretion of the legislators, provided that this discretion is exercised in a manner that is consistent with the principle of reasonableness. In a few judgments the Court has said that the rules governing proceedings in chambers by themselves are not at odds with the basic tenets of due process: therefore, it is possible (and sometimes even imperative) to interpret them so as to 'make room' for the procedural steps that, from time to time,

[24] The volume of academic writing on whether it is appropriate to resort to proceedings in chambers for contentious matters is monumental. Among the most significant and recent contributions to the debate, see Carratta (2010: 928–959).

[25] See in particular the judgment of the Italian Supreme Court issued *en banc* on 19 June 1996, no. 5629, published in *Giurisprudenza italiana*, 1996, I, 1, 1300.

are required by the fundamental guarantees surrounding the judicial enforcement of substantive rights.[26]

Be that as it may, over the years the number of 'special proceedings' dealing with both contested and non-contested matters has escalated, and so have the difficulties brought about by the overlapping of different legal sources, making it quite complex to identify the proper proceeding to be instituted. In 2011 the legislators resolved to engage in an effort to simplify the procedural landscape, a commendable goal that – unfortunately – the statute 'on the reduction and simplification of judicial proceedings'[27] has failed to achieve.

The idea underlying the statute was to reduce the special proceedings to only three procedural models already existing in the Code of Civil Procedure, that is, the ordinary proceeding, the proceeding in labour cases, and the summary proceeding. Unfortunately, not all special proceedings were taken into consideration, but only the ones regarding contested matters and governed by specific statutes; other exceptions were contemplated, for instance as regards family law, consumer law, and intellectual property (IP) law. In short, the statute on simplification applies only to some special proceedings of minor importance, and certainly not to the ones that crowd the courts' dockets. In addition, even for the proceedings affected by the so-called simplification new and complex rules had to be enacted so as to make the transmigration from the old rules to those of the 'proceeding of destination' viable.

In conclusion, the question remains whether non-contested matters do fall within the proper goals of civil justice, or whether to talk about non-contentious jurisdiction is a contradiction in terms. Already back in 1987, one of the most prominent Italian scholars in procedural law of the last century, the late Vittorio Denti, wrote that the notion of non-contentious jurisdiction belonged to the history of the doctrines and ideologies of civil procedure that were popular in the past but had lost their appeal in the contemporary cultural environment, in which there seemed to be no space left for great conceptual constructions (Denti 1987: 325–339). Drawing inspiration from this thought, this author thinks that both scholars and legislators should set aside any concerns about the true nature of non-contentious jurisdiction and address a more mundane issue: whether or not, in light of the present situation of Italian courts, overloaded with cases and lacking human and material resources, it still makes sense to entrust the judiciary with duties that – where the conflict between private individuals is over matters devoid of any public interest – could be discharged hopefully in a more efficient and less time-consuming way by administrative authorities.

---

[26] See, for instance, the following judgments issued by the Constitutional Court: no. 140 of 2001; no. 160 of 1995; no. 52 of 1995; no. 573 of 1989. All the judgments of the Court are published (in Italian) on its institutional website, at http://www.giurcost.org/decisioni/index.html (last accessed in August 2013).

[27] The statute referred to in the text is statute no. 150 of 2011. For an extensive commentary, see Carratta (2012: 928–959).

4.4 Conflict Resolution v. Policy Implementation: Courts Sometimes in Opposition to Policies They Are Expected to Implement

If one accepts the idea that courts are the enforcers of individual rights, insofar as these rights are infringed or even only threatened, one must also assume that the rights whose protection is the purpose of access to justice have been granted by substantive law in the process of implementing specific policies. Therefore, dispute resolution and policy implementation often intertwine, even though sometimes the policy implemented is difficult to identify. Equally difficult is to evaluate whether certain policies are truly consistent with what is conventionally deemed to be 'public interest', or whether they reflect the ideologies and the values of the ruling class: for instance, one may wonder whether 'public interest' has something to do with the fact that in Italy divorce can be petitioned only if 3 years have elapsed since the spouses' will of dissolving their marriage has been legally acknowledged in a court judgment rendered at the end of a separation proceeding, or in a court order ratifying a separation agreement.

In some recent cases the problem of policy implementation has taken an interesting turn when courts have opposed the very policy they were expected to implement. That has happened in the field of life-prolonging medical treatments applied to individuals in a permanent vegetative state, a field in which some courts have refused to abide by the governmental policy in favour of such treatments because of ethical reasons (allegedly the same reasons preventing the Parliament from passing any reasonable bills on living wills and advance directives concerning end-of-life care).[28] Similarly, courts have refused to implement the policy underlying the regulations on the expulsion of illegal aliens in cases concerning minors or individuals suffering from medical conditions. And, in light of the current debate on same-sex marriage, one can mention several judgments issued by Italian courts (including the Supreme Court) from which it is possible to infer a disagreement with the policy supported by a few components of the 'grand coalition' government presently in power, that is, a policy upholding a traditional concept of 'family': the judgments deal with the issue of child custody and support the view according to which the choice of the custodial parent cannot be influenced by the sexual orientation of either parent, since no scientific evidence demonstrates that the child's development is harmed in any way by the fact of being raised by a same-sex couple.[29]

[28] The case of Eluana Englaro, a young woman who had been injured in a car accident and had gone into a permanent vegetative state in 1992, forced not only politicians, but also Italian society at large to take a stand on a very controversial issue. Eluana's father petitioned several courts to be authorised to disconnect the medical equipment keeping his daughter alive; his applications were consistently rejected. Finally, toward the end of 2008, the Court of Cassation and the Milan Court of appeal on remand granted Mr. Englaro the right to discontinue the procedures by which Eluana was fed and kept alive: for an account of the case, see, among others, Gristina et al. (2012: 1897–1900); Turillazzi and Fineschi (2011: 76–80); Moratti (2010: 372–380); Luchetti (2010: 333–335).

[29] See, e.g., two judgments issued by the Court of Cassation, namely, judgment no. 601 of 8 November 2012 – 11 January 2013, and judgment no. 4184 of 15 March 2012, both available (in

In a wider perspective, it is worth mentioning that the issue of same-sex marriage has already been addressed by the Constitutional Court: the Court upheld a number of regulations of the Civil Code concerning marriage as the union between opposite-sex individuals and, by a convoluted argument, passed the 'hot potato' on to the Parliament, stating that it is the duty of the lawmaker to decide which kind of legal status is suitable for same-sex relationships. It is interesting, though, to emphasise that the Court, even if it refused to take a stand on the issue, for the first time acknowledged a same-sex couple as one of the 'social groups where human personality is expressed', groups that, under Article 2 of the Constitution, are recognised by the Republic as bearers of fundamental rights: henceforth, according to the Court, same-sex individuals have the right to live freely as a couple, and cannot be discriminated against because of their sexual orientation.[30]

4.5 Spokesperson of Public Interest: *Pubblico Ministero*

In the Italian system of civil justice, public interest has its own institutional spokesperson, that is, the public prosecutor (*Pubblico Ministero*, hereinafter PM). The Code of Civil Procedure provides for a limited number of hypotheses in which the PM has standing to sue or must intervene in the procedure (e.g. proceedings concerning the status of individuals, matrimonial cases, annulment of marriage on particular grounds); as a general rule, the PM is free to take part in any actions affecting public interest.[31]

More noteworthy is a peculiar power the PM at the level of the Italian Supreme Court is entitled to exercise: the PM can bring a final appeal against judgments that the parties have not appealed against or that are not subject to any appeals, for the sole purpose of empowering the Supreme Court to state the correct 'law of the case', on the assumption that the lower court did not address the questions of law

Italian) at http://www.articolo29.it/ (last accessed in August 2013). It is remarkable that the Court of Cassation, in the opinion of the latter judgment, cited extensively the decision of the European Court of Human Rights in *Schalk and Kopf v. Austria* (Application no. 30141/04), 24 June 2010, in which the Court, although denying that under the ECHR Contracting States have a duty to grant same-sex couples access to marriage, stated that since 'a rapid evolution of social attitudes towards same-sex couples has taken place in many Member States … the Court considers it artificial to maintain the view that, in contrast to a different-sex couple, a same-sex couple cannot enjoy "family life" for the purposes of Article 8. Consequently the relationship of the applicants, a cohabiting same-sex couple, living in a stable *de facto* partnership, falls within the notion of "family life", just as the relationship of a different-sex couple in the same situation would' (paragraphs 93–95).

[30] See judgment no. 138 of 15 April 2010, available (in Italian) on the Constitutional Court's website, at http://www.cortecostituzionale.it (last accessed in August 2013). For an engaging commentary on the judgment, see Romboli (2010: 1629–1635).

[31] The powers of the PM in civil cases are governed by Articles 69–73 of the Code. The author has chosen to translate the Italian expression 'Pubblico Ministero' into the English as 'public prosecutor', since this judicial body is more active in criminal cases. In fact, the PM has the monopoly on criminal prosecutions: see Article 112 of the Italian Constitution, according to which 'The public prosecutor has the obligation to institute criminal proceedings'.

raised by the case in the correct way.[32] This special final appeal brought 'in the interest of the law' does not affect the parties to the judgment at stake, but finds its justification in the peculiar role played by the Supreme Court as the judicial body in charge of watching over the proper and consistent interpretation of the law in force. Within this framework, the final appeal brought by the PM can be seen as an initiative expressing the public interest in triggering a mechanism that allows the Supreme Court to perform its institutional role. All that holds true in the framework of a theoretical overview of the rules whose purpose is to enhance the role of the Court as the 'guardian of the law'[33] in force; in practice, the heavy caseload makes it virtually impossible for the Court to perform its role, to the point that, in the perception of ordinary citizens, the final appeal simply is yet another chance the losing party is afforded in order to have an unfavourable judgment overturned. That depends on a unique feature of the Italian legal system, in which the final appeal is always as of right due to the constitutional rule according to which 'Appeals to the Court of Cassation in cases of violations of the law are always allowed'[34]: this rule prevents the legislators from establishing serious methods of case selection short of a constitutional amendment that is not likely to be passed any time soon. The issue of whether 'free access' to the Court of Cassation can be reconciled with the proper role a supreme court is supposed to play as the ultimate enforcer of the rule of law cannot be expanded here. Suffice it to say that a court that receives approximately 30,000 appeals and issues more than 25,000 judgments per year in civil matters alone can hardly be qualified as a real supreme court.

4.6 Issues to Be Determined by the Court Ex Officio

In spite of the popular idea according to which Italy, with a legal system belonging to the Civil Law tradition, adopts an inquisitorial model of adjudication, the principles of party presentation and party prosecution of a case are observed as general rules. Parties have full control over their case as far as its beginning, its development and its end are concerned. Furthermore, it is in the exclusive power of the parties to shape their case, whose scope is determined by the plaintiff's claim and the defendant's answer and defences. The possibility for the judge to determine *ex officio* issues that the parties have failed to raise is quite limited (e.g. issues concerning lack of jurisdiction or lack of standing to sue), and even when the law entrusts the judge with such a power, in practice the judge is more or less bound to relying on the parties' initiatives.

[32] On this special final appeal, provided for by Article 363 of the Code, see Silvestri (2012: 1366–1369).

[33] The role of the Court of Cassation is conventionally referred to with the expression *nomofilachia*, a neologism devised by a prominent Italian scholar (Piero Calamandrei) who authored a famous treatise on the Court and fathered this peculiar Italian expression by combining two Ancient Greek words, namely, νόμος (law) and the verb φυλάσσω (to watch, to have an eye upon). See Calamandrei (1920).

[34] See Article 111, sec. 7 of the Italian Constitution.

Italian scholars elucidate these rules making reference to the so-called *principio dispositivo* (principle of party disposition), one of the fundamental tenets of Italian civil justice. The substantive side of the principle is expressed by the rules governing the respective powers of the parties and the judge as to the shaping of the case[35]; the procedural prong of the principle implies, on the one hand, that only the parties can offer the evidence necessary to prove the facts they have stated in their pleadings and, on the other hand, that the judge is bound to relying only on this very evidence, except when a positive rule entrusts him or her with the power to call for evidence *ex officio*.[36]

4.7 Search for Truth: Slow Proceedings Do Not Advance the Cause of Accuracy

A naïve bystander could be inclined to infer that the notorious length of Italian civil proceedings shows how diligently the goal of determining the factual issues to every case brought before the courts in the utmost accurate way is pursued. Unfortunately, the reasons causing Italian civil justice to be unbearably slow have nothing to do with the aspiration of granting correct results to truth discovery in adjudication. In other words, accuracy in fact-finding is not the saving grace of Italian civil justice: on the contrary, the way in which the proof-taking stage of ordinary proceedings is structured, that is, as a non-concentrated sequence of fragmented hearings, spanning an indefinite period of time, does not advance the cause of accuracy in adjudicative fact-finding. The reasons are intuitive: time may affect the recollection of witnesses; documents may deteriorate, get misplaced or lost; and so on.

Only in the field of provisional measures are the scales tipped in favour of a swift response to situations in which a right is exposed to the risk of suffering an irrecoverable harm, while the need to reach an accurate result as to the factual issues at stake is postponed. If certain requirements are met, the provisional remedy is granted, in general *ex parte*, but its effects, at least in principle, are temporary, and conditional upon the fact that they are upheld by the outcome of a subsequent ordinary proceeding.[37]

4.8 'Hard Cases' or Mass Processing of Routine Matters?

At present, Italian civil justice is more about processing a huge number of ordinary cases than handling 'hard cases'. Cases of such a kind, raising new and often controversial issues, do occasionally end up before civil courts, but they are the exception, and not the rule.

---

[35] See Article 2907, sec. 1 of the Civil Code and Articles 99 and 112 of the Code of Civil Procedure.

[36] See Article 115, sec. 1 of the Code of Civil Procedure.

[37] For an effective account of Italian provisional measures, see De Cristofaro (2010: 278–296).

One of the most quoted sayings about 'hard cases' is 'Hard cases make bad law', but for Italy the reverse, that is, 'Bad law makes hard cases', is more suitable. 'Bad law' refers to statutes whose wording is so poor as to make their meanings difficult to interpret, but most of all to statutes implementing policies that sectors of Italian society perceive as undue government interference in the private lives of citizens.

Recent statutes dealing with issues touching upon bioethics have brought about 'hard cases': an example is the very restrictive and controversial statute on medically assisted procreation passed in 2004. The statute has gained an international reputation not so much for its contents, but because the very conservative approach to reproductive technologies it upholds has forced many Italians to engage in the so-called 'reproductive tourism' around Europe and beyond. The statute has been challenged several times before civil and administrative courts, and the Constitutional Court has repealed sections of it that were deemed to conflict with fundamental rights guaranteed by the Italian Constitution.[38] The final blow has been inflicted by the European Court of Human Rights that has pointed out the nonsense of the statute, finding it in violation of the right to respect for private and family life enshrined in Article 8 of the ECHR.[39] At present, it is unclear whether new legislative developments in the field of medically assisted procreation will take place.

Also old statutes still in force can provide ground for 'hard cases', as happened regarding the statute according to which a crucifix must or can be displayed in certain public buildings, including public schools. The case of the crucifix displayed in Italian schools has caused quite a stir within Europe. The issue, debated in several cases at the domestic level, eventually reached the European Court of Human Rights. The Second Section of the Court, with a judgment issued in November 2009,[40] ruled – *inter alia* – that there is 'an obligation on the State's part to refrain from imposing beliefs, even indirectly, in places where persons are dependent on it or in places where they are particularly vulnerable. The schooling of children is a particularly sensitive area in which the compelling power of the State is imposed on minds which still lack (depending on the child's level of maturity) the critical capacity which would enable them to keep their distance from the message derived from a preference manifested by the State in religious matters'.[41] Furthermore, the judgment stated that the display of the symbol of a particular faith in the classrooms of public schools infringes the right of parents to raise their children according to their beliefs, since the State, while exercising public authority, should have a 'neutral' approach, most of all in educational matters. In March 2011, on appeal brought by the Italian Government, the Grand Chamber of the Court reversed the 2009 ruling.[42] According to the Grand Chamber, 'There is no evidence before the Court that the display of a religious symbol on classroom walls may have an influence on pupils and so it cannot reasonably be asserted that it does or does not have an effect on

[38] See Hanafin (2013: 45–67); Minieri (2013: 214–222).

[39] *Costa and Pavan v. Italy* (Application no. 54270/10), 28 August 2012.

[40] *Lautsi v. Italy* (Application no. 30814/06), 3 November 2011.

[41] Ibid., at paragraph 48.

[42] Grand Chamber, *Lautsi v. Italy* (Application no. 30814/06), 18 March 2011.

young persons whose convictions are still in the process of being formed'.[43] In short, the Court denied that the display of the crucifix in a classroom amounted to an attempt by State authorities to impose on the pupils well-identified religious beliefs, and found no violations of the rights of parents to educate their children according to the creed of their choice.[44] In spite of the Grand Chamber's ruling, in Italy the issue is far from settled: many Italians (whether Catholic or followers of other religions) believe in the secularisation of the State, and think that the display of the crucifix, as well as of any religious symbols, in public buildings runs against at least two constitutional guarantees, namely, the principle of equality (Article 3 of the Constitution) and the right of religious freedom (Article 97 of the Constitution).

4.9 An (Almost) Unknown Concept: The Principle of Proportionality in the Treatment of Cases

The principle of proportionality is unknown to Italian civil justice, unless one is inclined to think that the rules of the Code of Civil Procedure providing for an allegedly simplified treatment of certain cases falling within a loose notion of 'small claims' show a certain degree of attention paid by the system to a use of judicial resources that is proportional to the amount at stake or the complexity of the issues raised by the case. The justices of the peace are the lay judges (or 'honorary judges', as they are called in Italy) handling 'small claims'. Actually, the jurisdiction of the justices of the peace shows that the claims they deal with are not necessarily so 'small': for instance, their jurisdiction based upon the value of the claim is up to €5,000, but it jumps up to €20,000 for cases in which the recovery of damages caused by car accidents is sought, not to mention the significant amount of subject matter jurisdiction justices of the peace are granted.[45]

As far as the procedure followed in front of the justices of the peace is concerned, a closer look shows that the 'simplified' procedure is just a rough copy of the procedure followed in 'proper court cases', meaning the ones falling within the jurisdiction of the ordinary courts of first instance, that is, the *tribunali*. Just to offer an example, before the justices of the peace parties must be assisted by lawyers, unless the amount at stake is below the risible threshold of €1,100.

In 2009, a new kind of summary procedure was made available for cases falling within the jurisdiction of the *tribunali*.[46] If the plaintiff chooses to submit a claim according to the forms of this new procedure, the court, either requested by the defendant or even *ex officio*, can order the case to be continued according to the

[43] Ibid., at paragraph 66.

[44] See, e.g., Zucca (2013: 218–229); Ronchi (2011: 287–297); Pin (2011: 97–149).

[45] On the justices of the peace, see Articles 7, 311–322 of the Code of Civil Procedure: Rota (2008: 291–332).

[46] The new *procedimento sommario di cognizione* is regulated by Articles 702 *bis*-702 *quater* of the Code of Civil Procedure: see Lupoi (2012: 25–51).

ordinary procedure *if* the issues raised by the parties are deemed unsuitable for summary adjudication. Could one say that a 'filtering mechanism' is at work here, allowing the court to apply a principle of proportionality as to deciding which cases deserve a full-fledged adjudication or may be dealt with in a more streamlined way? An affirmative answer to this question probably would imply ignoring that the establishment of the new summary procedure has been yet another attempt at speeding up the pace of litigation. Besides, one must keep in mind that the power allowing the court to order a procedural switch works only one-way: in other words, if a claim has been submitted in the form of an ordinary proceeding, it is impossible for the court to issue an order requiring the case to be disposed of through the new summary procedure, whatever the court's evaluation of the complexity of the case is.

If courts have no discretion as to decide which procedure is most suitable for the cases they process, even more so is it inconceivable that courts refuse to take into consideration cases deemed trivial or inappropriate: frivolous and groundless claims will end up being rejected, but not to entertain them would amount to a denial of the fundamental right of access to justice, and to a violation of the principle of equality.

4.10 Group Actions 'Italian Style'

The responsiveness of Italian civil justice to the contemporary problems of aggregate litigation is yet another example of its many paradoxes. If someone looked at the Italian law in force, he would find a wide variety of actions for the judicial enforcement of the rights belonging to a group of individuals: there are collective actions for injunctive relief, initially devised only for consumer protection under the pressure of EU law, but later on made available also in other areas such as labour law, anti-discrimination law, and environmental protection, just to mention a few. There are also class actions for damages available to consumers and users since 2009[47]; there are even what Italians call 'public class actions', that is, actions which groups can bring against public bodies when they have failed to act in spite of a specific duty to do so. Therefore, one might be inclined to think that the Italian legal system offers adequate relief to large-scale legal injuries. As everyone knows, appearances can be deceiving and this holds true also with reference to collective redress in Italy: the assortment of legal instruments available 'on paper' is offset by a disheartening lack of efficiency of these very legal instruments.

If one considers the Italian class action for damages, one is bound to notice that, in spite of the name (the literal translation of the Italian *azione di classe*), it is anything but a class action American-style. That, by itself, should not be seen as a negative factor, since most European legal systems have adopted forms of group

[47] The Italian 'class action' (which happens to be anything but a class action American-style) is provided for by Article 140 *bis* of the Consumer Code. An English version of this article, together with a commentary on its main contents, can be read in Calcagno (2011). See also Nashi (2010: 147–172); Silvestri (2009: 138–148).

actions that do not have much in common with true class actions; in addition, it is well known that, at the European institutional level, class actions are not envisaged as the viable pattern of a future pan-European collective redress mechanism.[48] Therefore, other reasons must explain the fact that, from the coming into force of the statute providing for class actions at the beginning of 2010, just a handful of them have been commenced. As of May 2013, out of the 26 actions initiated, 12 have been declared inadmissible at the preliminary stage of the procedure (that is, the stage at which the court certifies whether the class action is the appropriate form for the lawsuit), 14 are pending, and only one has been decided on the merits[49]: not exactly an outstanding performance, if one keeps in mind that in 2012 a number of amendments to the law in force were passed with the specific purpose of improving the viability of class actions.

A thorough analysis of the reasons why the Italian class action has turned out to be a blatant *debacle* is beyond the purpose of this paragraph. Just to list a few aspects that are critical and make Italian class actions quite 'unfriendly', one can mention that standing to sue is granted to each component of the class, personally or through a consumer association, but the alleged class is only a virtual one, since it takes shape in the development of the proceeding, through the mechanics of an opt-in procedure. It is well known that opt-in procedures are not very efficient, but in this regard – as mentioned above – Italy has made a choice shared by the majority of European Union Member States, states that have rejected opt-out approaches to collective litigation since they raise the concern of affecting the rights of individuals who could have become part of the class unknowingly or unwillingly. Rules governing *res judicata* also play an important role in the choice of opt-in versus opt-out, but it is not possible to elaborate on that any further.

The procedure is very complex, since it develops along two stages that can multiply if certain interlocutory decisions are appealed against. Collective settlements lack specific regulations, and complex issues may arise as regards other rules in force, for in instance the ones governing out-of-court mediation. Special provisions on financing and funding class actions are missing, and this lack is even more serious considering the chaotic situation Italy is experiencing due to some recent reforms affecting attorneys' fees.

[48] Recently, the European Commission took yet another stand against American-style class actions with some important documents issued with the view to outline a prospective model of harmonised group actions: see Communication from the Commission to the European Parliament, the Council, the European Economic and Social Committee and the Committee of the Regions, 'Towards a European Horizontal Framework for Collective Redress', COM(2013) 401/2, available at http://ec.europa.eu/justice/civil/files/com_2013_401_en.pdf (last accessed in August 2013); and Commission Recommendation on common principles for injunctive and compensatory collective redress mechanisms in the Member States concerning violations of rights granted under Union Law, C(2013) 3539/3, available at http://ec.europa.eu/justice/civil/files/c_2013_3539_en.pdf (last accessed in August 2013).

[49] These data are not official, since there are no official records of the class actions brought nationwide, but they seem reasonably reliable: see Osservatorio permanente sull'applicazione delle regole della concorrenza, Contatore azioni di classe, available at http://www.osservatorioantitrust.eu/index.php?id=885&L=5%27 (last accessed in August 2013).

The list of shortcomings could go on, but it seems pointless to insist on a theoretical evaluation of the rules governing Italian class actions: after all, these rules are 'empty boxes', bare rules subject to every kind of doctrinal interpretation, but on which courts, at least so far, have not produced a relevant amount of 'black letter law'.

4.11 Equitable Results or Strict Formalism?

In principle, Italian courts must decide cases by applying the law in force: this rule, laid down by Article 113, sec. 1 of the Code of Civil Procedure, is known as the principle of legality of court judgments. This principle is linked to the constitutional provision according to which 'Judges are subject only to the law.'[50] Against this background, the problem of how courts interpret the law arises, but it is settled that the principle of legality, by itself, does not have any direct bearing on the methods of statutory interpretation that courts might resort to, nor does it nullify a certain degree of discretion in the interpretative process.

Whether that means the Italian system of civil justice is more geared to strict formalism than to the attainment of equitable results is hard to say: certainly, the idea of courts as problem solvers is met with a good measure of scepticism in light of the poor performance of the justice system.

4.12 Rising Costs of Civil Justice: Is Access to Justice Becoming Illusory?

In Italy, civil justice is not free. Leaving aside the attorney's fees, the filing of a case requires the payment of a lump sum into the public purse: the amount varies according to the value of the claim and the type of proceeding that is initiated (e.g. an ordinary proceeding before a court of first instance, an enforcement proceeding and so on). Recent statutes have confirmed a steady trend toward the increase of such a tax burden, which is particularly high as regards appellate proceedings; numerous exemptions from payment have been repealed, too, even affecting cases in which the exemption had a social significance, such as labour cases.

The rationale behind the new arrangement of court fees is only in part the need to grant the State the cash flow necessary to meet the expenses required by the operation of the justice system: most of all, it is another step in the strategy aimed at reducing the caseload of the courts. And raising the costs of justice can be very effective in limiting access to the courts in a country, such as Italy, in which persons of limited financial means cannot count – unfortunately – on a modern and adequately funded

[50] Article 101, sec. 2 of the Italian Constitution.

system of civil legal aid. In this regard, it seems almost unbelievable that the issue of Italian legal aid has not yet found its way to the European Court of Human Rights. Even though it is well known that, according to the Court's case law, the ECHR does not impose any duty to grant across-the-board legal aid in civil cases on Signatory States,[51] the same case law states also that the rights granted under the Convention, and in particular the right to access to justice, are intended to be 'not rights that are theoretical or illusory but rights that are practical and effective'.[52] And the Italian legal aid schemes are so outdated and ineffective as to make the right to a fair trial just a chimera for a growing number of Italians.

4.13 Conclusion

Italy is a very litigious society, but there is no disagreement at all as far as the evaluation of the civil justice system: it does not work, and – which is probably even worse – nobody seems to know how to make it work. Users are unhappy, but the 'professional actors' are unhappy, too, and in this climate of general dissatisfaction the system stands still, *En attendant Godot*. Let us hope that sooner rather than later Mr. Godot shows up and works some magic.

References

Andolina I, Vignera G (1997) I fondamenti costituzionali della giustizia civile. Il modello costituzionale del processo civile italiano, 2nd edn, 7. Giappichelli Editore, Torino

Andrioli V (1979) Diritto processuale civile I: 52. Jovene, Napoli

Arieta G (1996) Procedimenti in camera di consiglio, Digesto delle discipline privatistiche – Sezione civile XIV. UTET, Torino, pp 435–459

Calamandrei P (1920) La Cassazione civile I. In: Opere giuridiche VI (edn. 1976). Morano Editore, Napoli

Calcagno N (2011) Italian class action: the beginning. Cardozo Electron Law Bull 17. Available at https://sites.google.com/site/cardozolawbulletin/home/spring-summer-2011?pli=1. Last accessed in Aug 2013

Carratta A (2010) Processo camerale (diritto processuale civile). In: Enciclopedia del diritto, Annali III. Giuffrè Editore, Milano, pp 928–959

Carratta A (2012) La "semplificazione" dei riti e le nuove modifiche del processo civile. Giappichelli Editore, Torino

Cipriani F (1997) Ideologie e modelli del processo civile. Saggi, 3, 103, 121, 157. ESI-Edizioni Scientifiche Italiane, Napoli

Cipriani F (2002) Il processo civile italiano tra revisionisti e negazionisti. Giurisprudenza italiana:425–427

---

[51] See, e.g., *Del Sol v. France* (Application no. 46800/99), 26 February 2002, at paragraph 20; *Essaadi v. France* (Application no. 49384/99), 26 February 2002, at paragraph 30.

[52] *Bertuzzi v. France* (Application no. 36378/97), 13 February 2003, at paragraph 24.

Cipriani F (2003) Il processo civile tra vecchie ideologie e nuovi slogan. Rivista di diritto processuale:455–466
Civinini MG (1994) I procedimenti in camera di consiglio I. UTET, Torino
Comoglio LP (1970) La garanzia costituzionale dell'azione e il processo civile, 131. Cedam, Padova
Comoglio LP, Ferri C, Taruffo M (2011) Lezioni sul processo civile I, Il procedimento ordinario di cognizione, 5th edn. 15. Il Mulino, Bologna
De Cristofaro M (2010) Provisional remedies. In: De Cristofaro M, Trocker N (eds) Civil justice in Italy. Jigakusha Publishing Corp., Tokyo, pp 278–296
Denti V (1970) Processo civile e giustizia sociale. Edizioni di Comunità, Milano, pp 56–74
Denti V (1987) La giurisdizione volontaria rivisitata. Rivista trimestrale di diritto e procedura civile:325–339
Genn H (2010) Judging civil justice. Cambridge University Press, Cambridge
Graziosi A (ed) (2011) I processi di separazione e di divorzio, 2nd edn. Giappichelli Editore, Torino
Gristina GR, Martin E, Ranieri VM (2012) Regulation of advance directives in Italy: a bad law in the making. Intensive Care Med 38:1897–1900
Hanafin P (2013) Law, biopolitics and reproductive citizenship. The case of assisted reproduction in Italy. Tecnoscienza Ital J Sci Technol Stud 4(1):45–67
Laudisa L (2002) Camera di consiglio – I) Procedimenti in camera di consiglio – Diritto processuale civile. In: Enciclopedia Giuridica Treccani VI. Istituto della Enciclopedia Italiana, Roma, pp 1–17
Luchetti M (2010) Eluana Englaro, chronicle of a death foretold: ethical considerations on the recent right-to-die case in Italy. J Med Ethics 36:333–335
Lupoi MA (2012) Recent developments in Italian civil procedure. Civil Proced Rev 3(1):25–51. Available at http://www.civilprocedurereview.com. Last accessed in Aug 2013
Minieri A (2013) Assisted reproductive technologies: a state matter. In: The interaction of national legal systems: convergence or divergence? Conference papers, 25–26 Apr 2013, Vilnius, pp 214–222. Available at https://jak.ppke.hu/uploads/articles/12417/file/Vilnius%20University.pdf#page=417. Last accessed in Aug 2013
Monteleone GA (2003) Princìpi e ideologie del processo civile: impressioni di un «revisionista». Rivista trimestrale di diritto e procedura civile 57:575–582
Moratti S (2010) The Englaro Case: withdrawal of treatment from a patient in a permanent vegetative state in Italy. Camb Q Healthc Ethics 19(3):372–380
Nashi R (2010) Note: Italy's class action experiment. Cornell Int Law J 43:147–172
Pin A (2011) Public schools, the Italian crucifix, and the European court of human rights: the Italian separation of church and state. Emory Int Law Rev 25:97–149
Porcelli G (2012) Commento alla legge 24 marzo 2001, n. 89, Previsione di equa riparazione in caso di violazione del termine ragionevole del processo e modifica dell'articolo 375 del codice di procedura civile. In: Carpi F, Taruffo M (eds) Commentario breve al codice di procedura civile, 7th edn. Cedam, Padova, pp 3391–3408
Priest GL (1989) Private litigants and the court congestion problem. Boston Univ Law Rev 69:527–559
Reich CA (1964) The new property. Yale Law J 73:733–787
Romboli R (2010) Il diritto "consentito" al matrimonio ed il diritto "garantito" alla vita familiare per le coppie omosessuali in una pronuncia in cui la Corte dice "troppo" e "troppo poco". Giurisprudenza costituzionale 2:1629–1635
Ronchi P (2011) Crucifixes, margin of appreciation and consensus: the Grand Chamber ruling. In Lautsi v Italy. Ecclesiast Law J 13(3):287–297
Rota F (2008) Giudice di pace (diritto processuale civile). In: Enciclopedia del Diritto, Annali, II, 1. Giuffrè Editore, Milano, pp 291–332
Saredo G (1874) Del procedimento in camera di consiglio e specialmente per gli atti di volontaria giurisdizione, 2nd edn. Libreria Nuova, Napoli, pp 29–31

Silvestri E (2009) Italy. In: Hensler DH, Hodges C, Tulibacka M (eds) The globalization of class actions. The Annals of the American Academy of Political and Social Science, spec 622(1):138–148

Silvestri E (2011) The never-ending reforms of Italian civil justice (2 August 2011). Available at SSRN: http://ssrn.com/abstract=1903863. Last accessed in Aug 2013

Silvestri E (2012) Commento all'art. 363 c.p.c. In: Carpi F, Taruffo M (eds) Commentario breve al codice di procedura civile, 7th edn. Cedam, Padova, pp 1366–1369

Silvestri E, Jagtenberg R (2013) Tweeluik – Diptych: Juggling a Red Hot Potato: Italy, the EU, and Mandatory Mediation. Nederlands-Vlaams tijdschrift voor Mediation en conflictmanagement 17(1):29–45

Taruffo M (1980) La giustizia civile in Italia dal '700 a oggi. Il Mulino, Bologna, pp 107–149

Taruffo M (2009) Cultura e processo. Rivista trimestrale di diritto e procedura civile:63–92

Turillazzi E, Fineschi V (2011) Advance directives in therapeutic intervention: a review of the Italian bioethical and juridical debate. Med Sci Law 51(2):76–80

Verde G (2002) Le ideologie del processo in un recente saggio. Rivista di diritto processuale 57:676–687

Verde G (2010) Diritto processuale civile 1. Parte Generale, 2nd edn. 27. Zanichelli, Bologna

Zucca L (2013) Lautsi: a commentary on a decision by the ECtHR Grand Chamber. Int J Const Law 11(1):218–229

Chapter 5
Goals of Civil Justice in Norway: Readiness for a Pragmatic Reform

Inge Lorange Backer

Abstract Norwegian civil justice has undergone thorough reforms in recent years. The adoption in 2005 of a new act on civil procedure – the Dispute Act – allowed for a consideration of the goals of civil justice. The wide competence of the ordinary courts of law to deal with cases of civil and administrative law as well as criminal cases is retained but the present trend is to confine the role of the courts to adjudication and to transfer non-judicial tasks to other bodies. In civil justice several goals are taken into account, in particular dispute resolution, implementation and enforcement of substantive law, clarification and development of the law, and also control of the Executive and the Legislature by way of deciding cases brought before the courts by the parties. None of these goals are given absolute priority and their relative importance may differ between the various court tiers. While offering new remedies to speed up proceedings and also to protect the public interest the rules of the Dispute Act may often be regarded as a pragmatic compromise between various goals and considerations. The Act seeks to promote swift, efficient and fair handling of cases and combines a quest for material truth and correct decisions with a right of the parties to dispose of the case.

5.1 Basic Features of the Norwegian Civil Justice System

Civil justice in Norway covers disputes between private parties as well as conflicts between a private party and the public administration. Norway has a unitary court system with courts of general jurisdiction handling civil as well as criminal cases, no separate administrative courts and very few specialised

I.L. Backer (✉)
Department of Public and International Law, University of Oslo,
Postboks 6706, St. Olavs plass, 0130 Oslo, Norway
e-mail: i.l.backer@jus.uio.no

A. Uzelac (ed.), *Goals of Civil Justice and Civil Procedure in Contemporary Judicial Systems*, Ius Gentium: Comparative Perspectives on Law and Justice 34,
DOI 10.1007/978-3-319-03443-0_5,

courts. Judicial review of administrative action lies with the ordinary courts of law and they also exercise constitutional control of legislation in so far as relevant in the cases brought before them.

In comparative law, the legal systems of the five Nordic countries may be regarded as a group of their own, distinct from the civil law and common law systems.[1] There is regular contact between the five supreme courts and between the five ministries of justice.[2] Topics relating to civil justice are usually included in the programme of the Conference of Nordic Lawyers, comprising judges, advocates, prosecutors, civil servants, and academics, which since 1872 is convened every 3 years (except in wartime) in one of the capitals to discuss topics of common interest relating to legal policy or current law. Civil justice is not expressly mentioned in the 1962 Helsinki Treaty of Nordic Cooperation, under which the parties are obliged to strive towards attaining the greatest possible uniformity in private law and to seek to establish uniform rules in criminal law.[3] Still, the systems of civil justice are broadly similar. There is, however, a marked difference between the Eastern Nordic countries (Finland and Sweden), which have separate administrative courts, and the Western Nordic countries (Denmark, Iceland and Norway), which do not. As regards civil procedure in the ordinary courts, the similarities are greater between the countries of each of the two groups of Nordic countries.

The Norwegian system of courts of general jurisdiction consists of three tiers: the district courts, the courts of appeal and the Supreme Court. There are now 65 district courts and six courts of appeal. In recent years, the district courts annually handled between 14,000 and 16,000 civil cases with an average handling time of about 5 months. The courts of appeal handled between 1,700 and 1,900 appeals against judgments; the average handling time was approximately 6 or 7 months.[4]

The conciliation boards operate in each of the (currently) 428 municipalities at a level below the district courts. They are composed of three lay judges elected by the municipal council. Dating from 1795, they have a long-standing tradition in Norwegian civil justice but no similar counterpart in any of the other Nordic countries.[5] Their original task was to provide a forum for mediation between the parties to the case with a view to reaching a friendly settlement, but they were also empowered to give judgments. By the 2005 Dispute Act reform their adjudicating powers were somewhat restrained and they are now regarded as a body with certain adjudicating powers and no longer included in the list of ordinary courts of law.

[1] See Malmström (1969: 147–149) and Zweigert and Kötz (1998: 277). Other authors prefer to regard Nordic law as belonging to civil (continental) law (maybe as a subgroup), see, e.g., Bogdan (1994: 88–90) and Bernitz (2000: 31–33).

[2] Contact between ministries is supported by a separate intergovernmental Nordic body, the Nordic Council of Ministers.

[3] Treaty of Nordic Cooperation, Helsinki 23 March 1962, Articles 4 and 5.

[4] Court Statistics published by the Norwegian Courts Administration.

[5] The conciliation boards were established at a time when Norway was united with Denmark. Similar boards were established in Denmark, but have now been abolished.

Norway has no comprehensive procedural code covering both civil and criminal procedure, as distinct from Denmark and Sweden. The main structure of procedural statutes was established by the 1915 Civil Justice Reform when three separate statutes dealing with, respectively, general court issues, the handling of civil claims and the enforcement of claims were enacted. In the past 15 years, Norwegian civil justice has been subject to a range of various reforms. The new Dispute Act was adopted in 2005[6] and took effect on 1 January 2008, replacing the former 1915 Act on Civil Procedure.[7]

5.2 Prevailing Opinions on Goals of Norwegian Civil Justice

The goals of civil justice may be discussed in various settings. The legislative intent and the views of judges, lawyers or scholars may differ. Sometimes no clear distinction is made between the goals and the tasks and functions of civil justice. The opinions may be difficult to ascertain; for example, no survey of judges' attitudes to the goals of justice has been undertaken in Norway and an explicit reference to the goals of civil justice is rarely to be found in judgments and awards.

In the Norwegian Dispute Act Reform of 2005, the goals of civil justice were considered in the commission report and the Government's bill. They recognise the importance of civil procedure for the implementation of substantive law as well as for dispute resolution, but do not discuss whether these two fundamental goals can always be reconciled or which of them should be given priority. In the Dispute Act itself, the goals are set out in the introductory section on the purpose of the Act. Section 1-1, first subsection, reads:

> This Act shall provide a basis for hearing civil disputes in a fair, sound, swift, efficient and confidence inspiring manner through public proceedings before independent and impartial courts. The Act shall safeguard the needs of individuals to enforce their rights and resolve their disputes, and the needs of society for respect and clarification of legal rules.

How the different goals should be balanced, and which goal should be given priority in case of conflict, is scarcely discussed in the preparatory works to the Dispute Act.[8] It may be taken as evidence of the pragmatic approach that is a characteristic of Nordic law and legal policy, which often seeks to find practical solutions to problems instead of developing solutions on the basis of a discussion of and deduction from general principles. Some of the dilemmas will be examined more closely below.

The procedural rules contained in the Act may suggest certain conclusions about prevailing goals. It appears that cost efficiency in dispute resolution is one goal; the establishment of material truth another, whilst respecting the right of the parties to

---

[6] Act of 17 June 2005 no. 90 relating to mediation and procedure in civil disputes. Translations into English and German are to be found in Lipp and Haukeland Fredriksen (2011: 135–447). The English translation can be accessed at www.ub.uio.no/ujur/ulovdata/lov-20050617-090-eng.pdf.

[7] For a survey of the reforms, see Backer (2007, 2011).

[8] See Strandberg (2011: 171–172).

dispose of the subject matter of the dispute. The goals of efficiency and cost reduction are further underlined by the major themes of the evaluation of the Act that is currently being undertaken in accordance with the promise given by the Ministry of Justice in the Government Bill at the instigation of the Ministry of Finance.

A civil dispute may be resolved by the parties reaching a settlement, possibly after mediation, or by a final judgment delivered by the court. The Dispute Act places greater emphasis on alternative dispute resolution and court mediation than its predecessor did and thus underlines the goal of conflict resolution. Dispute resolution by the courts need not, however, lead to a result which satisfies both parties even if they abide by the judgment. It has therefore been suggested that 'conflict treatment' would be a more appropriate description than dispute resolution.[9]

It may be argued that the Norwegian legislator is, in fact, as eager to keep people out of courts as to provide access to courts. As a main rule (with many exceptions[10]), mediation in the conciliation board is mandatory before a lawsuit can be filed in the district court. Court litigation can often be expensive, and there exist a vast number of appeal bodies or tribunals, particularly for consumer affairs, which may decide on disputes on the basis of written submissions by the parties. On the other hand, access to justice was improved by the Dispute Act introducing a special track for small claims and the possibility for class actions.

It must be admitted that in Norwegian procedural theory, the goals of civil justice tend to be only briefly discussed. The goals have been summarised in three points:

1. to resolve civil disputes between citizens and between citizens and public authorities,
2. to implement and enforce substantive law, in particular parliamentary and subordinate legislation, and
3. to clarify and develop the law.[11]

Sometimes a fourth point is added:

4. to control the Executive and the Legislature by way of judicial review of administrative action and control of the constitutionality of statutes and the legal authority of subordinate legislation.

With reference to conflicts between a citizen and a public authority, the latter goal may be seen as a necessary complement to the second goal (the implementation and enforcement of substantive law), but it can also be regarded as included in the first goal (resolution of civil disputes).

[9] Robberstad (2012: 3–4).

[10] Most of the exceptions refer to various types of cases, but claims exceeding NOK 125,000 where both parties have been assisted by a lawyer are generally exempt from mediation in the conciliation board.

[11] Skoghøy (2010: 3–4). Some authors address the question in terms of the functions or tasks of civil justice. Hov (2010 I: 138–139) asks what demands court procedure should fulfil: in particular, producing judgments that are correct in substance and confidence-inspiring proceedings that also are swift and cheap.

It has been suggested that the above-mentioned goals reflect and specify a superior goal – the protection of legal rights and positions.[12] In this context, it may be added that civil justice – together with criminal justice – serves to monopolise the use of coercion in the society.

As the courts have no legislative authority the third goal (clarification and development of the law) has a limited bearing. In Norwegian jurisprudence and legal theory, it has long been accepted and approved that courts should take an active attitude towards filling in gaps and lacunae in existing legislation and provide the necessary clarification of unclear law. In recent years, the courts appear more frequently to strike down, or refrain from applying, statutory provisions by virtue of constitutional and human rights provisions, even where opinions on the content of the latter provisions may be diverse.[13] A statement by the Government and the parliamentary committee in the preparatory works of the Dispute Act, to the effect that development of the law is a task for the courts only to some extent and in an interplay with the legislature, must be seen against this background.

The different goals play different roles at the various court tiers. It is generally agreed, and in accordance with the preparatory works of the Dispute Act, that the chief task of the first instance – the district courts – is to provide swift and efficient dispute resolution, the prime task of the courts of appeal is to correct erroneous judgments rendered by the district courts, while the Supreme Court has a particular responsibility to ensure the uniformity, clarification and necessary development of the law.[14]

While the Danish standard works in civil procedure do not engage in a discussion of the goals of civil justice, the opposite is true of the doctrine of civil procedure in Sweden.[15] One deep-rooted trend in Swedish procedural theory is to emphasise the goal of implementing and enforcing substantive law.[16] Other scholars, while retaining this view, hold that it can be reconciled with the goal of dispute resolution, and that the two are mutually supportive.[17] There are also dissenting views putting dispute resolution in the forefront.[18]

[12] Robberstad (2012: 2–3). She adds that from the users' perspective, civil justice may regarded as providing a forum for dialogue which the contesting parties are obliged to attend (2012: 4).

[13] In three different plenary decisions in 2010, the Supreme Court refused on constitutional grounds to apply new statutory legislation. All the judgments were delivered with dissenting opinions. There are several judgments where a statute was not applied due to the European Convention on Human Rights, which was incorporated in Norwegian law with precedence over other statutes by the Human Rights Act of 21 May 1999 no. 30.

[14] The role of the second tier – the courts of appeal – was discussed at the 39th Conference of Nordic Lawyers in Stockholm August 2011 following a report by the Icelandic professor Sigurður Tómas Magnússon. On the role of Nordic Supreme Courts, see Lindblom 2000b. Since then, the Norwegian Supreme Court has further developed into a precedential court.

[15] For a general survey, see Andersson (1997: 201–233).

[16] This view may, in particular, be attributed to Per Olof Ekelöf, see, e.g., Ekelöf and Edelstam (2002: 13 et seq).

[17] See for this view Per Henrik Lindblom, who has discussed the functions of civil justice in several works and articles, e.g. Lindblom (2000a: 41 et seq. and 2006: 289–291).

[18] See Lindell (2003: 89 et seq.).

5.3 Which Matters Fall Within the Scope of Goals of Civil Justice?

The prime subject of civil justice is to decide legal disputes. By a legal dispute is meant a dispute regarding the application of law on a set of facts; either the law or the facts, or both, may be contested between the parties. Norwegian courts cannot be resorted to in order to obtain a general statement of the law,[19] nor to decide on pure facts with no legal reference. Moreover, the balancing of interests involved in the exercise of administrative discretion falls outside the scope of the courts,[20] and, in many cases, the same goes for decisions taken by a private association affecting its members only. If an approval by a public body is needed in order to acquire a legal right or position, it is nowadays given by an administrative body and not by the courts, but the decision of approval or refusal may be challenged on legal grounds in a court of law.

By tradition, a number of tasks besides adjudication proper were vested in Norwegian courts, mainly the courts of first instance. They kept the land register and several other registers including the company and shipping registers. They dealt with matrimonial cases, administered matrimonial estates after divorce and estates of deceased persons (unless handled by the parties themselves) as well as bankruptcy estates, and, in a special procedure, decided upon compensation to be paid to landowners in the event of compulsory purchase.

During the last 30 years, however, the trend has been to concentrate the tasks of the courts to adjudication of contested claims. This trend appears to have been favoured by legislators and judges alike, without being opposed by the public. The present situation can be described as follows.

An enforcement title is required for the *collection of non-contested debt*. The Enforcement of Claims Act 1992 enumerates various kinds of enforcement titles, but for ordinary claims a judgment will be required. Such a judgment is commonly granted by the conciliation boards, a body composed of three lay judges elected by the municipal council, frequently in default proceedings on the basis of a complaint made by the creditor which has then been served on the debtor. The enforcement of a monetary obligation can now also be based on a written document which sets out the amount and foundation of the claim, provided it is communicated to the debtor and remains uncontested.

---

[19] It is now possible, however, for a petitioner with sufficient standing to obtain a judgment stating that a subordinate regulation issued by an administrative body is void, without having to link the claim to an individual decision or a particular set of facts. Before the Dispute Act, this was not accepted by Norwegian courts. A singularly clear exception is the constitutional right which the Norwegian Parliament has to ask the Supreme Court for its opinion on a point of law (Article 83 of the Constitution), but this right has not been used since 1945.

[20] Provided that the administrative body, when exercising its discretionary powers, has not infringed legal rules such as the European Convention on Human Rights or unwritten rules of abuse of administrative power.

The *enforcement of claims* is generally administered by the bailiffs, who may be organised as a separate body or linked to the local police. The rules on enforcement are laid down in the Enforcement of Claims Act 1992. An appeal against the bailiff's decision lies with the district court which must also decide on interim relief and certain other issues regarding enforcement.

The *keeping of registers* has been transferred from the district courts to administrative bodies. The company register, the register of mortgaged movable property and the marriage settlement register were transferred from the courts to the Brønnøysund Registers (which also handles numerous other registers) about 30 years ago. The ship registers are organised as a separate administrative body. The land register was computerised and centralised to the Norwegian Mapping Authority during the last decade. The transfers have deprived some small district courts of an important part of their tasks and may thus serve to cause a merger of certain local courts. The transfer of the land register, in particular, may also deprive the court of relevant information about the local community and reduce the courts' importance as a service centre for the public. Taken together, the transfer of civil registers may on the one hand reduce the role of the courts in the civil society and thus increase their relative function in criminal justice, but may on the other hand leave more time for civil adjudication.

The *administration of bankruptcy estates* continues to lie with the district courts, but most of the work is delegated to an advocate appointed as administrator of the estate. The administration of estates of deceased persons is normally avoided by the court appointing a trustee. The courts are rarely – if ever – called upon to administer the matrimonial estate after a marriage breakdown unless the division of the estate is heavily contested between the spouses.

The courts are given the task of *regulating the future relationship between the parties* in a limited number of cases only. Claims for separation, divorce or alimony are decided by an administrative body – the county governor – unless there is also a dispute on custody. Adoption decrees are made by the county governor. It is for the courts to issue a decree stating that a missing person is presumed to be deceased or to declare somebody incapable of managing his own affairs. Moreover, the courts are authorised to issue a decree for the dissolution of a company in special circumstances and for the annulment of a negotiable instrument.

Under specific statutes, *reallocation of land or covenants* in land may be decided by the courts, particularly by the special courts for reallocation of land. The administration of the these courts has recently been transferred from the Ministry of Agriculture to the Courts Administration, thus making the distinction between administrative bodies and courts less blurred. The ordinary courts are still authorised to decide on certain applications for compulsory purchase of a small area or the reallocation of covenants. In hydropower projects involving the regulation of watercourses, the courts have, in the special procedure of judicial assessment, certain limited powers to prescribe future obligations of the power company towards landowners and the local community.

The role of the courts in deciding by judicial assessment the *compensation for compulsory purchase* persists, but it has become less apparent as friendly settlements are strongly encouraged by the law. The task now includes the assessment of compensation for nature conservation areas where such compensation is provided by statute.

Lastly, the district courts perform the role of *notary public* which includes the confirmation of signatures and copies of documents, and the celebration of marriages. The profession of notaries, well known in continental law, does not exist in the Nordic countries.

It is fair to say that the above-mentioned procedures or cases play a limited role or none at all in determining the goals of civil justice generally. It can be noted, however, that efficiency is an important consideration behind the rules on collection of uncontested debts as well as enforcement of claims, although with regard to the latter, upholding the rule of law is as important. In the management of estates, conflict resolution is a major aim.

5.4 Protection of Individual Rights v. Protection of Public Interest

The prevailing opinion is probably that in civil justice a balance must be struck between the protection of individual rights and the protection of public interest.[21] It varies, of course, depending upon the particular case, to what extent the public interest may be affected. Generally, the public interest is more at stake in disputes between private parties and public authorities than in disputes between private parties only.

The role of the public interest in civil litigation has both procedural and substantive aspects. At the outset, if a public authority is a party to a case, it can be expected that arguments concerning the public interest will be presented to the court by the advocate for the public authority. There are, however, situations where this will not necessarily be so since the public interest may comprise considerations over and above those for which the particular public authority is responsible. In cases between private parties, considerations of public interest will often be less important, but it is also more likely that they will be overlooked by the private parties and their advocates. In either of these situations the question may arise whether the court is allowed or obliged on its own motion to bring in materials or considerations highlighting the public interest.

When interpreting and applying existing law, the courts will pay regard to common societal values and goals and to the public interest as set out in the relevant statutory provisions (including the provision stating the purpose of the act in question) and its

[21] The question has, especially in recent years, given rise to a debate on whether the courts – with a particular view to the Supreme Court – tend to favour the State rather than the individual. For a contribution in English, see Grendstad et al. (2010), who assert – in my view quite wrongly – that voting preferences by Norwegian Supreme Court justices are influenced by the political colour of the government by which they were appointed. For a comment see Føllesdal (2013).

preparatory works. This is regarded as a matter of substantive law rather than procedural law. A court of law is obliged to apply current law on its own motion (within the framework established by the claims and factual grounds invoked by the parties).

Some examples will illustrate that the balance between individual rights and the public interest varies. In a long series of judgments the Supreme Court has held that the regulation of private property – typically for purposes of area planning or nature conservation – will, in the absence of statutory provision, only give rise to a right to compensation for landowners in very exceptional circumstances. On the other hand, the Supreme Court has strengthened the authorities' duty to give convincing reasons for administrative decisions that *prima facie* appear to be unreasonable. In recent years there has been an increased willingness to modify or strike down statutory provisions on a constitutional or human rights basis without clear precedents.

In their application of procedural law, the overriding aim of the courts appears to be to achieve fairness for both parties. In 1983, a person who challenged the lawfulness of telephone tapping by the police was refused access to the court warrant for reasons of national security (NRt.[22] 1983, p. 1438); today, the courts are more likely to exercise an independent control in this respect.

The views of ruling elites or classes are clearly irrelevant for the application of the law and the courts will take account of government programmes only to the extent they are supported by or implemented through statutory legislation. Government White Papers and parliamentary debates may, however, highlight common societal values and goals that will be relevant legal arguments. Professional privileges will not as such be given priority by the courts. In a leading case from 1977 (NRt. 1977, p. 1035), the Supreme Court ruled that a patient is entitled to see his case record without the doctor's or hospital's consent; on the other hand, lawyers' confidentiality has been upheld on various occasions.

Even if Norwegian civil procedure at the outset is based on the contentions by the parties, the court is entitled to determine a number of issues on its own motion. *First*, it follows from above that the court determines the law regardless of, but assisted by, the parties' submissions. *Second*, in cases where the right of disposition of the parties is limited, the court is free to call for additional evidence and obliged to ensure that the evidence presented provides a sound and sufficient factual basis for its ruling, and the court may base its judgment on factual grounds that are not invoked by the parties. This applies to cases on personal status and legal capacity, custody cases, and other cases where public policy limits the parties' right of disposition.[23] The court may, however, only rule on the claims made by the parties to the case. *Third*, a number of procedural issues are to be decided by the court regardless of the contentions and submissions of the parties. They include questions of jurisdiction (except local venue), standing, *res judicata* and certain time limits for bringing a case.

[22] NRt. = Norsk Retstidende (Norwegian Law Gazette, reporting Supreme Court decisions).

[23] Admittedly, the scope of the latter concept, which is enacted in sec. 11-4 of the Dispute Act, is rather unclear, but it has the advantage of providing an adaptable instrument to ensure that the public interest is not overlooked or imperilled by court litigation.

Actors or bodies other than the parties have no general or statutory obligation to secure that the goals of civil justice will be reached in a particular case (except to abstain from interfering with the independence and impartiality of the court). Third parties with a real interest in the outcome of the case may intervene in a civil case for the benefit of a party. Moreover, associations and foundations as well as public bodies charged with promoting specific interests may intervene in cases falling within the purpose and normal scope of activity of the organisation. Such organisations may also offer written submissions on matters of public interest. There is no such institution in Norwegian (or Nordic) procedural law as the *ministère public* and a right of intervention in order to secure the ordinary goals of civil justice is not foreseen for anyone. In cases before the Supreme Court which raise the question of setting aside statutory rules for constitutional reasons or because of international obligations which are binding in municipal law,[24] the State – represented by the Ministry of Justice – is always entitled to appear in order to safeguard the State's interests with regard to the potential conflict of rules.

5.5 Seeking the 'Material Truth' or Providing Fair Trial Within a Reasonable Time?

Again, a fair balance must be struck between the goals of reaching the material truth and providing fair trial within a reasonable time.[25] This was already the aim of the great 1915 reform of civil procedure which introduced the principle of oral proceedings as well as the principle of presenting all relevant evidence directly to the deciding judge(s). It was then felt that oral proceedings would help in establishing the material truth as well as in promoting swifter proceedings. However, the means to achieve both aims simultaneously may be different today because of more complex litigation and new technology.

Recent years have seen still greater emphasis on a fair trial within a reasonable time.[26] This is demonstrated in the Dispute Act 2005 by the introductory section[27] as well as by various procedural remedies. They include time limits for the duration of the preparatory stage before the main hearing, for the main hearing and for

---

[24] It must here be borne in mind that Norway (and the other Nordic countries) has a dualistic legal system: international law becomes the law of the land only when transposed by a municipal act (although national law will be interpreted so as to conform with international law unless there are strong reasons for the opposite).

[25] In Norwegian procedural doctrine, Hov (2010 I: 138), appears to give a certain priority to the material truth. The goal of reaching a correct decision in individual cases may generally appear to have stronger support in Norway than in Sweden.

[26] In 2010, the average handling time for a case in the district courts was 5 months, in the courts of appeal 5.9 months, and in the Supreme Court 5.8 months.

[27] See section 1-1, first subsection, of the Dispute Act, quoted above under 5.2.

rendering judgment. These time limits are not compelling and may accordingly be adapted to the circumstances of the particular case, but the aggregate effect is reported in annual court statistics. The Act also provides several instruments to allow the judge to concentrate and speed up proceedings, including the right to refuse new claims, grounds or evidence to be introduced at a late stage when it will cause a delay. Rules requiring leave to appeal can also be seen in this light as they contribute to arriving at a final judgment at an earlier stage.

In cases where the right of disposition of the parties is limited, the court shall see to it that the case is sufficiently clarified with a view to reaching the material truth. In all cases, the court has a duty to give procedural guidance to the parties and may encourage a party to offer evidence and to take a position on relevant factual and legal issues, but must do so in a manner which does not preclude the impartiality of the court. Such guidance is particularly important with respect to a party who appears without counsel and serves to avoid a miscarriage of justice due to inadequate procedure on behalf of a party.

5.6 The Same Procedure for Everyone, Irrespective of the Importance of the Case, or a Principle of Proportionality (de minimis non curat praetor)?

The rules of civil procedure tend to have a general scope and to be applicable to all civil cases. Even so, and in the absence of specific rules for different types of cases, they may be formed in a manner which leaves the courts with considerable discretion to adapt the procedure to the needs of the particular case.

The principle of proportionality is one of the main principles underlying the Dispute Act 2005. It represents a true reform even if the principle was not unknown under the previous rules. The introductory section of the Dispute Act states in its second subsection that one of the means to achieve the purposes set out in the first subsection is that ‘the procedure and the costs involved shall be reasonably proportionate to the importance of the case’.

The principle is implemented by a number of provisions of the Dispute Act. The right of the parties to present evidence is limited to evidence on facts which may be of importance to the ruling to be made, and the scale and scope of evidence must be reasonably proportionate to the importance of the case. If it is not, the presentation of evidence may be limited by the court provided this will be in keeping with the general purpose of the Act. An award of compensation for costs is limited to necessary costs, having regard to whether it was reasonable to incur them in view of the importance of the case. At the request of a party, the court may dispose of unsustainable claims at the preparatory stage, without a main hearing, and the same applies if all objections made against a claim are unsustainable. An appeal against a judgment by the district court on an asset claim requires leave if the amount contested in the appeal is less than NOK 125,000 (currently ~€16,000).

For an appeal to the Supreme Court, leave is always required, but the main criterion is the significance of the legal issue raised with a view to its value as a future precedent, not the amount contested.[28]

Small claims (generally cases where the disputed claim does not exceed NOK 125,000) are handled in the district courts according to a special and simplified procedure. The judge has greater powers to administer the case and to provide guidance to the parties. It is thus hoped that litigation costs will be reduced because the parties do not need to be represented by counsel. Compensation for costs is limited to NOK 15,000 (~€2,000) and cannot include costs for presentation of unnecessary or disproportionate evidence. The oral hearing may be held in the form of a distance meeting by aid of audiovisual media, and, with the consent of both parties, the court may dispense with it in order to reduce litigation costs. Written submissions may be used as a basis for the judgment, and evidence shall be presented to the court only in so far as required on a balance of considerations to proper and cost-effective proceedings. Judgment shall be rendered within 3 months from the submission of the writ of summons and its reasons may be briefer than for ordinary judgments.

The introduction of the special small claims track and of class actions (below, 5.8) demonstrates that the Dispute Act aimed at providing access to justice even for small claims – which sometimes raise important issues of law or amount to huge sums taken together. For other small claims cases, rules on pre-trial obligations of information and on mediation are designed to encourage friendly settlements in order to avoid heavy litigation costs.

5.7 Trying 'Hard Cases' or Mass Processing of Routine Matters?

Whether the emphasis should be on trying 'hard cases' involving difficult questions of law or fact, or on mass processing routine matters, varies with the court tiers. The question of what is actually a routine matter – apart from obtaining an enforcement title for uncontested claims – is left aside here.

For the conciliation boards, mass processing of routine matters used to be – and still is – a primary objective, since this is the common lane for obtaining enforcement title for uncontested monetary claims.[29] In the district courts (courts of first instance) the emphasis is on securing efficient handling of a considerable number of cases, and each case is usually tried by a single judge. The president of the district court may, however, decide that three professional judges should sit on a case which involves particularly complex questions of law or fact.

[28] There are several examples where the monetary claim decided by the Supreme Court did not exceed €50, see for one NRt. 2006, p. 179 concerning a consumer's remedies against a faulty pair of boots.

[29] In 2004, the conciliation boards handled 218,000 cases, in 2011 117,000 cases. One reason for the reduction is that creditors may now succeed in obtaining enforcement title by communicating a written statement to the debtor.

In the court of appeal the emphasis is mixed. An appeal from the district court on a routine matter is unlikely to be admitted to the court of appeal for consideration if the contested amount is below NOK 125,000. Clearly unsuccessful appeals may be dismissed without an oral hearing if a panel of three judges agrees. Influenced by international human rights conventions, however, the Supreme Court has ruled that the panel must give reasons for such dismissals,[30] and an appeal lies to the Appeals Committee of the Supreme Court if the reasons given are insufficient. On the other hand, it is also a task for the courts of appeal to correct clear mistakes made by the district courts even with regard to routine matters.

'Hard cases' may come to a final judgment in the court of appeal, since only a small number of appeals from the courts of appeal are admitted for consideration by the Supreme Court. Even if the Supreme Court may consider the factual side in civil cases, only documentary evidence and court-appointed experts can be presented directly to the court and it may generally be said that appeal cases which depend on a difficult assessment of evidence are now unlikely to be admitted to the Supreme Court and will thus be finally decided in the court of appeal.

Formerly, it was widely held that the Supreme Court should be the ultimate guarantor for correct decisions. Over the years, a different view gained support and was adopted in the Dispute Act. Now the main goal for the Supreme Court is to resolve new questions of law which have not hitherto been addressed by it and where the answer may be doubtful. Far from all appeals to the Supreme Court have the qualities for this, and the necessary screening is brought about by a general requirement for leave to appeal which may be granted by the Appeals Committee of the Supreme Court (consisting of three judges) after a preliminary consideration of the appeal. Between 10 and 15 % of appeals from the courts of appeal are granted leave, and leave will usually be refused for appeals that will clearly involve a consideration of the facts. The Appeals Committee often makes use of its power to limit the leave granted to certain aspects of the appeal, but it does occasionally occur during the full proceedings that such a limitation was unfortunate. When the influx of appeals allow, leave to appeal may be granted in two or three cases of a similar nature with a view to joint or successive hearings that can better highlight the legal issue involved. Annually, the Supreme Court renders judgment in about 80 civil cases on appeal against a judgment by a court of appeal.

5.8 Bi-party Proceedings v. Resolution of Complex, Multi-party Matters

At the outset, Norwegian civil procedure is designed for simple, traditional disputes between two parties. Rules on joinder of claims and parties, and third-party intervention, allow for complex, multi-party disputes. Typical examples are compensation

[30] NRt. 2009, p. 1118. The Dispute Act was amended in 2010 to conform with this. Depending on the circumstances, in particular the appellant's arguments, it may be sufficient to refer to the reasons given by the district court.

cases after extensive disasters and real property cases involving joint ownership or commons with numerous rights holders. The courts have a long-standing tradition for dealing with the assessment of compensation for compulsory purchase involving a large number of properties, which is handled according to the special procedure of judicial assessment. Efficiency of justice is usually prompted by consolidating for joint hearing cases raising similar issues. The general goals of civil justice apply to complex and multi-party proceedings.

An alternative to multi-party proceedings is to single out one case with a view to obtaining a pilot judgment that will be accepted without trial in other similar cases. This was done, for example, regarding cases against banks concerning structured savings products which had caused an unexpected loss for the bank's customers.[31]

Judgments may, by way of the doctrine of precedent, affect the legal position of many individuals or large groups of the society. Courts will take account of such far-reaching effects when stating the law. Social regulation, however, is a matter for the legislature; the basic role of the courts is to decide legal conflicts between individual parties.

Certain procedural devices help the courts manage complex cases. The court may decide to split the proceedings and adjudication of separate claims if the proceedings will then be more efficient. Separate rulings may be given on certain topics, such as the grounds for a claim for damages as distinct from the assessment of the sum to be awarded, or grounds that may or may not lead to the determination of a claim, e.g. an objection on the basis of prescription, or the choice of law in private international law. In multi-party cases, evidence presented by one party applies in respect of all parties. In cases of judicial assessment involving compulsory purchase, the purchaser's obligation to pay for the landowners' legal costs may be restricted at the purchaser's request by requiring the landowners who do not have conflicting interests to engage one lawyer jointly instead of separate lawyers individually, thus reducing the total costs and generally promoting the efficiency of the proceedings.

Class actions were introduced in the Dispute Act for dealing with a large number of claims or obligations that are substantially similar.[32] As distinct from a joinder, the individual rights holders or debtors need not appear as parties to the case, but their interests will be defended by a class representative appointed by the court. As a main rule, the judgment will only be binding on individuals registered as class members ('opt in'), but the court may accept that it shall be binding on all individuals having a claim within the scope of the class action unless they have withdrawn from the action ('opt out'). The latter procedure can be used where the individual claims are so small that separate lawsuits would not be economically feasible. A class action may be brought by anyone qualifying as a member of the class in question or by an association or public body set up to promote specific interests,

---

[31] NRt. 2013, p. 388.

[32] Class actions have also been introduced in other Nordic countries, first in Sweden, strongly advocated by the Swedish professor Per Henrik Lindblom. See Lindblom (2008) for an account with an emphasis on the Swedish experience.

provided the action falls within the purpose and normal scope of the organisation. In any case, it is for the court to approve whether litigation should take place in the form of a class action or follow the ordinary rules including the possibility of joinder. There have been a number of class actions in Norwegian courts, but so far, the experience is limited.

5.9 Equitable Results and Substantive Justice or Strict Application of the Law in Favour of the Principle of Legality?

In Norwegian law, there is a strong tradition for seeking equitable results and substantive justice instead of formal justice. This is deeply rooted in legal reasoning which allows for considerations of reasonableness within the boundaries set by the law. The story goes that a Supreme Court justice towards the end of the nineteenth century expressed the view that 'never has the Supreme Court felt compelled to render a judgment which in its opinion would be unjust'. Later observers – judges as well as academics – hold that some qualification is needed and, indeed, it occurs that the Supreme Court sticks to a legal solution that the court may find unsatisfactory in real terms, thus leaving it to the legislature to change the law. The attitude to this question probably differs among the judges and where judicial restraint is preferred, it is chiefly out of respect for the legislature or because it may be unclear or left to a political assessment what the desirable rule should be. Inadvertent mistakes in the legislative process, however, tend to be corrected by the courts if possible, at least in the field of civil justice.

5.10 Problem Solving or Case Processing?

Even here the prevailing view is likely to be that both goals deserve to be pursued. The introduction and increased use of court mediation may be regarded as a means to obtain effective problem solving between the parties as well as to promote court efficiency, but it precludes the creation of new precedents where it is used. The trend in recent years, however, seems to be more bent on case processing than on problem solving. There is a stronger emphasis on the efficient case management which appears in the Dispute Act itself, court budgets and their statistical goals for case management, and continuing education of judges. On the other hand, there is also an awareness that efficient case processing must not go too far at the expense of actual problem solving. In certain cases or types of cases, the lack of problem solving can easily give rise to renewed or repetitive litigation which is not barred by the doctrine of *res judicata* if a different claim can be raised.

5.11 The Costs of Civil Justice: A Freely Available Public Service or a Quasi-commercial Source of Revenue for the Public Budget and a Source of Income for Lawyers?

Although subject to court fees, civil justice was originally largely perceived as a freely available public service, but the lawyer's salary had to be borne by the party. Nowadays, court fees as well as lawyers' salaries have risen to such an extent as to make civil litigation an expensive exercise for the ordinary citizen. Moreover, the Dispute Act allows counsel, without any specific permission, to be assisted in court by a deputy and this right is not restricted to complex cases. On the other hand, the Act gives the court power to reduce the amount claimed when awarding costs. As an example, in a case brought unsuccessfully by a consumer against a carpenter for faulty bathroom repairs, counsel for the defendant claimed costs for appeal court proceedings in the amount of NOK 320,000 (~€40,000), an amount almost equalling the consumer's claim for damages. The amount was reduced by 60 % by the court of appeal in its award of costs.

As distinct from consumers, businesses are entitled to deduct legal costs from their taxable income. The less well-to-do may be covered by legal aid schemes and ordinary citizens to some extent by insurance policy clauses. There are practically no legal services offered by the state or municipalities to the general public for court litigation. As a rule, citizens must engage counsel from private law firms, but some organisations, including trade unions, offer legal services to their members.

Court fees are calculated according to a specific statute on the basis of a court fee unit (termed R, which currently amounts to NOK 860 (~€ 110)). The court fee for an ordinary case in the district court amounts to 5 R if the main hearing lasts 1 day, with an addition of 3 R for each additional day of the main hearing and 4 R per day exceeding 5 days. The court fee for an appeal case amounts to 24 R (NOK 20,640 ~ €2,600) with a similar additional fee if the main hearing lasts more than 1 day. The court fee for a claim handled by the district court according to the special small claims procedure is 3.5 R (NOK 30,100 ~ €3,800).

The total amount of court fees nonetheless only covers about 10 % of the courts' budgets. In 2011, the total expenses for the district courts, courts of appeal and the Supreme Court were almost NOK 1,730 million (~€220 million) and the court fees collected amounted to almost NOK 166 million.

5.12 Orientation Towards the Users, or Self-Centred Goals?

It is probably not unfair to say that the goals of civil justice used to be somewhat self-centred within the judiciary and the legal profession at large and you can still come across the attitude that they should be no concern for the legislature or political authorities. The prevailing view is surely that it is also a matter for them, but there are proponents who hold that in order to secure the independence of the courts from the executive branch, the goals of civil justice are basically a matter for the Parliament.

Even when the goals of civil justice were perceived as a matter for the courts themselves, the needs of citizen users were never entirely left out of account. It is only in recent years, however, that the question of establishing their needs and wishes independently of judges and lawyers has arisen. As a part of the evaluation of the Dispute Act that is currently taking place, surveys and interviews with citizens who were parties to civil cases will also be used.[33]

References

Andersson T (1997) Rättsskyddsprincipen [The protection of individual community rights]. Iustus, Uppsala

Backer IL (2007) The Norwegian reform of civil procedure. Scand Stud Law 51:41–75

Backer IL (2011) The reform of Norwegian civil procedure. In: Lipp V, Fredriksen HH (eds) Reforms of civil procedure in Germany and Norway. Mohr Siebeck, Tübingen, pp 43–59

Bernitz U (2000) Nordic legislative cooperation in the new Europe – a challenge for the Nordic countries in the EU. Scand Stud Law 39:29–42

Bogdan M (1994) Comparative law. Kluwer/Norstedts Juridik/Tano, Göteborg

Ekelöf PO, Edelstam H (2002) Rättegång [Court procedure] I, 8th edn. Norstedts Juridik, Stockholm

Føllesdal A (2013) Much Ado about Nothing? Claims about political appointment to the Norwegian Supreme Court – and what to do – and not to do – about it. Tidsskrift for Rettsvitenskap 126:364–371

Grendstad G, Shaffer WR, Waltenburg EM (2010) Revealed preferences of Norwegian Supreme Court justices. Tidsskrift for Rettsvitenskap 123:73–101

Hov J (2010) Rettergang [Court procedure] I-II. Papinian, Oslo

Lindblom PH (2000a) Progressiv process [Progressive procedure]. Iustus, Uppsala

Lindblom PH (2000b) The role of the Supreme Courts in Scandinavia. Scand Stud Law 39:324–366

Lindblom PH (2006) Sena uppsatser [Late contributions]. Norstedts Juridik, Stockholm

Lindblom PH (2008) Group litigation in Scandinavia. Zeitschrift für Zivilprozess International 13:85–114

Lindell B (2003) Civilprocessen [Civil procedure], 2nd edn. Iustus, Uppsala

Lipp V, Fredriksen HH (eds) (2011) Reforms of civil procedure in Germany and Norway. Mohr Siebeck, Tübingen

Malmström Å (1969) The system of legal systems. Notes on a problem of classification in comparative law. Scand Stud Law 13:127–149

Robberstad A (2012) Sivilprosess [Civil procedure], 2nd edn. Fagbokforlaget, Bergen

Skoghøy JEA (2010) Tvisteløsning [Dispute resolution]. Universitetsforlaget, Oslo

Strandberg M (2011) Fordeler og ulemper ved partsprosessen, særlig med tanke på rollefordelingen mellom dommer og part [Advantages and disadvantages of civil procedure between parties, particularly regarding the roles of the judge and the parties]. Jussens Venner 46:165–181

Zweigert K, Kötz H (1998) An introduction to comparative law, 3rd edn. Oxford University Press, Oxford

[33] Demands and expectations of the modern judge were discussed at the 39th Conference of Nordic Lawyers in Stockholm August 2011 on the basis of a report by the Swedish Chancellor of Justice Anna Skarhed. One of the theses in her report is that an outside view on the judge and court activities is important but citizens' expectations can only be fulfilled within the rule of law and the justice system as adopted by democratic bodies.

Chapter 6
'American Exceptionalism' in Goals for Civil Litigation

Richard Marcus

Abstract American procedure has long been exceptional, a fact that baffles Americans and non-Americans alike. But focusing on the goals of civil litigation provides an important insight into why U.S. procedure is so different. Everyone around the world wants procedure that suitably balances accuracy with economy. But American procedure seeks to enable litigants in this country to go further, by enforcing public norms through private initiative, a major reason why it puts fewer obstacles in the way of prospective plaintiffs. That seems to be a uniquely American role for civil litigation, and largely explains the relaxed pleading, broad discovery, and jury trial features of American civil litigation.

6.1 Introduction

Identifying the goals of procedure may be more challenging in some ways in the common law world than in the civil law world because, as is true in many ways, the procedure of the common law world (like its substantive law) evolved organically and without any 'founding principles.' That does not mean that procedure is less valued in the common law world. To the contrary, for the U.S. 'due process' – the ultimate measure of procedure – is enshrined in two places in our Constitution.[1] Indeed, it is often said that Americans are much more concerned about procedure than people within other legal systems.

[1] The due process requirement appears in both the Fifth Amendment and the 14th Amendment of the U.S. Constitution. The Fifth Amendment limits the national government, and the 14th limits the state governments (and local governments acting under the states' authority). Both say that no person may 'be deprived of life, liberty, or property, without due process of law.'

R. Marcus (✉)
Hastings College of Law, 200 McAllister St, San Francisco, CA 94102, USA
e-mail: marcusr@uchastings.edu

A. Uzelac (ed.), *Goals of Civil Justice and Civil Procedure in Contemporary Judicial Systems*, Ius Gentium: Comparative Perspectives on Law and Justice 34,
DOI 10.1007/978-3-319-03443-0_6, © Springer International Publishing Switzerland 2014

As we shall see, particularly in the American setting, procedure also is measured importantly as it overlaps with or furthers the goals of substantive law; in this sense, one may speak of the overall purpose of civil justice as depending on the effectiveness of compensation and the other features of any civil justice system. Beyond that, owing to the peculiarly prevalent role litigation has played in important social and political developments in this country – illustrated most vividly by the civil rights movement of the 1950s and 1960s – procedure has remained central in the last half century to the larger political debate. That point was brought home by our Supreme Court's procedural decision in June 2013, that it lacked authority to decide the question whether states could deny same-sex couples the right to marry that couples of opposite sex enjoy.[2]

To complicate the picture, there is also the possibility that widely recognized purposes of procedure actually conflict with each other in important ways. For example, concerns about efficiency and accuracy may conflict if more costly procedure produces more accuracy. Similarly, to the extent one wants to use procedure to ensure law enforcement, one may downplay the goal of conflict resolution; conflicts may be regarded as desirable opportunities to enforce and articulate the law rather than unfortunate disruptions of social tranquillity that should be soothed over. Given these disputes about goals, we also can encounter debates about the costs of procedures that mask differences of view about the goals.

For the common law world, and for the U.S. in particular, there is no simple report on the goals of procedure. Instead, it is necessary to offer a complicated and ambiguous one, and to admit that it remains a hotly contested issue in the U.S.

6.2 The Historical Emergence of the Notion of Purposes of Procedure, and Resulting Debates

Although the concept of due process can be found as long ago as Magna Carta (1215), the concept that procedure must be explained or justified in terms of its purposes is of fairly recent origin in the Anglo/American world. Indeed, at first in England, it is said, there was only procedure; in the words of the Englishman Maine, 'substantive law has at first the look of being gradually secreted in the interstices of procedure' (Maine 1907: 389).

At first, then, procedure was the dominant feature of the common law. In the words of the American scholar Millar: 'Ever do we see that procedure has been the

[2] In Hollingsworth v. Perry, 133 S.Ct. 2652 (2013), plaintiffs sued the State of California and various state officials in federal court, claiming that they had a constitutionally guaranteed right to marry even though they were not of opposite sexes. The officials they sued refused to defend the law forbidding same-sex couples from marrying, which had been adopted by initiative election. The trial court permitted the proponents of the initiative to intervene in the case and defend the law, but the trial court held it unconstitutional and enjoined the state officials from enforcing it. The proponents of the initiative appealed, but the state officials did not. The Supreme Court held that they had no standing to appeal the trial court's ruling.

major element, substantive law the minor in the growth of the legal order, and that procedure has been signally procreative of the substantive rule' (Millar 1951: 4). But as Millar further explains, over time this relationship changes; 'the trend of development diminishes the place of procedure and enlarges that of the substantive law' (Millar 1951: 4).

In England, this development was markedly furthered by Jeremy Bentham, who applied utilitarianism to procedure (which he called 'adjective law') and rejected the notion that it had any inherent value: 'the whole of the adjective branch taken together may be said to have two specific ends: the one *positive*, maximizing the execution and effect given to the substantive branch; the other *negative*, minimizing the evil, the hardship, in various shapes necessary to the accomplishment of the main specified end' (Bentham 1843: 8). But Bentham qualified this view by emphasizing also that 'apparent justice ... in the eye of public opinion' was the critical objective: 'In point of utility, apparent justice is everything; real justice, abstractedly from apparent justice, is a useless abstraction, not worth pursuing, and supposing it contrary to apparent justice, such as ought not be pursued' (Bentham 1843: chp. III).

This objective points up one of the potential tensions or contradictions in identifying goals, for if 'real' and 'apparent' justice may be different things, it is possible that a procedure that responded to public desires (and therefore led to 'apparent' justice) might at the same time lead to results we would regard as conflicting with 'real' justice. For example, in a public that regarded divine intervention as the proper measure of guilt or innocence, methods that might strike us as fantastic might be adopted. Consider trial by ordeal, in which the accused is thrown into a pond. If the accused sinks, that supposedly shows that God is welcoming him into her bosom, signifying innocence, and if the accused floats that means God is rejecting him, signifying guilt. Actually, this sort of practice existed in England until a Papal Bull in 1215 forbade priestly participation in such spectacles, for without that blessing the premise of divine judgment disappeared. Except for those who accept the notion that divine judgments can be discerned by such techniques, the method was always ridiculous, but it may well have had wide acceptance in the populace, underscoring the potential contradiction between 'real' and 'apparent' justice.

Bentham's utilitarian attitude has been carried forward into the current times in the economic analysis of law made famous in the U.S. by Professor, and later Judge Posner. He asserted that the 'objective of a procedural system' is to minimize the sum of the cost of erroneous judicial decisions and the cost of operating the procedural system (Posner 1986: § 21.2). The U.S. Supreme Court adopted a variant of this approach for the constitutional due process requirement in 1976.[3] The notion is

[3] In Mathews v. Eldridge, 424 U.S. 319 (1976), the Court confronted an argument that due process permitted Social Security benefits to be terminated only after a live hearing. It rejected the argument, holding that due process should be dependent on factors like those endorsed by Posner: 'First, the public interest that will be affected by the official action; second, the risk of an erroneous deprivation of such interest through the procedures used; and finally, the Government's interest, including the function involved and the fiscal and administrative burdens that additional or substitute procedural requirements would entail.' In Connecticut v. Doehr, 501 U.S. 1 (1991), it extended

that the value of added or different procedures should be measured by the increase in accuracy they provide, and that improvement in accuracy should be balanced against the cost of the added procedures.

The prevailing law-and-economics analysis can prove elusive even to those schooled in its ways. But sometimes it can be instructive. A case decided by Judge Posner illustrates the point. Plaintiffs challenged the practice of the City of Chicago to treat a parking ticket as prima facie evidence of a parking violation, arguing that the officer who issued the ticket should be required to testify in every case there was a challenge to the ticket. Of four million tickets issued per year, about 67,000 were challenged. The judge assumed that testifying at a hearing would require about 2 hours of an officer's time, and that required attendance in court would use up the equivalent of 67 officers full time per year. Indeed, if those who receive tickets know the ticket will be dismissed unless the officer shows up, there will probably be more challenges. But the judge thought that the risk that proceeding without the officer would lead to an erroneous decision was only about 5 %, and that having the officer present would reduce the accuracy risk only by half, leading to an accuracy value of 2.5 % of the $55 ticket cost, or $1.38, what the judge described as a 'trivial amount'. In conclusion: 'These calculations are inexact, to say the least; but they help to show, what is pretty obvious without them, that the benefits of requiring the police officer to appear at every hearing are unlikely to exceed the costs.'[4]

Among some U.S. scholars, the Supreme Court's adoption of a law-and-economics attitude promptly drew criticism, in particular from Professor Mashaw, who warned that the Court had not properly attended to 'process values' with 'a calculus in which accuracy is the sole goal of procedure' (Mashaw 1976: 48). Professor Michelman urged more generally that 'dignity values' and 'participation values' should be recognized as important in addition to interests in accuracy (Michelman 1973: 1174–76). And Professor Dworkin argued that the 'psychological fact' that people generally mind an adverse decision that is taken facelessly is 'the sort of harm that figures in any decent utilitarian calculation' (Dworkin 1985: 97, 102). Somewhat from these seeds of dissent, there grew the 'procedural justice' analysis of procedures, which relied on empirical survey work to indicate which procedures were in fact important to people, and found that dignity and an opportunity to participate mattered separately from concern with the outcome (e.g., Did I win?) (Lind and Tyler 1988).

In sum, the twentieth century saw much work on the goals of procedure, but also illustrated ways in which there could be strong debate about purposes. For the present, the dominant 'due process' analysis in American courts is fairly strictly utilitarian in the sense adopted by Judge Posner, but the academic debate goes well beyond that. Unraveling those debates is the first challenge for one seeking to settle on goals.

---

this analysis to apply to judicial procedures the government makes available, changing the last factor so it focused on the interests of the party seeking to use the procedure rather than on the government's interest.

[4] Van Harken v. City of Chicago, 103 F. 3d 1346 (7th Cir. 1997).

6.3 Choosing Basic Goals – Conflict Resolution v. Policy Implementation

Even focusing primarily on utilitarian analysis, there is considerable room for debate. Assuming one has recognized procedure as 'adjective law,' which seeks to implement something else (substantive law), one is left to focus on whether it does that job effectively. But it turns out there is considerable room to debate what should be the goal of private civil adjudication, and that the resolution of this question is central to our inquiry. Professor Damaska introduced that notion a generation ago by positing a difference between what he called the 'reactive state' and the 'activist state' (Damaška 1986: chp. III).

One easy first answer is that the main goal of civil adjudication is conflict resolution – the focus of the 'reactive state'. At a very basic level, the State seeks to provide an alternative to self help. So long as procedure can inexpensively produce a result that satisfies the parties – or at least is not so unsatisfactory as to prompt them to resort to extrajudicial means of redress – it could be deemed adequate. But unduly high costs of using formal procedure would deter people from using the courts, perhaps sufficiently so that they would turn to self help instead, for self help is not subject to the limitations of due process.[5]

This orientation has been challenged, particularly regarding alternative dispute resolution. If dispute resolution were the sole objective, ADR might seem the perfect solution, resolving the dispute without involving the state. Most famously, in 'Against Settlement' Professor Fiss objected that '[t]he dispute-resolution story makes settlement appear as a perfect substitute for judgment … by trivializing the remedial dimensions of a lawsuit, and also by reducing the social function of the lawsuit to one of resolving private disputes' (Fiss 1984: 1085).[6]

Judge Edwards (a former law school professor) reacted to this debate by emphasizing that '[a]n oft-forgotten virtue of adjudication is that it ensures the proper resolution and application of public values', adding that 'there are some disputes that cannot be resolved simply by mutual agreement and good faith. It is a fact of political life that many disputes reflect sharply contrasting views about fundamental public values that can never be eliminated by techniques that encourage disputants to "understand" each other. Indeed, many disputants understand their opponents all too well…. One essential function of law is to reflect the public resolution of such irreconcilable differences' (Edwards 1986: 676–77). Similarly, Professor Brunet observed: 'The output of conventional litigation should be viewed as a public good – society gains more from litigation than would be produced were litigation

[5] See, e.g., Flagg Brothers, Inc. v. Brooks, 436 U.S. 149 (1978), holding that no due process protections applied to restrict sale of former tenant's possessions for failure to pay storage fees even though the possessions had been taken by the City Marshall in an eviction because the action of the storage company in selling the possessions was not 'state action'.

[6] For a critique of Fiss's argument, see Issacharoff and Klonoff 2009, who argue that Fiss himself conceived of the dimensions of court functions too narrowly, and regarded the values of full adjudication without sufficient critical distance.

left in the private market.... Litigation guides third parties. Litigation results in written opinions that apply necessarily vague positive law to concrete fact situations. Those opinions are expository – they refine and elaborate ambiguous norms' (Brunet 1987: 19–20). This view is particularly applicable, of course, to a common law system in which court decisions are 'the law' to a degree that is not usually true in a civil law system.

In sum, the objection launched as ADR was becoming much more popular in the U.S. was that it could erode or defeat the policy implementation objective even if (or perhaps because) it served the dispute resolution conflict resolution goal.

The same dividing line that influences enthusiasm for alternative dispute resolution also affects the content of procedural rules for cases handled in court. In the 1970s, Professor Scott explored these notions in his essay *Two Models of the Civil Process* (Scott 1975). He posited a 'conflict resolution model' and a 'behavior modification model'. The former would be concerned only with providing an alternative to retaliation or forcible self help, and therefore would be strongly inclined to leave unremedied 'wrongs' that would not excite retaliation. The latter, on the other hand, would expect civil litigation to serve as a way of altering behavior by imposing the costs of harmful activity on the wrongdoer. That orientation might focus most forcefully on the very instances in which the injured parties would be least likely to take action because their injury is trifling and the cost of taking action is large in comparison.

That division could affect the design of the class action, for example, as Professor Scott illustrated (Scott 1975: 940–45). One who favored the conflict resolution model would shy away from the consumer class action, for example, for that would stir up litigation where none would otherwise occur. That seemed to be the attitude of the U.S. Supreme Court in the 1970s, when it held that in class actions all class members must be individually identified and provided a chance to opt out even though each one would have little at stake, and that an aggregate recovery for the harm done would not be allowed (Scott 1975: 942–44).[7] But under the behavior modification view, one should favor creative use of the class action, as the California Supreme Court did in upholding its use for unidentifiable taxicab customers who were overcharged, permitting the court to order the taxi company to charge unduly low prices to future customers to take away its illegal profits from prior victims (Scott 1975: 940–42).[8] Those examples show that, even in the U.S., different choices about basic orientation can be made.

But this American debate does not capture all the possibilities. Consider the vigorous debates now ongoing in Europe about how to handle representative litigation in those countries (Hodges 2008). Putting aside distaste about 'excessive' American adversarial activity, one European view is that the American 'opt-out'

---

[7] Scott discussed Eisen v. Carlisle & Jacquelin, 417 U.S. 156 (1974), which required the named plaintiff who filed a class action to bear the entire cost of giving notice to all class members even though his individual claim was small and the class had approximately six million members.

[8] This discussion focused on Daar v. Yellow Cab Co., 433 P.2d 732 (Cal. 1967), which took a much more flexible attitude toward using the class-action device, as noted in text.

approach to class actions is fundamentally unacceptable for dignity and autonomy reasons. As Professor Stadler has observed, 'it is almost impossible to guarantee that all group members receive the information that a group action including their claims is pending', which makes the opt-out approach unworkable: 'In terms of their right to be heard and the right of every claimant to decide for him or herself whether to sue the defendant or not, [opt-out treatment] seems to be highly problematic' (Stadler 2010: 84–85). To American eyes, thus exalting the 'right' of every person with a €10 claim to decide whether it should be vindicated via a class action seems to place far too much weight on those autonomy interests; even Professor Stadler recognizes that the 'rational apathy of consumers' in that situation is a problem for her approach (Stadler 2010: 81).

6.4 The American 'Exceptionalism' Addition – Private Enforcement of Public Norms

The basic question about general orientation toward conflict resolution or behavior modification relates to a different question about procedural design – who does the enforcing? For most of the world, the answer is easy, almost automatic – enforcement is done by the state. But that is not the only way.

As Professor Scott also observed, one oriented toward the behavior modification model had to decide who should initiate the process: 'The creation of an administrative agency charged with the duty of enforcing the legal rules in these situations is one solution that has been tried. But a statutory instruction is not the same as an incentive for efficient enforcement' (Scott 1975: 939).

For most of the rest of the world, we Americans are informed, the administrative enforcement model is the favored method of achieving policy enforcement or behavior modification, and conflict resolution is the goal of private civil litigation. Of course, administrative enforcement is possible in the American legal system; as the Supreme Court recognized long ago in holding that a private employment discrimination class action could not go forward, the federal Equal Employment Opportunity Commission (EEOC) does not have to satisfy the same requirements to obtain classwide relief as a private plaintiff seeking certification of a class action.[9] The reality seems to have been, however, that such governmental enforcement has often not been sufficient to do the job. One looking for evidence of that shortfall of enforcement need only consider the multitude of reports that enforcement of securities laws in the period leading up to the 2008 financial crash was unduly lax, and the more recent reports that the federal Securities and Exchange Commission and other enforcement agencies are not funded sufficiently to do the job. Indeed, in 2009 the

[9] General Telephone Co. v. Falcon, 457 U.S. 147 (1982). The case held that plaintiff could not justify a class action under Fed. R. Civ. P. 23. The Court contrasted the situation of a private plaintiff with that of the EEOC, which has general enforcement power and 'may seek relief for groups of employees or applicants for employment without complying with the strictures of Rule 23'.

U.S. Securities and Exchange Commission (SEC) announced that it would seek help from third parties to fortify enforcement, citing staffing needs among other reasons for seeking this aid (Chung 2009).

As Professor Kagan has noted, this administrative shortfall results in part from American suspicion of intrusive government (Kagan 2001). He explains that people in the U.S., as in other post-industrial states, want aggressive protection from government, but they do not want the sort of big or intrusive government that would be necessary to provide that enforcement administratively. In these circumstances, the American reliance on private litigation can serve as an effective substitute for having government seek to enforce the law, including even those protections included only in administrative regulations and not in statutes.

Often Congress explicitly authorizes such private suits. A century ago, it introduced this technique in the Clayton Antitrust Act, which explicitly authorized those harmed by violation of the Sherman Antitrust Act (the federal antitrust law) to sue for 'treble damages' – three times their actual losses – and also guaranteed that they could recover their attorneys' fees if successful.[10] This early twentieth century model was repeatedly used by Congress and state legislatures beginning in the 1960s. Sometimes these authorizations for private enforcement promised a minimum monetary recovery, or offered claimants the chance to recover multiple damages, as with the Clayton Act. Usually they also promised the successful plaintiff an attorney fee award despite the American Rule that ordinarily the prevailing litigant must pay his own lawyer.

But it is not necessary for the legislature to authorize such private enforcement to permit it in the American scheme. The very heart of the common law system contemplates that the courts themselves will develop and enforce – via private litigation – the sorts of legal protections that are ordinarily adopted by legislative or administrative action in other legal systems. In the U.S., for example, the development of product liability law after World War II was almost entirely done by courts, and those product liability suits were intended to exert a decisive influence on industry. We are certainly told that they have; it is accepted Chamber of Commerce dogma that the risk of product liability suits weighs heavily on manufacturers. True, the American Rule regarding recovery of attorney fees still rules in such cases, but the American contingency fee system (coupled with the potential of high recoveries for emotional distress) offsets that feature and enables suits that would not be similarly workable in other countries.

Even when there has been legislative or administrative enforcement action, private enforcement can follow. Thus, by the 1970s it became commonplace for private plaintiff lawyers to use the Clayton Act to file damage class actions in the wake of a governmental antitrust enforcement action. And similar activity can be authorized on the courts' initiative even when not explicitly authorized by Congress. The most famous American example is probably securities fraud suit, which is not based on any Congressional authorization of private suits. To the contrary, Congress created the SEC, which in turn promulgated Rule 10b-5 forbidding fraud in

[10] 15 U.S.C. § 15.

connection with sale of securities. The SEC was authorized to enforce that antifraud provision, but after a time the courts concluded that it was not doing a vigorous enough job. In 1947 a district court therefore accepted a plaintiff's invitation to 'imply' a private cause of action for securities fraud in violation of Rule 10b-5, and in 1964 the Supreme Court endorsed this judicial invention.[11]

Not until 1995 did Congress implicitly endorse this judicial invention, and then it did so in a backhanded way by adopting the Private Securities Litigation Reform Act, which was designed to curb these suits, in part by imposing stringent pleading requirements and forbidding discovery until the complaint survived a motion to dismiss for failure to satisfy the pleading requirements. Yet when the Supreme Court first interpreted these new pleading requirements, the first line of its opinion said: 'This Court has long recognized that meritorious private actions to enforce federal antifraud securities laws are an essential supplement to criminal prosecutions and civil enforcement actions brought, respectively, by the Department of Justice and the Securities and Exchange Commission'.[12] So even Congress's efforts to curtail private securities fraud suits would be interpreted in a way designed to further the Court's – not Congress's – determination that these private enforcement actions are necessary.

---

[11] See J.I. Case Co. v. Borak, 377 U.S. 426 (1964). The Supreme Court has since become more cautious about whether to imply a private cause of action from congressional adoption of a regulatory statute. In Cort v. Ash, 422 U.S. 66 (1975), it ruled that the decision whether to do so should depend on whether there are indicia that Congress meant to create a private right to sue, and also whether the subject matter is one traditionally regulated by state law. The 1960s attitudes underlying the implication of a private cause of action for securities fraud have thus receded. But regarding securities fraud claims themselves the Court has not backtracked. As explained in the text, in 1995 Congress finally provided a backhanded endorsement for what the Court did in its 1964 decision by adopting legislation that recognized that such private suits had been commonplace for over 30 years and sought to curtail some aspects of them. The Court interpreted that legislation in the 2007 decision described in text, but with an eye to preserving the effectiveness of the private enforcement action it had created in 1964. One could regard the Court's conclusion that what Congress sought to do in 1995 must be tempered by what the Court had done three decades earlier as a form of effrontery. There is, after all, no indication that Congress affirmatively wanted the Court to do what it did when it inferred a private right to sue, although congressional inaction since the 1960s might be taken to be silent assent. Even so, the goal in 1995 was plainly to curtail what the courts had been permitting.

[12] Tellabs, Inc. v. Makor Issues & Rights, Ltd., 551 U.S. 308, 313 (2007). In that case, the Court was called upon to interpret the pleading requirements of the Act. Liability under the securities fraud laws requires a finding of scienter – the defendant's intention 'to deceive, manipulate, or defraud'. The Act required that the complaint 'state with particularity facts giving rise to a strong inference that the defendant acted with the required state of mind'. 15 U.S.C. § 78u-4(b)(2). The majority held that a complaint could be upheld 'only if a reasonable person would deem the inference of scienter cogent and at least as compelling as any opposing inference one could draw from the facts alleged'. Justice Scalia, dissenting, argued that the Act required more, reasoning that an equally cogent inference could not sensibly be found to be 'strong,' as required by the statute. Accordingly, he urged, an inference could be found sufficient only if it were the strongest, not merely equally strong. The skeptical might be inclined to suspect that the majority's interpretation reflected, to some extent, its commitment to preserving the vitality of private enforcement, even though Congress seemed intent on cutting that back.

Congress does take the lead on this point fairly often, however. As noted above, a century ago it authorized a private suit to enforce the antitrust laws. More recently, it has become much more active in authorizing similar regimes to enforce a variety of new enactments. The model for most of those was Title VII of the Civil Rights Act of 1964, the federal statute forbidding discrimination in employment. As extensively chronicled in Professor Farhang's 2010 book *The Litigation State* (Farhang 2010), there was a vigorous dispute in the U.S. Senate about how enforcement of these antidiscrimination provisions should be handled. The 'liberal' proponents of broad enforcement favored giving the main enforcement authority to the Equal Employment Opportunity Commission (EEOC). But they did not have enough votes to pass the measure, and needed to compromise with the Senate Republicans, who were responsive to business concerns that the EEOC would be full of zealots who would enforce the Act too vigorously. At the Republicans' insistence, therefore, primary enforcement authority relies on those who claim to be victims of discrimination; they can sue, and recover attorneys' fees if they prevail.

As Professor Farhang points out on the first sentences of his book, private enforcement has flourished: 'Next to petitions by prisoners to be set free, job discrimination lawsuits are the *single largest category* of litigation in federal courts. Over the past decade or so, the annual number of such lawsuits averaged about 20,000. Two percent of these job discrimination suits were prosecuted by the federal government, while 98 percent were litigated by private parties' (Farhang 2010: 3). Meanwhile, Congress repeatedly used the Title VII model during the quarter century after 1964 to create similar private enforcement regimes in a wide variety of other antidiscrimination, consumer protection, and other measures (Farhang 2010: chp. 5).

Like most civil law systems, most common law systems do not subscribe to this exceptional American arrangement. In the next section, I will address the procedural ramifications of this American choice, but I pause to note that other common law countries, particularly England, do not have a separation of powers arrangement and do rely much more heavily on governmental actors to enforce legislation. But this may be changing in the EU. Professor Keleman argues in his 2011 book *Eurolegalism* that for a variety of reasons the EU is gradually gravitating toward a variant of the adversarial legalism identified as American by Professor Kagan (Keleman 2011: chp. 1). Although the EU now relies on national judiciaries for enforcement, further integration along with this trend toward adversarial legalism may produce pressure to adapt procedure to effectuate enforcement through private litigation.

Furthermore, the notion of private enforcement is not entirely alien to European legal thought. Professor von Jhering, writing in the late nineteenth century, posited a duty to society for individuals whose rights are violated to seek vindication at law (von Jhering 1915: chp. IV). He began with the idea that the existence of legal rights itself creates a duty of the individual to insist on his rights for otherwise the abstract legal 'right' will have no actual force.[13] From that beginning, he then constructs a

[13] Von Jhering found that, at least when he was writing, the inclination to make this effort varied considerably among European nations. He said that 'the attitude which an individual or a nation assumes towards an attempt on its rights is the surest test of its character' (von Jhering 1915: 64). He added (von Jhering 1915: 65–66):

duty the individual owes to society to enforce his rights and thereby guard the similar rights of others that will be honored for fear of vigilant enforcement by anyone whose rights are violated.

This obligation, von Jhering argued, is parallel to the obligation of public officials to enforce public law and criminal law, and equally at risk if private actors do not act (von Jhering 1915: 72):

> The existence of all the principles of public law depends on the fidelity of public officials in the performance of their duties; that of the principles of private law, on the power of the motives which induce the person whose rights have been violated to defend them: his interest and his sentiment of legal right. If these motives do not come into play, if the feeling of legal right is blunted and weak, and interest is not powerful enough to overcome the disinclination to entering into a controversy and the indisposition to go to law, the consequence is that the principle of law involved finds no application.

So European soil contains some seeds that could support the sprouting of something like private enforcement of public law. And the step from a duty to enforce private law for the good of society to authority for private enforcement of public law seems a small one.

6.5 The Implications of Embracing Private Enforcement – Implementing American Exceptionalism

The more one conceives of private litigation as furthering a public enforcement purpose, the more one may be tempted to provide incentives to pursue it, and the more one may be inclined to equip those who do pursue litigation with the tools they will need to succeed. Thus, the goals of civil litigation largely explain American exceptionalism. If the prediction that the EU may resort more often to private enforcement is justified (Keleman 2011: chp. 1), moreover, it may predict ways in which pressures in the EU could emerge to promote similar provisions there in order to achieve similar objectives.[14] As Professor Strong has explained, there is a

---

> The best proof of this is afforded by the English people. Their wealth has caused no detriment to their feeling of legal right; and what energy it still possesses, even in pure questions of property, we, on the Continent, have frequently proof enough of, in the typical figure of the traveling Englishman who resists being duped by inn-keepers and hackmen with a manfulness which would induce one to think he was defending the law of Old England – who, in case of need, postpones his departure, remains days in the place and spends ten times the amount he refuses to pay. The people laugh at him, and do not understand him. It were better if they did understand him. For, in the few shillings which the man here defends, Old England lives. At home, in his own country, every one understands him, and no one lightly ventures to overreach him. Place an Austrian of the same social position and the same means in the place of the Englishman – how would he act? If I can trust my own experience in this matter, not one in ten would follow the example of the Englishman.

[14] For an argument along these lines, see Huang 2003. Huang argues that civil law systems should adopt American-style discovery and a preponderance-of-evidence burden of proof like the American one in order to foster law enforcement by litigation.

seemingly regulatory aspect at least to recent developments in EU Member States and the European Parliament (Strong 2012). Whether that proves true, and whether it might hold true for other features of litigation, may depend on the goals European countries have for litigation going forward.

One major feature of American litigation is that the stakes are higher. In part, that is due to the reliance (at least in theory) on juries – the ultimate private enforcement device, in a way. For some, reliance on jury trial is a critical feature of American civil litigation that is under threat because jury trials have become much less frequent than they were 50 or 100 years ago. Professors Burbank and Subrin, for example, argue that jury trials are 'constitutive of American democracy' (Burbank and Subrin 2011: 401). This peculiar feature of American procedure seems unlikely to spread even if it is rejuvenated in the U.S.

In another way, the higher stakes in American litigation are due to the prospect of large recoveries in many cases for pain and suffering and perhaps also for punitive damages. In yet another way, the stakes depend on the American Rule that each side must bear its attorneys' fees, win or lose. That rule – which some in this country call the 'only in America' rule – flows from the goal of facilitating private enforcement by protecting those who file lawsuits against ruinous liability if they lose. It may be that other countries would not follow where the U.S. has led on these subjects either.

But for our purposes, the most salient aspect is the magnetic force of private enforcement on relaxing burdens on plaintiffs. The relaxed 'notice pleading' requirements seemed designed to facilitate the commencement of suits. Although the American system expected that those who sue would first investigate and file suit only if they had a legitimate basis,[15] the American version of what the plaintiff must include in the complaint is notably less exacting than that used in the rest of the world.[16] Indeed, at least until recently the American formulation appeared almost to forbid dismissal on the pleadings.[17] There seems scant reason to expect that the rest of the world is moving rapidly toward the American

[15] See Fed. R. Civ. P. 11(b)(3) (requiring that factual contentions have evidentiary support, or be likely to have such support after discovery).

[16] Compare Rule 12, of the proposed Transnational Rules of Civil Procedure, ALI/UNIDROIT, Principles of Transnational Civil Procedure (Cambridge, New York, Madrid, Cape Town, Singapore, São Paulo, 2006) at 111, requiring that plaintiff state the facts and describe the evidence supporting the claim. Surely the actual pleading requirements vary from country to country, but the Principles' adamant rejection of 'notice pleading' strongly shows that there is a stark division between the U.S. model and the approach of the rest of the world.

[17] See Conley v. Gibson, 355 U.S. 41, 41, 45 (1957). The Court there said: 'we follow, of course, the accepted rule that a complaint should not be dismissed for failure to state a claim unless it appears beyond doubt that the plaintiff can prove no set of facts to support his claim which would entitle him to relief.' This formulation makes it sound like the plaintiff can ward off dismissal by saying nothing in the complaint. As Professor Hazard observed, 'Conley v. Gibson turned Rule 8 [the Federal Rule prescribing what a complaint must contain] on its head by holding that a claim is insufficient only if the insufficiency appears from the pleading itself' (Hazard 1998: 1685).

approach. To the contrary, there is some indication that the U.S. Supreme Court's movement toward requiring that claims be 'plausible' can be viewed as a shift toward the view of the rest of the world.[18]

More strikingly from the perspective of the rest of the world, the U.S. permits plaintiffs (and defendants) extremely broad discovery. As Professor Hazard has observed, in the U.S. '[b]road discovery is thus not a mere procedural rule. Rather it has become, at least in our era, a procedural institution perhaps of virtually constitutional foundation' (Hazard 1998: 1694). As Dean Carrington has explained, this attitude connects directly to the American election to rely on private enforcement: 'We should keep clearly in mind that discovery is the American alternative to the administrative state.... Private litigants do in America much of what is done in other industrial states by public officers working within an administrative bureaucracy' (Carrington 1997: 54). In order to enable them to do that work, discovery is broad gauged. 'Unless corresponding new powers are conferred on public officers,' Carrington adds, in America 'constricting discovery would diminish the disincentives for lawless behavior across a wide spectrum of forbidden conduct.'

The constitutional status of the right to jury trial also fits into this picture. Adjudicating cases using 'reasonableness' standards depends not on a professional judiciary, but instead on a lay jury:

> [M]any legal norms need community input for the decisions applying them to be accepted by the community. Issues such as negligence, intentional discrimination, material breach of contract, and unfair competition are not facts capable of scientific demonstration. Nor are these issues pure questions of law. Rather, they are concepts mixing elements of fact and law that become legitimate behavioral norms when the citizenry at large, acting through jury representatives, decides what the community deems acceptable (Burbank and Subrin 2011: 401–02).

And because there is a right to a jury trial, the judge cannot 'take the case from the jury' except in extraordinary circumstances.

None of these aspects of American procedure is intrinsically a feature of common law, as opposed to civil law, systems. In England, for example, Professor Zuckerman explains that '[j]ury trial declined [in the 19th century] because it was not being asked for' (Zuckerman 2003: 357 n.2). The American political commitment to the jury trial remains vibrant, in theory, even though the civil jury trial is becoming increasingly rare. More generally, as we can see, American exceptionalism depends largely on its embrace of the private enforcement goal.

[18] See Bell Atlantic Corp. v. Twombly, 550 U.S. 544 (2007) (requiring that antitrust complaint be 'plausible' before case can proceed to discovery); Ashcroft v. Iqbal, 556 U.S. 662 (2009) (rejecting claims against U.S. Attorney General and Director of the F.B.I. by mistreated prisoner on the ground that it was not 'plausible' that they were motivated by religious bias in authorizing wide investigation after the attacks of September 11, 2001).

6.6 'Easy' Problems Contrasted – Other Issues That Preoccupy Proceduralists

Much therefore flows from the choice of goals for a civil justice system, as already shown. But for many other things, there is no need to tarry long in terms of procedural design. For example, cost and delay are perennial concerns of proceduralists. But nobody is in favor of magnifying either as a matter of procedural design. Similarly, everyone is in favor of accuracy and efficiency, but these concepts need to be measured against one another. Recently in the common law world the notion of 'proportionality' has gained a considerable following. It makes abundant sense – the expenditure on litigation should be reasonable in light of the stakes. That notion was installed in the American discovery rules more than 25 years ago.[19] Professor Andrews tells us that Lord Woolf's reforms made proportionality a 'pillar' of modern English procedure (Andrews 2003: §§ 2.25–39) And Professor Piche has recently explored the vigorous adoption of proportionality in Quebec (Piche 2012). But the much higher stakes of American litigation make much higher costs 'proportional' in that litigation.

The challenge with these 'easy' principles is not so much one of determining whether they fit in general with the goals of civil justice, for both of them obviously do. But the hard part is determining how given principles should be balanced against one another in designing a procedural system. Instead, as in the U.S., one can build both into the system and leave it to judges to decide how they should be applied in specific cases when one side invokes one principle ('allowing me discovery will be efficient because it will provide a basis for deciding the case') and the opposing side invokes another one ('allowing discovery will be hugely expensive and won't produce anything of value'). Those individual determinations can be quite difficult, expensive, and time-consuming. They can also seem somewhat inconsistent with one another.

In the background lies the specter that haunts the American system – that the financial cost and other burdens of civil litigation will subvert the rights of the parties. This concern is raised most often from the defense side, relying on assertions that the cost of broad American discovery forces defendants to settle meritless cases because settling is cheaper than litigating successfully.

Many suggest that a loser pays rule would go far toward rectifying this situation, but that cuts against the American reliance on private enforcement; the fact that a plaintiff does not ordinarily risk paying for the defendant's lawyer makes the American contingency fee system work. But is important to appreciate that frustrating the merits due to cost afflicts prospective plaintiffs also, for the American Rule means they have to find a lawyer who will take their case for a share of the (contingent) recovery; regularly today we are told that it is too costly to litigate a claim for less than $100,000 in the American federal courts. For *all* categories of litigants, there is

---

[19] See, e.g., Fed. R. Civ. P. 26(b)(2)(C) (directing the court to curtail disproportional discovery).

an argument that the procedures justified by the private enforcement goal must be tempered to avoid defeating that goal.

With due respect, it is also worth noting that the less forgiving procedures of other countries may often defeat valid claims. A prospective plaintiff who lacks the means to assemble essential evidence without governmental assistance via discovery or otherwise may simply be denied relief even though the claim is actually fully justified. Easy access to court, as permitted in America, may for many claimants be the *only* real access to justice, and preventing this private enforcement may significantly erode legal protections for all.

6.7 Retreat from Private Enforcement?

As already indicated, the American commitment to private enforcement lies at the heart of many of the 'exceptional' features of its procedure. Put differently, this goal has shaped American 'exceptionalism.' And there is a suggestion that something like private enforcement could come to the fore in Europe (Keleman 2011: chp. 1).

But whatever the evolution toward private enforcement elsewhere, it is surely under challenge in America. For example, Professor Redish has denounced punitive damage awards (another American phenomenon widely decried in the rest of the world) as a violation of liberal democratic theory. He explains that 'the concept of punitive damages represents a perverse transfer of what is inherently public power to private individuals' (Redish and Mathews 2004: 3).

Class actions have become a more frequent focus of this sort of critique in recent years in the U.S., however, as illustrated by a Supreme Court decision in June 2013. As Professor Stadler recognized (Stadler 2010: 81), the problem of the small claims class action is a serious one. In the U.S., that problem is known as the 'negative value' class action – a case in which the claims are not large enough to support the cost of bringing the lawsuit.[20]

A central problem for the private enforcement idea is that the cost of litigation may often be much larger than the damages recoverable for violation of many of the laws American legislators want private litigation to enforce, such as regulations for loan terms or restaurants' disclosure of credit card numbers. American legislatures often respond to this problem by authorizing recovery of attorney fees for successful plaintiffs. Professor Farhang uses these features as indicia that the legislature sought to empower private enforcement (Farhang 2011: chp. 3). Despite those legislative efforts, additional costs or other obstacles may prevent effective private vindication.

[20] See In Re Monumental Life Ins. Co., 365 F. 3d 408 (5th Cir. 2004), which describes the case as 'what may be the ultimate negative value class action lawsuit' because the individual recoveries would be quite small but the cost of proving the case would be quite high. Perhaps an even better example would be Eisen v. Carlisle & Jacquelin, 417 U.S. 156 (1974), in which the claims of class members averaged about $100, but the Court held that Rule 23 required that the class representative had to shoulder the full cost of giving notice to all six million class members.

That sort of concern was before the U.S. Supreme Court in *American Express Co. v. Italian Colors Restaurant*,[21] an antitrust action in which plaintiff sought to recover $12,850, an amount that would be trebled to $38,550 under the 'treble damages' feature of the Clayton Antitrust Act if plaintiff won. The Act also provides that a successful plaintiff can recover its attorney fees. But attorney fee recoveries do not include the cost of expert witnesses, and the cost of hiring an economics expert to prove this antitrust claim would likely amount to about $1 million. As a result, according to plaintiff, the only way to sue effectively would be in a class action that would offer the possibility of a much larger recovery from which a percentage attorney fee could justify the lawyers' investment in an expert opinion. But American Express (the defendant) had inserted an arbitration clause in its contract with plaintiff that forbade class action arbitration. The question before the Court was whether the arbitration agreement should be enforced even though it might frustrate antitrust enforcement.

Dissenting Justices emphasized that 'Congress created the Sherman Act's private cause of action [by adopting the Clayton Act] not solely to compensate individuals but to promote "the public interest in vigilant enforcement of the antitrust laws."' Therefore, under the 'effective vindication rule,' the dissenters thought that the arbitration clause should not be enforceable because the Clayton Act's provisions would not provide meaningful relief. But the majority rejected this argument and held the clause enforceable, reasoning that 'the antitrust laws do not guarantee an affordable procedural path to the vindication of every claim.' The distinctive American goal has thus been challenged from on high, and also from other sources (e.g., Beisner et al. 2005). This relatively recent development may mean that a path to more complete American procedural harmonization with the rest of the world could open up because of a recalibration of proper goals for U.S. procedure.[22]

One must be cautious, however, about predicting any major revision of the goals of American procedure to remove their exceptional aspects. The Supreme Court's recent decisions curtailing class actions in some circumstances seem largely to reflect antagonism with the class action in particular, not the whole fabric of American exceptionalism. Moreover, these decisions were close decisions, generally by 5–4 votes. The multitude of statutory authorizations for private suits do not depend on class-action status. For example, the huge number of employment discrimination suits are almost all individual actions. The 'public interest' bar that promotes such litigation is vigilant and well financed. It will not soon go away. Legislatures that have sought to encourage private enforcement may fortify it more if confronted with broader judicial resistance. In short, even

[21] 133 S.Ct. 2304 (2013).

[22] There has, in fact, been a fairly broad-based challenge to the precepts of a number of distinctive American litigation characteristics, led most prominently by Professor Redish. His challenge relies on democratic theory for the proposition that all consequential legal determinations should be made by institutions that are accountable to the voters, and from this premise concludes that many U.S. doctrines that were adopted by judges lack legitimacy. For a critique of this approach, see Marcus 2013.

though the exceptional private enforcement goal of American procedure may have been challenged on its home ground, that challenge is not likely to win broad immediate acceptance.

6.8 Concluding Observations

America's procedural goals seem to have emerged gradually rather than being identified in advance and used to guide the framers in designing specific procedures. At least the framers did not say their plan in developing the new procedures was to pursue new goals that were hardly well known in the 1930s, when the new procedures were introduced. In retrospect, it seems that the private enforcement orientation grew somewhat organically over the twentieth century, mainly after the new procedural regime had been put in place.

It is impossible to say whether private enforcement would have emerged as a prominent feature of American civil litigation if the procedural reforms of the 1930s had not occurred. But it is also clear that conscious resistance to public enforcement sometimes contributed to the inclination to rely on private enforcement, as illustrated most graphically with the Title VII experience. More broadly, that orientation responded to an abiding American antipathy toward governmental activism coupled with growing enthusiasm for governmental protections against risks and improper behavior. Without necessarily engaging in penetrating analysis of what they were doing, American governmental institutions hit on empowering private enforcement as a technique for doing what the American people seemed to want. That orientation was peculiarly suited to, and probably quite dependent upon, American procedural exceptionalism.

So it turns out that much flows from the choice of goals of civil litigation. American procedure is exceptional because American procedural goals are exceptional. Whether that current reality is the result of careful and consistent choices about procedures seems secondary. The goal of public enforcement largely emerged after World War II, and there has recently been an effort in the U.S. to discredit the goal of private enforcement that seems now to explain so much about American procedure that baffles the rest of the world. Not surprisingly, those who challenge the private enforcement goal in the U.S. also seem to want to dismantle the procedural apparatus that supports it. Although it is difficult to claim that the current situation resulted from a consistent or coherent evolution, rather than happenstance, it is easier to say that strong interests favor preserving important features of this current arrangement because it serves distinctive American goals.[23] Those goals may change, but it is not clear that they will.

---

[23] Some in America denounce the effects of the private enforcement view as subverting the need to provide simpler, less costly procedures. A prominent and important example is Professor Maxeiner, who regards the complexities of American procedure as resulting from appropriation of contemporary litigation under the banner of public enforcement but actually for the primary

The absence of a comparable private enforcement goal probably helps explain why the procedures of the rest of the world differ so markedly from America's. But for the rest of the world, the goals might change also. One possibility is that something like American private enforcement might achieve a foothold in Europe, if Professor Keleman's predictions prove correct. Another is that European attitudes like those articulated by Professor von Jhering might achieve sway in the twenty-first century where they did not prevail in the nineteenth. If the power of states declines in the Information Age, that development could support a shift toward an American approach to private enforcement, which enables governmental protections to be enforced without a big government to do so.

Changing goals is rare and difficult, however. So there is a relatively small likelihood that either America or the rest of the world will actually change direction dramatically. For the present, it therefore seems likely that the distinctive American goals will continue to engage Americans, and the distinctive American procedures will remain in place. As a result, although both Americans and others will also seek to reduce cost and delay by improving efficiency and encouraging proportional use of procedure, the values they apply to those judgments will be quite different.

References

Andrews N (2003) English civil procedure. Oxford University Press, Oxford/New York

Beisner J, Shors M, Davidson J (2005) Class action "Cops": public servants or private entrepreneurs? Stanford Law Rev 57:1441–1473

Bentham J (1843) Principles of judicial procedures, with the outlines of a procedure code. The works of Jeremy Bentham, vol 2. William Tait, Edinburgh

Brunet E (1987) Questioning the quality of alternative dispute resolution. Tulane Law Rev 62:1–56

Burbank S, Subrin S (2011) Litigation and democracy: restoring a realistic prospect of trial. Harv Civil Rights Civil Lib Law Rev 46:399–414

Carrington P (1997) Renovating discovery. Ala Law Rev 49:51–78

Chung J (2009) SEC to enlist help on fraud. Financial Times, 1 April 2009, p 15

Damaška M (1986) The faces of justice and state authority. Yale University Press, New Haven/London

Dworkin R (1985) Principle, policy, procedure. In: A matter of principle. Harvard University Press, Cambridge, MA/London

Edwards H (1986) Alternative dispute resolution: panacea or anathema? Harv Law Rev 99:668–684

Farhang S (2010) The Litigation state. Princeton University Press, Princeton

Fiss O (1984) Against settlement. Yale Law J 93:1073–1090

Hazard G (1998) From whom no secrets are kept. Texas Law Rev 76:1665–1694

benefits of American lawyers. See Maxeiner 2011: 265–68. As he recognizes there, however, his view is a dissent from the widely-shared American academic consensus that public enforcement is a distinctive and central feature of American procedure. Thus, Professor Maxeiner quotes Professors Subrin, Woo, and Carrington and then explains that he does not accept their arguments. I am not disagreeing with those professors.

Hodges C (2008) The reform of class and representative actions in European legal systems. Oxford University Press, Oxford/Portland
Huang K-C (2003) Introducing discovery into civil law. Carolina Academic Press, Durham
Issacharoff S, Klonoff R (2009) The public value of settlement. Fordham Law Rev 78:1177–1202
Kagan R (2001) Adversarial legalism: the American way of law. Harvard University Press, Cambridge/London
Keleman RD (2011) Eurolegalism. Harvard University Press, Cambridge/London
Lind E, Tyler T (1988) The social psychology of procedural justice. Plenum Press, New York/London
Maine H (1907) Early law and custom. John Murray, London
Marcus R (2013) Bomb throwing, democratic theory, and basic values – a new path to procedural harmonization? Northwestern Law Rev 107:475–510
Mashaw J (1976) The Supreme Court's due process calculus for administrative adjudication in Mathews v. Eldridge. Univ Chicago Law Rev 44:28–59
Maxeiner J (2011) Failures of American justice in international perspective. Cambridge University Press, Cambridge/New York
Michelman (1973) The Supreme court and litigation access fees: the right to protect one's rights. Duke Law J:1153–1215
Millar R (1951) Civil procedure in the trial court in historical perspective. Law Center of New York University, New York
Piche C (2012) Figures, spaces, and procedural proportionality. Int J Proced Law 2:145–166
Posner RA (1986) Economic analysis of law, 3rd edn. Little, Brown and Company, Boston
Redish M, Mathews A (2004) Why punitive damages are unconstitutional. Emory Law Rev 53:1–53
Scott R (1975) Two models of the civil process. Stanford Law Rev 27:937–950
Stadler A (2010) Aggregate litigation – group/class actions in Germany. In: Gottwald P (ed) Litigation in England and Germany. GieseKing, Bielefeld
Strong S (2012) Regulatory litigation in the European UNION: does the U.S. class action have a new analogue? Notre Dame Law Rev 88:899–971
Von Jhering R (1915) The struggle for law. Callaghan & Co., Chicago
Zuckerman A (2003) Civil procedure. LexisNexis UK, London

Chapter 7
Civil Justice with Multiple Objectives

The Unique Path of Hong Kong's Civil Justice Reform

Peter C.H. Chan and David Chan

Abstract Litigants in Hong Kong had once endured a justice system that was both inefficient and unreasonably costly. Courts focused on substantive justice in the individual case and ignored broader concerns that are relevant in the delivery of overall justice to all. Undue delay, excessive litigation costs and other problems arising from an overly adversarial tradition threatened access to justice. The Civil Justice Reform in 2009 sought to change all that by introducing a reform agenda with multiple objectives, ranging from active judicial case management to the encouragement of settlement. While the adversarial principle is preserved, the excesses of adversarial proceedings once witnessed in the past are now curbed by the powerful case manager – the court. Aided by new procedural tools, courts make it their duty to achieve efficiency and cost-effectiveness in litigation. Procedural deadlines are strictly enforced and parties (concerned with the prospect of the court imposing an adverse costs order) would almost always attempt mediation. This chapter explores procedural aspects of the doctrinal shift in the administration of justice in Hong Kong since the Civil Justice Reform and examines the results of the reform. It also explores other goals of civil justice, such as the judiciary's attention to public interest as a goal of civil justice.

P.C.H. Chan (✉)
School of Law, City University of Hong Kong, Tat Chee Avenue, Hong Kong, China
e-mail: pchchan@cityu.edu.hk

D. Chan
Barrister-at-law, Hong Kong, Rooms 1323A-1328, Prince's Building,
10 Chater Road, Central, Hong Kong, China
e-mail: evadchan@netvigator.com

A. Uzelac (ed.), *Goals of Civil Justice and Civil Procedure in Contemporary Judicial Systems*, Ius Gentium: Comparative Perspectives on Law and Justice 34,
DOI 10.1007/978-3-319-03443-0_7,

7.1 Introduction

7.1.1 From a Single Predominant Objective to Multiple Objectives of Equal Importance

The Civil Justice Reform (CJR), which came into effect in April 2009, transformed the litigation landscape in Hong Kong. Before the CJR, the predominant objective of civil justice was almost completely about the pursuit of substantive justice in each individual case. Judges remained inactive and passive on matters of case management. Procedural deadlines were rarely observed, resulting in undue delay (Chief Justice's Working Party on Civil Justice Reform 2001: 2; Legislative Council Panel on Administration of Justice and Legal Services 2011: 1). Lawsuits were excessively lengthy with parties sometimes deliberately delaying the process for tactical purposes. In this kind of litigation landscape, procedural efficiency gave way to the overarching notion of 'justice on the merits' (Zuckerman 2009: 60–62 and 71).[1] Mediation was not specifically promoted by the courts as a core objective. Settlement was often left to the last minute before trial when most costs had already been incurred (Ma 2010: 5). Excessive litigation costs became a barrier to access to justice in Hong Kong (Chief Justice's Working Party on Civil Justice Reform 2001: 17). In some cases, the costs far exceeded the value of the claim. The problems encountered in Hong Kong were seen in other common law jurisdictions, such as England and Singapore.

Policy-makers began to notice the ramifications of the excesses of the adversarial system and the deficiency of a justice system that emphasized almost entirely the pursuit of substantive justice in each individual case. They realized that cost-effectiveness in the general management of the system, procedural expediency through strict enforcement of deadlines, a fair distribution of judicial resources and the optimal use of mediation were important notions for the overall success of any civil justice regime. It was against this background that the CJR was born, marking Hong Kong's transition from a system with a single predominant objective to a system that embraces multiple objectives of equal importance (Zuckerman 2009: 49).

This chapter critically examines the results of the CJR in the context of the goals of civil justice.

---

[1] The 'justice on the merits' approach is best encapsulated in *Birkett v. James* [1978] AC 297; Zuckerman (2009: 61) commented on the impact of this approach on civil litigation: 'The consequences of this approach were inevitable: a weakening of the normative force of the time limits, for litigants could rest assured that failure to comply with time limits would have no serious consequences for their case except in the most extreme situations. Even disobedience of peremptory orders i.e. "unless orders" on pain of specified sanctions would rarely have adverse consequences.'

7.1.2 Hong Kong's Unique Path of Reform: The Selective Adoption of the Woolf Reforms

One of the defining differences between the CJR in Hong Kong and the Woolf Reforms in England is that the CJR has been implemented by way of amendment to the Rules of the High Court (RHC) rather than by adopting an entirely new procedural code along the lines of the Civil Procedure Rules in England (CPR) (Chief Justice's Working Party on Civil Justice Reform 2004: 19).[2] While drawing inspiration from the English Woolf Reforms, the Chief Justice's Working Party on Civil Justice Reform (Working Party), for practical reasons, specifically rejected the adoption of an entirely new civil procedural code and instead favoured the selective adoption of reform measures.[3] It was argued by the Working Party that by cherry-picking, Hong Kong could benefit from reform measures that worked well in England (and in other common law jurisdictions) (Chan and Rogers 2013: 37)[4] and avoid 'the pitfalls revealed by the CPR experience, for example, in respect of measures carrying front-loaded costs' (Chief Justice's Working Party on Civil Justice Reform 2004: 16).[5] Further, the approach adopted by the Working Party tries 'to form a realistic view of the benefits likely to be achievable under local conditions' and asks 'whether such benefits can be achieved with less effort than by introduction of an entirely new code' (Chief Justice's Working Party on Civil Justice Reform 2004: 16). An example of a Woolf Reforms measure not adopted in the CJR is the use of pre-action protocols prescribed for all cases (i.e. by a general protocol) (Chief Justice's Working Party on Civil Justice Reform 2004: 73).[6] Apart from specific Woolf Reforms measures being rejected in the CJR, the level and methodology of adoption of key Woolf Reforms principles in the CJR also distinguishes Hong Kong from the English experience. For instance, reasonable proportionality is an underlying objective under the CJR in Hong Kong.[7] The Working Party did not follow the specificity of CPR 1.1(2)(c) in the English system given its tendency to generate 'uncertainty as to how it should be applied' (Chief Justice's Working Party on Civil

[2] See Recommendation 1.

[3] The Working Party cited the following (among other reasons) for rejecting the proposal to adopt an entirely new procedural code (Chief Justice's Working Party on Civil Justice Reform 2004: 15): 'If, for example, we were to adopt the CPR, every member of the legal community would have to learn not only what changes have been made and what new measures introduced, but also the new terminology and where exactly in the new rules equivalents – if they exist – of procedures presently contained in the Orders of the RHC are to be found. They would also have to familiarise themselves with the case-law that has developed in relation to the CPR in England and Wales and discard much of the familiar case-law illuminating the RHC.'

[4] See para. 1A/0/2.

[5] For example, reasons were given for the non-adoption of the pre-action protocols (Chief Justice's Working Party on Civil Justice Reform 2004: 58–73).

[6] See Recommendation 5.

[7] RHC O. 1A, r. 1(c).

Justice Reform 2004: 51).[8] Instead, the Working Party preferred it to be 'a reminder that commonsense notions of reasonableness and a sense of proportion should inform the exercise of a judicial discretion in the procedural context', while noting that elements of the proportionality principle have already been reflected in the existing procedural rules (Chief Justice's Working Party on Civil Justice Reform 2004: 53–54).[9]

7.2 Prevailing Opinions on the Goals of Civil Justice

After April 2009, the prevailing opinions on the goals of civil justice surround the CJR, in particular the underlying objectives set out in the amended RHC which guide the exercise of procedural discretion of courts.[10] The parties to any proceedings and their legal representatives must assist the court to further the underlying objectives.[11] In *Chevalier (Construction) Co Ltd v. Tak Cheong Engineering Development Ltd*,[12] Lam J (as he then was) referred to an observation made in an English case that civil justice is a 'co-operative process to which solicitors, counsel and judges all make their contributions'.[13] Implementing the underlying objectives has become the core goal of civil justice in Hong Kong.

The CJR targeted the excesses of the adversarial system (such as undue delay and excessive complexities within the system) and sought to improve the cost-effectiveness of Hong Kong's civil procedure without changing the fundamental adversarial nature of proceedings. The reform was 'subject to the fundamental requirements of procedural and substantive justice' (Chief Justice's Working Party on Civil Justice Reform 2004: 19).[14] As a result of the CJR, there has been a qualitative shift in the Hong Kong civil justice system from the predominant emphasis on 'justice on the merits' (or substantive justice) to a 'three-dimensional concept of justice' under which 'efficiency and expedition are as important as the correctness

---

[8] See para. 102.

[9] See paras. 105 and 106.

[10] RHC O. 1A, r. 1 reads:

'The underlying objectives of these rules are –

(a) to increase the cost-effectiveness of any practice and procedure to be followed in relation to proceedings before the Court;
(b) to ensure that a case is dealt with as expeditiously as is reasonably practicable;
(c) to promote a sense of reasonable proportion and procedural economy in the conduct of proceedings;
(d) to ensure fairness between the parties;
(e) to facilitate the settlement of disputes; and
(f) to ensure that the resources of the Court are distributed fairly.'

[11] RHC O. 1A, r. 3.

[12] HCA 153/2008, 23 February 2011.

[13] HCA 153/2008, paras. 20–21.

[14] See paras. 31 and 34.

of the outcome' (Zuckerman 2009: 49 and 71). The goal of civil justice has transcended the search for pure substantive justice and embraced a multi-faceted agenda to (among others) promote efficiency and reasonable proportionality, as well as to encourage settlement. To achieve this agenda, extensive case management powers were conferred on the judge.[15] The judge may exercise these powers on application or of his or her own motion.[16] The new judicial case management regime encompasses both procedural powers[17] and substantive powers[18] of case management.[19]

The CJR is by no means a shift to the inquisitorial approach. Parties are still actively involved in an ordinary civil lawsuit. The principle of party-presentation is deeply entrenched. What the CJR has done is to curtail the 'excesses' of the adversarial system and concurrently retain 'the best features of the adversarial system' (Legislative Council Panel on Administration of Justice and Legal Services 2010: 1).[20] An example of this philosophy at work is discovery.[21]

Zuckerman argued, 'The civil court provides a law enforcement service. The role of the civil court is not merely to mediate disputes but to give effect to our rights and enforce them' (2009: 53). It is unrealistic to devote every possible resource to a particular case regardless of its importance. To effectively discharge its public function, the court must distribute resources fairly and appropriately (2009: 53–54).[22] The system must reduce the overall cost and time of litigation by encouraging ADR, active judicial case management and a continued effort to streamline procedures. The saved cost and time can be devoted to the improvement of the overall quality of adjudication (2009: 56–57). Zuckerman further observed that a 'public service will be considered adequate if it is effective, efficient and fair', which he described as the 'three imperatives' of any public service (2009: 54). He added, 'Justice is a finite commodity that has to be distributed fairly amongst all' (2009: 68). Hong Kong civil justice aspires to strike a delicate balance in judicial case management to achieve these imperatives.

The extent to which the underlying objectives could be enforced depends largely on the court's exercise of its discretion (Zuckerman 2009: 56). The court must be bold and principle-centred in exercising its case management discretion and enforce procedural deadlines (Zuckerman 2009: 62–69). If the court is not determined

[15] RHC O. 1B, r. 1.

[16] RHC O. 1B, r. 2.

[17] For instance, the power to adjourn or bring forward a hearing: RHC O. 1B, r.1(2)(b).

[18] For instance, the power to exclude an issue from consideration: RHC O. 1B, r.1(2)(j).

[19] Despite the express conferral of extensive case management powers on the court, the Working Party warned, 'It should, however, be made clear that the Working Party is not in favour of unwarranted proactivity by the court. The case management powers are there to curb the excesses of the adversarial system, not to displace that system' (Chief Justice's Working Party on Civil Justice Reform 2004: 55).

[20] See para. 3.

[21] As the Working Party recommends, a modified regime of discovery should aim at enforcing compliance with the present rules instead of narrowing the scope of discovery (Chief Justice's Working Party on Civil Justice Reform 2004: 246).

[22] Also see RHC O. 1A, r. 1(f).

enough to enforce deadlines and too readily grants relief from sanctions, the old problem of delay would continue (Zuckerman 2009: 70). Courts in Hong Kong are generally determined in enforcing deadlines after the CJR. 'Unless orders' (i.e. peremptory orders) are now more commonly made by judges as compared to the past (when an unless order would be imposed only after multiple delays or applications for extension of time).[23] In *Nanjing Iron & Steel Group International Trade Co Ltd and others v. STX Pan Ocean Co Ltd and others*,[24] the Court of First Instance (CFI) struck out the plaintiff's claim for inordinate delay on the basis that such a delay[25] was contrary to the underlying objectives.[26] The Court of Final Appeal (CFA) elaborated on the test for striking out for want of prosecution in *The Liquidator of Wing Fai Construction Company Limited (in compulsory liquidation) v. Yip Kwong Robert*.[27] The CFA stated that Reyes J (as he then was) in *Nanjing Iron & Steel Group International Trade Co Ltd* 'was not saying that simply because the delay was both inordinate and inexcusable, this was somehow enough to justify a striking out order being made.'[28] It must be founded on the abuse of the process of the court, namely that the 'delay causes a substantial risk that a fair trial is not possible'.[29] It is reiterated by the CFA that with the 'combination of greater case management by the courts' and 'peremptory orders more readily made', 'applications to strike out for want of prosecution, should now be consigned to history'.[30] However, where such application is made for the 'straddle' cases,[31] striking out for want of prosecution 'should only be used in plain and obvious cases' and 'must be a remedy of last resort'.[32]

---

[23] *The Liquidator of Wing Fai Construction Company Limited (in compulsory liquidation) v. Yip Kwong Robert* (FACV 3/2011, 8 December 2011), at para. 32(5)(b), p. 14. In breach of the 'unless order', parties are prohibited from proceeding with the matter, i.e. filing of the defence, which inevitably would result in judgment on liability against the defendant.

[24] HCAJ 177/2006.

[25] In this case, 2 years passed after the commencement of court proceedings.

[26] In the judgment, Reyes J said: 'Under the present CJR regime, that would seem to me to be sufficient cause to strike out the claim. In the absence of some compelling reason, it is contrary to the underlying objective in Order 1A, Rule 1(b) ("to ensure that a case is dealt with as expeditiously as is reasonably practicable") for a party to allow an action to languish for 2 years once the same has been commenced. I am unable to see any compelling reason in this case. There simply is no excuse for such a long delay.'

See HCAJ 177/2006, para. 13.

[27] FACV 3/2011, 8 December 2011.

[28] FACV 3/2011, para. 75(6), 31.

[29] FACV 3/2011, paras. 75(2) and 75(3), 29.

[30] FACV 3/2011, paras. 70–72, 28.

[31] Cases that were commenced prior to the CJR taking effect.

[32] FACV 3/2011, paras. 65, 69 and 75(6), 31. Non-expiry of the limitation period, a factor which used to militate against an order for striking out under *Birkett v. James* [1978] AC 279, is no longer relevant consideration under the CJR. The first author had previously argued (Chan 2011: 194): '*Birkett v. James* contradicts the spirit underpinning the CJR. While the CFA is reluctant to overrule *Birkett v. James* altogether, it does not change the fact that the CJR signifies a fundamental change in the concept of civil justice ... So while *Birkett v. James* remains technically "good law",

7.3 Matters Regarded to Be Within the Scope of the Goals of Civil Justice: Non-contested Matters (e.g. ADR, Enforcement)

The goals of civil justice are not strictly limited to litigation. The Hong Kong courts consider non-contested matters (such as enforcement and ADR) to be of great significance.

The civil justice system in Hong Kong encourages ADR.[33] The successful resolution of disputes through ADR saves costs and time. It also helps preserve the future relationship between the parties. Under Practice Direction 31 (PD 31), procedures are in place to encourage parties to settle their disputes through mediation. Settlement negotiation by itself does not amount to ADR and PD 31 applies to mediation only.[34] The court may impose an adverse costs order on the successful party that had unreasonably refused to submit to mediation. PD 31 states, 'In exercising its discretion on costs, the Court takes into account all relevant circumstances. These would include any unreasonable failure of a party to engage in mediation where this can be established by admissible materials'.[35] The court, however, will not make any adverse costs order where the party has engaged in mediation to the minimum level of participation agreed to by the parties or as directed by the court prior to the mediation, or where the party has a reasonable explanation for not engaging in mediation.[36] In exercising this discretion, the court is guided by PD 31 and case law. The leading case is *Halsey v. Milton Keynes General NHS Trust*,[37] in which the English Court of Appeal held:

> In deciding whether to deprive a successful party of some or all of his costs on the grounds that he has refused to agree to ADR, it must be borne in mind that such an order is an exception to the general rule that costs should follow the event. In our view, the burden is on the unsuccessful party to show why there should be a departure from the general rule. The fundamental principle is that such departure is not justified unless it is shown (the burden being on the unsuccessful party) that the successful party acted unreasonably in refusing to agree to ADR.[38]

Halsey highlighted a number of factors that may be relevant when determining whether a refusal to mediate was unreasonable.[39] The court is only entitled to con-

---

it should have very limited application (i.e. only for "straddle" cases). This relic of the past should not prevent the courts from dispensing with the old notion of "justice on the merits" ... Wherever the rules allow flexibility, discretion must be exercised in such a way that best promote the underlying objectives. Anything otherwise would defeat the purpose of the CJR.'

[33] RHC O. 1A, rr. 1(e), 4(2)(e) and 4(2)(f).

[34] Para. 3 of PD 31.

[35] Para. 4 of PD 31; also see RHC O. 62, r. 5(1)(aa).

[36] Para. 5 of PD 31.

[37] [2004] 1 WLR 3002.

[38] See [2004] 1 WLR 3002, 3009.

[39] [2004] 1 WLR 3002, 3009.

sider statements made in the mediation certificate on the question of costs.[40] Stakeholders generally regard the PD 31 regime as effective (Chan et al. 2014 forthcoming):

> An experienced mediator is of the view that the use of mediation does not prolong delays, especially if the case is suitable for mediation. He is also of the view that the mediators are generally skilful and the parties are willing and committed to resolving their disputes by mediation. A leading litigation practitioner commented that, after the CJR, the court is more successful than before in facilitating settlement. Under the new environment, parties are much more active in considering settlement (usually through mediation) at an early stage of proceedings. This increases the likelihood of settlement.

Hong Kong civil procedure takes enforcement seriously. Depending on the nature of the judgment, a plethora of enforcement measures are available in the event that the unsuccessful party refuses to comply with the judgment (Wilkinson, Cheung and Booth 2011: 851), for example, writ of *fieri facias*,[41] garnishee order,[42] and charging orders.[43] These enforcement measures can be used concurrently (Wilkinson, Cheung and Booth 2011: 851).

7.4 Protection of Individual Rights v. Protection of Public Interest

7.4.1 Attention to Public Interest as a Goal of Civil Justice

7.4.1.1 Public Interest Litigation

Public interest litigation in Hong Kong takes the form of judicial review.[44] The debate focuses on the extent to which the court should adjudicate on matters concerning public interests (such as environmental protection) when cases of this nature inevitably overlap with the political domain (Kong 2009: 328). It is observed that 'there is a growing trend in the use of judicial review applications by NGOs and political activists as a means of raising public concern and framing political issues in terms of legal entitlements' (Kong 2009: 328).

---

[40] *Bhana, Angela Mary v. Ocean Apex Trading Limited* (1732/2009). By way of background, the court will receive a mediation certificate that provides information on (a) whether or not the plaintiff or defendant was willing to attempt mediation with the view of settlement; and (b) if the plaintiff or defendant was unwilling to attempt mediation, the reasons for not willing to do so.

[41] RHC O. 47, for seizure and sale of personal chattels.

[42] RHC O. 49, for application of any debt due or accruing due to the judgment debtor from the garnishee in satisfaction of the judgment debt.

[43] RHC O. 50, as security created over shares, stocks and landed property beneficially owned by the judgment debtor.

[44] RHC O. 53.

7.4.1.2 CJR Features

Statement of truth: Proceedings for contempt of court may be brought against a person if he makes a false statement in a document verified by a statement of truth without an honest belief in its truth.[45] The Working Party believed there is an important public interest to prevent a party from knowingly misleading the court and other parties and that contempt proceedings must remain available in support of that public interest (Chief Justice's Working Party on Civil Justice Reform 2004: 125).[46]

Exclusion of irrelevant or marginally relevant evidence: While the court does not have the authority to exclude admissible evidence, the court may exclude evidence on the basis that it is 'insufficiently relevant'.[47] The Working Party believed that public interests (and third party interests) are better served if the court is empowered to 'stop what has been demonstrated to be an unjustifiably prolix examination or cross-examination of a witness'. The Working Party provided the rationale for excluding evidence under such circumstances (Chief Justice's Working Party on Civil Justice Reform 2004: 309–310)[48]:

> While the evidence might initially have been relevant and admissible, repetitions and reiterations may take further evidence along the same lines across the 'insufficiently relevant' line and justify intervention by the court. Such an approach would be consonant with existing principle and authority and would be reactive rather than proactive.

Vexatious litigants: While access to court is a constitutional right in Hong Kong, there are strong public policy grounds to impose reasonable restrictions on this right in relation to vexatious litigants. New measures have been introduced to deal with vexatious litigants (Chief Justice's Working Party on Civil Justice Reform 2004: 237–238).[49]

Rights of third persons: The civil justice system in Hong Kong takes the rights of third parties seriously. An example is the interpleader relief under RHC Order 17. Where a claim is made by a third party to any property taken or intended to be taken by a bailiff in execution, the bailiff may apply to the court for interpleader relief.[50]

---

[45] The reform introduced the requirement that all pleadings (together with the further and better particulars of the pleadings) must be verified by a statement of truth. The effect of the statement of truth is that the pleader believes that the facts stated in the pleadings are true. See RHC O. 41A, r. 2.

[46] See para. 258.

[47] *Vernon v. Bosley* [1994] PIQR 337, quoted in the Final Report (Chief Justice's Working Party on Civil Justice Reform 2004: 308–309). In fact, this is always within the power of the court under RHC O. 24 discovery. For instance, where the plaintiff sought specific discovery against the defendant, and the latter contested such application, the court may dismiss the application on the ground that the documents sought are irrelevant to the issues of the case.

[48] See Recommendation 99. Also see PD 11.3 on restricted application order and restricted proceedings order. This practice direction took effect on 2 April 2009.

[49] See Recommendations 67 and 68.

[50] See RHC O. 17, r. 1(1)(b).

The third party must give notice of his claim to the bailiff. Upon receipt of such notice, the bailiff must immediately give notice to the execution creditor and the execution creditor must,

7.4.2 Preservation of Legal Professional Privilege as a Goal of Civil Justice

7.4.2.1 Overview

Discovery and inspection of documents[51] are vital to all civil proceedings in Hong Kong.[52] Documents which are relevant to the key issues between the parties should be disclosed.[53] Their production, however, is not without limitations. Legal Professional Privilege (LPP) is the cornerstone of Hong Kong's justice system, be it civil or criminal.[54] Their importance has been stone-etched into the guides and codes that regulate the conduct of lawyers in Hong Kong. The policy rationale underlying LPP, as Mr. Justice Bokhary PJ (as he then was) has explained, is:

> It is obviously conducive to the due administration of justice that clients candidly reveal the unvarnished truth to their lawyers. And of course the law is not so naïve as to imagine that such candour can confidently be expected in practice if disclosure of the contents of client-lawyer communications may be compelled, to a client's prejudice and contrary to his wishes.[55]

As to the fundamental nature of LPP, Mr. Justice Bokhary PJ (as he then was) further stated that:

> [the] rule constituted by this privilege is a rational and practical one which exists in the public interest and involves an important right belonging to the client. In Hong Kong this right is a constitutional one. It is contained in the confidential legal advice clause of art. 35 of the Basic Law. By this clause it is provided that 'Hong Kong residents shall have the right to confidential legal advice' – a right which our courts will always be vigilant to accord proper protection.[56]

---

within 7 days after receiving the notice, give notice to the bailiff informing the bailiff whether he admits or disputes the third party claim. If the execution creditor disputes the claim or fails to give the required notice within the 7-day period, the bailiff may apply to the court for interpleader relief: see RHC O. 17, r. 2. Upon the bailiff's application to the court, in less complex cases (e.g. where the question at issue between the claimants is a question of law and the facts are not in dispute), the court may summarily determine the question at issue between the claimants and make an order accordingly on such terms as may be just: see RHC O. 17, r. 5(2); also see Wilkinson, Cheung and Booth (2011: 884–886). Where the court cannot summarily determine the question, it may order that an issue between the claimants be stated and tried: see RHC O. 17, r. 5(1).

[51] RHC O. 24, and O. 24 of the Rules of the District Court, Cap 366H (RDC).

[52] Purposes of discovery include: (1) to enable the other party to know the case it has to answer; (2) to avoid the other party being taken by surprise; (3) to encourage settlement, by knowing the strengths and weaknesses of the parties' cases.

[53] *Commerciale Du Pacifique v. The Peruvian Guano Co.* (1882) 11 QBD 55.

[54] There are two categories of LPP: (1) legal advice privilege, which protects all confidential *communications*, whether written or verbal, between a client and his legal adviser in his professional capacity for the purpose of receiving or giving legal advice; (2) litigation privilege, which protects communications between a client and a third party (e.g. an expert), communications between the client's lawyer and a third party, and other documents, that are produced or brought into existence for the dominant purpose of getting information or legal advice for, or conducting or helping in the conduct of, pending or contemplated litigation.

[55] *Solicitor v. Law Society of Hong Kong* (2006) 9 HKCFAR 175, 185 (paras. A-B).

[56] (2006) 9 HKCFAR 175, 185 (paras. C-F).

7.4.2.2 Guides and Codes Regulating Legal Professional Privilege

The guides and codes that regulate the conduct of Hong Kong lawyers in relation to LPP are as follows.

Hong Kong Solicitors' Guide to Professional Conduct (Principle 8.01):

> A solicitor has a duty to hold in strict confidence all information concerning the business and affairs of his client acquired in the course of the professional relationship, and must not divulge such information unless disclosure is expressly or impliedly authorized by the client or required by law [i.e. disclosure ordered by the Court or required under various Ordinances, e.g. Prevention of Bribery Ordinance, Cap 201] or unless the client has expressly or impliedly waived the duty.[57]

Code of Conduct of the Bar of the Hong Kong Special Administrative Region (Paragraph 116):

> A barrister employed as Counsel is under a duty not to communicate to any third person information which has been entrusted to him in confidence, and not to use such information to his client's detriment or to his own or another client's advantage. This duty continues after the relation of Counsel and client has ceased. A barrister's duty not to divulge confidential information without the consent of his client, express or implied, subsists unless he is compelled or permitted to do so by law.

7.4.2.3 Solicitor v. Law Society of Hong Kong

Solicitor v. Law Society of Hong Kong[58] involved the Law Society of Hong Kong's statutory powers to appoint inspectors to assist it in verifying compliance by solicitors with the rules governing their conduct and activities. The statute provides that where inspectors reasonably suspect that any documents are relevant to the performance of their task, they may require a solicitor to produce those documents even if they are subject to solicitor-client privilege. To protect the client's interests, the statute provides that the documents produced may only be used for the purposes of an inquiry or investigation under the statute. In other words, such documents may not be used against the client. After considering that safeguard and other safeguards provided by the statute, the Court of Appeal (CA) was satisfied that such production was compatible with the client's constitutional right to confidential legal advice. The CA therefore dismissed the solicitor's constitutional challenge to so much of the statute as provided that production cannot be resisted on the ground of privilege.

Apart from Article 35 of the Basic Law of Hong Kong as highlighted by Mr. Justice Bokhary PJ, article 41 extends the prescribed rights and freedom to persons in Hong Kong other than Hong Kong residents.

The aforesaid principles were revisited in another Court of Final Appeal case, *Akai Holdings Ltd (in compulsory liquidation) v. Ernst & Young (a Hong Kong*

[57] Duty of confidentiality continues even after termination of retainer or death of client.

[58] (2006) 9 HKCFAR 175.

firm),[59] which involved documents (transcripts and notes) created by a liquidator during a series of private examinations and interviews in the process of companies winding-up, pursuant to section 221 of the Companies Ordinance, Cap 32 (CO). The issue was whether these documents would be subject to discovery in the ordinary civil litigation. The Companies Court and the CA ruled that as the nature of private examinations and interviews is inquisitorial, litigation privilege does not extend to protect the documents and information obtained in the course of the non-adversarial proceedings. The appellant argued that this view, 'if correct, would mean that the product of non-adversarial proceedings that are inquisitorial can never be the subject of legal professional privilege even if the intended use of such product is dominantly connected with adversarial litigation in real prospect' (para. 96).

Mr. Justice Bokhary PJ, after considering the evidence contained in the documents, ruled that LPP, in particular litigation privilege, should apply in relation to the documents in question, and allowed the appeal. He opined that, 'in resorting to private examinations and interviews… the liquidators did so for the dominant purpose of bringing the transcripts and notes of those examinations and interviews into existence for them to be placed before the legal advisers of the company in liquidation in order to obtain legal advice in connection with litigation that was in active contemplation and therefore in real prospect at the time'. It was found that there was 'no evidence that any other purpose could have been the dominant one… the question of whether there is evidence on which to make a finding of fact is a question of law': *Devi v. Roy*[60] and *ADS v. Brothers* (see para.101).[61]

7.4.3 Issues That the Court Should (in the Context of the Goals of Civil Procedure) Determine Ex Officio

To put into effect the underlying objectives, the courts are vested with the power to make order of its own motion.[62]

An interesting area which perhaps better illustrates issues that the court should determine *ex officio* can be found under RHC Order 18, rule 19. With the implementation of the CJR, words are added to the effect which gives power to the court on its own motion at any stage of the proceedings to strike out, order amendment of pleadings or endorsement, order action to be stayed or judgment to be entered. In *Park Young Sook v. Sharon Melloy*,[63] the plaintiff's action against a family judge was dismissed upon the CFI's own motion on the basis that the family judge 'is immune

[59] (2009) 12 HKCFAR 649.

[60] [1946] AC 508.

[61] (2003) 3 HKCFAR 70.

[62] RHC O. 1B, r. 2.

[63] HCA 763/2010, 30 June 2010.

from legal action in respect of acts done in performance of her judicial function',[64] under Article 85 of the Basic Law.[65]

In *Park Young Sook v. Sharon Melloy,* the plaintiff, acting in person, claimed against a family judge based on the allegation that the judge had conspired with the plaintiff's ex-husband to make orders and rulings against the plaintiff in a matrimonial matter. The family judge applied to strike out the plaintiff's statement of claim under RHC Order 18, rule 19(1)(a) on the ground that it disclosed no reasonable cause of action.

Upon reading the plaintiff's statement of claim, To J realized that the claims were 'against a judge of the District Court who is immune from legal action in respect of acts done in the performance of her judicial function under Article 85 of the Basic Law' (see also section 71 of the District Court Ordinance, Cap 336 ('DCO')). To J therefore requested appearance of the plaintiff to explain the same to the plaintiff and to ask her to show cause as to why an action could be brought against the judge before requiring the attendance of the judge in order to save costs.[66] In doing so, To J had in mind the underlying objectives under RHC Order 1A: 'I had in mind the underlying objectives as stated in Order 1A of the RHC, i.e. to increase cost-effectiveness of any practice and procedure and to ensure that the case can be dealt with as expeditiously as is reasonably practicable and with a sense of reasonable proportion and procedural economy'.[67]

After hearing the plaintiff, Hon To J found that her claims against the judge were based on bare assertions,[68] and the orders of the judge upon which she complained of were previously appealed by the plaintiff and refused.[69] Upon his own motion,[70] To J struck out the plaintiff's statement of claim[71] and dismissed the action.[72]

The plaintiff appealed To J's decision. The CA refused to grant leave to appeal.[73] Subsequent to this judgment, the plaintiff successfully obtained leave from the CA to again file notice of appeal against To J's decision in order to adhere to the proper procedure.[74] The final outcome of this case is still pending at the time of the writing of this chapter.[75]

---

[64] HCA 763/2010, para. 2, 2.

[65] Also see section 71 of the District Court Ordinance, Cap. 336.

[66] HCA 763/2010, para. 2, 2.

[67] HCA 763/2010, para. 2, 2.

[68] HCA 763/2010, para. 25, 10.

[69] HCA 763/2010, para. 29, 10–11.

[70] RHC O. 1B, r. 2.

[71] RHC O. 18, r. 19(1)(a).

[72] HCA 763/2010, para. 30, 12.

[73] HCMP 1373/2010, 19 August 2010.

[74] HCMP 1727/2010, 30 September 2010.

[75] At the time of this report, there is no further decision under this case. The last judgment is 30 September 2010.

Subsequent to *Park Young Sook v. Sharon Melloy*, it is noted that the courts are more ready to invoke this power in dealing with vexatious or frivolous proceedings: see Chan and Rogers (2013: 416), in particular, para. 18/19/3A.

7.4.4 Intervention of Other Actors to Secure the Goals of Civil Justice

The Hong Kong judiciary is independent from the government and legislature. Therefore, as a general principle, intervening in the judicial process is forbidden by the Constitution.[76]

However, executive interventions do occur in certain proceedings. An example is company winding-up proceedings.[77] Involvement, assistance and interventions of the Official Receiver are expected. Official Receivers[78] can be appointed as a liquidator[79] in a compulsory winding-up situation. One of the liquidator's rights is to bring or defend proceedings in the company's name.[80] This right tallies with its obligation to realize the assets and eventually distribute dividends to interested parties. As such, a liquidator's intervention, for example in a civil action against the company,[81] helps to protect the interest of the company's creditors.[82]

7.5 Establishing the Facts of the Case Correctly v. Fair Trial Within a Reasonable Time: Entrenching the Principle of Proportionality

7.5.1 Fair Trial Within a Reasonable Time

Common law courts are concerned with legal truth and not material truth. The principle of party-presentation is deeply entrenched. On this basis, and coupled with the underlying objective of the CJR[83] to ensure that a case is dealt with as

---

[76] Article 85, the Basic Law of the HKSAR. The courts of the Hong Kong Special Administrative Region shall exercise judicial power independently, free from any interference.

[77] Another example is bankruptcy proceedings against the individual.

[78] It is also possible for persons other than Official Receiver to be appointed as provisional liquidator and liquidator. However, a company and an undischarged bankrupt cannot be appointed as a liquidator: s. 278 of the CO.

[79] And also a provisional liquidator before a winding-up order is made. See ss. 193 and 194 of the CO.

[80] S. 199 of the CO. The liquidator can appoint solicitors to assist in discharging such duty.

[81] No legal proceedings could be commenced or continued against the company without leave from the court: s. 186 of the CO. The liquidator may consent to or oppose application made by the plaintiff of the civil action for leave to continue the same. For example, *Re B+B Construction Company Ltd* (HCCW 114/2001, 28 June 2001).

[82] The liquidator acts on behalf of all unsecured creditors of the company, not just the petitioner. If the action is successfully contested, more assets will be available for distribution to creditors.

[83] Even before implementation of the CJR, there were mechanisms available for the court to expedite cases. For example, RHC O. 24, r. 4 allows a court to order that an issue or question between the parties should be determined first before discovery. However, this rule is rarely applied, even

expeditiously as is reasonably practicable,[84] fact-finding within a reasonable time has become a core goal of civil justice. For example, under RHC Order 58, rule 1(5), the court should only allow new evidence to be adduced for an appeal from Masters[85] on special grounds being shown.[86] Before the introduction of this provision, there was no limitation for a party appealing against a Master's decision to adduce new evidence.[87] This old practice, inevitably, escalated time and expenses incurred by the parties since new round(s) of affirmations would have to be filed, which RHC Order 58, rule 1(5) aims to defeat. The said objective is further enforced by the new RHC Order 24, rule 15A, which allows the court to make an order limiting discovery.[88]

Notwithstanding the above, the importance of a fair trial is not compromised under the CJR.[89] Fair trial is ensured by the front-loading of the facts-gathering exercise before the action is commenced.[90] For example, pleadings, witness statements and expert reports are now required to be verified by a statement of truth that the facts contained therein are true (and opinions honestly held in the case of expert report),[91] so that deviation (and consequently amendments of pleadings and filing of

---

when the discovery fight between the parties took 6 years: e.g. *Alexina Investments Ltd & Anor v. Keysberg Ltd & Ors* (HCA 6359/1992, 27 March 2002).

[84] RHC O. 1A, r. 1(b).

[85] *Aggressive Construction Company Limited v. Yick Wai Cheong* (HCA 1889/2008, 29 June 2009). See also *Fortis Insurance Company (Asia) Ltd v. Lam Hau Wah Inneo* (CACV 86/2010, 28 October 2010).

[86] The special grounds that apply to appeals against Masters' decisions are those as set out in *Ladd v. Marshall* [1964] 1 WLR 1489: (1) 'the evidence could not have been obtained with reasonable diligence for use' at the hearing below; (2) 'the evidence must be such that, if given, it would probably have an important influence on the result of the case, though it need not be decisive'; (3) 'the evidence must be such as is presumably to be believed'.

[87] Such appeal was therefore, in substance, a rehearing of the same application.

[88] See *Wong Tze Ming v. Dr. Woo Chi Pang, Victor & Anor* (HCPI 472/2009, 27 July 2012). The Personal Injuries Master considered application by the defendant for specific discovery of certain documents from the plaintiff which may show his pre-existing condition. The Master found that the documents were relevant to the issues in the case, thus there was no reason for her to exercise the discretion in achieving the underlying objectives of RHC O. 1A to limit the defendant's application pursuant to RHC O. 24, r. 15A.

[89] RHC O. 1A, rr. 1(c) and 1(d).

The importance of a fair trial is not compromised under the CJR as shown in the case of *Choi Chun Ming v. Cosco-HIT Terminals (Hong Kong) Ltd* [2009] 3 HKLRD 402. The plaintiff sought to adduce additional evidence after trial date had been set down and despite in the Listing Questionnaire he had confirmed that no additional evidence would be adduced. After considering the importance of the new evidence required to be adduced, and that the likely prejudice suffered by the defendant could be compensated by appropriate costs order, Fung J allowed plaintiff's application.

[90] RHC O. 24, r. 7A. Pre-action discovery has been enlarged by the CJR to cover any actions and not merely personal injury actions. See and compare the 1 July 1997 version of s. 41 of the High Court Ordinance, Cap 4, and the current version.

[91] RHC O. 41A, rr. 2 and 4(1).

supplemental statements and reports) are avoided.[92] The parties will also be tied down to their respective cases at the earliest possible stage of the proceedings, which also serves the purpose of expediting the entire process.[93]

Further to the above, it is common practice under the CJR[94] for the court to require that parties set out and, if possible, agree to the key issues that should be dealt with at trial, so as to save time and costs.[95]

7.5.2 *Entrenching the Principle of Proportionality*

An underlying objective of civil justice in Hong Kong is that procedure should be proportional.[96] The principle of proportionality carries with it a mixture of user-oriented and institutional objectives. There have been cases (pre-CJR) where the cost of litigation exceeded the value of the claim. Promoting proportionality has an institutional dimension in that resources of the court can be distributed more evenly (and fairly) (Zuckerman 2009: 54). This has an immense impact on access to justice.

---

[92] In the case of *Tong Kin Hing v. Autron Mauritius Corp.* [2010] 1 HKLRD 77, as per Rogers VP: 'Hence the seriousness of the statement of truth cannot be brushed aside. It may not be an affidavit or an affirmation but the Rules themselves treat the statement with similar seriousness. The requirement of a statement of truth is important. Its purpose is to focus the mind of the relevant party and to deter sloppy or speculative pleadings and prevent dishonest cases being put forward...the requirement serves to help the Court and the parties to achieve the underlying objectives which are set out in Order 1A Rule 1 of the Rules of the High Court:...In my view, when faced with a situation where a pleading has been verified in circumstances where it has been demonstrated that the verification should never have been made, the Court should be very slow to permit any amendment to that pleading. If the part of the pleading that is defective is the central part of a claim then the Court may well consider that the pleading should struck out and the party left to whatever course is open to him in bringing new proceedings. It is a matter of discretion and in exercising that discretion the Court recognises that the primary aim in exercising its powers is to secure the just resolution of disputes in accordance with the substantive rights of the parties. Hence, there can be no hard and fast rule, but the onus lies heavily on the party in default. In this case I consider that the pleading was so defective that it is not a matter of simple amendment; it is a matter of reconstituting any claim.'

[93] The issues between the parties can be identified at an early stage by reference to their respective pleadings. This, in turn, will assist in limiting the scope of documents to be discovered, i.e. documents relevant to the issues of the case: *Re Estate of Ng Chan Wah* (HCAP 5/2003). Another positive side of frontloading costs on fact-finding is that lay clients will be in a better position to explore settlement at an earlier stage of the proceedings.

[94] Such practice was available in the District Court even before implementation of the CJR: see RDC O. 18, r. 22. However, it is interesting to note that such a mechanism never was and is not now available under the RHC. However, see n. 95 below.

[95] Practice Direction 5.2, para. 6: parties should focus on relevant issues. Proliferation of efforts on irrelevant factual or legal disputes should be avoided. Listing Questionnaire to be filed before Case Management Conference (CMC) or Pre-trial Review (PTR) (Appendix C to PD 5.2) also requires solicitor or counsel to attach a one-page summary of the issues to be tried.

[96] RHC O. 1A, r. 1(c).

7.6 Channelling and Other Methods of Dealing with 'Hard Cases'

The goals of civil justice, in the aspect of 'hard cases' versus mass processing of routine matters, are achieved in Hong Kong by channelling. Civil cases are divided amongst the three main levels of first instance courts[97] in accordance with the amount of quantum claimed.[98] In the District Court (DC) and the CFI, the workloads are further distributed according to the nature of the claim. For example, Family Court[99] and Companies Court[100] are within the structure of the DC and the CFI, respectively. Judges may also be assigned with particular duties, for example, managing the Employees' Compensation List in the DC, and Commercial List, Personal Injuries List, Construction List, Arbitration List and Admiralty List, etc. in the CFI.

Whilst judges are primarily tasked with presiding over trials, interlocutory applications[101] are mostly processed by Registrars and Masters.[102]

Apart from the above, other specialty tribunals are set up in Hong Kong to avoid expense and delay.[103] For example, the Labour Tribunal has certain exclusive jurisdiction over employment matters,[104] whilst the Lands Tribunal has jurisdiction over certain land matters.[105] Nevertheless, mechanisms are available for these tribunals to decline jurisdiction and transfer cases to the CFI and DC, for example, where complex and complicated issues are involved.[106]

7.7 Multi-party Matters: The Beginnings of Representative Litigation

Most lawsuits in Hong Kong are bipartisan proceedings. However, it is possible to initiate third party proceedings. A defendant who has given notice of intention to defend may claim against a third party by issuing a third party notice containing a

---

[97] Namely, Small Claims Tribunal (SCT), District Court (civil jurisdiction), and the High Court (CFI, civil jurisdiction).

[98] Jurisdiction up to HK$50,000 (about 5,000 EUR) for SCT (Schedule to Small Claims Tribunal Ordinance (Cap 338) (SCTO)); HK$1,000,000 (about 100,000 EUR) for District Court (s. 32, DCO); and unlimited civil jurisdiction for the CFI.

[99] Responsible for matrimonial matters, e.g. custody of children and ancillary relief.

[100] Responsible for companies matters, e.g. winding-up of companies, shareholders disputes.

[101] E.g. discovery, amendments of pleadings, CMC, etc. PTR are usually fixed 1 month before the trial and presided over by the trial judge.

[102] Interlocutory applications that involve complex and complicated issues are often dealt with by judges sitting in chambers.

[103] Legal representation is not allowed in the Labour Tribunal (s. 23 of Labour Tribunal Ordinance, Cap 25) and the SCT (section 19(2) of SCTO). In addition, formal rules of evidence do not apply in the Labour Tribunal (s. 27) and the SCT (s. 23(2)).

[104] See Schedule to the Labour Tribunal Ordinance, Cap 25.

[105] See s. 8 of the Lands Tribunal Ordinance, Cap 17.

[106] See s. 10 of Labour Tribunal Ordinance and section 8A of the Lands Tribunal Ordinance.

statement of the nature of the plaintiff's claim, and either of the nature and grounds of the claim made by the defendant (against the third party) or of the question or issue required to be determined.[107] The availability of third party proceedings is to 'prevent multiplicity of proceedings and to prevent the same question being tried twice with possibly different results' (Wilkinson, Cheung and Booth 2011: 254).

Hong Kong has no class actions regime. Currently, the only avenue that deals with multi-party disputes is provided under RHC Order 15, rule 12. The court may appoint a defendant to act as representative of other defendants being sued on the application of the plaintiff. A judgment or order rendered in representative proceedings will be binding on all the parties so represented.[108] However, representative proceedings suffered from the problem of lack of certainty and the absence of detailed rules that govern its operation (Chief Justice's Working Party on Civil Justice Reform 2004: 240).[109] Hong Kong is in need of a full-fledged statutory regime for multi-party litigation that encompasses areas such as the conduct of proceedings, protecting representative claimants, costs and the disposal of the case.[110] With this goal in mind, the Class Action Subcommittee of the Law Reform Commission of Hong Kong issued the *Consultation Paper on Class Actions* in November 2009 to seek stakeholders' views on the subject. Following the consultation, a detailed report on class actions was published in May 2012.[111]

7.8 Resolving Tensions Between Substantive Justice and Legal Formalism

The tension between substantive justice and legal formalism can be understood on three levels.

Firstly, adjudication under the common law system demonstrates unique characteristics. While the court would generally apply the principles in the case law, it is possible for the court to come to a decision divergent from the precedent by distinguishing the case on its facts or on policy considerations. Hence, the nature of common law allows greater leeway on the part of the judge to tailor a solution for a specific problem and produce relative substantive justice.[112]

Secondly, on a procedural level, the tension is between the need to enforce deadlines and the importance of finding a just solution on the basis of merits. Before the CJR, the adherence to the notion of 'justice on the merits' (or substantive justice)

---

[107] RHC O. 16, r.1(1). Also see Wilkinson, Cheung and Booth (2011: 256).

[108] RHC O. 15, r. 12(2); also see Class Action Subcommittee of the Law Reform Commission of Hong Kong (2009: 1).

[109] See Recommendation 70.

[110] Class Action Subcommittee of the Law Reform Commission of Hong Kong (2009: 2), see para. 6.

[111] The Law Reform Commission of Hong Kong (2012).

[112] For further discussion, see Chan (2012: 320).

resulted in the court's indulgence with non-compliance (Zuckerman 2009: 70). With the implementation of the CJR, a major challenge is how effectively could the court enforce procedural deadlines, while at the same time, give due regard to the merits of each party's case (Zuckerman 2004: 231).

Thirdly, on the level of fact-finding, common law courts are concerned with legal truth and not material truth. The principle of party-presentation is deeply entrenched. While judges are conferred substantive case management powers, the judge has no *ex officio* investigatory powers. The court strictly follows the procedural rules of fact-finding.[113]

7.9 Problem Solving Through 'Constructive Discussions' with the Court

In Hong Kong, it is never the case that the courts are merely performing case-processing functions.[114] In fact, it is very common to have constructive discussions between legal representatives and the presiding Master or Judge during CMC or PTR as to, for example, how to narrow down the issues between parties, whether certain facts can be agreed amongst the parties, whether additional evidence should be obtained and what further steps should be taken. Useful directions and/or suggestions from the bench are unexceptional. Furthermore, courts are contented to be used as the mechanism for resolving impediments amongst the parties. For example, lack of mutual trust between the litigants in matrimonial matters is habitual, so much so that disputes as to who[115] should hold, for the time being, proceeds received from the sale of matrimonial properties are almost universal, which in turn hinder progress of the main cause. In these situations, problems are often resolved by having the proceeds paid into court pending distribution.[116]

In one ancillary relief case (handled by the second author of this chapter as counsel for the wife), disputes between husband and wife (who was granted custody of the children) as to who should hold in trust maintenance money (in a lump sum) for the children was resolved by the court suggesting to them that the funds could be paid into court, and they would have to make monthly application to the court for release of the same for the children. The husband and wife, fearing such arrangement would bring about great inconveniences and adversely affect the children's livelihood, quickly resolved their differences in this regard.

[113] Even when the court exercises discretion, it is because of case management needs rather than an attempt to leave no stone unturned in the name of substantive justice. Fact-finding remains a party-driven exercise conducted on the basis of the court's case management regime.

[114] This is especially true after implementation of the CJR, where judges actively participate in case management.

[115] Including parties' legal representatives.

[116] See, for example, *CPK v. CY* (FCMC 7599A/2007).

7.10 Costs of Civil Justice: Free, but at the Cost of a Deficit

Save for minimal fees payable by litigants,[117] civil court services in Hong Kong are available to the general public at no expense. Unsurprisingly, the Hong Kong judiciary usually runs at a deficit.[118] The costs for maintaining the courts, therefore, come primarily from Hong Kong taxpayers through the government. It is unlikely that, in the foreseeable future, this system in Hong Kong will change, since the society as a whole emphasizes and desires the accessibility of justice by the general public. Whilst the common perception is that justice is reserved only for the rich, the Hong Kong government, judiciary and the legal profession have endeavoured to change this perception.[119] Nevertheless, limitations in these services are unavoidable and many, so much so that an overhaul of the civil justice system is required.[120] A change in the current system will be seen as a regression.

7.11 Mixing User-Oriented and Institutional Objectives

The goals of Hong Kong civil justice have a strong orientation towards the users. While enhancement of procedural efficiency yields institutional benefits of lowering the caseload of the court system, the CJR was implemented not for pure institutional reasons or to serve self-centred goals. The fundamental objective is to improve access to justice for the user. For instance, an important goal of the CJR is to enhance the cost-effectiveness of civil procedure.[121] The court is obligated to

---

[117] E.g. fees for issuance of writ in the High Court and the District Court are HK$1,045 (about 100 EUR) and HK$630 (about 60 EUR), respectively, at the time of the writing of this chapter.

[118] As shown in the Hong Kong Judiciary Annual Reports 2007–2012, the Hong Kong judiciary runs at a deficit. For example: (1) in year 2010–2011, the expenditures and revenue amounted to HK$998,167,000 and HK$572,894,000 (HK$163,657,000 from fees); (2) in year 2009–2010, the expenditures and revenue amounted to HK$973,620,000 and HK$643,913,000 (HK$175,454,000 from fees), respectively; (3) in year 2008–2009, the expenditures and revenue were HK$943,863,000 and HK$468,815,000 (HK$177,524,000 from fees), respectively; (4) in year 2007–2008, the expenditures and revenue were HK$886,622,000 and HK$438,646,000 (HK$158,818,000 from fees), respectively; and (5) in year 2006–2007, the expenditures and revenue amounted to HK$856,736,000 and HK$498,836,000 (HK$222,079,000 from fees), respectively. It should be noted, however, that there was a surplus in the year 2011–2012, where the expenditures and revenue were HK$1,033,928,000 and HK$2,061,950,000 (HK$174,909,000 from fees), respectively.

[119] For example: free legal advice from Duty Lawyer Service; Bar Free Legal Service Scheme; pro bono services from law firms; free legal consultations in district and legislative councillors' office; increased upper limit of means test for Legal Aid eligibility.

[120] With the emphasis now placed on mediation amongst litigants, it is hoped that the number of argued cases and therefore the corresponding expenditures of public funds would decrease.

[121] RHC O. 1A, r. 1(a).

take into account the underlying objectives in exercising its discretion as to costs.[122] This would incentivize the parties to consider the underlying objectives seriously before making any decisions to incur costs. The enhancement of efficiency has the effect of lowering costs, which in turn is conducive to improving access to justice for the user.[123]

The principle of proportionality carries with it a mixture of user-oriented and institutional objectives (as explained above).

The encouragement of settlement (especially via mediation) also has the user in mind.[124] A settlement through mediation usually involves less time and costs, which is directly in line with the interests of the users. Of course, a regime that effectively promotes settlement also has an institutional benefit of lowering the caseload of the court system. Other measures to improve access to justice include measures to assist unrepresented litigants, taking into account their relative disadvantageous position.[125]

7.12 Concluding Remarks

The successful implementation of any civil justice reform requires an appropriate deployment of judicial resources and an acute awareness among judges of what the core goals of civil justice are. Inevitably, judges need to prioritize under different circumstances. For instance, Hong Kong's system demonstrates a strong orientation towards the users and their rights of access to justice. By comparison, given the social circumstances, institutional goals take precedence in Mainland China where courts are much more inclined to serve policy objectives as a priority over the needs of individual litigants.

The CJR transformed the litigation landscape in Hong Kong.[126] Civil justice now embraces a multi-faceted agenda. Judges are guided by the underlying objectives in adjudication and fully understand that the culture of non-compliance with procedural deadlines in the past must be eradicated for the CJR to be successful (Zuckerman 2009: 60–62). Procedural efficiency has become a priority of the Hong Kong judiciary and a core goal of civil justice. According to the Legislative Council Panel on Administration of Justice and Legal Services (2010, 2011), on the whole,

---

122 RHC O. 62, r. 5(1)(aa).

123 The cost regime in Hong Kong suffers from structural defects. Lawyers are paid by the hour. In some cases, the litigation cost far exceeded the value of the claim. Efforts to address this issue can be seen in the Law Reform Commission's report on conditional fees: see The Law Reform Commission of Hong Kong (2007).

124 RHC O. 1A, r. 1(e).

125 See Chief Justice's Working Party on Civil Justice Reform (2004: 464), see para. 865.

126 See Chan et al. (2014 forthcoming).

the CJR was regarded as a success upon its first 2 years of implementation.[127] This view is supported by statistics.[128]

The CJR is premised on the notion that by empowering the courts in case management, the goals of civil justice are best served. While the fundamental adversarial nature of proceedings remains the same, judicial proactivity in managing the litigation timetable would determine *how* the various goals of civil justice are achieved. An inefficient procedural system could hardly enforce the principles and objectives of justice. Procedural efficiency is therefore the foundation for achieving any goal of civil justice.[129]

References

Chan PCH (2011) Three years of civil justice reform: constructing a cost-effective and efficient civil procedure in Hong Kong. Acta Universitatis Lucian Blaga 2:181–202

Chan PCH (2012) The enigma of civil justice in imperial China: a legal historical enquiry. Maastricht J Eur Comp Law 19(2):317–337

Chan P, Rogers M (eds) (2013) Hong Kong civil procedure 2013. Sweet & Maxwell, Hong Kong

Chan P, Chan D, Chen L (2014 forthcoming) China: Hong Kong. Selective adoption of the English Woolf reforms. In: van Rhee CH, Fu YL (eds) Civil litigation in China and Europe: essays on the role of the judge and the parties, Ius Gentium: comparative perspectives on law and justice 31. Springer, Dordrecht/Heidelberg/London/New York

Chief Justice's Working Party on Civil Justice Reform (2001) Civil justice reform: interim report and consultative paper (21 November 2001). Available at: http://www.civiljustice.gov.hk/eng/archives_ir_download.html. Last accessed 16 Aug 2013

---

[127] See Legislative Council Panel on Administration of Justice and Legal Services (2011: 41), para. 87. Also see (2010: 2, para. 5).

[128] The average time from commencement to trial in the CFI has decreased from more than 1,000 days (where commencement occurred pre-CJR) to 167 days (the first year following the CJR). This figure further diminished to 155 days in the second year following the CJR. However, the statistics should be qualified in that the post-CJR sample (number of hearings) was substantially less than the pre-CJR sample. In relation to the average time from commencement to trial in the CFI, six scenarios were reported: (1) where both date of commencement and date of trial were on or before 1 April 2009, the average time was 1,013 days (totalling 212 hearings); (2) where the date of commencement was on or before 1 April 2009 and the date of trial was between 2 April 2009 and 31 March 2010, the average time was 1,132 days (totalling 251 hearings); (3) where the date of commencement and date of trial were between 2 April 2009 and 31 March 2010, the average time was 167 days (totalling 16 hearings); (4) where the date of commencement was on or before 1 April 2009 and the date of trial was between 1 April 2010 and 31 March 2011, the average time was 1,356 days (totalling 194 hearings); (5) where both date of commencement and date of trial were between 1 April 2010 and 31 March 2011, the average time was 155 days (totalling 18 hearings); and (6) where both date of commencement and date of trial were between 2 April 2009 and 31 March 2011, the average time was 277 days (totalling 70 hearings).

See Legislative Council Panel on Administration of Justice and Legal Services (2010: 10), Table 6.1. Also see (2011: 11), Table 6.1.

[129] See Chan et al. (2014 forthcoming).

Chief Justice's Working Party on Civil Justice Reform (2004) The final report of the chief justice's working party on civil justice reform (3 March 2004). Available at: http://www.civiljustice.gov.hk/eng/archives_fr_download.html. Last accessed 16 Aug 2013

Class Action Subcommittee of The Law Reform Commission of Hong Kong (2009) Consultation paper on class actions (executive summary) (5 November 2009). Available at: http://www.hkreform.gov.hk/en/publications/classactions.htm. Last accessed 16 Aug 2013

Hong Kong Judiciary Annual Reports (2007–2012) Available at: http://www.judiciary.gov.hk/en/publications/publications.htm. Last accessed 16 Aug 2013

Kong K (2009) Public interest litigation in Hong Kong: a new hope for social transformation? Civ Justice Q 28(3):327–343

Legislative Council Panel on Administration of Justice and Legal Services (2010) The first year's implementation of the civil justice reform from 2 April 2009 to 31 March 2010 (LC Paper No. CB(2)591/10-11(06), December 2010). Available at: http://www.legco.gov.hk/yr10-11/english/panels/ajls/papers/aj1221cb2-591-6-e.pdf. Last accessed 16 Aug 2013

Legislative Council Panel on Administration of Justice and Legal Services (2011) The first two year's implementation of the civil justice reform from 2 April 2009 to 31 March 2011 (LC Paper No. CB(2)713/11-12(01), December 2011). Available at: http://www.legco.gov.hk/yr10-11/english/panels/ajls/papers/aj1221cb2-713-1-e.pdf. Last accessed 16 Aug 2013

Ma G (2010) Efficiency at all costs – true or bluff? In: Meggitt G (ed) Civil justice reform – what has it achieved? Sweet & Maxwell/Thomson Reuters, Hong Kong, pp 3–9

The Law Reform Commission of Hong Kong (2007) Report: conditional fees (July 2007). Available at: http://www.hkreform.gov.hk/en/publications/rconditional.htm. Last accessed 16 Aug 2013

The Law Reform Commission of Hong Kong (2012) Report: class actions (May 2012). Available at: http://www.hkreform.gov.hk/en/publications/rclassactions.htm. Last accessed 16 Aug 2013

Wilkinson M, Cheung ETM, Booth CN (2011) A guide to civil procedure in Hong Kong, 4th edn. LexisNexis, Hong Kong

Zuckerman AAS (2004) Enforcing compliance with deadlines. Civ Justice Q 23:231–243

Zuckerman AAS (2009) The challenge of civil justice reform: effective court management of litigation. City Univ Hong Kong Law Rev 1(1):49–71

Chapter 8
Social Harmony at the Cost of Trust Crisis: Goals of Civil Justice in China

Fu Yulin

Abstract This chapter addresses 'social harmony' as the ultimate goal of civil justice in China and its adverse impact on the public's trust in the justice system. The author introduces and analyses this issue in three dimensions: statutory law, judicial policy and comments from scholars. This chapter attempts to view the situation in the context that China's justice system has been undergoing rapid transition following continuous reforms. As the author indicates, although the law provides diverse and vague purposes of civil procedure, in practice the goal of dispute resolution always takes precedence over rights protection, with the ultimate policy goal of 'social harmony'. The pre-eminence of this fundamental policy goal, coupled with the common use of informal procedures and the tradition of judicial mediation, creates a civil justice with the following main features: (1) emphasis on dispute resolution especially by judicial mediation, while neglecting protection of private rights and justice; (2) overemphasis on speed or efficiency; (3) the dualism of 'ordinary' and 'summary' procedures; (4) preoccupation with routine cases while lacking mechanisms to handle hard cases; (5) user orientation (as intended by lawmakers) being usually ruined by judges' super-power and discounted by some binding opinions of the Supreme People's Court.

8.1 Background: Civil Justice in Transition

In Mainland China, the principal source of law in civil justice is The Civil Procedure Law of the People's Republic of China (CPL) issued by the National People's Congress (NPC). The various opinions (so-called 'judicial interpretations') issued

F. Yulin (✉)
School of Law, Peking University, 316 Chen Ming Building,
Haidian District, Beijing 100871, China
e-mail: fuyulin65@126.com

A. Uzelac (ed.), *Goals of Civil Justice and Civil Procedure in Contemporary Judicial Systems*, Ius Gentium: Comparative Perspectives on Law and Justice 34,
DOI 10.1007/978-3-319-03443-0_8,

by the Supreme People's Court (SPC) are important sources, even to the extent of acquiring the status of 'the constitutional law of the judges'. Accordingly, the goals of civil justice and its orientation are largely revealed in these documents. Certain goals are also determined or influenced by the edicts of the Chinese Communist Party (CCP) and even by public lectures of SPC leaders.

For more than 30 years after the establishment of 'New China', before the 'test' CPL was first enacted in 1982 (CPL 1982), civil justice was governed by the 'Sixteen Characters Guideline' promulgated by the SPC in the form of judicial policy documents of the CCP, namely 'relying on the masses; based on investigation and research; resolving disputes on the spot; and taking mediation as the primary way'. Civil cases were mainly disposed by judicial mediation, while judgments were rarely rendered. Under these guidelines, civil procedure in China was defined as a 'unified, internal autonomous institution', which included 'a set of steady trial mode' (Yaxin Wang 2004: 89).

The CPL 1982 established the principle of civil judicature, as substitution for the 'Sixteen Characters Guideline'; and the 'mediation as the primary way' principle was replaced by the principle of 'emphasizing mediation' (Art. 6). Under CPL 1982, civil justice had '[to] regard facts as the basis and regard law as the yardstick' (Art. 7). Mediation was still the dominant approach with judges who acted mainly as mediators rather than as neutral umpires, though judges were supposed to render judgment in time if the parties failed to settle after judicial mediation.

The first civil procedure law in China with some modern features is the current CPL enacted in 1991 (CPL 1991). The CPL 1991 aimed to enhance the position of the parties and protect their procedural rights, thereby tremendously improving procedural transparency and normalization and controlling what used to be the unlimited powers of judges. In the meantime, courts were required to 'conduct mediation under the principles of free will of the parties and legality; if mediation fails, the courts shall enter a judgment in a timely manner' (Art. 9). Furthermore, as a response to increasing judicial errors and corruption, CPL 1991 extended the scope of the parties' means of recourse against judgments by making it possible for them to challenge legally effective judgments. At the same time, rules of prosecutorial supervision over civil adjudication were introduced.

In the 1990s, as a step to implementing CPL 1991, the SPC initiated judicial reforms aimed at enhancing procedural transparency and formalization as well as establishing the parties' burden of proof in fact-finding. The results of these reforms are crystallized in two important judicial interpretations of the SPC, one on the mode of trial (SPC 1998) and the other on evidence (SPC 2001). As a result, the new concepts of party autonomy, open trial and due process, burden of proof and limitation of evidence presentation, judicial professionalism, etc. were broadly known and generally accepted by judges and lawyers.

However, while the parties had to bear the burden of proof, procedural powers remained firmly in the hands of judges. It appears that judges, lawyers and parties were all not particularly accustomed to their new roles, especially when it came to the rules of evidence and following formal procedures. Meanwhile, the dramatic increase of caseload led to the overuse of the summary procedure.[1] All these factors led to more judicial errors, and consequently to more complaints against courts and judgments of questionable quality. The rising number of reported judicial errors and the increasing difficulties with enforcement compelled a partial revision of the CPL 1991 in 2007, which made it easier for the parties and the procurators to challenge legally effective judgments (i.e. to reopen proceedings) and added certain relief measures at the enforcement stage. Furthermore, against the political background of 'social harmonization', since the turn of this century, there has been a tendency of a general retreat of the judiciary in that the courts are often viewed as a tool to promote policies and serve political needs.[2]

After 20 years of its enactment, the CPL 1991 was revised comprehensively in 2012 (CPL 2012).[3] The CPL 2012 was devoted to procedural diversity based on a variety of values and goals. The orientation was still to promote the parties' procedural participation and trial transparency, to control judicial discretion, to deter fraudulent behavior on the part of the parties, and to regulate judicial supervision and the retrial of effective judgments. At the same time, small claims became a special procedure added to the summary procedure. Mediation acquired an almost compulsory status. In order to help channel cases away from the courts, settlement agreements by out-of-court mediation shall become enforceable after judicial confirmation and commercial arbitration awards shall be reviewed mainly on procedural grounds.

Hopefully, the on-going judicial reform presided over by the Political and Judiciary Commission of the CCP is devoted to enhancing judicial independence, procedure transparency and professionalization, as well as to eliminating local government intervention in the judicial process. These policies should greatly influence civil justice in the future.

8.2 Prevailing Opinions on the Goals of Chinese Civil Justice

8.2.1 Statutory Definitions

The goals of civil justice are not clearly and uniformly indicated in the CPL 2012. Art. 2 provides:

> The tasks of the Civil Procedure Law of the People's Republic of China are to protect the litigation rights exercised by the parties, to ensure that the people's courts find facts, to distinguish right from wrong, to apply the law correctly, to try civil cases promptly, to

[1] This situation is particularly serious in the basic people's courts, which are responsible for disposing about 80 % of all civil cases in China.

[2] Compare the annual reports of the Supreme People's Court with the reports of the Central Committee of the Chinese Communist Party before/around the same time.

[3] The current Civil Procedure Law of China is CPL 2012 as a revision of CPL 1991; unless indicated otherwise, the provisions referred to in this chapter are under CPL 2012, i.e. the 2012 version of CPL 1991.

> affirm the rights and obligations in civil affairs, to impose sanctions for civil wrongdoings, to protect the lawful rights and interests of the parties, to educate citizens to voluntarily abide by the law, to maintain the social and economic order, and to guarantee the smooth progress of the socialist construction.

Though Art. 2 provides the 'tasks' (not 'goals') of civil procedure and speaks of 'law' rather than of 'civil justice', it is the only available statutory instrument that sheds light on the goals of civil justice. In November 2011, the NPC for the first time clearly announced that the 'goals' of the 'modification of the CPL' are 'to resolve disputes properly, to protect the parties' lawful rights and interests, and to promote the harmony and stability of society'. Accordingly, the goals of civil justice can be read as 'dispute resolution' and 'protection of rights', under the overarching goal of maintaining 'social harmony'.

8.2.2 Academic Opinions

As for academic opinions, there were no consistent 'prevailing opinions' on the goals of civil justice in China, although a number of doctrines were advanced by individual scholars, such as rights protection, legal order maintenance, dispute resolution, due process assurance, etc. However, in contrast to the prevailing policy among courts and judges, an increasing number of scholars argue that the function of the civil justice system should be in declaring and protecting the lawful rights of the parties. They also emphasize the importance of establishing a 'legal order' (as opposed to a 'social order') in addition to the dispute resolution function of procedure (Tang 1997).

By way of background, the goal of promoting the role of litigants in disposing of their private disputes during the country's transition to a market economy was already advocated by some scholars in 1990s. Though for a long period before the reform, the 'central tasks of the CCP' (CCP 2006) was to use civil justice as a political tool. Thus, since the turn of the century the goal of 'private rights protection' has been superseded by the goal of 'maintaining social order'. Judicial mediation became again the preferred means of civil dispute resolution under the policy goal of 'social harmony/peace' (as opposed to establishing a 'legal order') (SPC 2007). Under these circumstances, scholars in the field of civil procedure still argued that the goal of protection of 'legal rights' should have a more prominent place. They urged the courts to exercise their 'adjudicatory function' in declaring legal norms and upholding justice.

8.3 Goals of Procedure in Various Matters Entrusted to Civil Justice

Under Art. 3 of the CPL,

> … the provisions of this Law shall apply to civil actions accepted by a people's court regarding property or personal relationships between citizens, between legal persons, between other organizations or between citizens and legal persons, citizens and other organizations or legal persons and other organizations.

The task of Chinese civil justice is to process many different types of legal matters. The scope of civil justice covers contentious cases of civil disputes and labor disputes, non-contested cases of declaration of missing persons, death, civil incompetency or limited competency, and unclaimed property; cases of application for a repayment order (collection of debt or dunning procedure); cases of judicial confirmation of mediation agreements concluded outside courts by ADR, etc. (see e.g. Arts. 194 and 214 CPL).

Moreover, the courts undertake cases of enforcement, including enforcement of judicial decisions by the courts in civil cases and the decisions regarding property in criminal cases, arbitral decisions by labor arbitration committees and commercial arbitration committees, and enforceable instruments issued by notary offices (Art. 238). Remarkably, the enforceable judicial decisions include not only judgments and orders, but also judicial mediation agreements. Similarly, enforceable arbitral decisions also include mediation agreements entered in proceedings before labor arbitration committees and commercial arbitration committees. As a unique Chinese trait, the mediator is usually the same person as the adjudicator (i.e. judge or arbitrator).

The goals of civil justice discussed above in Sect. 8.2 are largely understood as the goals of the civil procedure for litigation in contested matters. However, general provisions in the CPL, in particular the ultimate goal of 'maintaining social harmony', may also be extended to other matters disposed by the court, including non-contested matters. Since the judiciary focuses on the resolution of disputes, instead of verifying and protecting legal rights, more than 70 % of civil cases are disposed by judicial mediation or settlement.

In spite of the fact that CPL requires judges who conduct mediation to find facts and discern between right and wrong, guidelines for judicial behavior and decision-making in mediation are never as clear as in adjudication. Moreover, the lack of consistency of judgments makes things worse. These problems were becoming more and more apparent to jurists. In response, the SPC introduced in recent years 'guiding cases' (by collecting and publishing 'model' judgments) with a view to establish consistency in jurisprudence. However, it is hard for the parties and potential parties to discover what the law is in their civil cases unless judicial policy pays more attention to the goal of legal rights protection in routine litigation. In our view, when civil litigation is concerned, the goal of maintaining social order should clearly be redefined and focused on legal order, not on social peace.

The main goal of enforcement and bankruptcy proceedings, according to the prevailing opinion, is to realize the creditor's legal rights by forcing the debtor to perform his obligations because the right has already been verified and affirmed in judicial decisions without any further 'dispute'. But in practice, under the overarching goal of 'social harmony', bankruptcy is rarely established so as to avoid unemployment, which is a risk for social harmony. Instead, settlement at the enforcement stage is encouraged pursuant to the notion of 'maintaining social harmony'. Under Art. 230 of the CPL, settlement during enforcement should be entered by the creditor and debtor themselves, without the court's involvement except for 'recording the provisions of the settlement agreement in the enforcement transcripts, to which both sides shall affix their signatures or seals'. But in practice the courts are inclined to mediate a settlement and in most cases this would mean that the creditors have to partially waive their rights.

In the long run, policies aimed to maintain 'social harmony' proved to be counterproductive, because they encouraged debtors to infringe the rights of creditors, knowing that the court was likely to push for a settlement anyway. This contributed, in no small part, to the undesirable situation of 'difficulties of enforcement' in China. Fortunately, the trend to protect creditors' legal rights and to sanction defaulting debtors is embodied in new policies implemented since the 2007 revision of the CPL and will dominate the drafting of the Enforcement Law, which will be a stand-alone piece of legislation separate from the current CPL.

The goal of the dunning procedure of debt collection is no doubt to protect the creditors' rights through an expedited means at low cost. Yet this goal failed in practice as regulations made it too easy for the debtor (at no cost at all) to present an objection, thereby changing the non-contested case into a 'dispute'. As a result, the creditor would have to file a lawsuit bearing the costs, and enduring possible delay and problems relating to the docketing of the case. During the time when the creditor is initiating an action, the debtor's financial position might have changed (e.g. assets might have been dissipated). Given how easy it is to file frivolous objections, Chinese creditors rarely resort to the dunning procedure despite its supposedly expedited nature. As such, cases resorting to the dunning procedure account for no more than 1 % of all first instance civil cases.[4]

8.4 Rights Protection Overshadowed by Public Interest

In the context of a 'socialist' society based on public ownership, the ideas of protection of public interest permeate civil justice. The goal of protecting public interest is too often implemented by conferring disproportionate powers on the judge to intervene and narrow down the domain of the parties' free disposition with their private rights.

Under CPL 1991, the parties were entitled to excise or dispose with their procedural or substantive rights in civil proceedings (Art. 13); the CPL 2012 added here the principle of good faith. Where a plaintiff requests withdrawal of the action before a judgment is pronounced, the court shall overrule such a request in cases where the parties' disposition of rights violates interests of the state, social/public interests, or third party interests (Art. 145). For the same reason, the appellate court may exercise a full review of the lower court judgment, disregarding the scope of the appeal. The same grounds authorize the court to refuse the enforcement of an arbitral award.[5] Even if judges have considered policy factors in adjudication, very

[4] The CPL 2012 therefore modified the mechanism of debt collection. Where the debtor objects to a court order for payment, litigation should be initiated directly, unless the party applying for the order for payment refuses to institute an action.

[5] However, these rules are very rarely applied in practice.

rarely would they explain such considerations in the judgment unless the parties clearly presented and defended this issue.

A special regime exists regarding family and labor cases where public interest is additionally and specifically protected. In family cases, judges must consider the interests of the child and the elderly, ethics and local custom. In these cases mediation is a mandatory and compulsory process before judgment. In labor litigation, both statutory law and common practice are inclined to protect the employee. In labor cases, public policy considerations are usually declared in judgments, no matter whether or not presented by the parties. For instance, in labor cases, judges adjudicate along policy lines to protect employees; the employee party even has a privilege in respect to means of recourse over the employer party. For several types of urgent claims, awards entered by labor arbitration committees are final with regard to the employers, who can only file for judicial review if they can prove that the award falls within the strict grounds of review; while the employee party can file for proceedings if they are dissatisfied with the arbitral award (Arts. 47–49, Mediation and Arbitration Law of Labor Dispute 2007).

CPL 2012 added in Art. 55 an important new type of 'public interests litigation':

> For conduct that pollutes the environment, infringes upon the lawful rights and interests of numerous consumers or otherwise damages the public interest, an authority or relevant organization as prescribed by law may institute an action in a people's court.

But since no law to date defines what the 'authorities or relevant organizations' are who have *locus standi* to initiate public interest proceedings, it remains a topic for debate. Also, the new provision failed to address the need for a special procedural design in such cases, which may have a great and significant impact on the public at large.[6]

Furthermore, as exceptions to the principle of open trial, civil cases involving national security, commercial security or privacy can be heard *in camera*. Despite the overwhelming view that confidential communications between parties in certain relationships should be privileged and protected (e.g. among relatives and professional relationships such as the one between a lawyer and a client), the rules of evidence under CPL 2012 did not incorporate such an approach.

In practice, policy considerations do influence judicial decisions very frequently. These considerations are not openly reasoned in judgments despite having a profound impact on judicial decision-making. It is difficult for judges to ignore policy considerations when the overriding ideology of the courts (against which the performance of a judge is evaluated) requires civil justice to produce the 'integration of legal and social effect'.

Usually, the interests of the state regarding the work of civil justice are clearly declared in various formal or informal documents (including speeches by the

---

[6] In contrast, there are some substantive provisions in Chinese law that impose more onerous burden of proof rules regarding certain dangerous industries and some highly specialized professions.

leaders of the Supreme People's Court). Local interests are not so openly set out in policy documents issued by the local courts. These documents are more or less public and act as guidelines for judges (and parties) in relation to legal customs and practices within the local jurisdiction. Some of these documents may include local policies which are de facto binding, as long as they are not against national laws or the opinions of the Supreme People's Court. The problem, however, is that there is no way for the parties to challenge the policies expressed in these documents except for the usual reliefs (i.e. appeals and retrials) available to revoke the lower court's decision.

The prevailing view in doctrine is that policy matters should be properly considered and determined by the court exercising its own discretion, with publicized reasoning in the judgment. National interest and security issues should be decided *ex officio*; and other matters such as governmental programs, suppression of illegal activities, reasons of national security, confidentiality obligations, professional privileges, etc. should be presented by the parties. But this idea may be too new for the legal community to be accepted. On the contrary, the public questions the legitimacy of policy influencing civil adjudication. Lawyers are particularly sensitive to these policy considerations and to how the court exercises its discretion when considering policy factors. Few judges would openly accept that they have been influenced by policy and still fewer explain such policy reasons in their judgments. This is likely to be the case even where lawyers expressly request the court to take extra-judicial factors into consideration.

However, extra-judicial influences occur frequently through non-official channels. Examples of such influences are government officials calling the court or issuing a memorandum to the courts; the masses filing administrative petitions against the court or staging protests on the internet or at people's congresses; procuratorates or different branches of government or the CCP and experts commenting on legal issues at a party's motion; or, occasionally, pursuant to the court's invitation, and so on. Sometimes, such extra-judicial interventions are kept on the record of the 'judicature committee' of the court and are only accessible to those who have power of 'judicial supervision' and never to the parties or the public. The extent of influence on the judges depends on the approach taken by the individual judge and the level of pressure from the outside. So if a judgment is entered in line with certain interests of local or national government, the only record of such consideration is in the record of the panel meeting and the 'judicature committee' conference.

Hopefully, the new round of judicial reform initiated by the Political and Judiciary Commission under the CCP (with the involvement of the Supreme People's Court) may change the traditional financial and personnel dependence of courts on local sources and might mitigate local interference with the judiciary. It is the first step towards judicial independence, though there is a long way to go. Of course, considering China's geographical size, local diversity should be taken into consideration in the reforms. But it should be achieved best by granting more prominence and autonomy to local legislation and jurisprudence. Unfortunately, this issue has not been addressed in any reform agenda to date.

The prosecutor in China is deemed to be the legal representative of the interests of the state and the public, and is authorized to challenge legally effective judgments in civil procedure. Under Art. 129 of the Constitution, the procuratorate is a state organ for legal supervision. Accordingly, the procuratorate's supervision over judicial activities is stipulated as a basic principle of the CPL (Art. 14). Since 1991, the procuratorate has been authorized to challenge effective judgments and mandate the courts to reopen cases to correct judicial errors. The causes of re-adjudication listed in the current CPL are as many as 13. Furthermore, since 2012, the procuratorate also has authority to supervise the enforcement proceedings.

Debate on the procuratorates' supervisory power over judicial activities has never ceased since its introduction in the CPL 1991. Scholars mainly agree that the procuratorates' power and authority should be limited to a narrow list of circumstances or cases. Examples of such cases would be the decisions passed contrary to judicial precedents (if a system of judicial precedents emerges in the future); violations of public order and good customs; litigations dealing with mass torts and public interests; and bankruptcy cases affecting social and economic order.

However, in spite of criticisms directed at prosecutors' wide powers in civil proceedings, the procuratorates' supervisory powers survived and were even augmented in the most recent reforms in China. In CPL 2012, the procuratorates fulfilled their ambition to retain and even extend their present powers by acquiring the authority to supervise the courts in enforcement proceedings.

8.5 Truth v. Speed: Expediency Always Has Precedence

Since the 1990s, the courts have been endeavouring to strike a balance between the wish to establish the facts correctly and the need to provide effective protection of rights within an appropriate timeframe. Paradoxically, the overemphasis on procedural expediency has resulted in a high rate of appeal (as a consequence of the parties' complaints about judicial errors) and frequent retrials, making the whole system increasingly inefficient and costly.

Under the CPL, a civil case of first instance is required to be closed within 6 months in the ordinary procedure and 3 months in the summary procedure. Second instance proceedings (i.e. final instance) must conclude within 3 months. The CPL 2012 added a new small claims procedure under which the decision of the basic people's court shall be final (Art. 162). Failure to dispose a case within the required period is a serious procedural error and may result in disciplinary sanctions against the judge(s) under the current judicial assessment system. Eighty percent of civil cases are within the jurisdiction of basic courts where 90 % of cases are disposed using summary procedure (i.e. within 3 months). Moreover, many basic courts carry out a so-called 'fast track' reform in which a case must be concluded within 30 days. In some basic courts the right to appeal may be waived by the agreement of the parties even if the amount in dispute exceeds the threshold for small claims.

In order to help courts close cases within the set deadlines, the SPC provided a rule which urges the parties to produce evidence in a timely manner (SPC 2001: Art. 33):

> The court notice requesting the parties to produce evidence shall specify the principle and requirements regarding burden of proof, the circumstances under which the parties concerned may plead the people's court to investigate further and collect evidence, the time period prescribed by the people's court for producing evidence and the harmful consequences for failure to produce evidence within the prescribed time period. The time period for producing evidence may be agreed upon by the parties concerned subject to affirmation by the people's court. If the time period for producing evidence is designated by the people's court, the designated time period shall not be shorter than 30 days.

In practice, the parties hardly have any opportunity to set a time period and the courts rarely give the parties more than 30 days to produce evidence.

The policy that efficient disposition of cases always has precedence, even at the price of violating elementary legal certainty and the principle of effective remedy, let alone the accuracy of adjudication, may result in serious damage to judicial credibility. The lack of uniformity of decision-making, the increase in the number of public complaints, and the abuses of the retrial procedure undermine public trust in China's civil justice system. Moreover, complaints against judicial errors lead (like the overemphasis on procedural expediency) to a high rate of appeals and frequently cause retrials, making the whole system increasingly inefficient and costly.

Concerned with this situation, many scholars call on the courts to slow down the proceedings so as to allow adequate time to promote fairness in adjudication (Li 2009). The SPC and many local courts are trying to distinguish complex from simple cases. The former should produce model judgments, while the latter should embody efficiency. The CPL 2012 attempts to adopt the scholars' suggestion of 'diversification of civil procedures' and make the rule of 'the time limit for provision of evidence' more flexible. See e.g. Art. 65:

> Where it is difficult for a party to provide evidence within the time limit, the party may apply to the people's court for an extension, and the people's court may appropriately extend the time limit upon application of the party.
>
> Where a party provides any evidence beyond the time limit, the people's court shall order the party to provide an explanation; and if the party refuses to explain or the party's explanation is not acceptable, the people's court may, according to circumstances at hand, deem the evidence inadmissible or adopt the evidence but impose an admonition or a fine on the party.

These modifications aimed to give more space for accuracy of fact-finding and fairness in the proceedings. Compared with the time taken in the courts of other jurisdictions, China is at the top when it comes to speed of civil proceedings – but only if we calculate the time needed to render an individual (first instance) judgment.

So the dilemma in China currently is not how to balance between accurate and fair proceedings, but how to balance between correct decisions and swift but (very likely) inaccurate judgments.[7]

---

[7] In this context, I would say that incorrect justice cannot be efficient; mistaken justice is equal to no justice at all.

8.6 The Perils of 'Hard Cases' and Innovative Decisions

A 'hard case' in practice has a fuzzy meaning and entails a much broader scope than the academic understanding of the concept (Suli 2009). Apart from the cases involving difficult legal issues, cases with complicated facts or politically (or socially) sensitive cases may also be understood to be within the range of this notion. In order to distinguish between these two groups of cases, I will refer to the latter as 'difficult cases', as opposed to the narrowly defined 'hard cases'.

All difficult cases including hard cases are not welcomed by courts and frequently get refused at the beginning of the proceedings, i.e. at the docketing stage. Usually the reason for refusal is that the court in question has no jurisdiction over the matter. The SPC issued in the 1990s several opinions directing lower courts not to accept certain new types of cases on a temporary basis.[8] Though these instructions were fiercely criticized by some scholars, it seems that it was reasonable to exercise jurisdictional restraint in relation to cases that make courts vulnerable to policy influence, or force them to make decisions without ripe and consistent legal basis. This is only natural in all situations where judicial power has not acquired a status strong enough within the whole political structure to make a final and determinate ruling in novel situations. What is more, the local courts frequently refused to docket cases typically falling in the courts' civil jurisdiction when such types of cases were closely related to social policies or premised on new legal rules. Even if such cases luckily survived the strict 'docketing check', they have been mostly mediated by the courts, thereby avoiding the need to address difficult issues that are likely to arise in adjudication. So it is hard for the public to secure a judicial decision in a difficult case because the hotter the case, the greater the chance that it will be settled by mediation or result in the plaintiff's withdrawal.

Apart from the weak status of courts in comparison with other actors, particularly those from political circles, the other important reason for the precarious position of the judiciary is the dominance of the doctrine according to which social harmony as the prevailing goal of civil justice needs to have the key influence in the actions of each and every judge. Due to this postulate, judges regard their cases as a trouble to resolve, rather than as an incentive to protect a harmed right and draw adequate inferences from violations of legal norms. Judges tend to place attention solely on the opportunities to get rid of disputes that trouble them. They prefer to avoid the big trouble (hard cases) and refrain from creating new trouble (risk of innovation and judicial law-making). Under the pressure of their heavy caseload, of the imperative to reach the goal of social harmony, and of various forms of outside

[8] Among such cases were e.g. disputes arising from rural land rights (these were regarded not to be typical 'civil' cases because of their dependence on political reforms of the economic structure in society). Another example where SPC ordered the courts to refuse cases was tort claims arising from stock transactions that were socially sensitive and difficult to be dealt with by the courts, because the stock market was undergoing institutional reforms with a very scarce legal basis in substantive law.

'supervision' over the courts, judicial reaction is regularly to choose the easier road: to avoid difficult cases altogether.

It is fair to say that in a transitional society such as China, the SPC as the highest court actually plays a very important role in defining and clarifying new legal issues. However, the SPC achieves that not by rendering judgments in hard cases, but by issuing brief replies to legal questions presented by lower courts on specific cases or by issuing general opinions in the form of comprehensive regulations. Both types of SPC opinions are public and binding. Moreover, at the end of 2011, after several years of preparation, the SPC published the first batch of 'guiding cases' (four cases including two civil), and as of the present time the fourth batch has been published. This new mechanism of law interpretation has the purpose 'to sum up the experience of the judicature and unify the application of law'. These 'guiding cases' are not only judgments of the SPC but also judgments of selected lower courts, edited and published by the SPC. The prestige associated with the fact that a lower court judgment was chosen to lead the practice of other courts might encourage judges to accept more difficult cases. What is more important, the present judicial reforms strive to guarantee the courts' independence from outside interference; release the judges from the pressure of administrative evaluation; promote a regular way of control of judgments through appeals rather than the present system of 'reports' to higher court authorities; and separate difficult cases from routine matters, and strengthen the functions of the panel in deciding difficult cases. All these efforts may change the attitude towards difficult cases and encourage Chinese courts to start issuing decisions with the force of precedents, assuming in such a way more important duties besides routine settlement of simple disputes with the goal of maintaining social harmony.

8.7 The Rise of the Principle of Proportionality

It is widely accepted in China that cases should be disposed by different procedures in accordance with their respective nature and social weight, and to afford as much attention to the cases as they deserve (Fu 2011). This concept was partly embodied in the two types of procedures provided in CPL 1991, although the procedures have been criticized – the 'ordinary procedure' (the formal procedure) as not formal enough, and the 'summary procedure' as not simple enough.

The CPL 2012 promoted further the principle of proportionality. As a form of summary procedure, a small claims procedure is introduced (one instance procedure with no appeal). Under the special procedure, judicial confirmation of an out-of-court mediation agreement is now possible. The dunning procedure for debt repayment is simplified. Parties are encouraged to waive the ordinary procedure and choose the summary procedure by agreement. On the other hand, the ordinary procedure is being developed in the direction of formalization and professionalization. The ordinary procedure conducted by a collegial panel (as opposed to a single judge) is, as highlighted above, more formalized and specialized, so that cases that are complex, of greater social importance, or where the disputed amount is significant, would be given more attention. The CPL 2012 added a channel of case separation at the pre-trial stage (Art. 133) and adopted the rules of evidence production which are in line with the earlier SPC's opinions. Presently, more weight and importance is given to the formal notice to the parties and to detailed reasoning in judgment and orders.

In practice, the reforms regarding classification of proceedings began much earlier and have been going much farther than the revision of the CPL. Most basic courts with heavy caseload adopted 'fast track' pilot schemes that made the litigation process more efficient and flexible than the 'summary procedure' and brought about a higher rate of settlement through mediation. A series of directions from the SPC emphasized the deliberation of the panels. In the intermediate and high courts, complex and difficult cases are processed by elite panels and even decided by the 'judicature committee' of the court. Unfortunately, the CPL 2012 failed to separate the procedures in family cases and labor cases from general cases, and the legal criterion for channeling cases from 'ordinary procedure' to 'summary procedure' is still not sufficiently clear. Since the selection of procedures is mainly kept in the judges' hands, their discretionary power sometimes results in the tendency to push all cases in the direction of summary proceedings, no matter whether it would have a negative impact on due process or the protection of the harmed rights.

8.8 Multi-party Matters – A New Concept in the Pursuit for Brave Adjudicators

The aforesaid principles of civil justice are equally applicable in resolving simple bi-party matters and complex multi-party matters. The multi-party procedure is devised to consolidate cases with similar legal and/or factual grounds and resolve them simultaneously so as to avoid conflicting judgments, and at the same time maintain social order, enhance judicial efficiency and level the playing field between parties of different bargaining powers so as to achieve greater fairness. In practice, however, judges are reluctant to process multi-party cases and even refuse to take on class actions because of their complexity, unmanageability and unpredictability. These actions also entail greater political interference due to the high level of social attention they may attract. Those class actions which are accepted by the courts are mainly resolved by judicial mediation or withdrawn after settlement. This fortifies the notion that the goal of dispute resolution is comparatively more important than the protection of rights.

8.9 'Active Justice' and Legality

In Chinese legal culture and judicial custom, achieving an equitable result and substantive justice has always been the priority, and less emphasis is placed on strict legal formalism or entrenchment of the principle of legality. In the 1990s, some judicial reformers and researchers advocated a new concept that the goal of justice and the correct legal solution could be achieved by strict application of law. This new concept resulted in the official recognition of the judicial principle 'take facts as the basis and laws as the criterion'. However, before this concept and judicial principle had an opportunity to be universally adopted by judges, an antithetical concept of 'active justice' started, in recent years, to be implemented. It aims at rectifying situations where the application and interpretation of the law contradicts the necessary results of substantive justice. This may be seen as a regression since the concept of 'active justice' resembles the said cultural preference for equitable results over legal formalism, and adheres to the political pursuit of 'unification of legal and social effect' in civil justice. Nevertheless, most scholars and some elite judges insist that the application of 'active justice' should not infringe judicial functions provided under the CPL: otherwise the judiciary will be nothing more than a mere political tool.

8.10 Problem Solving v. Case Processing: What Is More Important?

Is it the dominant view that the civil justice system needs to approach cases by trying to find adequate resolution of the underlying problems or is it that cases have to be efficiently resolved by means requiring the least effort and expense by the competent authorities? In China, the answer to this question is both complicated and self-contradictory. On the one hand, time limitations to close a case within 3–6 months under the CPL and statistical evaluation of judicial performance strongly compel the courts and judges to focus on case processing. On the other hand, political requirements and judicial policy declared by the central authorities are based on a problem-solving philosophy (*An Jie Shi Liao*, or 'to end the problem while closing the case'), which requires judges to find adequate resolution of the dispute. However, the concept of 'adequacy' in Chinese legal culture does not mean 'legally adequate' (as appraised by the law) or 'legitimate' (as appraised by natural law or the common sense of the public), but denotes 'acceptable' (as appraised by the parties). Based on this philosophy, if a party is dissatisfied with the judgment, even though it is final and effective, the party may still petition to various authorities, including courts, procuratorates, the ombudsman (*xinfang* or 'letters and visits'), offices under the People's Congresses, the government, or the Politics and Law Commission of the CCP, etc. A record of such complaints may shed a negative light on the judge in relation to his or her evaluation, regardless of the fact that only less than 1 % of these petitioned cases may be retried by a procedure called 'adjudication supervision'.

In the light of the above, the goal of Chinese civil justice is to give consideration to both problem solving and case processing. Ironically, neither objective is fulfilled. The dominant view of scholars is that the Chinese civil justice system needs to approach cases with a view to finding adequate resolution of the underlying problems. Unless 'adequate resolution' of disputes is recognized as '*legally* adequate', this goal of civil justice remains unattainable.

8.11 Courts as Suppliers to Local Treasury: The Trends of Commercialization of Civil Justice in Modern China

In China, there is no constitutional right of 'access to justice'. The notion of 'due process' is also not recognized.[9] In the 1980s and early 1990s, the courts operated like commercial institutions where incomes were generated from litigations in local courts to cover budgetary deficits. Since the early 1990s, financial reform has become an important part of judicial reform, with the financial budget being separated from the courts' income derived from legal fees. Nevertheless, at present, the majority of local governments still make budgetary plans for their courts based on the amount courts are able to 'contribute' to the local treasury. Given such a background, the Chinese civil justice system remains a quasi-commercial source of revenue for the public budget.[10]

Impervious to criticisms against the regulation of litigation fees and coupled with the custom that the courts draw money from local governments, judicial independence is hanging by a thread. There are scholars who support the view that civil justice should not be regarded as a freely available public service. The rationale behind this is that when civil proceedings are used only by a fraction of taxpayers (as a public service which has been financed by all taxpayers) to resolve their private disputes and protect their own interests, it would only make sense if the litigants shared the costs to a higher degree. Moreover, civil procedure is regarded as a means to balance procedural rights and obligations between the parties through the allotment of litigation costs. Since the regulation of litigation fees in 2006 was promulgated, the reduction of some fees and/or rate of some fees has contributed to a noticeable increase of caseload and frivolous litigations. The predominant view is that new rules which would increase litigation fees are required to rectify this problem.

8.12 Instead of a Conclusion: Chinese Civil Justice in Pursuit of User Orientation

The NPC's original intention was that the civil justice system should cater for the needs of the users. But several factors have undermined this intention. The first factor is that the participants in the legislative process are mainly senior judges and top-notched professors, procuratorate, and only a small number of lawyers. Since

[9] Instead, citizens are entitled to the basic right to complain against officials and/or government branches under Art. 32 of the Constitution of the PRC; and this so-called 'right of complaint' is ridiculously read as the constitutional source of right of petition against effective judgments with probable 'errors'.

[10] In an attempt to collect money, even the Supreme People's Court introduced some unreasonable charges which were beyond statutory regulations, causing a reaction by the State Council that issued a new regulation on litigation fees drafted by the Treasury Department in 2006.

lawyers in China do not enjoy the same status and bargaining powers as they do in the West, the original intention of the NPC was diluted, albeit scholars among the group usually fight for the rights of the litigants. Secondly, the current CPL is so arduous and outdated that the judiciary in practice places heavy reliance on 'judicial interpretations' issued by the Supreme People's Court, which naturally embeds its own goals, not the goals of those whose rights are at stake.

From the users' perspective, the goal of civil justice established by CPL, in particular the protection of private rights, is neither sufficient nor entrenched; the aim to provide efficient dispute resolution is negated by the notable defects in judicial process and the courts' refusal to accept some complex/sensitive cases. The goals of maintaining social order and educating people are almost unachievable because of the easy and frequent challenges of effective judgments. This may be a reason that in the revision of the CPL the drafters in the NPC pay more attention to the suggestions of independent scholars who support the concept that civil justice should embrace an orientation towards the users whose rights and interests are at stake.

Acknowledgements The author would like to thank Prof. C.H. (Remco) van Rhee, Mr. Peter C.H. Chan and Prof. Alan Uzelac for their comments.

References

CCP (2006) The Decision of the Central Committee of the Communist Party of China: decision to construct socialist harmonious society, 11 October 2006

CPL (1982) Civil Procedure Law 1982

CPL (1991) Civil Procedure Law 1991

CPL (2012) Civil Procedure Law 2012

Hao Li (2009) Prefer to being slower but better. Peking University Law Review 2009/4

SPC (1998) Several Provisions on the Issues Concerning the Civil and Economic Trial Mode Reform 14

SPC (2001) Some Provisions of the SPC on Evidence in Civil Procedures 33

SPC (2007) The Supreme People's Court: opinions on providing judicial guarantee for the construction of socialist harmonious society, 30 January 2007. No.2 法发[2007]

Suli (2009) Legalism, popular will and hard case. Peking University Law Review 2009/1

Weijian Tang (1997) Market economy and looking into the future of civil procedure law. Forum of Politics and Law 1/1997

Yaxin Wang (2004) Procedure, institution and organization: routine procedures in grass-roots courts and the transformation of governance structure. Social Sciences in China 2004/3

Yulin Fu (2011) Small claims vs. procedures classification/systematization. Tsinghua Law Review 3/2011

Chapter 9
Civil Litigation in Russia: 'Guided Justice' and Revival of Public Interest

Dmitry Heroldovich Nokhrin

Abstract The wish to live in an era of change was considered a curse in ancient China. 'An era of change' most Russians call the 20-year period that passed following the collapse of the Soviet Union. During this time even the basic legal categories repeatedly changed their meaning, being sometimes filled with a new content and sometimes restored to the former Soviet standards. The current state of Russian legal doctrine is characterized by simultaneous borrowing of Western and rebirth of Soviet concepts. In this chapter the author presents the rather diverse views on the goals of civil justice among Russian scholars, and assesses the actual practical problems in implementing them in the Russian judicial system. The author also shows the main trends in the development of procedural law and hints at the mistakes, which the Russian legal elites seem to be destined to make over and over again.

9.1 Prevailing Opinions on the Goals of Civil Justice

9.1.1 A Positivist Survey of Hierarchy of Aims and Tasks

In Russian legal doctrine 'justice' is usually understood in two ways. In the broad sense (as 'civil jurisdiction') it covers the activities of numerous bodies involved in the multi-faceted processes aimed at protection and securing of individual rights and legal interests.[1] In the narrow sense, which is represented in older, traditional

[1] According to this meaning of civil justice, it is composed of bodies such as courts, enforcement services and bailiffs, mediators, registrars of all kinds, notaries, etc. This is a common view in contemporary doctrine (e.g. Reshetnikova and Yarkov 1999: 3–4); such a view was rarely expressed by Soviet scholars (see Osipov 1973).

D.H. Nokhrin (✉)
The Constitutional Court of the Russian Federation,
Senatskaya ploschad 1, 190000 Saint Petersburg, Russia
e-mail: Dmitriy.Nohrin@ksrf.ru; sanctum1181@gmail.com

A. Uzelac (ed.), *Goals of Civil Justice and Civil Procedure in Contemporary Judicial Systems*, Ius Gentium: Comparative Perspectives on Law and Justice 34,
DOI 10.1007/978-3-319-03443-0_9, © Springer International Publishing Switzerland 2014

Russian literature, 'justice' covers only the process of judicial decision making and the procedural activities pertaining to this process.[2]

The latter approach is sometimes narrowed even more by excluding private arbitration from the scope of civil justice, by reference to the 'public' and 'authoritative' nature of the term 'justice'. The tension between 'public' and 'private' arbitration is from time to time demonstrated by the opinions of the Supreme Arbitration Court (SAC) of the Russian Federation, which is the highest instance in the system of state commercial courts (not to be confused with voluntary arbitration as a private dispute resolution mechanism). The SAC is continuously attempting to put into question legal provisions that empower arbitrators to deal with disputes that concern real estate, or have some public law element (e.g. when arbitration decisions transfer rights to expensive property, or cause modification of rights registered in land registers, or affect the interests of third parties).[3]

The constitutional concept of civil justice, which is often referred to in jurisprudence and legal writings, was formulated in 2001 by the Constitutional Court of the Russian Federation[4] in following way:

> The administration of justice is a special kind of realization of state power. Carrying out justice, the court applies general legal provision (norm of law) to the concrete circumstances of the case. … To dispense justice should be understood not as the whole of legal proceedings, but as a part of them, which consists in the passing of acts of judicial authority concerning the resolution of issues submitted to the court, i.e. judicial acts resolving the merits of the case at hand. … [In these acts] the court determines the legal status of the parties, i.e. applies norms of law to the circumstances of the concrete legal dispute. Exactly by resolving the case as to the merits (Articles 126, 127, 128 of the Constitution of Russian Federation) and ruling the decision according to the law (Article 120 of the Constitution), the court carries out "justice" in its proper meaning, which is the goal of civil proceedings, and through this implements the rights and freedoms that are directly applicable (Article 18 of the Constitution). Legal acts, though carried out by courts, that do not determine the legal status of the parties and are not aimed at the resolution of the merits of the case, are not covered by the concept of "dispensing justice"…; these acts solve mainly procedural issues arising during the trial: from declaring the application admissible to the execution of the court decision.

---

[2] This view was widely accepted in Soviet textbooks of civil procedure. It was provided in the two most popular textbooks of Soviet times: see Chapter 12 'Competence of courts' by A.A. Dobrovol'skii in Avdyukov et al. (1970: 99–102) and Chapter 3 'Competence of judicial bodies over civil cases' by V.F. Taranenko in Vorob'ev et al. (1967: 50–60).

[3] The first such attempt took place in 2006 when the SAC applied to the Legislative Assembly of the Russian Federation with the project of statutory amendments focused on exclusion of certain kinds of legal disputes from the competence of arbitration, among which were mentioned disputes concerning real estate or the rights thereto; disputes on the rights to the results of intellectual activity demanding registration, patent or certificate delivery; other disputes connected with the possibility of assignation of the judgment-established duties on the third parties. These amendments were greatly criticized by the legal and business communities, so in the end they did not pass. Later the SAC attempted to quash these norms by means of constitutional grounds, but no incompatibility with the Constitution was found by the Constitutional Court of Russia. (See Judgment of 26 May 2011 No. 10-P.)

[4] See Constitutional Court Judgment of 25 January 2001 N 1-P.

The consideration and resolution of disputes, and elimination of uncertainty in the legal relationship between the parties, is traditionally regarded as a basic element within the concept of 'justice'. Russian courts carry out rather various activities and a part of their powers is not connected with consideration of civil disputes. Powers of the court in issues of judicial inspection and administration in this meaning do not concern 'justice' (at least not in the narrow sense).[5]

The peculiar feature of the Russian legal system is the heavy influence of legal positivism and especially of normativist ideas. The procedural law is no exception. Almost everything is directly fixed in the norms of law, including many legal concepts of broad, abstract and not quite clearly shaped meaning. The same is true for the goals of civil proceedings which are also defined in legislation. The federal legislation is frequently inconsistent, so the goals are sometimes called 'aims of civil justice' and sometimes 'procedural tasks'.[6]

Article 2 of the Code of Civil Procedure (CCP) of the Russian Federation contains the same dualism of 'aims' and 'tasks' of civil proceedings. The following aims of civil procedure are listed:

1. protecting the infringed or challenged rights, freedoms and legitimate interests of people, institutions, rights and interests of the Russian Federation, Russian Federation entities, municipal units, other entities that participate in civil, labour or other legal relationship;
2. strengthening of law and order and protecting the principle of legality;
3. prevention of future violations of law; and
4. forming of a respectful attitude towards the law and the court (the latter is deemed to be the 'educational' or 'didactic' purpose of civil proceedings).

Achievement of these objectives is ensured by the main task allocated by procedural legislation – correct and timely consideration and resolution of civil cases.

A similar, slightly extended list of aims is repeated in Article 2 of the Code of Arbitration Procedure (CAP) of the Russian Federation that governs procedure before commercial (arbitration) courts:

1. to protect the violated or disputed rights and legitimate interests of persons performing entrepreneurial and other economic activities, as well as the rights and legitimate interests of the Russian Federation, of the constituent units of the Russian Federation, of municipal entities in the sphere of entrepreneurial and other economic activities, public authorities of the Russian Federation, public authorities of the constituent units of the Russian Federation, local government bodies, other bodies and state officials in that sphere;

[5]This view is shared by A.T. Bonner (1971: 194), N.A. Gromoshina (2002: 26–27), N.A. Chudinovskaya (2008). The opposite view is followed by G.A. Zhilin (2010).

[6]For more detailed information on differentiation of the concepts of 'purpose (aim)' and 'objective (task)' of civil legal proceedings, please refer to Zhilin's study of the notion of the goals of justice (2010: 52–60). The term 'procedural aim' is usually defined as the socially necessary and desirable general result of court proceedings; and by 'procedural task' most understand the special and immediate aim of the process.

2. to ensure the accessibility of justice in the sphere of entrepreneurial and other economic activities;
3. to provide a fair and public hearing within a reasonable time, by an independent and impartial court;
4. to consolidate the rule of law and prevent offences in the sphere of entrepreneurial and other economic activities;
5. to form respect for the law and the court;
6. to assist the establishment and development of business relations and the formation of customs of trade and business ethics.

The 'aims' or 'goals' in the cited norms obviously contain categories of different value and ranking. Summarizing the views of Russian scholars on the goals of civil procedure, the following hierarchy of goals can be construed.

The main goal of legal proceedings in civil cases consists in the protection of infringed or wrongfully challenged rights that are subject to court jurisdiction. It is the main social mission of the court as a body of civil justice. It is also a reflection of the duty of the state to protect individual rights and freedoms by all means of state power, including judicial power, as expressly provided in the Constitution (Articles 2, 17, 18, 45, 46).

This goal is achieved by the accomplishment of the *basic task* arising before the court, which is correct and timely resolution of civil cases. This basic task is composed of a number of *particular tasks* that are performed by the court during certain stages of the proceedings. Among them are the accessibility of justice (mainly important at the initial stages of the proceedings) and the task of fair and public hearing, carried out at the main stage of the proceedings on the merits. Apart from these tasks, the specified separate stages of the process have as well their own aims, which we can refer to as *particular aims*. According to this approach, the 'aim' of a separate stage of the proceedings will be the realization of a concrete procedural right or rights, and a 'task' – the consistent and correct application of the procedural means established by the law with the view to realization of the relevant 'aim' ('particular aim') of a stage.

Thus, the aim of the commencement stage of process in a court of the first instance is the realization of the right to a court, which is reached by bringing the matter before the court and by declaring the case admissible (Zhilin 2010: 136–150). The aim of the preparatory stage of proceedings consists in ensuring the correct and timely consideration and resolution of a case.[7] The hearing on the merits of the case, as the central stage of civil proceedings, has a particular aim and task which coincides with the basic aim and task of the proceedings. Tasks of the procedures regarding the means of recourse against judgments (appeal, etc.) are both correct and timely examination and elimination of judicial errors. The aim of these procedures also coincides with the general (ultimate) aim of civil procedure.[8]

[7] See Art. 148 CCP and Art. 133 p. 3 of the CAP.

[8] This scheme of the aims and tasks of civil process was first proposed by G.A. Zhilin (2000). It summarizes almost all of the more or less serious domestic studies of the subject.

Particular aims and tasks of certain stages of civil procedure often draw the attention of legal scholars. For example, K.I. Komissarov (1971: 7) attributed correction of miscarriages of justice and maintenance of legality in justice to the aims of courts of supervising instance. The control of legality and correctness of judicial decisions was referred by him as the direct task of the procedure, and keeping uniformity of practice before inferior courts – as a derivative task.

The auxiliary aims of civil procedure, in pursuit of which civil justice participates along with other public authorities, are realized through consideration of all civil cases by all the courts of the country. These are the strengthening of law and order; prevention of rights' violation; and promoting respect for the law and the judicial system.[9] Yet the goal of 'legality' is not considered specific for the judicial system: the Public Prosecutor's Office, the Ministry of Justice and the police – all have this same goal. However, this goal has a specific procedural dimension, because it should maintain legal certainty and predictability. This aspect was targeted in several decisions of the European Court of Human Rights concerning the practice of successive annulments and remittals of final judgments that was evaluated as incompatible with the European Convention on Human Rights. This resulted in the reform of specific Russian supervisory procedure, which will be addressed below.

Relevant for the discussion about the goals and aims of procedure is also the ideological and philosophical underpinning of the doctrine. The background approach to the goals of procedure may be libertarian (the one advocating absolute primacy of individual rights) or may be solidarist (the one which emphasizes the need for mutual balance of the individual rights and of a society as a whole).

In general, Russian legal scholarship is solidarist. It agrees that the basic aim of civil process – rights' protection and, through this, the search for the truth and equity – is a part of the broader aim of social harmonization and the search for the social truth. The search for the truth and equity demands 'finding the right balance between contrary interests of the parties on the one hand, and public interest of the state in establishing law and order on the other hand' (Dan'kov 2005).

9.1.2 'Extraneous' and 'Imposed' Goals of Russian Civil Procedure

Evaluating Russian doctrine and statutory provisions on the goals of civil procedure we can state that in reality the basic goals, despite all the social changes did not change much in the past decades. If we remove from CCP 1964 all references to socialism, we will see that the old law listed the same goals as those presently in force. In my opinion, there is nothing surprising about this fact, as the nature of justice itself did not change in Russia.

---

[9] The given understanding of auxiliary aims was shared by A.T. Bonner (1989: 14–15), I.M. Zaitsev (1990: 15), G.A. Zhilin (2000: 16–24, 59–60), N.A. Chechina (1972: 53–57).

The considerations above in Sect. 9.1.1 were mainly rooted in positivist analysis of legal provisions and leading textbooks of civil procedure. However, they should be expanded by pointing to some other goals that are not expressly stated in legal provisions, but nevertheless define the vector of changes in civil procedure of modern Russia. We can state that these 'extraneous goals' are not primarily of a legal but of a political character.[10]

Among such 'extraneous' or 'imposed' goals we can mention the goal of *socialization of civil procedure*. In the past, we could observe two distinct trends in the ideology of procedural law in Russia: one can be called paternalistic and the other – liberal. The goal of socialization is usually associated with a paternalistic trend, which needs a bit of illustration.

In two main branches of Russian court jurisdiction – civil and commercial – these goals seem to be different. It is held that civil courts of general jurisdiction, though dealing with private law cases, cope with many matters that contain an intrinsic element of public interest. These courts are entrusted with the protection of social rights, such as those in labour cases and administrative cases. In these cases an individual, opposed by companies or by the state, is usually a weaker party and may require some additional assistance by the court. So, in Russian (conventional) civil procedure the paternalistic approach is rather common; it caters to the individuals' interests and stands for the goal of socialization of justice, i.e. for easing the accessibility of justice or availability of legal aid (Briksov et al. 2011: 45, 127, 134–140). On the other hand, commercial courts commonly deal with economic relations based on the principles of private initiative, autonomy and competitiveness. Therefore, in the sphere of commercial jurisdiction the liberal trend dominates, strongly supporting free disposition with disputed rights and competitiveness of the process.[11]

Another prominent goal that defines current tendencies in Russian civil procedure is a goal of improving efficiency of the judiciary. The features on the agenda that aim at maintaining and improving the efficiency of Russian civil justice can be divided into two groups: structural and functional. Among the first are projects to establish specialized courts, such as administrative courts, which should relieve the burden of cases from courts of general jurisdiction. Specialized courts for protection of intellectual property rights are already established within the system of general[12] and commercial courts.[13]

[10] In my opinion, the goals of civil justice can be divided into 'normative goals', which are inherent, attributive, constant (proclaimed in the legislation) and 'imposed goals', which are extrinsic, modal, temporary (defined mainly by the considerations of political pragmatism).

[11] See, e.g., V.V. Yarkov's reasoning on functional principles of commercial procedural law (Absaljamov et al. 2010: 69–77).

[12] Federal Law of 2 July 2013 N 187-FZ 'On Amendments to Certain Legislative Acts of the Russian Federation on the protection of intellectual property rights in the information and telecommunications networks'.

[13] Federal Constitutional Law of 6 December 2011 N 4-FKZ 'Amendments to the Federal Constitutional Law "On the Judicial System of the Russian Federation" and the Federal Constitutional Law "On Arbitration Courts in the Russian Federation" in connection with the establishment of the Court for intellectual property rights within the system of commercial courts'.

The functional means of efficiency improvement are diverse. Among them are introduction of special written procedure in simple cases[14] and implementation of the concentration principle in first instance court proceedings, where a case should be prepared for consideration so that it could be heard in one single court hearing. Accordingly, rules on early evidence disclosure are introduced, as well as sanctions in the form of unfavourable consequences for the uncooperative party.[15] Recent legislative amendments also introduced pecuniary liability for judges and bailiffs if they fail to consider and decide a case or enforce a judicial decision within proper time.[16]

Undoubtedly, courts do implement certain state policies. The goal of policy implementation is often understood as subsidiary one, for it is not a specific goal of courts and of civil justice in general. Numerous state bodies implement state policies, including policy concerning justice (the Ministry of Justice, the President, the Government and the Federal Assembly). The state organs often have to protect the same values as the justice system.

However, the aim of policy implementation is nowadays not very appreciated among scholars because our domestic authorities are – I could say desperately – trying to foster judicial independence, and accepting the idea that a judge can be a policy-maker seems to be in contradiction with the idea that the judge should be impartial and unbiased, and not subject to any extraneous influences. But policy goals, as will be showed later, indeed exist, however reluctantly accepted.

9.2 Protection of Individual Rights and Public Interest: The Problem of Balance

Under Article 18 of the Russian Constitution rights and freedoms of a person and a citizen are directly operative. But frequently there are situations when absolutization of individual rights would lead to negative consequences for large groups of citizens. According to the Constitution (Art. 55 p. 3), rights and freedoms can be limited only by a federal law and only to the extent necessary for protection of fundamental principles of the constitutional system, morality, health, the rights and lawful interests of other people, for defence of the country and security of the state. Providing balance between private and public interests is indeed an important general objective. However, law has to be applied in action, and therefore it will be interesting to observe concrete examples of attempts to find such balance.

[14] Federal Law of 25 June 2012 N 86-FZ 'Amendments to the Code of Arbitration Procedure of the Russian Federation in connection with the improvement of summary proceedings'; see also: Federal Law of 9 December 2010 N353-FZ 'Amendments to the Code of Civil Procedure of the Russian Federation'.

[15] Resolution of the Plenum of Supreme Arbitration Court of 20 December 2006 N 65 'On the preparation of the case for trial'.

[16] Federal Law of 30 April 2010 N 68-FZ 'On compensation for the violation of the right to trial within a reasonable time, or of the right to enforcement of a judicial act within a reasonable time'.

9.2.1 Protection of Proprietary Interests of the State

Under special legislation regulating the state budget,[17] the limitation of actions, established by civil legislation of the Russian Federation, did not extend to the actions of the Russian Federation that arose in connection with the granting of budgetary funds on a returnable and compensative basis, including claims on payment of percentages and/or other payments provided by a contract, including claims on unjust enrichment and indemnification. This rule should be applied, in particular, to the relations that arose prior to 1 January 2008 (the date the law in issue came into force).[18]

Commercial courts of Russia in a number of cases ruled that it was not possible to apply the disputed norms retroactively to the legal relations that had already been covered by the statute of limitation before that provision came into force. They also considered that the given norms extend only to the budgetary relations, which are not by their nature civil, and do not cover contracts, concerning the transfer of budgetary funds, concluded between commercial organizations. The Supreme Arbitration Court initiated a constitutional procedure against these provisions. The Constitutional Court in its Judgment of 20 July 2011 upheld the cited position of state arbitration courts.[19]

9.2.2 Compensation for Undue Administration of Justice

The European Court of Human Rights (ECtHR) in the 'pilot' judgment adopted by the Chamber in the case of *Burdov v. Russia (no. 2)*[20] expressed a grave concern with the problem of non-enforcement or delayed enforcement of domestic judgments in Russia, which in the Court's assertion very frequently occurred in cases concerning the payment of pensions, child allowances, compensation for damage sustained during military service or compensation for wrongful prosecution. Thus, the Court obliged the Russian Federation to implement in the national legal system certain mechanisms to cope with such flaws. The Federal Law of 30 April 2010 N 68-FZ 'On compensation for the violation of the right to trial within a reasonable time, or of the right to enforcement of a judicial act within a reasonable time' (the Compensation Act) was enacted in the wake of this judgment.

---

[17] See point 4 of Article 93.4 of the Budgetary Code of the Russian Federation (as enacted by the Federal Law of 26 April 2007 N 63-FZ).

[18] See Article 5 (part 6) of the Federal Law of 26 April 2007 N 63-FZ.

[19] This judgment was followed by amendment of the disputed provision in Federal Law of 12 November 2012 N 189-FZ. Claims of the state can now be brought to court within a 5-year period since the time of violation. This period for limitation of actions is still longer than is common, but at least the legislator has successfully overcome the issues of retroactivity and uncertainty.

[20] *Burdov v. Russia (no. 2)*, no. 33509/04, 15 January 2009.

The law provides pecuniary liability of the state for the actual omission by courts or bodies of compulsory enforcement that resulted in a violation of the right to trial and enforcement within reasonable time. However, it is clear from both the wording of the Compensation Act and its interpretation by the Supreme Court that in the sphere of enforcement this remedial tool can only be applied to situations connected with non-enforcement of judgments establishing pecuniary obligations of the state and not to those imposing obligations in kind (such as provision of housing, housing maintenance and repair services, provision of a car for a disabled person, etc.). This had been addressed by the ECtHR in Chamber Judgments of 17 April 2012 in the cases of *Ilyushkin and Others v. Russia* (application nos. 5734/08 et seq.) and *Kalinkin and Others v. Russia* (nos. 16967/10 et seq.), which concerned 50 members of the Russian armed forces who suffered excessive delays in enforcing judicial decisions ordering the Russian authorities to provide them with housing. The Court also communicated a number of applications concerning the issue with a view to a possible pilot judgment.[21] The first approximation that can be considered a preliminary solution of the mentioned problem was the Constitutional Court ruling where the mechanism that allows converting obligations in kind into pecuniary obligations was proposed.[22]

9.2.3 Protection of the Public Morals

The issue of public morality can be vividly illustrated by the decision of the ECtHR in the case of *Alekseyev v. Russia* (21 October 2010). Mr. Alekseyev, together with other individuals, was an organizer for a number of marches to draw public attention to discrimination against the gay and lesbian minority in Russia. The decisions of Moscow officials contained refusals to hold these marches on the grounds of protection of public order, health, morals and the rights and freedoms of others, and on preventing riots. Courts of general jurisdiction, guided by corresponding provisions of the law on processions and meetings, as well as by reasons of morals and public safety, refused to repeal the challenged decisions.

Evaluating these considerations, the ECtHR pointed out that the mere risk that a demonstration might create a disturbance was not sufficient to justify its ban. If every probability of tension and heated exchange between opposing groups during a demonstration resulted in the demonstration's prohibition, society would be deprived of hearing differing views on questions which offended the sensitivity of the majority opinion, which is contrary to the principles of the European Convention on Human Rights. The Russian government stated in their submissions to the Court that such events had to be banned as a matter of principle because gay propaganda was incompatible with religious doctrine and public morals, and could harm children and adults who were exposed to it.

[21] *Gerasimov and 14 other applications v. Russia*, no. 29920/05.

[22] Decision of the Constitutional Court of Russia of 1 November 2012 N 2008-O.

Avoiding an estimation of how good the reasons of domestic courts were, of Tverskoy district court of Moscow in particular, as well as those of other officials in the case of Mr. Alekseyev, all these bodies pretended to follow what they thought to be traditional Russian ideas on law and morals. They declared in particular that homosexuals in Russia were not exposed to any real discrimination, because Russian legislation did not recognize sexual orientation as a circumstance in any way significant as a discriminatory basis, leaving thereby its protection out of the legal sphere, since this was a free choice of an individual. The courts also rejected the claim that the inability to conclude gay marriage constituted discrimination, as the same legal consequences could be reached by other legal means[23]: gay partners could settle their mutual proprietary rights through a standard civil contract, they could inherit each other's property by means of a last will and testament, they could even adopt children, because according to Russian law single foster parents were allowed.[24] It was concluded that legislation provides to gays a full set of remedial features, so no special changes were required and no real discrimination was confirmed to exist. That is why the demands to organize a Gay Pride parade had been regarded not as a struggle against discrimination, but as an attempt at homosexual propaganda. As commonly believed in Russia, research shows that sexual orientation is determined by genetic and other medical factors only for a small percentage of homosexuals. Many choose this orientation because of its socializing effect – under the influence of gays in their milieu and due to their specific subculture (Plummer 1975).[25] This is why the propaganda of homosexuality would enter into contradiction with the morals of the society, increasing the threat of public disturbance and acts of violence.

9.2.4 Protecting the Tradition in Family Relations

Courts of the Russian Federation traditionally treat with awe social rights given to women in connection with motherhood. Thus they are extremely reluctant in admitting men to the sphere of such rights, in particular when men appear in typically 'female' roles, for example, in the role of a single parent.

[23] Sophisticated arguments on why marriage should only be understood as the conjugal union of husband and wife, in many aspects similar to considerations common for Russian authorities, can also be found in the West (Sherif Girgis et al. 2010).

[24] This reasoning has been continued by the authorities outside of the *Alekseev* case – in connection with the adoption of a corpus of legislative acts, both regional and federal, aimed to ban the promotion of homosexuality. Protecting the interests of children is declared to be the main cause of its acceptance. The authorities now speak openly about the inadmissibility of the adoption of children by homosexual couples, as this adoption is not in the interests of the child and is at odds with the provisions of the UN Convention on the Rights of the Child, which enshrines the right to a family in its historical sense as the right to mother and father.

[25] Grounds for such a conclusion are sometimes found in literature that was originally intended to contend prejudices against homosexuals. See, for example, reasoning concerning 'pushing the right buttons: halting, derailing, or reversing the "engine of prejudice"' (Marshall and Hunter 1989: 147–157).

Such a situation had happened to Mr. Markin, a Russian military serviceman, who unsuccessfully tried to uphold his right to parental leave. His applications in this connection were considered by the Constitutional Court of Russia, which held:

> Owing to the specific demands of military service, non-performance of military duties by military personnel *en masse* must be avoided as it might cause detriment to the public interests protected by law. Therefore, the fact that servicemen under contract are not entitled to parental leave cannot be regarded as a breach of their constitutional rights or freedoms, including their right to take care of, and bring up, children guaranteed by Article 38 § 2 of the Constitution of the Russian Federation. Moreover, this limitation is justified by the voluntary nature of the military service contract ... By granting, on an exceptional basis, the right to parental leave to servicewomen only, the legislature took into account, firstly, the limited participation of women in military service and, secondly, the special social role of women associated with motherhood. (Decision of 15 January 2009 N 187-O-O)

The reasoning concerning 'special social role of women associated with motherhood' was later regarded in the *Konstantin Markin* case as gender prejudice by the European Court of Human Rights.[26] It should be noted that attempts to reconsider preconceived gender stereotypes traditionally cause negative reactions in Russia.

9.2.5 Institutional Mechanisms for the Protection of Public Interests

In Russia, an institution traditionally designed to protect public interests and the interests of the state is the Public Prosecutor's Office. Article 45 of the Code of Civil Procedure regulates the participation of the public prosecutor in civil cases. The public prosecutor has the right to institute civil court actions for the purpose of protecting the rights, freedoms and legitimate interests of individuals, of an indefinite circle of persons, or of interests of the Russian Federation, entities of the Russian Federation, and municipal units. The Code of Arbitration Procedure (Art. 52) contains similar provisions, except for the option of bringing a suit in favour of a concrete individual. The action in favour of the concrete citizen can be brought by the public prosecutor under rules of the CCP only in cases when the citizen, because of a poor state of health, age, incapacity and other good reasons, cannot address the court himself.

In civil proceedings governed by the CCP the prosecutor may also participate in cases concerning eviction, illegal termination of employment and compensation of the harm caused to life or health. In these cases, seeking the goal of strengthening obedience and respect for the law, he can make an official statement ('conclusion') as to whether the acts subject to the court's investigation were executed by the respective officials in strict compliance with the law.

[26] See ECHR Judgment of 7 October 2010 (Application No. 30078/06).

Certain problems may occur when the prosecutor, for example, initiates the process of eviction in favour of the municipal unit and at the same time participates in the case as the 'unbiased' provider of legality, issuing a 'conclusion' on compliance with the law. In such an example, two conflicting procedural functions coincide – the function of a party (plaintiff) and the function of an impartial body for the protection of legality. Such a conflict may lead to the breach of the right to a fair trial and, in particular, infringes the balance of the procedural rights of the parties. The Constitutional Court has done much to deal with this problem, and nowadays that kind of practice is almost unheard of.[27]

The other instrument of public interests protection is the procedure of supervision (*nadzor*). The supervision procedure even caused certain tensions in relations between Russia and the Council of Europe as this procedure was repeatedly found by the ECtHR not to be in correspondence with the European Convention on Human Rights, mainly in connection with the *res judicata* principle and the principle of legal certainty.[28] This procedure allowed the changing of the final and binding judicial decision on the basis of violation of uniformity in the application of law, or if the challenged decision violated the rights and legitimate interests of the general public or public interests (Art. 387 CCP, Art. 304 CAP).

Subsequently these provisions of the CCP and CAP were amended, partly also due to the decisions of the Constitutional Court.[29] The most important changes are: (1) shortening of the period during which bringing of supervisory appeal is admissible (now it is 6 months from finality of the challenged act); (2) obligatory requirement of appealing against the disputed decision (duty to exhaust ordinary means of recourse); (3) elimination of the Supreme Court officials' power to bring 'supervisory reports' *ex officio*; and (4) narrowing the possibility of repeated consecutive supervisory reviews in the courts of different level.

Recently, the procedure of supervisory review was totally redesigned and is currently organized in a more conventional way. From 1 January 2012 it has been almost fully replaced by the reformed cassation procedure and the 'old-fashioned' supervision is now only possible in the presidiums of highest courts on a limited number of occasions.

---

[27] Decisions of the Constitutional Court of the Russian Federation of 20 June 2006 N 165-O and N 176-O (cases of Ms. Frenkel and of Ms. Abdurakhmanova, evicted as a result of process initiated by the Solntsevsky interdistrict public prosecutor). At present, it is held that the right of individual occupation, according to Russian housing law, does not as such affect the essence of the public right of possession to the extent that would make the prosecutor's initiative necessary; therefore, public bodies, executing powers in the sphere of public property, should initiate this kind of proceedings, in particular regarding eviction, by themselves, enabling the prosecutor to perform his primary task of providing legality.

[28] See, in particular *Ryabykh v. Russia*, Judgment of 24 July 2003; *Zasurtsev v. Russia*, Judgment of 27 April 2006; *Nelyubin v. Russia*, Judgment of 2 November 2006.

[29] See Federal Law of 4 December 2007 N 330-FZ; Constitutional Court Judgment of 5 February 2007 No. 2-P.

9.2.6 Maintaining the Uniformity of Law

Throughout the Soviet and post-Soviet period judicial supervision was intended to be the procedure aimed at securing the uniformity of law. However, in 2008 the Supreme Arbitration Court recognized that the existing supervision procedure was not an effective tool for that purpose.[30] Thus, the function of providing uniformity was imposed as well on re-trial procedure for new and newly discovered circumstances. According to this Resolution, if the decision of the Presidium or the Plenum of SAC contains any 'new' interpretation of legal provisions, which is indicated to have retroactive force, any interested person involved in any already resolved analogous case may demand retrial of that case on the basis of such decision of SAC and revision of an existent final decision.

This initiative of SAC had been found consistent with the Constitution,[31] and later was legislated in the amendments introduced to the Code of Civil Procedure[32] and the Code of Arbitration Procedure.[33] These amendments conferred on the Supreme Court the same power of retroactive application of its changed interpretation of law in cases considered and finally decided by the courts.

At present, most experts agree that this innovation granted to the highest courts a new tool to control the activities of subordinate courts, which works against the principles of judicial independence and legal certainty.[34] The new regulation has already borne fruit. During 2011–2013, the Constitutional Court had an influx of appeals brought by various entities, whose cases were reconsidered as a result of the introduction of the new mechanism.[35] For example, a large number of commercial enterprises was subject to remarkable changes in case law on mortgage disputes. The Supreme Arbitration Court found that in case of changes (concerning the sum of the debt, percentages, etc.) in the contract between the creditor and the debtor, whose obligation is secured by a mortgage provided by a third party, the mortgage remains as is and the consent of the mortgagor for such changes in the contract is not required. The present legal interpretation was given a retroactive power in the Judgment of the Presidium of SAC of 17 March 2011 N 13819/10. This allowed unscrupulous lenders and borrowers to act in collusion, which resulted in the bankruptcy of some of the major players in the mortgage market.

---

[30] See Resolution of 14 February 2008 N 14 of the Supreme Arbitration Court.

[31] Judgment of the Constitutional Court of 21 January 2010 No. 1-P.

[32] Federal Law of 9 December 2010 N 353-FZ 'On amendments to the Code of Civil Procedure of the Russian Federation'.

[33] Federal Law of 23 December 2010 N 379-FZ 'On amendments to the Code of Arbitration Procedure of the Russian Federation'.

[34] In its most colourful form this concern was expressed in the dissenting opinions of judges Gennadiy Zhilin and Mikhail Kleandrov to the aforementioned Judgment of the Constitutional Court.

[35] For illustration: Judgment of the Constitutional Court of the Russian Federation of 8 November 2012 N 25-P (upon the complaint of JSC 'Transnefteprodukt'); Decision of 28 June 2012 N 1252-O (upon complaint of JSC 'Fabrika proizvodstva platkov'); Decision of 29 November 2012 N 2348-O (upon complaint of LLC 'Eksima') etc.

Another controversial initiative was carried out internally within the Supreme Arbitration Court for the past 7 years. This is the so-called 'prejudicial request' or 'request for a preliminary ruling'. Russia's understanding of such a request has little in common with the procedure of the same name provided in Art. 267 of the Treaty on the Functioning of the European Union. The 'preliminary ruling Russian-style' should be organized in the way that a trial court, when faced with the legal issue that has not been uniformly resolved in case law, is obliged to request from a higher court a preliminary ruling on the subject.

This question has been raised repeatedly in the speeches of the President of the Supreme Arbitration Court and in the publications of its judges (Neshataeva 2007). According to various experts, this initiative threatens at least three important procedural principles: the principle of judicial independence (since the trial judge will be bound by an abstract view of a higher court), the right to a trial by a competent court (because the consideration of the case on the merits will effectively be transferred to the higher court), and the right to a fair trial (because in case of appeal, the higher court will be bound by its own previously expressed opinion).[36] Currently, the legislation on this issue is in the stage of development under the auspices of the Supreme Arbitration Court. Hopefully, this 'guiding' tool, which is being designed for one purpose only – to achieve maximum 'controllability of justice' – will not be implemented hastily, as it sometimes happens in Russia.

9.2.7 Protecting Third Parties' Rights

The task of protecting the rights of third parties evolved gradually from a minor issue to a task of major importance. This development is mainly due to the strengthening of dispositive features of civil proceedings.

The 2002 Code of Arbitration Procedure was the first procedural statute that clearly granted the parties who did not participate in the first instance proceedings the right to appeal against the decision, if they supposed that the challenged decision affected their rights and duties. In such a way third parties may use the procedures of appellation, cassation and supervisory review (Art. 42). The Code of Civil Procedure, enacted later in the same year, unfortunately did not follow the Code of Arbitration Procedure, allowing the third party only a limited number of means for quashing such decisions – either in the process of supervision, or by submitting their claim in a separate legal suit.

The problem of accessibility of appellation and cassation procedures for third parties finally became a constitutional issue. The Constitutional Court acknowledged the right of third parties to bring cassation appeals against the court decisions, which allegedly affected their rights.[37]

---

[36] Khalatov (2011) and Smol'nikov (2012) give an illustration of vivid discussion, concerning the issue, on the pages of their internet blogs.

[37] See CC Judgment of 20 February 2006 N 1-P. As to the appellation procedure, the analogous right was recognized for the third parties in the Judgment of 21 April 2010 N 10-P.

9.2.8 *Fostering Judicial Independence (or Hindering Intervention of the Civil Sector)*

Among the most recent means supposed to ensure the judicial independence is the legislative initiative of the government aimed at preventing so-called 'non-procedural appeals'. 'Non-procedural appeal' is an appeal to the judge lodged by persons who are not parties to the proceedings, or an appeal filed by trial participants but in a form that is not provided in procedural law. Non-procedural appeal is, pursuant to new legislation, no longer allowed.[38]

With the adoption of this Act, the process of formation of a full-fledged institution of *amicus curiae* in Russia will become extremely difficult. The persons and entities that dared to intervene on behalf of public interest by submitting to court legal opinions, materials, reports and other evidence that could affect the judgment, such as representatives of non-governmental organizations and other civil society organizations, under the new regulation face the risk of being subject to persecution.

9.3 The Clash of Two Truths: 'Material' v. 'Formal' Truth

In Soviet civil procedure, the principle of material truth was considered an important part of the principle of legality. The construct of 'material truth' was contained in Article 14 of the Code of Civil Procedure of 1964:

> The court is obliged, without being limited to the material and arguments presented by the parties, to take all measures provided by law for comprehensive, full and objective investigation of the real circumstances of the case and of the rights and duties of the parties.

In theory, the noted principle was understood as a requirement addressed to courts (or, even broader, to all law practitioners) that their decisions strictly and fully correspond to the objective reality.[39] This legal approach was based on philosophical doctrine of dialectical materialism, which recognized the objective cognoscibility of the events of the past. Most scholars of that time (S.V. Kurylev, M.A. Gurvich, O.V. Ivanov, M.K. Treushnikov) considered the finding of 'material truth' as the main goal of procedure, stating that it should be found even if it is contradictory to the interests of the parties. The public character of Soviet civil procedure was thereby highlighted, in accordance with the doctrine of 'socialist legality'. Upon discovering that parties' actions were 'unlawful', the court had broad powers in the struggle against alleged deviations: it could make special court rulings, imposing on

---

[38] Federal Law of 2 July 2013 N 166-FZ 'On Amendments to Certain Legislative Acts of the Russian Federation'.

[39] See Alekseev (1982: 321) and Treushnikov (1998: 9–12).

parties the duty to eliminate certain illegalities; rulings obliging the prosecutor to initiate criminal investigation when the court during the trial suspected that a criminal offence had been committed; and it could even initiate criminal proceedings on its own motion in cases of impending urgency. The search for the 'material truth' was an argument to justify the application of supervisory reports by officials of the highest courts and the Public Prosecutor's Office. Subsequently, this changed corresponding to the changes in the state policies, as well as to the changes of paradigm in scholarship.

Many contemporary jurists appreciate the concept of 'formal truth' (among such – Yarkov, Reshetnikova, Murad'yan), understanding the process of judicial cognition as the process of infinitely approaching the truth, the absolute of which is objective, but can hardly be reached with usage of the limited means that are at the court's disposal (Bernam et al. 1996: 26). Besides, the concept of 'material truth' does not correspond well to the competitive and dispositive nature of modern process. The rule of 'reasonable doubt' is fully integrated in law, and decisions are considered just if they are substantiated by the evidence provided by the parties. The limitation of court investigative powers fosters procedural economy, shortens the time needed to process the case, and is focused on providing effective protection of rights in an appropriate time.

The doctrine of 'legal truth' as 'procedural truth' is advanced by Professor Zhilin (2010), who develops a concept which is not purely formal (because formal truth might presuppose that established facts do not correspond with real facts), nor can it be considered objective (because the means available for fact-finding are limited, so complete objectivity can hardly be reached). Therefore, the concept of 'procedural truth' shares features of both, but coincides with neither of the two.

9.4 Equitable Results as a Result of Strict Formal Application of Law

Reaching equitable results and observing the principle of legality are both equally important goals of civil justice. It is commonly considered that an equitable result is a result which is in strict correspondence with law. The task of reaching such a result and the task of correct application of the law, and thus of strengthening of the legality, coincide and cannot be opposed to each other. Of course, sometimes acts of legislation do not correspond with the meaning and intention of the hierarchically higher norms (in particular, the norms of the Constitution and of the European Convention on Human Rights). In such cases the problematic norms are disqualified with the help of the highest court instances.

If the court of civil jurisdiction during the process comes to the conclusion that certain norms of applicable law contradict the provisions of higher rank, it is a duty of the court to address the Constitutional Court and submit specific query, suspending the process until the Constitutional Court rules on this issue.

9.5 Proportionality Principle and Discretionary Filtering of Appeals

9.5.1 General Considerations

Logically, 'hard and important' cases have more chances to reach the higher court instances, so the decisions on them are more likely to become precedential. Simple cases most likely will find their resolution in the courts of lower instances. Thereby, we can say that a specific system of automatic regulation and 'channelling' of cases depending on their complexity naturally exists in the civil process.

The court cannot elude the claim addressed to it, otherwise it would construct a 'denial of justice', which is unacceptable and unconstitutional. That is why the Code of Arbitration Procedure does not have a norm that would allow refusal to start the process, so it starts even if the court is not competent to consider the claim (in this case the court can discontinue the process later after finding the obstacle). Article 134 CCP allows the court to refuse initiation of the process in a limited set of circumstances, such as (1) where the court is obviously incompetent to resolve the issue and other judicial procedure (possibly referring to other branches of judicial power) is clearly established in the legislation for that kind of issue; (2) when the power to initiate a process is only provided for specific officials (this concerns protection of the public interest or of the rights and interests of an 'unidentified set of persons'); (3) when the final judicial act on the issue already exists. It is not allowed that the court refuse to file the claim while suggesting that the challenged acts have nothing to do with the rights of the claimant.[40]

However, the mechanisms of case filtering involving court discretion actually exist in the procedures of cassation and supervision. In these proceedings the rejection to accept respective means of recourse does not form 'denial of justice' due to the 'extraordinary nature' of these procedures. Before such an appeal could be considered on the merits by the Presidium (or College) of the appropriate higher court, it should pass two preliminary stages, successful passage of which depends on the complexity and importance of the case, and the extent to which possible judicial error affects the rights of the parties or public interests. This preliminary examination of the case is not very detailed in the CCP, thus it provides flexibility and allows the court to focus on important practice-forming cases.

Hence, in general, all the cases that are brought to court should be considered irrespective of their complexity and importance. However, there may be certain peculiarities in the way of handling simple cases. Some of the claims if they are indisputable and supported by certain forms of evidence can be resolved in the form of an order of the court, not by the court judgment (Chapter 11 of the Code of Civil Procedure). This order can be easily quashed if the debtor objects to it. When this happens the case is heard in a regular way. Analogously, in arbitration courts if the

[40] Decisions of the Constitutional Court of 08 July 2004 N 238-O, of 20 October 2005 N 513-O, of 24 January 2006 N 3-O.

claim is not contested or acknowledged by the respondent, or the claim deals with an insignificant sum, the case can be considered in the simplified procedure. Such legal proceedings are held in the absence of the parties. The court evaluates only written evidence and arguments on substance of the claim presented in writing.[41]

9.5.2 'Deformalization' of the Procedure

Recent amendments to procedural legislation reveal strong tendencies of 'deformalization' and simplification of court procedure.

The Federal Law of 25 June 2012 N 86-FZ changed the procedure for summary proceedings in the arbitration process. The judge hears the case summarily without summoning the parties after the expiry of the deadlines set by the court for the presentation of written evidence and other documents; the ability of the parties to call for the 'full' procedure is limited by the specific circumstances listed in the law.

The same tendencies can be illustrated in the example of reshaping 'private appeals' (i.e. *ex parte* appeals on procedural matters) in Russian civil procedure. The proceedings in such appeals is differentiated from regular appeals, allowing both written (*in absentia*) and oral ('internal') appeals. The procedure also depends on the type of appealed decisions. Under new rules,[42] the private appeal of the party or corresponding statement of the prosecutor brought against the procedural decision of the court of first instance shall be considered without notice to the persons involved in the case.[43] An exception is the decisions on the stay or termination of the proceedings or on the abandonment of the application without consideration. The legislator took into account that in procedural appeals attention is paid not to the facts of the case, but to the examination of plainly formal procedural matters, so the need for oral proceedings and the personal presence of the parties at the hearing is considerably reduced.

These changes were assessed in the Judgment of the Constitutional Court of the Russian Federation of 30 November 2012, No. 29-P. The amendments were considered to be compatible with the Constitution as far as the right of the parties to be informed of the filing of such 'private appeals' was guaranteed. Moreover, parties should have an opportunity to get acquainted with the essence of an appeal, and respond to it by notifying the court of their opinion in writing. The norms on 'private appeals' also presuppose the right of the court to hold oral hearings regarding disputed procedural issues if it is necessary; if the court, having estimated the complexity and importance of the issue, decides to hear it in the presence of the parties, the latter should be informed of the time and place of the hearing and given the right to present their opinions orally.

---

[41] See Chapter 29 of the CAP.

[42] See Article 333 and Article 244.6, fifth paragraph CCP.

[43] This norm was enacted by the Federal Law of 9 December 2010 N 353-FZ.

It seems that cited amendments to procedural laws coincide with the stance taken by the Constitutional Court, according to which the legislature should establish such institutional and procedural conditions for the exercise of procedural rights that would meet the requirements of procedural efficiency, economy in the use of remedies, and thus would ensure the fairness of the decision, without which the balance between public and private interests is unattainable; the neglect of the principle of procedural economy entails the unnecessary and meaningless waste of time, financial and human resources of the state.[44]

The indicated trends of simplification of particular aspects of civil proceedings cannot be considered ill-founded and have an objective basis. But the question of how well these changes fit the Russian legal system remains. The answer to this question may depend on the existing level of trust people have in the domestic judicial system.

9.6 Concluding Remarks

'Era of changes' always means not only a time of instability, unpredictability and uncertainty but also the space for new opportunities, for hope and dreams. The Russian domestic legal system is obviously not inert and unchangeable, so there are still possibilities for its improvement. In my opinion, despite all the flaws the democratic trends in the Russian system of civil justice will eventually prevail, and a solid basis for a trustworthy and independent judicial system will be finally built. The more intense the cooperation in the legal sphere between Russia and the international community is, the easier the achievement of this task will appear. Broader involvement of Russian scholars and judicial professionals in the global exchange of ideas and their access to major international legal forums give grounds for optimism. Final success is, however, far from certain. The only certain conclusion that can be provided so far is that the struggle for democratic, transparent and equitable justice in Russia is far from over, and many structural deficiencies are yet to be overcome in reaching this goal.

References

Absaljamov AV, Arsenov IG, Vinogradova EA, Degtjarev SL, Polonskij BJ, Razd'jakonov ES, Reshetnikova IV, Skuratovskij ML, Yarkov VV, Kuznecov EV, Komarov IS (2010) In: Yarkov VV (ed) Arbitrazhnyj process: uchebnik [The arbitration process: textbook]. Infotropik Media, Moscow

Alekseev SS (1982) Obschaya teoriya prava [General theory of law]. 2. Yuridicheskaya literatura, Moscow

[44] Judgment of 19 July 2011 N 17-P.

Avdyukov MG, Averin DD, Anosova SV, Dobrovol'skij AA, Kleinman AF, Kovaleva EN, Loginov PV, Smyshlyaev LP (1970) Sovetskii grazhdanskij process: Uchebnik [Soviet civil process: textbook]. Moscow State University, Moscow
Bernam W, Reshetnikova IV, Yarkov VV (1996) Sudebnaya reforma: problemy grazhdanskoj yurisdikcii [Judicial reform: problems of civil jurisdiction]. Publishing of Humanitarian University, Yekaterinburg
Bonner AT (1971) Nekotorye problemy socialisticheskogo pravosudiya [Certain problems of socialist justice]. In: Shakarian MS (ed) Trudy VYuZI. Tom 17: Voprosy grazhdanskogo processual'nogo prava [Works of All-Union Extramural Institute of Law. Vol. 17: Problems of civil procedural law]. VYuZI, Moscow
Bonner AT (1989) Princip zakonnosti v sovetskom grazhdanskom processe [Principle of legality in the Soviet civil procedure]. RIO VYuZI, Moscow
Briksov VV, Ganicheva ES, Gorokhov BA, Zhilin GA, Zaitsev VY, Kalinin VV, Nikitin SV, Novik-Kachan MY, Prikhod'ko IA, Tolcheev NK, Fokina MA, Fursov DA, Kharlamova IV, Khudenko KI (2011) In: Zhilin GA (ed) Kommentarii k Grazhdanskomu processual'nomu kodeksu Rossiiskoi Federacii: postateinyi [Commentary to the Civil Procedure Code of the Russian Federation: itemized]. Prospect, Moscow
Chechina NA (1972) Vospitatel'naya funkciya sovetskogo grazhdanskogo processual'nogo prava [Educational function of the Soviet civil procedural law]. Izdatel'stvo LGU (Leningrad State University), Leningrad
Chudinovskaya NA (2008) Ustanovlenie yuridicheskih faktov v grazhdanskom i arbitrazhnom processe [Establishing of facts in civil and arbitrary process]. Wolters Kluwer, Moscow
Dan'kov AA (2005) Balans chastnogo i publichnogo interesov i ego znachenie v pravoprimenitel'noi deyatel'nosti [Balance between private and public interests and its value for the application of laws]. Problemy Mestnogo Samoupravleniya [Problems of local government] 16(4). Available at: http://www.samoupravlenie.ru/16-05.htm Last accessed 24 July 2013
Girgis S, George R, Anderson RT (2010) What is marriage? Harv J Law Pub Policy 34(1):245–287
Gromoshina NA (2002) K voprosu o vidah grazhdanskogo sudoproizvodstva [Towards the problem of types of civil procedure]. In: Uletova GD (ed) Zaschita prav i zakonnyh interesov grazhdan i organizacii: Materialy Mezhdunarodnoi nauchno-prakticheskoi konferencii [Protection of rights and legal interests of citizens and organizations: Materials of international conference]. Part 2. Publishing of Kuban' State University, Krasnodar/Sochi
Khalatov S (2011) O sovetakh starshikh tovarischej [On the advices of elders]. Available at: http://blog.pravo.ru/blog/arbitr_sudoproizvodstvo/1258.html. Last accessed 25 July 2013
Komissarov KI (1971) Zadachi sudebnogo nadzora v sfere grazhdanskogo sudoproizvodstva [Aims of judicial supervision in the sphere of civil justice]. Sverdlovskii yuridicheskii institut, Sverdlovsk
Marshall K, Hunter M (1989) After the ball: how America will conquer its fear and hatred of gays in the 90s. Doubleday, New York
Neshataeva TN (2007) Formirovanie edinoobraznoj sudebnoj praktiki i vozmozhnosti vvedeniya procedury preyudicial'nogo zaprosa v processual'noe zakonodatel'stvo Rossii [Formation of uniform court practice and possibility for implementation of prejudicial request procedure into procedural legislation of Russia]. Zakonodatel'stvo [Legislation] 5:52–55
Osipov JK (1973) Podvedomstvennost' yuridicheskih del [Jurisdiction in legal matters]. Sverdlovsk: Sverdlovskii yuridicheskii institut. Republished in 2004. Rossiiskii ezhegodnik grazhdanskogo i arbitrazhnogo processa [Russian yearbook of civil and arbitrational process] 3: 721–829. Publishing house of Saint-Petersburg State University, Saint-Petersburg
Plummer K (1975) Sexual stigma: an interactionist account. Routledge & Kegan Paul, London
Reshetnikova IV, Yarkov VV (1999) Grazhdanskoe pravo i grazhdanskii process v sovremennoi Rossii [Civil law and civil procedure in contemporary Russia]. Norma, Moscow/Yekaterinburg
Smol'nikov D (2012) VAS obsudil preyudicial'nyj zapros s Sudom ES [SAC have discussed prejudicial request with ECHR]. Available at: http://zakon.ru/Blogs/vas_obsudil_preyudicialnyj_zapros_s_sudom_es/2650. Last accessed 25 July 2013

Treushnikov MK (1998) Sudebnye dokazatel'stva [Judicial evidence]. Gorodets, Moscow

Vorob'ev MK, Gurvich MA, Kurylev SV, Marysheva NI, Sergun AK, Taranenko VF, Trubnikov PY, Shakaryan MS (1967) In: Gurvich MA (ed) Sovetskii grazhdanskii process: Uchebnik [Soviet civil process: textbook]. Vysshaya shkola, Moscow

Zaitsev IM (1990) Tselevye ustanovki grazhdanskogo sudoproizvodstva [Goals of civil justice]. In: Volozhanin VP (ed) Problemy reformy grazhdanskogo processual'nogo prava i praktiki ego primeneniya [Problems of reform of civil procedural law and of practice of its application]. Sverdlovskii yuridicheskii institut, Sverdlovsk

Zhilin GA (2000) Tseli grazhdanskogo sudoproizvodstva i ih realizaciya v sude pervoi instancii [Goals of civil procedure and their realization in the court of the first instance]. Gorodets, Moscow

Zhilin GA (2010) Pravosudie po grazhdanskim delam: aktual'nye voprosy: monografiya [Justice in civil matters: actual issues: monograph]. Prospect, Moscow

Chapter 10
Battle Between Individual Rights and Public Interest in Hungarian Civil Procedure

Miklós Kengyel and Gergely Czoboly

Abstract This chapter addresses the main issues of the goals of civil justice in Hungary. It begins with a summary of the prevailing opinions on the issues, then deals with the correlations between the protection of individual rights and public interests, and the role of the truth in Hungarian civil procedure. Subsequently, the following issues are discussed: the matters within the scope of civil justice, the differentiation of procedures and the application of proportionality, the resolution of multi-party matters, the absence of formalism and the user-orientation of civil procedure in Hungary.

10.1 Oscillating History: From Liberal to Socialist Concept of Procedural Goals (and Back)

According to the *dualist conception* encountered frequently in academic legal literature, civil action is aimed at the enforcement of subjective rights and the protection of legal order. In different historical eras one or the other aim may be given more emphasis. In the nineteenth century the liberal approach to legal action laid down as the sole requirement that legal action 'should lead to the resolution of the legal dispute in the simplest, shortest and most certain way' (Gaul 1968: 36). Only a few decades later the 'preservation of legal peace' and the protection of 'the legal order as a whole' were again moved to the foreground in socialist civil action. Socialist procedural law went even further when at the centre of civil action it placed the revelation and assertion of objective truth (Klein and Engel 1927: 188).

M. Kengyel (✉) • G. Czoboly
Faculty of Law, University of Pécs, 48-as tér 1-3, 7622 Pécs, Hungary
e-mail: kengyel.miklos@ajk.pte.hu; czoboly.gergely@ajk.pte.hu

A. Uzelac (ed.), *Goals of Civil Justice and Civil Procedure in Contemporary Judicial Systems*, Ius Gentium: Comparative Perspectives on Law and Justice 34,
DOI 10.1007/978-3-319-03443-0_10,

10.2 Civil Justice with 100 Procedures for Non-contested Cases

The main function of the court is to decide in contested matters, but it also encompasses non-contested issues; however, the extent and significance of non-litigious procedures varied greatly during the last century.

The modernization of the Hungarian legal system took place in the last third of the nineteenth century. The term 'voluntary jurisdiction' appeared in the legal literature at that time, which was replaced in the second half of the twentieth century by the term 'non-litigious procedures'.[1] Neither in the nineteenth century nor in the twentieth century were these procedures regulated comprehensively, because their codification always played a *secondary* role to that of the litigious procedures. During the legislation of the codes of civil procedure of 1911 and 1952, litigious procedures were incorporated into statutes whose purpose was to put the codes of civil procedure into force. Nevertheless, in 1952 the result was a voluminous regulation, the 105/1952 (XII. 28) MT decree. It contained in 58 paragraphs the rules of the courts' non litigious procedures[2] and the regulation of the notary public's procedures, including the general provisions of the non-litigious procedures. It could have been the starting point of a unified regulation, if there had been the will for the codification. Instead of this, a separate regulation of these procedures had begun.[3]

The number of non-litigious procedures increased quickly due to separate legal acts, but the legal regulation did not lose its clarity. By this time the unified regulation did not seem as hopeless as 20 years later, when the explosive growth of the procedures of voluntary jurisdiction took place in several waves. The first wave – after political changes – brought back those non-litigious procedures which existed in our legal system before but during the decades of socialism atrophied or were set aside (e.g. company registration, insolvency procedures, dissolution proceedings, etc.) The second wave was the result of deliberate codification, when procedures of voluntary jurisdiction were created by dozens of major substantive and procedural legal acts (e.g. Act XXII of 1992 on the Labour Code, Act LXXI of 1994 on Arbitration, Act LIII of 1994 on Judicial Enforcement, etc.). Finally a 'stealth' codification must be mentioned, which means that the legislator created non-litigious procedures in the most unexpected situations due to considerations of legal policy.

[1] The term 'non-litigious' was first mentioned by Sárffy (1946: 9–11); after this the use of term became common.

[2] Regulation on provisional measures, termination of the matrimonial community property, declaration of death, order for payment procedure, annulment of securities and documents and succession procedure.

[3] e.g. pl. 6/1958. (VII. 4.) IM rendelet regulates the succession procedure, 1/1960 (IV. 13) IM rendelet regulates the declaration of death, 9/1969 (XII. 28.) IM rendelet regulates the procedures concerning the industrial property rights.

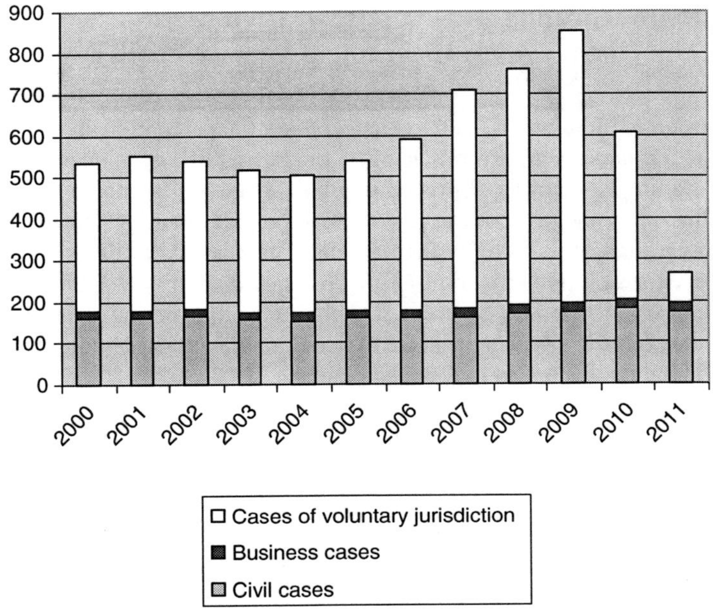

Fig. 10.1 The number of civil cases at first instance courts and cases of voluntary jurisdiction in Hungary between 2000 and 2011 (thousands of cases) (Kengyel 2013)

The current situation can be summarized as follows: presently approximately *one hundred* non-litigious procedures exist in Hungary (more at Sect. 10.7), and the number of legal acts regulating these procedures is nearing *sixty* (Varga 2010). Only article 13 of the 105/1952. (XII. 28.) MT decree can be considered a common rule, according to which, unless the specific legal act which regulates the procedure of voluntary jurisdiction provides otherwise, or otherwise following from the nature of the procedure, the provisions of the Code of Civil Procedure shall be applied adequately.

In connection with the ratio of the number of contentious procedures and proceedings of voluntary jurisdiction exact statistical data are available. The following diagram contains the number of litigious (civil and business) and non-litigious proceedings of the courts between 2000 and 2011. It shows that the number of non-litigious proceedings is much higher than the litigious ones. While the number of litigious cases is relatively constant, the number of non-litigious proceedings – which are particularly sensitive to economic processes – increased most dynamically during the years of the economic crisis, which affected Hungary also. In 2010 this process was disrupted, the explanation for which lies – *unfortunately* – not in the upturn of the economy, but in the fact that order for payment procedures making up the majority of non-litigious proceedings have been transferred from the jurisdiction of courts to the competence of notaries (Fig. 10.1).

10.3 Reinterpreting the Purpose of Civil Action: The History of an Incomplete Success

In the academic literature of the twentieth century the perception about the purpose of civil action underwent several changes. In the first half of the century – despite the fact that the Code of Civil Procedure of 1911 did not lay down either the purpose of the Act or the tasks of the court – legal protection of the parties was moved to the foreground. Accordingly, Jancsó (1908: 12), and later Falcsik, defined the goal of civil action as the resolution of civil law disputes by 'public authority', while Magyary (1924: 1–2) regarded this goal to be, on the one hand, the enforcement of the plaintiff's private law interests and, on the other hand, legal protection for the defendant against an unfounded claim.

The definition of the goal of civil action was often intertwined with the requirement of the revelation of truth. In Falcsik's view, parties must accept what is laid down in the court judgment as the truth. 'This is the truth the recognition of which is due to external factors, the judicial power of the state and the form of judgment: the formal truth. – A court judgment corresponds to the substantive truth only if it fully enforces the idea of law in the specific legal case and as a consequence, fully satisfies one's sense of justice' (Jancsó 1908: 12).

In 1952 the purpose of the Act was moved to the beginning of the Code. The original text of § 1 of the Code of Civil Procedure provides: 'The aim of the present act is to ensure the resolution in court procedures of legal disputes arising in connection with the rights attached to the person and property of the citizens of the state, the state and other legal persons on the basis of material truth.' Névai (1953: 25) laid down the enforcement of socialist legality as the general goal of civil proceedings and the resolution of the given legal dispute as its specific goal.

The amendment of 1957 of the Code of Civil Procedure modified the terms contained in § 1: 'citizen of the state' was replaced by 'citizen', while 'material truth' was changed to 'truth' without any attribute. Following this the text of the Act remained unchanged for more than 40 years. Instead of the 'misinterpreted' material truth, academic legal literature started using the term of 'objective truth'. In accordance with the purpose of the Act as well as § 3 thereof the court was to establish the objective truth that reflected objective reality even if the party did not comply with his obligation of proof.

In socialist *academic literature*, apart from Névai, it was Farkas (1956: 23–27) who dealt with the purpose of civil action in more detail and who again placed emphasis on the protection of subjective rights – in contradistinction to the dominant perception: 'The goal of civil action is to provide legal protection with regard to the injured or endangered right or legal relation.' One of the primary and most important basic conditions of this is that the court must reveal the facts of the case in accordance with the truth.

After the democratic political transition almost a whole decade had to pass before the basic principles and some legal institutions of the Code of Civil Procedure were changed in compliance with the requirements of the era. The process of transformation was rendered even more difficult by the fact that – despite expectations – no new Act was passed. This caused the situation in which the two main principles of the Code of Civil Procedure, the principle of party control and the principle of oral hearing, already appeared with a renewed content in the amendment of 1995, while the purpose of the Act was reformulated only in 1999.

In accordance with the amended § 1: 'The purpose of the present Act is to ensure the impartial resolution by court proceedings of legal disputes arising in connection with the property and personal rights of natural and other persons while enforcing the basic principles defined in the present chapter.'

Forty-seven years after the entry into force of the Code of Civil Procedure the legislator gave up the goal of ensuring the resolution of civil law disputes based on the truth. At the same time the legislator relieved the court of its obligation contained in § 3 (1) that during the civil action the court shall endeavour to find out the truth. The legislator explained these essential changes by the fact that the content and meaning of the 'requirement of justice' expected of the court and the Code of Civil Procedure itself had become obsolete in several respects, the earlier formulation defining the goal and intended purpose of the Act was considered outdated. The Constitutional Court declared as early as the beginning of the 1990s that there was no constitutional guarantee relating to the revelation of the material truth.[4] The new goal that has replaced the just resolution of legal disputes – in accordance with the requirement of fair process contained in Article 6 of the European Convention on Human Rights – *is to ensure the impartial resolution of legal disputes.* This is guaranteed by the requirement that the court shall proceed in accordance with the reformulated principles of the Code of Civil Procedure.

According to the new perception, instead of the revelation of truth, the Code of Civil Procedure is to guarantee the 'justness of the process itself'. The most important content elements of procedural justice include: regulation in accordance with the principle of legal security, an independent (impartial) judicial proceeding, respect for the principle of party control and the fair (equitable) division of advantages and disadvantages between the participants of the proceeding based on mutuality (Gadó 2000: 18–19).

The reinterpretation of the purpose of civil action *did not meet with complete success* either in theory or in practice. On the other hand, the 10 years that have passed since the amendment have revealed various problems connected with the process of distancing from the past, socialist/paternalistic concepts of civil justice.

The issues that the court should determine *ex officio* changed over time. Contrary to the socialist transcript of the principle of party control of the scope and nature of civil proceedings, the socialist version of the principle of party control of the facts and means of proof did not gain ground in Hungarian civil procedural law. As a result of the spirit of the Code of Civil Procedure of 1911, the parties' duty to supply evidence for the legal proceedings and the ordering of evidence to be taken officially became amalgamated in a moderate way, which even in the 1950s protected Hungarian civil procedure from the application of an inquisitorial system (Gáspárdy 2000: 22).

---

[4] Dec. 9/1992 (I. 30.) Constitutional Court.

After the democratic transition, the 1995 amendment provided the duty to supply details for the legal action with a new basis. According to the new rule, the court may order the taking of evidence *ex officio* only when the law allows it, consequently proving the facts required to decide the action is solely the task of the parties. The modification of § 164 (2) restricted the possibility of officially ordering evidence to be taken to a narrow circle defined by the Act, by which it wanted to ensure the absolute effectiveness of the principle of party control of the facts and means of proof. By this solution, the legislature did not return to the moderate regulation (the principle of mixed system) applied by the 1911 Code of Civil Procedure but to the model applied by liberal civil procedure in the nineteenth century.

In Hungarian civil procedure, the public prosecutor has an obligation to ensure that the goals of civil justice are being reached. But due to historical events, the intervention of the prosecutor is very limited. The content of the 1952 Code of Civil Procedure found an expression in the principle of party control of the scope and nature of civil proceedings. The law divided the power of disposition concerning the legal action among the parties, the court and the prosecutor. With this, the conventional right of disposal became in practice illusory because all the procedural acts of the parties fell under the control of the court (and the public prosecutor). The personal and property legal disputes of the citizens – in accordance with the paternalistic-*ètatique* approach of the era – happened in front of the 'caring eyes' of the prosecuting attorney and under the 'provision' of the court.

However, the four decades of socialist civil procedure cannot be defined as a uniform period because, at the beginning of the 1970s in Hungary, the situation was suitable for reducing the dominance of the judge and the prosecutor. The third amendment to the Code of Civil Procedure (Act XXVI of 1972) restricted the possibility of the initiation of a court action and intervention by prosecutors and took steps to increase the weight and responsibility of the parties in the legal action, for the sake of improving the efficiency of the procedure. At the beginning of the 1970s the monopoly of the public prosecutor's office over legality was terminated. Act V of 1972 was based on the concept that guarding the observance of legality was not solely the task of the prosecutor, but legality control by prosecutors closely fitted into the coherent system of organizational and procedural guarantees of legality. Consequently, the prosecutor did not have to take part in so many trial and non-trial procedures as before. This was the message of the amendment of Art. 2/A of the Code of Civil Procedure, which tied the bringing of an action to an important public or social interest or the disability of the entitled person to mount a legal defence. After 1973 the number of legal actions commenced by prosecutors decreased considerably.

The 1995 amendment repealed § 2/A titled 'Rights of prosecutors in civil action' and regulated the legal status of prosecutors in § 2 (2)–(6) titled 'Initiation of a court action and the task of the court'. In accordance with Dec. 1/1994 (I. 7) AB, the general entitlement of the prosecutor to commence actions has been maintained in cases where the entitled party is unable to protect his rights for any reason. According to the point of view of the Constitutional Court, this restriction on the constitutional right of autonomy is an unavoidable restriction and corresponds to the constitutional provision of Art. 51 (3) of the Constitution, according to which the protection and ensuring of constitutional public order, of the rights and legal interests of citizens (and their organizations) is also the task of the public prosecutor's office. At the same time, the amendment revived with a different content the action by the prosecution which was described as unconstitutional in 1994. In comparison with the previous regulation, the most important difference is that *action by the prosecution is not possible in general but only when the entitled party is unable to protect his rights for any reason.* Thus action by the prosecution in legal proceedings cannot be regarded as an independent right but, according to the preamble, this is 'a dynamic element' of the right of initiation of a court action, that is, participation in an already ongoing legal action by virtue of the same consideration that would have established the right of filing of action in the specific case.

10.4 Running Away from 'Material Truth': Speed Above Correctness?

Academic legal literature has been concerned with the question in the form of *Fixigkeit vor Richtigkeit* (speed above correctness) for centuries (Kengyel 2010: 78–79). As a matter of fact this question cannot be given an answer that would be applicable to all times and situations. Depending on the era or the country, one or the other aspect has been or could be given greater emphasis. In Hungary – as a result of the bad experiences of past decades – the endeavour to a trial within a reasonable time has become more intensified. Despite the fact that 70 % of civil cases and 50 % of criminal cases are resolved within half a year,[5] both types of proceedings are considered unacceptably long by the media and public opinion. The contradiction between the facts and the subjective evaluation may be explained by the fact that numerous proceedings attracting public attention are protracted as a matter of fact, which leads the public to negative conclusions about all proceedings. Every year the legislature – yielding to pressure from public opinion – takes newer and newer measures with a view to accelerating proceedings, which measures do not always achieve their goal and cannot in any case replace a comprehensive reform of civil proceedings.

At present the creation of a new code of civil procedure to replace the Act of 1952 is not on the agenda, but academic legal literature has already formulated requirements relating to it (Osztovits 2010: 158–163; Kengyel et al. 2010: 135–158). One cannot exclude a future return to the notion of truth either, which may repeatedly bring up the debate surrounding the question of *Fixigkeit vor Richtigkeit* (Földesi 2003: 467–473).

As for ourselves, we do not oppose the declarative re-appearance of the concept of truth in civil procedure, and so it is expected by the majority of the judiciary and

[5] Altogether 10 % of civil cases and 20 % of criminal cases last longer than a year.

by the public seeking justice. We share the view of the great Austrian jurist Franz Klein that legal action without truth is a 'rattling mill running with no loads'. However, we consider it more important that a future new code of civil procedure should define the aim of proof more specifically than the present one. On the basis of the present terminology of the Code, proof is nothing else but an activity directed at the clarification of the facts of the case and establishing the facts which are needed to decide the action. In view of its content, it is less by far than the concept of proof applied by József Farkas, which is also authoritative at present (Farkas and Kengyel 2005: 32). Our *de lege ferenda* suggestion is that the legislature should state, concerning proof, that the court – unless the law provides otherwise – shall make sure through its discretion whether the facts necessary to decide the action are true or untrue. Besides the philosophical concept of truth, it would be worth considering – at least at the level of legal literature – a return to the concept of material and formal truth which was banished from socialist civil procedure as early as the 1950s. Civil procedure cannot lack the latter one either, since judicial decisions based on the rules of the burden of proof are essentially founded upon formal truth. If the court establishes the truth or untruth of facts, it makes a decision in accordance with the material truth.

Another substantial part of the change of model between 1995 and 2000 was – besides the alteration of the aim of civil action – the dimming of the role of the judge. The 1999 amendment to the Code of Civil Procedure put even more emphasis on the principle of party control of the scope and nature of civil proceedings by the re-formulation of the fundamental principles of the Code, by the modification of the existing provisions and by the establishment of new rules. The modified § 3 (1) lays down the exclusive right of the party interested in the dispute to institute legal proceedings, which right may only be restricted by law. § 3 (2) in declaring that the court – unless provision is made to the contrary – is bound by the petitions and declarations submitted by the parties, extends the application of the principle of party control of the scope and nature of civil proceedings over the whole proceedings. Thus, the Code now makes it clear that the parties are the 'masters of the case', they determine the subject matter of the proceedings and thus the procedural scope of action of the court. At the same time, the court is bound to prevent any procedural action of the parties and their representatives which is contrary to the requirement of good faith in the exercise of rights (§ 8 HCCP). Consequently, the parties' right to disposition is not unlimited, it may only prevail within the framework of another principle, the exercise of rights in good faith.

Everybody agreed that the judge needed to be relieved from unnecessary burdens, so the 'hyperactivity' of the socialist era had to be changed with a different role for judges. The modifications between 1995 and 1999 seemed to find this new role in the contemplative judge. In conformity with this, supplying evidence and details in proceedings became solely the task of the parties and the modification did not allow the ordering of proof officially – contrary e.g. to the 1911 Code of Civil Procedure – even for practical purposes, because it would restrict the right of the parties to self-determination.

However in other countries of Europe (and the world) just by the turn of the millennium the contemplative judge was being replaced by a more active participant in the procedure. This process began in the last decades of the twentieth century largely as a result of a global legal, sociological research called the *Access-to-Justice Project* (Cappelletti and Garth 1978–1979). The ideal of social civil procedure (Klein 1901) became highly respected again and the enhancement of the court's role in the action became the most important guarantee of an efficient, quick and reasonable procedure.

The change in the relations between the court and the parties is most conspicuous in the common law legal systems where the passivity of the judge is very deeply rooted. The idea of managerial judges already appeared in the 1980s, moreover it became partially realized in the USA (Murray 1998: 319–338). The entering into force of the new English Civil Procedure Rules meant the real turning point which, in an unprecedented way, cover the whole of civil procedure and further contain basic principles at the beginning of the Act. The new Act wants to remove the judge from his centuries-long inactivity, and therefore encourages more activity in the course of the establishment of the facts of the case, proof, the conduct of legal proceedings and, last but not least, in ensuring the rights of the parties.[6]

Seeing this procedure, we can observe the third change of model of our civil procedure within a century with some alarm. In the middle of the 1950s, mechanical and uncritical acceptance of Soviet legal institutions replaced the German-Austrian orientation of values; nowadays we are approaching a – partly-outdated – English-American model of civil procedure. (Meanwhile, the world is moving in the direction of convergence concerning judicial powers and the parties' right to disposition.) (Kengyel 2003: 301–322). Even besides the fulfilment of legal duties of legal harmonization, enough 'playing field' is left for the Code of Civil Procedure, which should be filled with legal institutions based on Hungarian procedural traditions rather than with the development of a newer model of litigation. The judge's role in civil litigation does not have to be re-invented since it was defined precisely by Géza Magyary (1924: 36) nearly a century ago: 'It must be up to the party whether he wants a legal defense or not but it must not depend on him how the proceedings are conducted or how long they last.'

10.5 The Ideal of Mass Processing: Mandatory Payment Order Procedure

The Code of Civil Procedure of 1952 – as opposed to Hungarian civil procedural conventions – did not contain special procedural rules relating to claims of small value (small claims proceedings). The dogma of general first instance proceedings, which laid down the application of the same procedural rules with regard to all cases except for so-called extraordinary actions, was broken through only in 2008, when the legislator prescribed the application of simplified procedural rules during the

[6] Civil Procedure Rules, para. 1.4 (1)–(2).

adjudication of claims with a value of less than one million forints (approx. €3,700). The aim of the amendment was to formalize and accelerate procedures based on Council Regulation (EC) 861/2007 establishing a European Small Claims Procedure. Two years later claims with a value exceeding 400 million forints (approx. €1.5 million) were classified as high profile cases and again rules differing from the general ones were laid down for them with the aim of accelerating the procedure (§ 24 of Act LXXXIX of 2011). Both amendments support the propositions contained in Sect. 10.4 above as well, namely that there is an intensified endeavour on the part of the legislator to give priority, over the revelation of truth, to the resolution of legal disputes within a reasonable time, be it a small claim or a high profile ('hard') case.

In connection with the mass processing of cases, the order for payment procedure should be mentioned, which is in Hungary the most important filter mechanism. It is *obligatory* in the case of claims with a value not exceeding one million forints (approx. €3,700). The value limit is rather high – even in a European comparison – compared especially to the value limit of €2,000 contained in the Regulation relating to the European small claims procedure. Proceedings must be filed with the notary, who, in the event the conditions are met, issues the order for payment, which comes before the court only if a statement of defence is submitted against it. The order for payment procedure that has been transformed into a lawsuit is conducted by the court in accordance with the simplified rules relating to small claims.

10.6 Recent Shift Towards the Proportionality Principle

As it was described above, proportionality was introduced to the Hungarian civil procedure in 2009 and 2011, when special procedural rules were developed for the small and to the high profile cases. The *trichotomy of the procedure* is not unique in European legal developments as the English system after the Woolf reform shows us. However, the method of the case differentiation in these legal systems is not very similar and the difference does not only arise from the different legal traditions. In spite of this, the idea of case differentiation served the same purposes in both countries: to reduce costs and to accelerate procedure. The theoretical basis of both was that it is inappropriate to use the same procedural rules in cases with different complexity and significance. According to Lord Woolf, it is necessary to depart from the old approach, where 'time and money are no object' and to move to another, where human and other *resources are allocated effectively*. These reasons can be found in the preamble of the Hungarian reform act too. From this principle it should logically follow that in cases of less financial value fewer resources should be used than in cases with more financial value. The English reform aimed to develop a needs-oriented system to achieve the optimal resource allocation. Differential case management was the main instrument in achieving this goal. While in cases allocated to the small claims track the parties can only use restricted resources and the style of the trial is more direct than cases allocated to the fast track or to the multi-track. This is not the case in Hungarian small claims procedure. It can be observed that the

Hungarian legislator designated certain, well-definable areas of the cases where the length of procedure can be shortened, sometimes at the expense of the normal cases, instead of applying a comprehensive reform. The Hungarian reform only limits the parties' autonomy, shortens the deadlines and applies priority treatment in certain cases.

The mentioned reforms represent a shift in Hungarian civil procedure compared to the previous rules, because it broke with the ideology of the single first instance procedure and introduced a differentiated one. By introducing separated procedures for smaller claims the legislator did not enter onto new terrain, because a *summary procedure* had already existed from 1893. These rules were incorporated into the Code of Civil Procedure of 1911[7] and the summary procedure was replaced by the procedure of the district courts (Kengyel 2010: 533). This procedure had several differences from the procedure of the tribunals, which was the general first instance procedure. Examples of this divergence include the fact that the parties had verbal contact with the court outside the oral hearings as well, and in the procedure before the district courts there was no pre-trial hearing (Magyary 1924: 66). The later Code of Civil Procedure from 1952, which was built on socialist principles, *abolished the divergence* and established a new and single first instance procedure. The socialist civil procedure treated the single first instance procedure as dogma (Kengyel 2010: 533). After the political transition, the legislator did not return to the previous rules from 1911, but modified the existing code and the single first instance procedure.

The reforms from 2008 to 2011 changed the previous status and – following both Hungarian tradition and foreign examples – it divided the first instance procedure.[8] As a result of the reforms, there are *three types of first instance procedures*: the small claims procedure, the normal procedure and a procedure for cases with prioritized significance.

Regarding cases with small financial weight, the legislator aimed to accelerate the procedure, so the reform limited the scope of party control, introduced stricter rules for non-attendance at trial and prescribed shorter deadlines to the court. In practice, limiting party control means that the right to change the claim, to present motions to take evidence and to file a counterclaim is limited in time as compared to normal cases. In the case of small claims, possibilities of appeal are also limited.

In normal procedure the plaintiff can *change his claim* before the time when the hearing preceding the giving of judgment in the first instance is adjourned (§146 1); in small claims procedure the plaintiff can make changes to his claim on one occasion, only after the defendant's counter-plea is presented on the merits, during the first hearing (§ 391/A).

In small claims procedure the party can present motions for the taking of evidence in principle on or before the first day of the hearing (§ 389). This seems a very strict rule, however the law gives several exceptions: in the event of any change made in the claim, or counterclaim to prove the changed parts of the claim, or with the consent of the other party. And according to § 389 (6) HCPC, the party shall be

[7] Act I of 1911 on the Code of Civil Procedure.

[8] Preamble of Act XXX of 2008, General part, para. 2.

entitled to present his request for the performance of taking of evidence before the hearing preceding the giving of judgment in the first instance is adjourned, even if he presents any fact or evidence, or any binding court or other official decision, which he was unaware of before the deadline normally prescribed for the presentation of such motion without any fault on his part, or if he has learned about the decision becoming definitive after this deadline, and if he is able to produce credible proof to that effect. This exception aims to prevent the reintroduction of the *Eventualmaxime* into Hungarian civil procedure. However, it gives the opportunity to the other party to use various tactics that in practice result in the reintroduction of the *Eventualmaxime*, because the law allows request for performance of taking of evidence only if the party was 'unaware' of the existence of the fact or evidence before the deadline. In cases where the party did not know about the future relevance of the evidence, he can be trapped. This makes the procedure suitable for 'ambush tactics', where the defendant can present his arguments only at the first hearing, where the not sufficiently prepared plaintiff cannot respond to the defendant's evidence. So the plaintiff has to request the taking of all evidence – which is merely possibly relevant – to prevent such tactics, which as a result – contrary to the intentions of the legislator – can make the entire procedure more complex.

With the procedure for cases with prioritized significance the legislator aimed to increase the efficiency of procedure in 'high profile cases'. To achieve this, the deadlines were shortened, the obligation of the courts to inform the parties was abolished and cross-examination was introduced. In this procedure the court has to hear the cases in priority proceedings without the motion of the parties (§ 386/B). In this type of procedure some deadlines are shorter than in the others: for example the court must examine the statement of claim without delay, not later than 8 days from the time of delivery to the court, and has to set the date of the hearing within 60 days from the same time (§ 386/C). The law gives less time for the preparation of the expert's report, so the expert has to give his report to the court within 30 days, 60 days in complex cases. For the purpose of deciding the dispute, the court – contrary to the other procedures, where it is obligatory – does not have to inform the parties in advance concerning the facts for which the taking of evidence is required, the burden of proof, and also on the consequences of any failure of the evidentiary procedure (§ 386/J).

In summary, the Hungarian reform did not differ essentially between procedures. There is no difference between the procedures neither from the aspect of preparation of procedure, nor in the style of the trial. The parties can use the same evidence in every procedure and the judge has no obligation to be more interventionist or active in smaller cases. Instead of an active case management, the reforms abolished the judge's task in high profile cases to inform the parties in advance concerning the facts for which the taking of evidence is required, the burden of proof, and also on the consequences of failure to produce evidence.

The new rules have not made procedures better suited to the characteristics of the types of cases, therefore they have not improved resource allocation. The legislator has only utilized some acceleration techniques for a distinct group of cases *as a testing ground* so the legal practice can test it and give feedback on the operation of it. This method would not be unique in the history of Hungarian civil procedure, because Alexander Plósz, the developer of the Code of Civil Procedure of 1911, used the summary procedure in 1893 as a testing ground for the reform of the normal procedure (Kengyel 2010: 533).

10.7 Bi-party v. Multi-party: Traditional Approach with a Touch of Novelty in Special Fields

Hungarian civil procedure traditionally concentrates on the handling of bi-party proceedings. In general, if there are more parties involved in one dispute, the rules of joinder of parties apply. In special cases, like environmental or consumer disputes, representative actions are available too.

The Hungarian Code of Civil Procedure renders the joinder of parties possible in two cases. Accordingly, several claimants may file a joint action and several defendants may be jointly sued if, on the one hand, the subject matter of the lawsuit is a joint right or obligation which may be adjudged uniformly only, or the decision made in the lawsuit would affect the joint litigants even without their participation in the lawsuit (necessary/compulsory joinder of parties), such as in an action filed for the termination of joint ownership. Or, on the other hand, if the claims to be asserted originate from the same legal relationship; or the claims to be asserted are founded on a similar factual or legal basis (permissive joinder of parties). This latter type of the joinder of parties is grounded on expedience, the former, as indicated by its name, is grounded on necessity.

The type of the joinder used has a vital effect on the relations between the parties. In cases of the compulsory joinder of parties, any litigants' procedural acts (except for settlement, recognition or waiver of a right) have an effect also on the joint litigant who has missed some deadline or closing date, or who has failed to perform some act provided that he has not subsequently rectified his omission. If the procedural acts or pleadings of the joint litigants of this type diverge from each other, the court must adjudge them with regard to the other data of the lawsuit as well. In case of a permissive joinder of parties, no joint litigant's acts or omissions constitute an advantage or a disadvantage for the other joint litigant.

In environmental matters, collective forms of injunctive and compensatory redresses are available; however, the latter is very limited. According to Article 99 of the Act LIII of 1995 on the General Rules of Environmental Protection (hereinafter GREP), NGOs are entitled to intervene in the interest of protecting the environment and file a lawsuit against the user of the environment in the event the environment is being endangered, damaged or polluted. In this case, the party in the case may request the court to enjoin the party posing the hazard to refrain from the unlawful conduct (operation), or compel the same to take the necessary measures for preventing the damage. In the event of endangerment to the environment, the prosecutor is also entitled to file a lawsuit to impose a ban on the activity, according to Article 109 of the GREP. In connection with the relationship of the two collective redresses, the order of the Chief Prosecutor of Hungary no. 3/2012. (I.6) states that public prosecutors shall cooperate with NGOs in order to coordinate their activities.

NGOs can directly sue the polluter in general, independently of an administrative procedure, so even in the omission of the authority.

A special collective compensatory redress is granted by Article 103 of the GREP. It states that if the injured party does not wish to enforce his claim for damages against the party causing the damage – on the basis of a statement pertaining to this made by the injured party within the period of limitation – the Minister may enforce said claim to the credit of the environmental protection fund.

10.8 Impartial Resolution Before the Revelation of Truth

The objective of the Hungarian Code of Civil Procedure declared in § 1 and § 3 of the Act was changed in 1999 and the revelation of truth as an objective was replaced by the impartial resolution of the legal dispute. The change did not lead to the prevalence of strict formalism, this has never been a characteristic of modern Hungarian civil procedure, but the requirement of legality has increased, which has been given expression primarily in the reformulated principles of the Code of Civil Procedure.

10.9 Problem Solving or Case Processing?

It is not possible to provide a straightforward answer to the question whether the dominant attitude of Hungarian civil justice is problem solving or case processing. While litigants expect the resolution of their dispute from civil proceedings, judicial government demands efficiency from courts. With the economic crisis the pressure on the courts has increased; in Hungary several legislative packages have recently been adopted aimed at increasing the efficiency of criminal and civil proceedings. They are directed – especially with regard to small claims – at solutions requiring the least effort and expense. However, only the spread of electronic proceedings can mean a satisfactory solution in Hungary. Besides small claims, in so-called high profile cases as well (see Sect. 10.4), special rules were adopted with the purpose of increasing the efficiency of case resolution. In the latter, however, the aim is to reduce not the expenses but the length of lawsuits, because these types of lawsuits are generally considered to be rather protracted.

10.10 From Generosity to an Institutional System of Legal Aid

From Socialism Hungary inherited a generous legal aid system, which practically granted exemption from costs in litigation relating to certain groups of cases (maintenance, guardianship, employment disputes, etc.). After the democratic transformation of the political system the significant increase in lawyers' and experts' fees led to a rise in the costs of litigation. The earlier situation where the majority of costs reductions were connected with the subject matter of the lawsuit and not the income of the grantee *became untenable*.

The setting up of a state legal aid system functioning at an appropriate level was laid down as an indispensable condition for Hungary's accession to the European Union.[9] Act LXXX of 2003 on Legal Aid changed existing regulation fundamentally. The institutional system built up gradually since 2004 renders it possible to provide support to a wider circle and in a more differentiating way, which is also adjusted to Community regulation (Kengyel and Harsági 2010: 125–140).

The new legal aid system is aimed at covering the costs of legal protection to the extent of neediness. At the same time, it should be noted that the high costs are not caused by court fees but by lawyers' fees and other ancillary expenses, which – as a result of the uncertain outcome of lawsuits – also means a burden for those otherwise granted cost reduction.[10]

10.11 Orientation Towards the Users? The Limited Promise of Procedural Justice

The Hungarian Code of Civil Procedure does not define the *goal* of civil action but that *of the Act* (see Sect. 10.3). This objective is also applicable to the civil justice system itself, and, out of the participants of proceedings, mainly to the court, whose task is to ensure the impartial resolution of legal disputes. This formulation, which has been contained in the text of the Act since 2000, promises less to litigants than the earlier regulation, which – as has been mentioned above – laid down as the aim of legal action the resolution of legal disputes based on the truth, since the new regulation guarantees merely procedural justice.

References

Cappelletti M, Garth BG (eds) (1978–1979) The Florence access-to-justice project. Giuffré, Milan
Farkas J (1956) Bizonyítás a polgári perben. Közgazdasági és Jogi Könyvkiadó, Budapest
Farkas J, Kengyel M (2005) Bizonyítás a polgári perben. KJK, Budapest
Földesi T (2003) A jogban alkalmazott igazság terminusról és annak háttérbe szorulásáról a magyar polgári eljárásjog újabb fejlődésében. Magyar Jog
Gadó G (2000) Az eljárási igazságosság a polgári perben. Magyar Jog

[9] Council Directive 2002/8/EC of 27 January 2003 to improve access to justice in cross-border disputes by establishing minimum common rules relating to legal aid for such disputes. Official Journal L 026, 31/01/2003 P. 0041–0047.

[10] If the party who has been granted exemption from costs loses the lawsuit, he shall bear the costs awarded to the opposing party (§ 86, HCCP).

Gáspárdy L (2000) Modern magyar perjogtörténet. Novotni, Miskolc
Gaul H (1968) Zur Frage nach dem Zweck des Zivilprozesses. Archiv für die Zivilistische Praxis
Jancsó G (1908) Magyar polgári törvénykezési jog. Lepage, Kolozsvár
Kengyel M (2003) A bírói hatalom és a felek rendelkezési joga a polgári perben. Osiris, Budapest
Kengyel M (2010) Magyar polgári eljárásjog. Osiris, Budapest
Kengyel M (2013) Economic analysis of civil litigation in Hungary. In: Recent trends in economy and efficiency of civil procedure. Materials of international conference 9–10 of May 2013. Vilnius University Press, Vilnius, pp 112–129
Kengyel M, Harsági V (2010) Civil justice in Hungary. Jigakusha Publishing Corporation, Tokyo
Kengyel M, Cserba L, Gadó G, Kiss G (2010) Kell-e új Polgári perrendtartás? In: Huszonkilencedik Jogász Vándorgyűlés. Budapest, pp 135–158
Klein F (1901) Zeit- und Geistesströmungen im Prozesse. Klostermann, Vienna
Klein F, Engel F (1927) Der Zivilprozeß Österreichs. J. Bensheimer, Mannheim
Magyary G (1924) Magyar polgári perjog, 2nd edn. Franklin, Budapest
Murray P (1998) Civil justice reform in America: the 1990 civil justice reform act and its consequences. Zeitschrift für Zivilprozeß International
Névai L (1953) A magyar polgári perjog alapelvei. In: A magyar polgári perjog főbb kérdései. Budapest
Osztovits A (2010) Az új magyar Polgári perrendtartás szükségességéről. Magyar Jog
Sárffy A (1946) Magyar polgári perjog. Grill Károly Könyvkiadóvállalata, Budapest
Varga I (ed) (2010) A polgári nemperes eljárások joga. ELTE Eötvös Kiadó, Budapest

Chapter 11
(In)compatibility of Procedural Preclusions with the Goals of Civil Justice: An Ongoing Debate in Slovenia

Aleš Galič

Abstract Slovenian doctrine acknowledges that the following belong among the goals of civil justice: the resolution of disputes, vindication of the parties' rights, affirmation of substantive legal order and its underlying social values and policies, promotion of uniform application of law and development of law through case law, predictability and legal certainty. However, the key issue concerns the relation between all these goals, especially in the case of procedural instruments, which are compatible only with some of these goals, while they adversely affect the others. In Slovenia, a heated debate concerning the goals of civil justice has emerged especially in regard to the introduction of 'preclusions' – the judge's power to disregard facts asserted and evidence adduced past the time limits that are imposed, whether by the law itself or set by the court. The author therefore presents the regulation of preclusions following the latest reforms of Slovenian civil procedural law. Herein, the notion of such powers of the judge are critically assessed from the viewpoint of the goals of civil justice.

11.1 Introduction

Legal scholars and courts in Slovenia do not offer any surprising or exotic definitions concerning the goal of civil justice. It is usually referred to (in a manner of enumeration, although not necessarily in exactly the same order) as (1) the resolution of disputes, (2) vindication of the parties' rights, (3) affirmation of substantive legal order and its underlying social values and policies, (4) promotion of uniform application of law and development of law through case law, (5) predictability and

A. Galič (✉)
Department of Civil Procedure, Faculty of Law, University of Ljubljana,
Poljanski nasip 2, 1000 Ljubljana, Slovenia
e-mail: ales.galic@pf.uni-lj.si

A. Uzelac (ed.), *Goals of Civil Justice and Civil Procedure in Contemporary Judicial Systems*, Ius Gentium: Comparative Perspectives on Law and Justice 34,
DOI 10.1007/978-3-319-03443-0_11,

legal certainty.[1] Such an all-embracing enumeration can hardly be disputed, however, at the same time it is not very useful. The key question remains unanswered. Namely, the question of the relation between all these goals, especially in regard to procedural institutes and devices, which are compatible only with some of these goals, while they adversely affect the others. Do some of them need to be given precedence in certain circumstances? These dilemmas arise much more at times of discussions, which accompany reforms of certain procedural instruments, than on an abstract level. This occurred, for example, at a time of the advancing promotion of alternative dispute resolution, especially mediation (as well as promotion of in-court settlements), when the critical question, whether the goal of settlement of the individual dispute is not overemphasized, appeared. A critical question is put whether this disproportionately affects the goal of affirmation of legal order and – since judicial authority might be deprived of an opportunity to resolve an important legal question – also goes at the expense of the uniformity of case law, legal certainty and the development of law. At the time of preparation of the reform concerning access to the Supreme Court, which introduced the leave to appeal system in 2008, polemic controversies concerning the goals of civil justice, when it comes to access to the Supreme Court, arose. Should the decision-making of the Supreme Court predominantly serve the individual purpose or – which clearly is the case since the reform – a public purpose?[2] At the same time, the discussion regarding the reform made it clear that proceedings before the Supreme Court should not be aimed at mass processing of cases, rather the qualitative aspect should be in the foreground: the number of cases which the Supreme Court needs to examine comprehensively must be relatively low, so that supreme court judges may fully concentrate their legal research, debate and reasoning on the cases which are of general importance. When the court fees were raised, debates arose on the issue, whether the trial is solely in the interest of the party (who must also pay fully for it) or does it pursue public objectives as well (so that a litigation in court cannot be seen merely as a 'payable service'). Increasingly common are critical warnings (especially in connection to consumer cases and competition law) that the standard structure of civil procedure does not enable proper protection of collective or diffuse interests and collection of mass monetary claims.

---

[1] See, e.g., Ude (2002: 30–31, 57 et seq.), Ude et al. Vol. 1 (2005: 25), Juhart (1956: 3 et seq.). Compare also decisions of the Slovenian Constitutional Court, U-I-302/09 of 12 May 2011 and U-I-164/09 of 4 February 2010.

[2] With the introduction of the 'leave to appeal system' in Slovenia the public purpose of adjudication in the Supreme Court, oriented foremost to the effects of its decisions on the future, is clearly emphasized. This public function consists of safeguarding and promoting the public interest of ensuring the uniformity of case law, the development of law and offering guidance to lower courts and thus ensuring predictability in the application of law. The private purpose of the just and correct resolution of every individual case, thereby striving to fulfil the expectations of litigants in the case at hand, is not the primary goal of the Supreme Court.

However, none of the aforementioned changes and reforms of procedural instruments stirred up so many and such heated debates about compatibility with the goal(s) of civil justice as the introduction (in 1999; strengthened in 2008) of the judge's power to disregard facts asserted and evidence adduced past the time limits that are imposed, whether by the law itself or set by the court. In Slovenian legal terminology this instrument is referred to as 'preclusion' (*prekluzija*, following the German procedural concept of *Präklusionen*). The discussion regarding the goals of civil justice in Slovenia in the last 15 years was mostly affected precisely by debates concerning preclusions (and the strengthening of other procedural demands and expectations). It is not only a question of balance between the desire to reach accurate results and the need to ensure a trial within reasonable time. It is also a matter of determining many other relationships concerning the goals of civil procedure.[3] With the regulation of preclusions questions such as how to find a proper balance between strict formalism and the wish to reach equitable and fair results, as well as how to determine the balance between the protection of individual rights and the public interest,[4] emerge.

The introduction of 'preclusions' has – for the first time in Slovenian civil procedure – been inevitably linked with more judicial discretion in organizing proceedings and the possibility to adapt the conduct of proceedings to the characteristics of the specific case. Hence, the question of the proportionality between state resources offered for the resolution of a single dispute and the social and economic importance of this dispute ('proportionality between the case and the procedure'[5]) is clearly emphasized in the context of this procedural instrument as well.

The promotion of procedural sanctions for late facts and evidence, like all other procedural instruments, which are based on the expectation that parties (their counsels) will diligently and actively prepare and participate in litigation, inevitably requires a clarification of another dilemma concerning the goals of civil justice. Should the court also be pursuing a kind of a welfare function in civil proceedings – remedying omissions and the lack of diligent preparation of the litigants in order to reach adequate results on the merits, a goal which can get dangerously close to state paternalism. Or should another goal of civil justice, autonomously procedural, have precedence here? Namely, the goal to promote the liberal concept that the party must be perceived as a person who has the capacity and hence the responsibility for his own choices. Concerning that same issue, the question as to what the goals of civil justice are is closely linked to the question of whose responsibility it is to strive for achieving these goals at all. Is it the sole responsibility of the court or of the parties (actually: the bar) or should the question again be posed as, how to strike a proper balance between them?

---

[3] These relationships are summarized by Uzelac (2012: 113).

[4] See ibid.

[5] Compare: ibid.

11.2 In Pursuit of a New Balance: Restrictions on Late Factual Allegations and Evidence in the 1999 Civil Procedure Act and Its 2008 Amendment

Under the Yugoslav Civil Procedure Act – 1976, parties were free to submit new facts and evidence until the end of the last session of the main hearing and – except in commercial cases – even during an appeal. It was left entirely to the parties to decide at what stage of proceedings they wished to present relevant facts and evidence. After the independence of Slovenia in 1991, the Yugoslav Civil Procedure Act continued to apply until 1999, when the first Slovenian Civil Procedure Act[6] (CPA) came into force. It was only then that a certain system of procedural sanctions for late facts and evidence was introduced in the regulation of civil litigation.[7] Pursuant to Art. 286 CPA, parties may assert new facts and evidence at the first main hearing at the latest. At subsequent main hearings the parties are allowed to present new facts and new evidence only if they were not able to submit them at the first main hearing through no fault of their own. The same restrictions apply to new facts and evidence which a party wishes to rely on at the appellate stage of proceedings.

After more than 10 years of practical experience with the described system of 'preclusions' as procedural sanctions, it can be established that they produce effects foremost on the level of 'general prevention', whereas they are not rigidly applied in practice. Nevertheless, it would be wrong to conclude that the case law on the procedural sanctions of preclusion is so permissive that they would merely remain a dead letter. Time limits regarding the presentation of facts and evidence are very much alive in the perception of attorneys and judges alike and the procedural sanctions attached to them sufficiently feared.[8] Since the system of preclusions produces effects on the level of prevention, the prediction that the courts would lose more time determining issues of 'justified reasons for default' than regarding the merits of the case[9] did not prove to be correct either. It must be stressed, however, that precisely due to the requirement that all facts and evidence should in principle be put forward already during the first session of the main hearing, the judge's responsibilities connected with this session are strengthened as well. This applies both to the expectation that the judge himself should diligently prepare for the hearing as well as to his duty to discuss relevant factual and legal aspects of the case with the parties and to offer them 'hints', feedback and observations in order to supplement and clarify their positions.

[6] *Zakon o pravdnem postopku*, Official Gazette, No. 26/99.

[7] Of course, preclusion of new facts and evidence is not the only sanction for default and inactivity. A judgment by default can be entered in case of the total passivity of the defendant (Art. 318 CPA). Furthermore, the facts that were not explicitly denied or were denied in an unsubstantiated manner will be presumed to be admitted (Art. 214 CPA).

[8] For the confirmation of the sanction of preclusion see e.g. Judgments of the Supreme Court of Slovenia No. II Ips 84/2008 of 26 November 2009, No. II Ips 400/2009 of 21 October 2010, No. III Ips 142/2009 of 2 April 2010 and No. III Ips 44/2008 of 24 November 2009.

[9] For this view See Wedam Lukić (1996: 317).

It is acknowledged both in the case law[10] as well as in legal writing[11] that preclusions restrict parties' right to be heard and thus they should be applied carefully and with a proper balance (proportionality) between competing policies. A too restrictive approach to preclusions can amount to a breach of the right of the parties to be heard.[12] The system does not amount to a (re)introduction of a rigid *Eventualmaxime*.[13] As explained above, a party may put forward new facts and evidence even at later stages of litigation provided that the party was not culpable for default as regards the late submission. The notion of 'culpability for default' is interpreted with a degree of flexibility.[14] Justified excuses include not only the circumstance that a party only subsequently learned of a certain fact or piece of evidence, but also the circumstance that it was only in the course of ongoing proceedings that certain hitherto not submitted facts and evidence appeared relevant for the case.[15] The courts realistically accept that 'unexpected shifts' do sometimes occur in litigation, resulting in different facts appearing as legally relevant only at a later stage of proceedings.[16]

The 1999 Civil Procedure Act made some important steps towards the concentration of proceedings. However, it remained 'half-way'. The described system of sanctions for submitting facts and evidence late did not allow for the proper organization of the preparatory stage of litigation in general. It was not able to prevent the common – however, from the aspect of the efficiency of proceedings, outright fatal – practice that attorneys filed further preparatory briefs as late as during the main hearing. Such practice resulted either in frequent adjournments of hearings or in the inability to ensure their adequate quality (on account of new arguments, facts and evidence, which neither the court nor the opposing party had a chance to adequately consider).[17]

---

[10] E.g. the decision of the Supreme Court of Slovenia No. II Ips 289/2010 of 26 July 2012, Judgment of the Supreme Court of Slovenia No. II Ips 449/2008 of 10 July 2008, Judgment of the Supreme Court of Slovenia No. II Ips 1083/2007 of 10 March 2011.

[11] E.g. Wedam Lukić (2012: 1391), Trampuš (2002: 1549).

[12] Judgment of the Supreme Court of Slovenia No. II Ips 197/2009 of 7 April 2011.

[13] Judgment of the Supreme Court of Slovenia No. III Ips 14/2010 of 20 December 2011.

[14] See, e.g., Decision of the Supreme Court of Slovenia No. II Ips 302/2011 of 26 April 2012.

[15] Šipec (1999: 1206), Ude et al., Vol. 2 (2006: 600).

[16] Decision of the Supreme Court of Slovenia No. III Ips 14/2010 of 20 December 2011. Courts also acknowledge that the preclusion concerns facts and evidence and not new legal analysis and legal arguments (Decision of the Supreme Court of Slovenia No. II Ips 302/2011 of 26 April 2012). If the opposing party puts forward certain facts or evidence only at the first oral hearing, the party is not precluded from rebutting this material by later submitting new facts and evidence concerning the same issue (Judgment of the Supreme Court of Slovenia No. II Ips 197/2009 of 7 April 2011). A motion that the expert should supplement his expert opinion (within limits of the initial *thema probandum*) does not count as a fresh proposal for evidence (Judgment of the Supreme Court of Slovenia No. II Ips 191/2007 of 16 December 2009). What is stressed is also the inherent link between the duty of the judge to pose adequate questions and promote clarification, on the one hand, and the effect of procedural preclusions, on the other (Judgment of the Supreme Court of Slovenia No. II Ips 449/2008 of 10 July 2008).

[17] Compare Betetto (2004: 37).

The Slovenian CPA was substantially reformed in 2008.[18] The system of procedural sanctions for delays in litigation was strengthened and more importance was placed on the preparatory stage of litigation. In order to enable the other party's right to be heard and to organize his case, the first party is now obliged, whenever possible, to file new preparatory briefs[19] in sufficient time for them to be served on the other party with adequate time before the main hearing. This rule strives to achieve that the main hearing does not need to be adjourned in order to enable the other party to consider the newly submitted arguments in the opposing party's brief (Art. 286a/4 CPA). Furthermore, judges now have the power *sua sponte* to require (and to impose binding time limits for this purpose) that parties submit further written observations, comments or clarifications of their factual assertions, evidence which they wish to offer or which has already been taken (e.g. comments on a submitted expert opinion[20]), to comment on issues of law or to consider arguments put forward by the opposing party (Art. 286a/1 CPA).[21] If the judge exercises the aforementioned powers, he can ensure that the parties' standpoints are clearer and more complete and that it is at least clear which facts are really relevant for the case and, in addition, which of those facts are disputed, and thus which issues the main hearing should concentrate on. The judge may exercise these powers to set binding time limits either during the oral hearing (in order to adequately prepare for the next session of the oral hearing) as well as in written form during the time between hearings. In either case, a proper sanction is attached to the aforementioned requirements. If a party does not observe them, he is precluded from making submissions at the later stages of the proceedings (including the first session of the main hearing) unless justified reasons caused the default or if the admission of belated submissions would not significantly delay the proceedings.

The system of procedural sanctions for facts and evidence submitted late under the 1999 CPA applied only to phases of litigation after the first session of the oral hearing. In earlier stages of litigation (including the first oral hearing) there were no restrictions as to when the parties should put forward (and if necessary, clarify, supplement and substantiate) facts and evidence they wanted to rely on. Since the parties were entirely free to put forward entirely new arguments, facts and evidence (e.g. a proposal to hear an additional witness) as late as during the first oral hearing, the promoted goal that whenever possible the litigation should terminate after only one, but thoroughly prepared, oral hearing, was clearly frustrated. On the other hand, the strict requirement that all facts and evidence be submitted already before the main hearing would be incompatible with the judge's duty to provide

[18] *Zakon o spremembah in dopolnitvah Zakona o pravdnem postopku (ZPP-D)*, Official Gazette, No. 45/2008.

[19] *Pripravljalne vloge*. In German: *vorbereitende Schriftsätze*.

[20] Experience shows that after the introduction of the power of the judge to set binding time limits for preparatory briefs that this instrument has been most often (and with positive results) used in the context of commenting on the expert opinion Voglar (2009: 1655).

[21] See in detail: Ude et al. Vol. 4 (2010: 219), Voglar (2009: 1649), Bergant Rakočević (2008: 1597).

clarification, hints and feedback (Art. 285 CPA).[22] This duty aims at encouraging parties to supplement their insufficient assertions of relevant facts and to designate adequate means of proof. If the law imposed a strict sanction of preclusion already prior to the oral hearing and if at the same time the timeframe during which the judge can exercise the aforementioned duty were not extended to the earlier (written) stage of proceedings, such a system would make the performance of the mentioned role of judges impossible. In addition, it must be taken into account that not all cases are suitable for a written preparatory procedure. Depending on the characteristics of the individual case, it might sometimes be plausible and more effective to clarify issues during the oral hearing and not by an exchange of written briefs and court orders beforehand.

This issue was also addressed by the 2008 CPA amendment. Judges can now pose questions and require further clarifications in writing *even before the first session of the main hearing* and can also require parties to offer further evidence or to supplement their factual assertions and to give necessary clarifications (Art. 286, par. 2 and 3, CPA). Thus, if a judge is properly active (e.g. by giving hints and feedback by means of written procedures) already before the first session of the main hearing, parties need to react in the same manner and put forward corresponding additional facts and evidence, in line with the judge's questions, hints and observations. Otherwise they will be precluded from asserting such facts and adducing such evidence at the first oral hearing (Bergant Rakočević 2008: 1598).[23] The judge's responsibility to give hints and feedback and to pose questions in order to encourage the parties to supplement and clarify their submissions, submit additional facts and means of proof, and rectify ambiguities and contradictions in their pleadings has been an essential element of Slovenian civil procedure for a long time (Art. 285 CPA). The novelty of the aforementioned CPA amendment of 2008 is actually an expansion of this role with regard to time (from the oral hearing to the preparatory stage of the procedure) and form (from a purely oral form to a written one). But the substance and purpose of this activity of the judge remains unchanged.[24]

Neither of the aforementioned tools necessarily amounts to a fundamental change in the judge's manner of directing the proceedings. In fact, already before the implementation of the 2008 reform, judges in Slovenia often required parties to file further written observations and clarifications, to consider, for example, an expert opinion, or to submit means of evidence (e.g. documents that were cited but not actually yet submitted) (Dolenc 2007: 70). What was missing, however, was a sanction due to non-compliance. Under the system applicable before the 2008

---

[22] See the Explanatory memorandum to the draft amendment of the Civil Procedure Act 2008 EVA: 2007-2011-0001, Poročevalec Državnega zbora, Vol. 21/08, p. 135.

[23] Compare the judgment of the Ljubljana Court of Appeals No. I Cpg 888/2010 of 13 October 2010.

[24] See the Explanatory memorandum to the draft amendment of the Civil Procedure Act 2008 EVA: 2007-2011-0001, Poročevalec Državnega zbora, Vol. 21/08: 136. See also the Decision of the Slovenian Constitutional Court No. U-I-164/09 of 4 February 2010, Bergant Rakočević (2009: 1658).

reform, parties were safe from any negative adverse consequences due to failing to observe set time limits, e.g. to present in writing their comments regarding an expert opinion (Betetto 2010: 12). This amounted, in my opinion, to a serious systemic deficiency in the organization of civil procedure. With the implementation of the 2008 reform the situation changes: if the court set a time limit for the filing of new preparatory submissions and this time limit was not met, new submissions made after the time period has expired are admissible only if the court is convinced that admitting them will not delay the resolution of the dispute or if the party provides adequate justification for the delay (Art. 286a/2 CPA).

What should not be neglected is the positive effect of the timely collection of procedural material from the viewpoint of the goal of promoting settlements. From this viewpoint, it is very useful if the parties can early enough realistically assess the strengths and weaknesses of their position – also in light of the arguments invoked and evidence disclosed by the opposing party. If a party cannot know before the main hearing what arguments and evidence are 'in the hands' of his opponents, he cannot realistically assess his prospects of success. In such a case, settlement negotiations during the early stages of litigation can hardly be effective (Brus 2007: 336; Trampuš 2002: 1549).

11.3 Proportionality Between Case and Procedure: Flexibility and More Judge's Discretion in Organizing the Conduct of Proceedings

The described system of procedural sanctions is flexible. The judge is empowered but not obliged to set a binding time limit – either before or after the first session of the main hearing. The decision whether to conduct proceedings in such a manner is left to the judge's discretion (Voglar 2009: 1654). This is also a proper solution. Cases can differ greatly – some are easily resolved, some involve difficult questions of law, some involve difficult questions of facts and a time consuming process of taking evidence, highly qualified attorneys participate in some (sometimes in a mutually co-operative manner, sometimes in a rather hostile atmosphere), while in others lay parties represent themselves. Therefore, a flexible system (in which it is left to the judge to decide whether to request that further information be provided in written briefs and, if so, within what time limit) is more appropriate than a rigid system of time limits imposed by law (Bergant Rakočević 2008: 1602). It is also plausible that a judge can decide, in accordance with the particularities of the given case, whether at an early stage of litigation he will adopt a written preparatory procedure (requiring parties to file further written briefs), or whether an oral hearing will take place and the case discussed orally with the parties.

There are of course numerous reasons that justify the filing of new briefs and submitting fresh facts and evidence not only at the first but also at subsequent hearings. This, however, should be left to a flexible interpretation of the notion of 'justified reasons' (Šipec 1999: 1206; Ude 2002: 284). The common feature of most modern reforms of civil procedure is such that more room is provided for the judge to adapt the conduct of proceedings and its time-frame to the characteristics of each particular case. This is achieved by granting the judge greater powers of discretion or by extending the use of open-ended terms in procedural legislation, relying more upon general principles and legal standards (e.g. 'good faith', 'due diligence', 'good administration of justice', 'prevention of abuse of rights') or by providing for different 'tracks' concerning the preparatory phase of proceedings. In Slovenia, however, very few are willing to support this trend.[25] The widespread perception is exactly the opposite. Such procedural rules are often rejected with aversion as being 'unclear', 'too vague', 'unreliable and unpredictable', therefore open to abuse and arbitrary decision-making. Clearly, the objections to greater discretion and powers to adapt the proceedings to the particularities of each case are an expression of a lack of trust in the judges and the judiciary in general. It is thus not surprising that a stiff procedural order that left the judges no place to adjust the conduct of proceedings was characteristic of the old, socialist civil justice.[26] That was the period when the judiciary was denied the position of an independent branch of state power. Another fact that is not surprising is that the resistance to greater judicial discretion today is expressed by exactly those politicians and attorneys who demonstrate general mistrust in courts. However, giving the judges more powers to adjust the conduct of proceedings to the characteristics of each individual case is strongly opposed, perhaps as a sign of serious lack of self-confidence, by some judges as well.[27]

11.4 Preclusions and the Goal of Doing Justice on the Merits

When a country goes through a period of fundamental changes in its political and economic order a critical re-evaluation of the goals of civil justice is essential. Polemics and discussions concerning the goals and possible reforms of civil justice that have flourished over the last 20 years should thus be perceived as a welcoming occurrence. The problem, however, is that the debates have (too) often been burdened with an excessive amount of ideology and increasingly also populism and demagogy. Opinions and proposals expressed in these debates often reflect a

[25] A prominent Slovenian intellectual (and one of the leading dissidents in the period of socialism) Dr. France Bučar observed: 'We degraded judges to mere bureaucrats. A judge must have a personality and be worthy of having confidence in him. But because of the totalitarian past in Slovenia, we thought that every step of the proceedings should be prescribed in detail for the judge to follow. However, if you prescribe their every move, judges will not strive for justice, they will seek only their own protection. Judges need more discretion.' Cited by: Mekina (2008: 10).

[26] As Uzelac observes, judicial discretion in this paradigm was often viewed as behaviour that inevitably leads to arbitrariness, therefore endangers legal certainty as the fundamental value of decision-making as well. Uzelac (2004: 77).

[27] See the Note on the draft of the Civil Procedure Act Amendment, Celje Court of Appeals President's office, dated 22.6.2007 (submitted in the course of the law-drafting debate).

complete ignorance of a comparative perspective concerning civil justice systems in the world and their reforms. In addition, they are frequently based on a serious lack of knowledge concerning the historical origins of procedural instruments and principles. One-sided and simplified answers are typically offered, whereby the lack of competence is often disguised and compensated for by invoking strongly worded phrases, appealing prejudices, fears and other emotions. Such polemics were already common in the time when the first Slovenian CPA was drafted in the 1990s. It was typical for that period that the truth-finding and the substantive aspect of dispute determination were often flatly denied any significance. It was a widely accepted perception that the goal of acceleration of proceedings should be achieved through a more passive role of the judge and that instruments such as the judge's duty to ask appropriate questions and to promote clarification, the so called 'substantive procedural guidance' (*materielle Prozessleitung*) should be abolished.[28] Simplifications and misperceptions in the sense that a judge has an active role in the 'East' (that is, in the Soviet style of civil procedure) but remains passive in the 'West' were common.[29] The conviction that 'effectiveness of proceedings' equals nothing but speed was also widespread. The substantive quality of adjudication and the desirability that the judicial process should result in accurate determinations of facts and law remained completely neglected.

After some rather calm years an ideologically burdened discussion on civil justice re-emerged in connection with the 2008 CPA amendment. There were many similarities with the debates from the 1990s. Again, a lack of any comparative perspective and complete ignorance of civil justice systems along with their contemporary reforms in other countries was oftentimes reflected in these discussions. Again, simplified and one-sided concepts as to the goals of civil justice were offered. Only these were the exact opposite from those offered in the debates in the 1990s. Just as it was typical for the debates in the 1990s to deny any significance of justice on the merits and the accuracy of court's findings of facts and law, the goal of doing justice on the merits, which is inseparably linked to the finding of true facts, is now generally perceived as the one single goal of civil justice. This perception is often accompanied by an absolute resistance to any binding time limits for bringing forward new material as well as for procedural sanctions against non-compliance with such time limits. These supposedly prevent the court from doing justice on the merits. Some authors perceive the binding of such time limits as a major impediment to the vindication of rights and are thus supposedly incompatible with the constitutional right of an effective access to justice. The 'effectiveness' of access to justice is – exactly the opposite as in the debates of the 1990s – understood exclusively in the sense of substantive accuracy of the judgment, not relating to time and costs at all. The strengthening of

---

[28] This was (as noted, e.g., by Rechberger (2008: 108) typical also in other Central-Eastern European ex-socialist countries in the early years of transition.

[29] Typically Šipec (1999: 1201), Koman-Perenič (1997: 801). It is superfluous to say that these were serious misconceptions, since the concept of an active judge in the Yugoslav Civil Procedure Act in fact derived from the Austrian (Franz Klein's) ZPO and was not a result of legislative changes after the introduction of socialism.

procedural obligations, combined with the system of sanctions (as implemented by the 2008 CPA reform), is perceived as a formalization of the procedure and as an expression of an (assumed) trend that a goal of reaching substantive justice is fading.[30] It has often been said (and it is already becoming a standard clause in briefs and appeals of certain counsels) that the '... novelties in civil procedure pursue a goal to enable the judge to get rid of the file easily by imposing procedural hurdles and engaging in procedural manoeuvres without examination on merits'.[31] Certain authors (attorneys-at-law by profession) even go so far as to suggest that the single paramount principle of civil justice is establishing the truth and that imposing any legal obstacles, which prevent the court from finding the truth, is a 'step back in time' and 'far from being compatible with a contemporary idea of civil justice'.[32] One can only conclude that such views amount to an outright 'resurrection of the idea of material truth' in a manner not different from the one promoted in the early years of firm communist rule.[33]

Such a simplified view of the goals of civil justice cannot be supported. It is not disputed that from the viewpoint of a private individual litigant (leaving aside numerous co-existing public purposes of civil justice) the main goal of civil justice is enforcement of individual substantive rights. In order to fulfil this goal the court is expected to accurately determine facts and correctly apply the law (it goes without saying: with overriding respect for party autonomy and free disposition). In addition, this determination must, if it is to have any practical value, be reached without undue delay. The question how the procedural sanctions of disallowing late facts and evidence as well as of disregarding late filed preparatory briefs are compatible with the goal of enforcement of individual rights is posed. Those who oppose such procedural sanctions are (at least to a certain extent) ready to acknowledge that preclusions have positive effects on the acceleration of proceedings. Nevertheless, they claim that this result is reached on account of the main element of enforcement of individual rights – the expectation that the court's judgment will reflect true facts and a correct application of the law (Jelačin 2008: 10; Varanelli 2012: 6; Ilc 2008: 20).

I believe that such a reproach, although nowadays quite often expressed in Slovenia, is not well founded. The judge's powers to disallow late facts and evidence are not mutually exclusive with the purpose of doing justice on the merits. Intensification of the expectation that the parties shall bring forward facts and means of evidence (as well as all available material and arguments in general) in a timely

30 Typically Wedam Lukić (2009: 64): 'Today, it is increasingly becoming a common view that it is fair if the party loses the case only because she was not diligent enough and had not on time submitted facts and evidence ... But justice is not done!'

31 Typically: Jelačin (2008: 10).

32 Varanelli (2012: 6). In a similar manner: Jelačin (2008: 10): '... do not pursue the overriding principle – reaching a decision correct in the factual and legal aspect. Hence any obstacles on the path towards this goal are a step back and not forward.'

33 Typically Kamhi (1957: 23), who (in his textbook of 1957) argued that 'in contrast to a bourgeois state a socialist state is deeply interested in achieving the goal of finding the real truth in every single litigation, regardless of how unimportant and minor the dispute seems to be'.

manner (under the threat that late facts and evidence shall be disregarded) is not aimed at enabling the judge to 'get rid of the matter easily by means of excessive formalism without deciding it on the merits'. On the contrary, this device is designed to ensure not only acceleration but also a better substantive quality of judicial decision-making in every individual case.

Extended and intensified procedural requirements for the timely submission of facts and means of evidence (along with some other procedural tools[34]) should primarily be understood as a clear message to the parties (their counsels) that a diligent and active preparation for their case is necessary.[35] A diligent and active preparation of all participants of the civil process, not only the judge but the parties and their counsels as well, can only be beneficial for the substantive quality of judicial process. The accuracy of this finding is probably not denied even by those who oppose the introduction of procedural sanctions against delay. The approach that accepts the idea that the parties and their counsels should diligently prepare for litigation, while at the same time opposes any adverse consequences (labelling them as 'repression'), should they fail to do so, appears to be simple demagogy. How the goal of active, serious and diligent preparation of the parties and their counsels can then be effectively achieved remains unanswered. The problem here is that incentive for the parties to be active cannot be achieved only as a 'request', without any adverse consequences for non-compliance. A system of sanctions must be attached to the imposed time limits, otherwise it would remain entirely without effect. In addition, the parties should be well aware of the fact that the judge is – if necessary – determined to enforce procedural sanctions for delay and that he will not too leniently relieve them from sanctions against delay. The judge's active role in case management and judicial control of litigation, including the duty to promote clarifications and to give hints and observations, can undoubtedly not only save time and cost of litigation but can benefit the substantive quality of the judgment as well. These positive effects can, however, be attained only along with the appropriate activity of the parties (Zobec 2009: 1373).

The opponents of the system of binding time limits for submission of facts and evidence forget that the introduction of sanctions against non-compliance does not necessarily mean they shall often be implemented in practice. It is not unrealistic to expect that in most cases time limits and court orders are respected and that the culture of compliance will prevail. These sanctions predominantly pursue a preventive effect. This is based on the presumption that submissions of facts and means of evidence as well as preparatory briefs of parties and their counsels shall result from a diligent and timely preparation for the trial and that they shall be presented in a systematic and comprehensive manner already before the trial. If we trust in the

[34] E.g. the rule that, in principle, facts which are not expressly denied are considered admitted and that the party should indicate with sufficient precision which factual assertions of his opponent are denied and to reflect on them, and so that merely a flat 'denial of all facts' does not suffice. Such is also the rule that the party must designate the means of evidence, and at the same time sufficiently indicate the facts they relate to and why they can be relevant.

[35] From the viewpoint of a legal counsel: Slivnik (2008: 1607).

competence of attorneys and their adherence to professional standards, and if time limits for bringing forward facts and means of evidence and for further preparatory briefs are sufficiently long, it is not unrealistic to expect that the culture of compliance shall prevail.

11.5 Balance Between Results Achieved and Time and Cost Spent: Mutual Responsibility of the Parties and the Court

It would be wrong to perceive the introduction of binding time limits for putting forward facts and evidence and preparatory briefs as a means of 'passivization' of the court. It is true that the introduction of the system of preclusions imposes an additional burden on the parties and their attorneys to diligently prepare for their case. This, nevertheless, does not mean that the judge's responsibility to exercise control over litigation and to take an active role in preparation of the trial is diminished. The introduction of binding time limits with appropriate sanctions for the parties is intrinsically bound up with the requirement that the judge himself will also diligently and timely prepare for the case. The introduction of the system of preclusions means that the duty of the judge to pose appropriate questions, to promote clarification and the overall responsibility for the case management and achievement of justice is gaining and not losing in importance (Wedam Lukić 2003: 1671; Bergant Rakočević 2008: 1602; Betetto 2010: 12). Precisely because the court is able to refuse new statements of facts and new evidence, submitted in the later stages of proceedings, it is becoming more important for the court to properly fulfil its obligations to stimulate the parties to supplement and to clarify their submissions and, if necessary, state new facts as well as offer new evidence already in the first session of the main hearing (Trampuš 2002: 585). A mutual responsibility of the parties and the judge to strive for a focused main hearing and overall concentration of proceedings, as well as for a substantive justice, is clearly needed (Dolenc 2008: 1574; Voglar 2009: 1654). A judge who is himself not diligently prepared for the case cannot effectively exercise his powers in directing the parties to give further clarifications and supplementations, nor can he decide whether conditions for disregarding new facts and evidence are fulfilled. In addition, sanctions for belated submission of facts and means of evidence may not be imposed in cases where the court itself has delayed the proceedings because of insufficient judicial clarification and case management.[36]

Hence the introduction of a system of preclusions in fact imposes an additional burden of diligent preparation for the first session of the main hearing for both – the parties as well as the judge. It therefore might not come as a surprise that the system of preclusions is opposed not only by numerous attorneys but by certain judges as

[36] Judgment of the Slovenian Supreme Court No. II Ips 449/2008 of 10 July 2008.

well. In fact, instruments that were introduced by the 2008 reform and designed to enable a comprehensive preparation for the trial are still insufficiently used in practice. These tools require diligent preparation before the trial, thus good knowledge of the file and a serious preliminary legal analysis by both the judge as well as the attorneys. However, such a preparation cannot be expected from a judge who cannot rid himself of the old habit of having 'the first serious look' at the file only at the first hearing and only then truly starting to work on the case. Inevitably, such a judge will neither be able to correctly apply the statutory provisions concerning binding time limits nor will he be able to exercise his duty to pose appropriate questions and promote clarification at the preparatory stage of proceedings.

11.6 Do Procedural Sanctions and Preclusions Prevent the Goal of Doing Justice on the Merits? The Experience of Socialist Yugoslavia

Starting from the early 1950s Yugoslavia opted for a version of socialism that was the least repressive and at the same time the most economically prosperous of all the (then) socialist countries.[37] As a logical consequence thereof Yugoslav civil justice did not suffer from the same degradation as did its counterparts in the Soviet bloc countries. For example, the principle of respect for party autonomy was adequately recognised in the law. Nevertheless, practice often tended towards a much more paternalistic approach.[38] As explained above, the Yugoslav socialist concept of civil procedure was characterized by accentuated responsibility and (expected) activity of the judge, on the one hand, and by the non-existence of sanctions against the parties' belated submission of facts, evidence and preparatory briefs, on the other. Both were an expression of the paramount importance placed on the 'principle of material truth'.[39] This was partly an expression of the ideological view that courts (i.e. the state) are omnipotent and should be able to find the truth to ensure substantive justice and to affirm 'socialist legality' without any hindrances.[40] This was combined with the perception that there should be as many levels of 'control' as possible

[37] Yugoslavia managed to stay out of the Soviet bloc and remained equally close to the Western countries (with unrestricted and visa-free travel to these countries for individuals as well). Private business was allowed to a bigger extent and the system of a 'centrally planned state economy' did not apply. Major trade partners of Yugoslavia were (West) Germany and Italy. In the northern parts of Yugoslavia (Slovenia, Croatia) English (and not Russian) was the first foreign language taught already in primary schools.

[38] Uzelac observes that inquisitorial elements and judicial activism of the Austrian procedural legislation were not interpreted as a warrant for concentration, publicity, directness and efficiency any more, instead they became instruments of socialist paternalism Uzelac (2004: 295), compare also Dika, Uzelac (1990: 394).

[39] See n. 33 above.

[40] For such an ideological foundation concerning the doctrine of the primacy of the material truth see Kamhi (1957: 22–24). For a critique of such an approach see, e.g., Uzelac (2010: 380 et seq.).

(Uzelac 2010: 390). Secondly, it was an expression of a certain disrespect for the autonomy of the individual and his ability to be responsible for his acts and omissions. Thirdly, it was – at least as a result – an expression of a certain scepticism regarding the bar as an independent legal profession and lawyers' ability to effectively accomplish their role of protecting the rights of their clients.

However the experience in Slovenia from the period such a system was in force demonstrates that the high importance assigned to the substantive aspect of adjudication ('material truth') often led to results exactly the opposite of those it strove to achieve. It was precisely the procedural system that lacked adequate sanctions against the parties' inactivity and delay that caused the goal of substantive justice to fade. The lack of effective tools that would enable the timely gathering of procedural materials resulted in frequent adjournments of hearings, in a 'piecemeal' manner of the presentation of facts and evidence and in culpably delaying a case's progress. Through such practice, proceedings often became too formalized and bereft of substance.[41]

Court hearings that are degraded to a mere 'meeting point' for an exchange of further preparatory briefs do not embody the ideal of the quest for substantive justice (Bergant Rakočević 2008: 1602; Betetto 2010: 12). And neither do hearings which are immediately adjourned following a party's putting forward further evidentiary proposals or following a finding that certain documentary evidence, although already relied upon by one party, has not yet been adduced (disclosed) to the court and the opposing party. It is entirely incompatible, not just from the viewpoint of speed, but as well from the viewpoint of substantive justice, if essential new arguments and fresh evidence are adduced only at the hearing itself. If the hearing is then adjourned, because respect for the opposing party's right to be heard so requires, it did not fulfil its purpose of the substantive determination of the dispute. If, on the other hand, the hearing is not adjourned despite the belated submission of new material, and the court requires the opponent to respond immediately, both the opponent and the court alike are taken by surprise. This jeopardizes not only the procedural guarantees of the right to be heard and of the equality of arms, but the goal of justice on the merits as well. If neither the court nor the opposing party has enough time to reflect on new arguments and fresh facts and evidence, it is difficult for the court to properly steer the hearing and exercise its duty to ask appropriate questions and promote clarification. Even more importantly, it is difficult for the opposing party to make such quality counter-arguments 'on the spot' as he could have if he had had sufficient time beforehand. A further consequence of the former Yugoslav procedural system was that often when the oral hearing had already commenced it still remained unclear which facts were actually material for the case (Plauštajner 1997: 812). In addition, in most cases it remained unclear which facts were really in dispute, since a litigant's response to the factual allegations of the opposing party was reduced to mere (but at that time sufficient) escape (*salvatory*) clauses that 'everything is denied unless expressly admitted' (Slivnik 2008: 1611). The attorneys' tactics of adducing an excessive amount of documentary evidence

[41] See, e.g., Betetto 1995: 10, in general for Yugoslavia Uzelac 2010: 384 et seq.

'in a bundle', thus without indexation and without precise indication as to which factual allegations it refers and without proper references to its particular contents, was common as well.

Another feature of the style of litigation in the former system was the frequent use of 'ambush tactics' by attorneys. As there were no time limits for the adduction of fresh evidence and no obligation regarding advance disclosure (even of documents in possession of the party who himself relied on them), parties often filed documentary evidence only at the oral hearing. They counted on the other party's being taken by surprise (admittedly, though, such late disclosure of relevant evidence was often not a result of any deliberate tactics, but a mere consequence of negligent preparation for the case, or, more frequently, a tool that enabled the achievement of a desired adjournment of the hearing[42]). The idea that it is precisely in the interests of justice – not only procedural, but substantive as well – that evidence in the hands of one party should be disclosed to the other party in a timely fashion, such that both the opposing party as well as the court can properly consider it, found no response. And all this was done, supposedly, in the name of the 'quest for material truth'.

Most importantly, the paternalistic expectation that the judge is required to supplement any insufficient diligence, inactivity, incompetence or lack of research and analysis of the case by the attorneys led to results which were disastrous not only from the viewpoint of delay, but also from the very viewpoint of pursuing substantive justice. Since attorneys were aware that any insufficient knowledge and research of their client's case would need to be rectified by the activism of the judge, they increasingly became completely inactive and negligent in the preparation and conduct of their clients' cases (Betetto 1995: 10; Uzelac 2004: 300).[43] There was (and to some extent still is) a widespread misperception among attorneys that the rule of *iura novit curia* (the court knows the law) means that attorneys are not expected to undertake any legal analysis and put forward any legal arguments or references as to the settled case law at all. This system which enabled attorneys to attend court hearings totally unprepared, whereby these hearings were reduced to a mere formality with the exchange of further briefs and evidentiary proposals, followed by another adjournment, inevitably also resulted in the passivization of judges. It simply did not pay off either for judges to prepare diligently for the hearing, if it was very likely that the parties would put forward new material therein which would shed an entirely different light on the case. Hence, it was increasingly common that not only the parties' legal counsels but also judges appeared at hearings totally unprepared and with little

[42] See also Uzelac (2010: 384).

[43] From the viewpoint of an attorney Slivnik (2008: 1611 et seq.) notes that it is simply unfair (and is not a real incentive for a future diligent preparation) if an attorney comes to a hearing properly and diligently prepared just to see that his colleague 'on the other side' did not prepare at all but is then for this very same reason greatly assisted by the active judge in order to remedy his incompetence or (and) negligence.

or no real knowledge of the case and its factual and legal bases.[44] It was only after the first oral hearing had already commenced that the judge had a truly serious look at the case file for the first time. Understandably, when the habit of a lack of diligent preparation for the hearing prevailed, numerous adjournments of hearings were actually preferred by all – attorneys and judges alike.[45]

It is indicative that even procedural sanctions, which at that time were already available against a culpable delay in submitting facts and means of evidence and preparatory briefs, were rarely used (except for a judgment by default in the event of the defendant's total and repeated passivity). A party that was guilty of delay could be ordered to pay the opponent the costs incurred by such a delay (for example, for the need to reschedule a hearing). However, the court could not impose such 'wasted cost order' *ex officio*, but only upon the motion of the opposing party. But such requests were extremely rare in practice (nevertheless, the practice of submitting preparatory briefs, facts and evidence late was endemic). This is not really surprising since attorneys who made requests for a 'wasted cost order' due to the culpable delay of the opposing party's attorney were soon labelled by their colleagues as not being loyal to the bar. In this context, it is not irrelevant that the system of attorneys' fees did not stimulate attorneys to strive for a focused trial or avoid a piecemeal manner of litigation.

Commenting on the everyday practice of socialist civil justice in Yugoslavia, Judge Betetto (1995: 10) later observed:

> Precisely in the name of the quest for material truth, the system imposed burdens only upon judges. But because it failed to include appropriate sanctions which would make them active, this system enabled parties to 'fall asleep' (with honourable exceptions). The law enabled them to attend hearings unprepared and to file further briefs there, while the judge had to 'beg them' to adduce evidence.

It is probably inherent in human nature that the introduction of a procedural system that imposes the entire burden of and responsibility for the preparation and substantive quality of adjudication exclusively upon the judge will sooner or later result in the passivization of the parties and their legal counsels. In fact, it is proper economic behaviour not to engage in additional work if one (here: an attorney) can be sure that his omissions and lack of diligent preparation will not result in any adverse consequences since they will necessarily and effectively need to be rectified by another person (here: the judge at issue). The substantive quality of

[44] In this regard it should be noted that this 'habit' developed in a system which in theory was based on the idea of a very active and dominant role (and responsibilities) of the judge in litigation. This should be contrasted to the purely adversarial style of civil justice, where the judge's lack of knowledge of the file before the trial was actually its inherent and logical part.

[45] Another expression of Yugoslav 'judicial paternalism' and its disproportionate accentuation of the principle of 'material truth' was the wide open possibility of further appeals, enabling for a nearly full review. The 'wide open doors' to the second and third tiers of jurisdiction led to a further disastrous consequence, namely the changing mentality of litigants and their attorneys. Since they could be confident that there was still 'time to catch up later', they simply too often did not take the procedure in the first instance court as seriously as they should and could have. Furthermore, also the quality of the adjudication in the first (and even in the second) tier of jurisdiction probably decreased, as the judges knew that they did not have the 'responsibility of the last word'.

adjudication cannot benefit from such practice. For the effectiveness of civil justice, not only concerning time and cost, but from the viewpoint of substantive justice as well, it would be lethal if the perception prevailed that the attorney, although a legal professional, can remain confident that there will be no adverse consequences for his client's case even if he completely fails to exercise due diligence in preparing for the case, since the entire burden of the goal of achieving a just result to the process remains on the court.

For all of the above-mentioned reasons, it would be wrong to perceive the introduction of procedural sanctions against non-compliance with the requirement to put forward facts, evidence and preparatory briefs in a timely fashion as an expression of excessive formalism. This does not concern adopting an overly formalistic approach to procedural requirements in order to prevent parties from having their case examined on the merits. Not only the right to be heard and prompt adjudication, but also the substantive accuracy of adjudication are promoted by requiring all available materials and arguments to be available and made known to the opposing party and the court already before the oral hearing (Zobec 2007: 1060).

11.7 The System of Binding Time Limits and the Goals of Civil Justice: The Assessment of the Slovenian Constitutional Court

In 2009 the Slovenian Constitutional Court confirmed that the system of binding time limit for submitting facts and motioning for evidence does not violate constitutional procedural guarantees.[46] The Constitutional Court admitted that the system of preclusions constitutes an interference with the right to be heard as determined in Article 22 of the Constitution, however, this interference is proportionate with the justified aim it pursues – acceleration and concentration of proceedings. The Constitutional Court holds that this aim can be attained only when appropriate activity and diligence of the parties to proceedings is involved. It is thus necessary that the statutory regulation be designed in such a way that it forces the parties to prepare themselves diligently and in a suitable timeframe for the civil proceeding on their own, which also significantly facilitates a greater quality of the content of the judicial protection.[47] For such a request to be effective, a proper system of sanctions must be attached to it. Thereby, the responsibility lies with the legislator as well as in every particular case with the judge to find the right balance between ensuring concentration and acceleration of the proceedings, on the one hand, and a correct judgment from the point of view of substantive law, on the other. When trying to balance these principles, the result should not be that one of the principles (completely) excludes the other or that one of the principles would always prevail.[48]

---

[46] Decision of the Slovenian Constitutional Court No. Up-2443/08 of 7 October 2009.

[47] Ibid.

[48] Ibid.

Another decision of the Slovenian Constitutional Court also stressed the positive effects of the introduction (by the 2008 CPA amendment – see above, Sect. 11.2) of the court's powers to exercise its duty to provide clarifications in the written form already before the main hearing.[49] As explained, a system of procedural sanctions (disregarding late facts and evidence) is also attached to these powers. Provided that the judge himself has diligently prepared for the trial, these new statutory instruments can ensure that procedural materials be collected in the shortest time possible, already before the main hearing. In this decision the Constitutional Court also stressed that a relation of incumbent interdependence exists between the judge's duty to provide clarifications (exercised already in the preparatory phase of proceedings) and the sanction of disallowing facts and evidence, submitted in default. If there is no proper activity (observations, hints, requests for clarifications and supplementations) from the side of the judge already in the written preparatory procedure, sanctions disallowing new facts and evidence before the first oral hearing cannot be allowed as well.[50] The Constitutional Court also stressed that the new statutory instruments can contribute not only to the concentration and acceleration of proceedings, but to substantive quality of adjudication as well. Furthermore, it stated that by introducing such instruments the legislature corrected the previously existing systemic deficiency regarding the regulation of civil procedure.[51]

The Slovenian Constitutional Court, therefore, very positively evaluated the extended system of procedural sanctions of disregarding new facts and evidence as it was introduced by the 2008 CPA amendment. It clearly emphasized the principle that the responsibility or burden to contribute to efficient and expeditious proceedings, as well as to the substantive quality of judicial protection, also falls on the parties. Thereby, it should be noted that the very same Constitutional Court otherwise has little or no understanding for procedural novelties which amount to an excessive formalization of procedure. The aforementioned 2008 CPA amendment indeed included such novelties, many of which have already been declared unconstitutional by the Constitutional Court. Such novelties were introduced in the text of the CPA amendment only in a very late stage of the legislative procedure, upon initiative of the Ministry of Justice or certain judges.[52] The rule that a claim filed by an attorney is immediately stricken out, without the possibility of rectification, if it does not fulfil all formal criteria (Art. 108/2 CPA)[53] or if a correct power of attorney is not submitted (Art. 98/5 CPA) has already been declared unconstitutional by the

[49] Decision of the Slovenian Constitutional Court No. U-I-164/09 of 4 February 2010.

[50] Ibid.

[51] Ibid.

[52] This should be taken into consideration in contrast to the provisions which extended the judge's powers to disregard late facts and evidence (including an extension of the judge's responsibility to provide clarification). These were formulated on the basis of extensive comparative research and explanatory memoranda and were subject of in-depth discussions in the study group responsible for drafting the reform.

[53] Decision of the Slovenian Constitutional Court No. U-I-200/09-14 of 20 May 2010.

Constitutional Court.[54] The Constitutional Court also annulled strict procedural sanctions of automatically striking out a claim in cases where the claimant did not attend the main hearing[55] and the sanction of an automatic judgment by default, if it was the defendant who did not attend the main hearing (regardless of whether he had previously duly filed a defence plea).[56] The rule that the service of a claim to a physical person can always be validly effected on the address, entered in the official administrative register, regardless of whether the addressee actually (still) lives at that address and regardless of whether the addressee could, upon reasonable effort actually be found at a certain other address (Art. 143 CPA), has also been declared unconstitutional since it disproportionally restricts the constitutional right to be heard.[57]

All the aforementioned issues prove that a real danger of abuse of procedural instruments leading to a pure formalization of proceedings without any real benefits of legitimate aims of civil justice truly exist, and that they can put the fairness of the trial in jeopardy. It must, therefore, be constantly and critically assessed whether both the legislature and the judge in every individual case have managed to find a proper balance between the goals of concentration, speed and procedural economy on the one hand, and the goal of achieving justice on merits on the other. Furthermore, the quest for a proper balance must also include the aspect of adequately protecting procedural guarantees such as the right to be heard. Review of the case law of the Slovenian Constitutional Court, however, shows that an individual assessment must be made in each specific case, since it is not possible to attach the label of a 'mere formalization of procedure' to every accentuated procedural requirement or every procedural sanction. The system of the judge's powers to disregard late facts and evidence proves that such requirements and sanctions attached to cases of non-compliance, can, if applied properly, benefit all of the aforementioned aims of civil justice.

11.8 Conclusion

I have attempted to account for the desire for more intensified activity and the responsibility of parties to contribute to the goals of the civil justice (especially from the view of both substantive quality as well as speed), giving practical arguments. Put simply, if there are three people in a boat (a judge and two parties or their representatives), the boat will proceed with greater ease and speed if all three are

---

[54] Decision of the Slovenian Constitutional Court No. U-I-74/12-6 od 13.9.2012. On the contrary, such a requirement is not inadmissible in procedure on a further appeal on points of law (on account of specific features of the procedure in the Supreme Court and acknowledging that the main content of the right of access to court has already been achieved in the lower courts; the procedure in the Supreme Court may thus be more formal); Decision of the Slovenian Constitutional Court No. U-I-277/09 of 14 June 2011.

[55] Decision of the Slovenian Constitutional Court No. U-I-164/09-13 of 4 February 2010.

[56] Decision of the Slovenian Constitutional Court No. U-I-161/10-12 of 9 December 2010.

[57] Decision of the Slovenian Constitutional Court No. U-I-279/08 of 9 July 2009.

compelled to row. There is no need for ideological arguments here. However, the other side repeatedly offers them. Those who categorically oppose any system of procedural sanctions for non-observance of time limits for asserting facts and evidence like to present themselves as liberal protectors of human rights and justice itself, while labelling those who advocate the responsibility and activity of parties as 'repressive'. Nevertheless, it might be even easier to claim just the opposite – namely, the concept that a party should not bear responsibility for his actions and decisions is not liberal at all. Such a concept is paternalistic. On the contrary, it is respect for human dignity that requires that a party be given the capacity and therefore the responsibility for his own choices. Denial of responsibility is in fact a denial of autonomy and hence freedom. Correspondingly, advocating that the law preserves the systematically built-in expectation that an attorney's negligent and incompetent work will be remedied by the judge (the court), thus opposing the demand for legal counsels to perform their work diligently and competently, in fact expresses a great distrust towards the bar. Precisely the expectation that attorneys should contribute to the quality of civil justice is an expression of trust therein. This expectation enables the bar to assume its proper role in society. Denying the role the attorney is supposed to play in civil proceedings would in the last instance lead to the position the bar 'enjoyed' in the communist countries of the Soviet bloc – i.e. first the disappearance of attorneys from the courtroom, then from society in general, finally to the disappearance of the bar itself as an independent profession.

An ideologically burdened debate is simply not needed. First of all, because opposition to the system of disregarding facts and evidence submitted late (and to any kind of expectations regarding the activity of the parties in general) in the name of material truth, that is, justice on the merits, often simply does not sound sincere. Civil procedure without procedural sanctions and binding time limits for submitting facts and evidence, as experience in Slovenia has clearly proved, has regularly resulted in the fact that both attorneys as well as judges come to hearings totally unprepared. Invoking the principle of material truth and emphasizing the goal of a substantively correct decision in such a system is, realistically speaking, usually only a transparent excuse to postpone the start of serious work (studying the law, learning the facts, selecting appropriate means of proof, etc.) to a later time or even the expectation of the legal counsel that the work he should perform and should be able to perform himself, will be done by someone else (the judge). Moreover, general human experience probably confirms that a system without time limits regarding any kind of work does not necessarily mean that more substantive work will be done and that it will be of a higher quality. Perhaps the work will only begin at a later time.

But the most important lesson that can be learnt from debates in Slovenia concerning the relation between the goals of civil justice and introduction of procedural sanctions and preclusions is that there are no black and white answers out there. What remains – for the legislature as well as for the judge in every specific case – is to seek out the proper balance between the goal of reaching a substantively correct decision, on the one hand, and using the adequate resources and time that can be devoted to that goal, on the other. The principle that is emphasized the most in the modern development of civil procedure is precisely proportionality. What is strived for is finding the most efficient distribution of the responsibilities and burdens of all participants in proceedings in order to find the optimal balance between the goal of comprehensive substantive examination of the merits of the case, on one hand, and speed and efficiency in reaching this decision, on the other. Proportionality means not only assessment from the point of view of the specific parties to the case at hand, but also assessment from the standpoint of the administration of justice in general. An individual case should be allotted a fair and appropriate share of the limited public resources allotted for the justice system and, put simply, all other litigants waiting in the queue for their turn in court should also be taken into account.

References

Bergant Rakočević V (2008) Materialno procesno vodstvo v pisnih fazah postopka in razmerje do prekluzije [Material procedural guidance in the written stage of litigation and its relation to preclusions]. Podjetje in delo 6–7:1597–1606
Bergant Rakočević V (2009) Prekluzije in posebni procesni položaji [Preclusions and specific procedural phases]. Podjetje in delo 6–7:1656–1664
Betetto N (1995) Ob predlogu novega ZPP [On the draft of the new civil procedure act]. Pravna praksa 341:10–11
Betetto N (2004) Pospešeni pravdni postopek [Accelerated litigation]. Pravna praksa 29:36–38
Betetto N (2010) Vloga sodnika v postopku na prvi in drugi stopnji [The role of the judge in the first and second instance proceedings]. Pravni letopis 1:9–22
Brus M (2007) Prvostopenjski civilni proces po nemškem ZPO [Litigation in first instance courts pursuant to the German ZPO]. Podjetje in delo 2:336–369
Dika M, Uzelac A (1990) Zum Problem des richterlichen Aktivismus in Jugoslawien. Zbornik Pravnog fakulteta u Zagrebu 40:391–416
Dolenc M (2007) Materialno procesno vodstvo v luči odločb Ustavnega sodišča [Material procedural guidance in the case law of the constitutional court]. Pravosodni bilten 1:65–75
Dolenc M (2008) Materialno procesno vodstvo – sredstvo za racionalizacijo postopka ali dodatno breme in prelaganje odgovornosti? [Material procedural guidance – a tool for the rationalization of proceedings or an additional burden and discharging of responsibilities?]. Podjetje in delo 6–7:1568–1576
Ilc J (2008) Pravdno represivni postopek – k noveli ZPP-D [Repressive civil procedure – remarks concerning the CPA amendment]. Odvetnik 40:19–21
Jelačin M (2008) Novela ZPP-D, njene skrite pasti in pravne praznine [The CPA amendment, its hidden traps and legal loopholes]. Pravna praksa 25:10–12
Juhart J (1956) Civilno procesno pravo [Civil procedure]. Univerzitetna založba, Ljubljana
Kamhi S (1957) Građanski sudski postupak [Civil procedure]. Veselin Masleša, Sarajevo
Koman-Perenič L (1997) Izpeljava ustavnih določil v civilnih procesnih zakonih [The application of constitutional norms in civil procedural laws]. Podjetje in delo 6–7:795–806
Mekina B (2008) Demontaža države. Mladina 28:9–11
Plauštajner K (1997) Položaj upnika v sodnih postopkih [The position of a creditor in court proceedings]. Podjetje in delo 6–7:807–814
Rechberger W (2008) Die Ideen Franz Kleins und ihre Bedeutung fur die Entwicklung des Zivilprozessrechts in Europa. Ritsumeikan Law Review 28:101–110
Šipec M (1999) Med liberalnim in socialnim civilnim procesom [Between a liberal and social civil procedure]. Podjetje in delo 6–7:1200–1209

Slivnik A (2008) Materialno procesno vodstvo – spodbuda za boljše ali slabše delo [The judge's duty to ask questions and promote clarification – an incentive for better or worse work]. Podjetje in delo 6–7:1607–1612

Trampuš Z (2002) Materialno procesno vodstvo in sodna poravnava [Substantive procedural guidance and court settlement]. Podjetje in delo 6–7:1545–1560

Ude L (2002) Civilno procesno pravo [Civil procedure]. ČZ UL, Ljubljana

Ude L, Galič A, Betetto N, Rijavec V, Zobec J, Wedam Lukić D (2005–2010) Pravdni postopek – zakon s komentarjem [Civil procedure – the act with the commentary], vols 1–4. GV Založba/ČZ UL, Ljubljana

Uzelac A (2004) Accelerating civil proceedings in Croatia – a history of attempts to improve the efficiency of civil litigation. In: van Rhee CH (ed) History of delays in civil procedure. Maastricht University, Maastricht, pp 283–313

Uzelac A (2010) Survival of the third legal tradition? Supreme Court Law Rev 49:377–396

Uzelac A (2012) Goals of civil justice – general report. In: Maleshin D (ed) Civil procedure in cross-cultural dialogue. Eurasia context. Statut Publishing House, Moscow, pp 111–136

Varanelli L (2012) Sodišče in ocenjevanje dokazov v civilnem postopku [The court and the assessment of evidence in civil procedure]. Pravna praksa 2:6–8

Voglar M (2009) Prekluzije in sankcije po ZPP-D v praksi: izkušnja sodnika [Preclusions and sanctions pursuant to the CPA-D amendment in practice: experience of a judge]. Podjetje in delo 6–7:1649–1655

Wedam Lukić D (1996) Pravica do sodnega varstva civilnih pravic in obveznosti [Right to judicial protection of civil rights and obligations]. Zbornik znanstvenih razprav PF v Ljubljani 1:303–321

Wedam Lukić D (2003) Vloga in odgovornost sodnika v civilnem pravdnem postopku [The role and responsibilities of the judge in litigation]. Podjetje in delo 6–7:1667–1676

Wedam Lukić D (2009) Profesor Stojan Cigoj in civilno procesno pravo [Professor Stojan Cigoj and law of civil procedure]. In: Pavčnik M (ed) Stojan Cigoj: 1920–1989: zbornik razprav s simpozija SAZU ob 20-letnici smrti. SAZU, Ljubljana, pp 55–64

Wedam Lukić D (2012) Ustavnopravni vidiki izvajanja dokazov v pravdnem postopku [Constitutional aspects of taking of evidence in civil procedure]. Podjetje in delo 6–7:1384–1393

Zobec J (2007) Predlagane novosti glede zamudne sodbe in posledic izostanka ter glede vmesne sodbe [The proposed novelties concerning the judgment by default and the interim judgment]. Podjetje in delo 6–7:1045–1065

Zobec J (2009) Zloraba procesnih pravic [Abuse of procedural rights]. Podjetje in delo 6–7: 1369–1383

Chapter 12
Judicial Activism as Goals Setting – Civil Justice in Brazil

Teresa Arruda Alvim Wambier

This chapter was inspired by the intelligent and well-posed questions of Professor Alan Uzelac. On many issues I found it difficult to provide a simple yes or no answer. What was needed was to find a very delicate balance between the contrasted positions. If to some this may seem like sitting on the fence, I would argue that it is not the case. It is just the way things really are.

Abstract The goal of civil justice in Brazil is to resolve disputes between individuals and also to solve problems generated by inappropriate activities of the government. Nowadays, we do have neutral and impartial judges, but circumstances, such as the huge number of suits and appeals, and also a considerable and undesirable level of bureaucracy create difficulties for the judiciary to perform well.

12.1 Opinions on the Goals of Civil Justice: From Resolving Individual Disputes to Judges as Legislators

The goal of civil justice in Brazil is, according to most Brazilian legal writers (academics), to resolve conflicts or disputes[1] between A and B[2] in accordance with the law.[3] When we say 'in accordance with the law', in Brazil we mean

[1] Our Code of Civil Procedure was conceived in a very individualistic society. Thus, its structure is in fact suitable to resolving disputes between individuals and not group conflicts. Zavascki (1997: 173).

[2] Although, as will be seen below, we have a very well-developed class action system, it is not in our Code of Civil Procedure.

[3] In fact, contemporary legal writers recognise that civil procedure also has social and political goals. It serves to allow individuals to exercise their citizenship. Dinamarco (2009: 135).

T.A.A. Wambier (✉)
Catholic University of São Paulo, Rua Hildebrando Cordeiro, 30, Ecoville, Brazil
e-mail: teresa@wambier.adv.br

A. Uzelac (ed.), *Goals of Civil Justice and Civil Procedure in Contemporary Judicial Systems*, Ius Gentium: Comparative Perspectives on Law and Justice 34,
DOI 10.1007/978-3-319-03443-0_12,

statutory law, as Brazil is a civil law jurisdiction.[4] This is a typical academic approach.

But, in fact, on many occasions civil justice has the goal of solving problems generated by inappropriate activity of the government[5] and, in these cases, judges have to decide based on norms which are verbally formulated with the use of vague or cloudy concepts and legal principles, which sometimes are not even written. In statutory law these cases are normally resolved in the context of class actions.[6]

Exactly in this kind of conflict between society, represented by one of its bodies, and the government, the serious issue of judicial activism arises. Judges have to 'create' solutions, ways to solve problems, because in most cases they have to find a way to resolve conflicts which were not previously thought of by the legislator. Many times judges act as if they were part of the administrative branch of the government (*pouvoir exécutif*).[7]

Judges sometimes act as if they were the legislative branch of the government because they have to resolve disputes having the last word on a very important legal issue (*quaestio juris*). Usually, these disputes involve a large group of people (class actions), but not necessarily. In these conflicts or disputes, the final word of the judiciary is *law* (completes the real meaning of the norm) and prevents new disputes involving the same theme.

This is a very relevant new role of the judiciary, mainly related to the courts which are at the top of the structure of the judiciary.

In 2004, there was an amendment to our Federal Constitution, which included in our legal system what we call *súmula vinculante*. This could be roughly translated as 'binding precedent', but it is not at all a precise translation, because, in fact, it is not a precedent: it is a 'summary' of a line of precedents issued by the Brazilian Supreme Court (STF), which denotes its 'opinion' on a specific *quaestio juris*, and must necessarily be respected or adopted by all other courts and judges, and by the administrative branch.

This legal concept, *súmula vinculante*, is the most expressive example of this last function or role of the judiciary: 'creating' law. Thus, since the above-mentioned amendment, the Supreme Court can, in a very peculiar way, create law, but always respecting the formal limits established by the Brazilian Constitution that provides

---

[4] Although there are some typical characteristics of common law systems: e.g. small claims are treated in a special fashion and, as was said before, we also have class actions, inspired by the North American system. Barbosa Moreira (1998: 87).

[5] In fact, inappropriate activity of the government generates lawsuits and also their conduct during proceedings is not always ideal, but there are unfortunately not very reliable statistics on this problem.

[6] There are often nowadays lawsuits (normally class actions, but not only these) against the Government to obtain medicines (RE 607381/SC – STF) or a specific medical treatment (REsp 872733/SP – STJ) or the restructuring of hospitals and maternities for them to respond in an adequate fashion to the needs of the underprivileged (REsp 1041197/MS – STJ).

[7] The judiciary can exceptionally play this role, mainly when the government refuses citizens the attainment of essential goods, in relation to their social rights. (*Arguição de Descumprimento de Preceito Fundamental* nº 45).

a very specific procedure which must be followed. The 'precedent' is said to be 'binding', because, as said before, other judges, courts and bodies of public administration must obey what has been decided by the Supreme Court, as if its decision were a rule. Of course, to understand this trait of the Brazilian legal system, it is convenient to remember that Brazil is a civil law jurisdiction, so we are not familiar with *stare decisis* as in common law systems.

This peculiar legislative activity of the Supreme Court can take place when a controversy over a constitutional issue creates a state of uncertainty and there is a large number of claims with the same cause of action.

Initially, this innovation, now familiar to the legal community (lawyers, judges, courts and so on), caused some apprehension. For some, the peculiar legislative activity of the Supreme Court is a threat to the autonomy of the three branches of government, because it means that this court performs the typical role of the legislature (Wambier et al. 2005: 374). Others are concerned about the decrease in judicial 'creativity' and, therefore, the loss of independence of the judges and the courts, to the detriment of democracy itself (Shimura 2005: 761).

The exception was made because there were more pros than cons. In fact, with its peculiar legislative activity the Supreme Court can perform a relevant role, imposing the application of constitutional principles such as legal predictability, uniformity, legal certainty and equality. Furthermore, the adoption of binding *súmulas* also allows rationalization of the judicial activity and provides dispute resolution in a reasonable time (Martins 2009: 313). As a result, the role of the Supreme Court contributes effectively to reducing social tensions (Shimura 2005: 762). Since the aforementioned constitutional amendment, there have been 32 binding *súmulas*, created within the limits established in the Brazilian Federal Constitution.

The Federal Constitution also provides a very peculiar procedure that can be used, in case a judge, court or any body of public administration does not respect the *súmula vinculante* of the Supreme Court. It is a special claim, called *Reclamação*, that one can file before the Supreme Court and that has, as cause of action, the disobedience of a *súmula vinculante*. But there are some restrictions, for instance: this claim cannot be filed when the disobedience happens in a judicial act, which may be challenged by an appeal to the very same Supreme Court, according to procedural law.[8]

12.2 Brazilian Specialty: Class Actions

Generally speaking, social regulation is the task of the legislative and administrative branches of government. When something does not work or works badly, the judiciary should intervene, provoked by an individual party. However, a special feature of

[8] Thus: Rcl 11859 AgR, Relator Ministro Teori Zavascki, Tribunal Pleno, julgado em 23/05/2013, publicado em 14/06/2013.

civil justice in Brazil is the availability of a class action, where action may be filed by an entity expressly authorized by statutory law.

The Brazilian system of class actions is very well developed.[9] In fact, complex matters are frequently handled within this context. In class actions, mainly when they are filed against the government, courts have to exercise the complex functions of social regulators. For example, an action was filed against the *Prefeitura de São Paulo* (City Council) and the judge ordered it to reserve vacancies at a day care centre for mothers to leave their children when they go to work.[10] The regulatory role, often exercised by class actions, is being increasingly considered one of the main goals of civil justice in Brazil (Mancuso 2004; Dinamarco 2001; Lenza 2003; Leonel 2002).

Brazilian *class actions*[11] are a rather well-developed field of our civil procedural law. Today, we have a sophisticated system of class actions. Brazilian legislation is very detailed in what concerns the kinds of rights which are protected; *res judicata*,[12] *lis pendens*,[13] and other important aspects are expressly dealt with.

Class actions can be considered a powerful device to improve access to justice and to balance a lack of power over companies and government. Class actions are a device to resolve disputes over rights or duties found in society to which no one is specially or specifically entitled, and sometimes claims of various plaintiffs revolving around some legal issue.

Which point, or points, actually makes class actions different from individual ones? Mainly two points: standing and *res judicata*. Rules of standing and *res judicata* are two sides of the same coin. A class action is brought by a representative claimant (collective standing) without the express consent of all the represented persons. And the outcome of the action shall bind the group as a whole.

In Brazil, class actions can only be brought by those identified by the statute: social unions, associations, prosecutors of the Office of the Attorney General (*Ministère Public*) and so on. Judges cannot evaluate the adequacy of representation on a case-by-case basis, as in the USA.

In the *res judicata* regime there is something special: specific rules of *res judicata* in Brazilian class actions do not bind absentees if the judgment is not favourable to their interests. And, furthermore, there shall be no *res judicata* at all if there is a

[9] We could speak of a scientific revolution (Venturi 2007: 24).

[10] See REsp 736.524/SP, Rel. Min. Luiz Fux, STJ, 21/03/2006.

[11] On the subject: Gidi (1995), Barbosa Moreira (1991), Grinover (1986, 2002, 2005), Gomes Junior (2008), Mazzilli (2011).

[12] Latin for 'the thing has been judged', meaning the issue before the court has already been decided by another court, between the same parties. Therefore, the court will dismiss the case before it as being useless. Example: an Ohio court determines that John is the father of Betty's child. John cannot raise the issue again in another state. Sometimes called *res adjudicata*. Available at http://dictionary.law.com/Default.aspx?selected=1825 access 04/07/2011.

[13] Latin for 'a suit pending', a written notice that a lawsuit has been filed which concerns the title to real property or some interest in that real property. Available at http://dictionary.law.com/Default.aspx?selected=1172 access 04/07/2011.

defeat due to insufficient evidence. The same class action can be brought again if new evidence is found and presented.

We now talk about (a) diffuse rights, (b) collective rights and (c) homogeneous individual rights. These three types of rights correspond to three kinds of class actions, each with a slightly different procedure and scope of judgment.

1. A diffuse right (Mazzilli 2011; Prade 1987: 57–58; Mancuso 1987: 49; Figueiredo 1988: 105; Grinover 1984: 30–31; Bastos 1981: 40; Rocha 1992: 174–175; Benjamim 1995: 93) belongs to a universe of indeterminate people, not previously connected and linked only by factual circumstances. For example, we all have the right to breathe clean air or live in an ecologically balanced environment.[14]
2. A collective right (Cassales 1996; Benjamim 1995: 94; Mazzilli 2011) belongs to a specific group, where persons are linked to each other by a legal relationship, pre-existing the lawsuit (Watanabe 2005: 803), e.g. rights which belong to a specific professional category, such as lawyers[15] or fishermen.
3. The homogeneous individual rights (Mazzilli 2011) are the 'old' rights (as the *droit sujectif* of French law) which can be the object of a collective treatment, if they have a common origin (Dinamarco 2001: 60).

An example of these rights emerges from the situation of clients of a bank from which excessive fees have been charged; or that of a consumer enticed by false advertising, for example, to acquire beverages that contain prizes in the bottle tops but that, due to printing errors, nullify the right to the prize; and also those consumers who purchase vehicles produced with factory defects; or people who take out loans that contravene national legislation or omit essential information.[16]

Those who can take the initiative of filing claims against (or suing) the State, companies, etc. 'represent' a group of persons, the community or the whole society. They are specifically mentioned or named by statutory law. In Brazil, we did not adopt the system of adequate legitimacy or standing.

The effects of the final decision on the case affect all those who are 'represented' unless the decision is based on a lack of evidence. In this case, the claim can be presented again.

The inversion of the burden of proof is also possible, that is, it is possible for a judge to decide not to apply the rule, according to which, each of the parties has to produce evidence of the allegations of fact that he or she made. These proceedings are normally used (employed) in environmental matters, consumer law and in general questions or problems related to financial institutions.

[14] On this subject: REsp 28222/ SP 1992/0026117-5 rel. Mina. Nancy Andrighi. Available at: https://ww2.stj.jus.br/revistaeletronica/ita.asp?registro=199200261175&dt_publicacao=15/10/2001

[15] REsp 331403/ RJ – Rel. Ministro João Otávio de Noronha, DJ 29/05/2006. Lawyers could only claim for something related to their professional group.

[16] TRF 2ª Região. Agravo em Ação Civil Pública 2006.02.01.004411-3, rel. Desembargador Federal Frederico Gueiros. DJ. 13/06/2007.

12.3 Matters Regarded to Be Within the Scope of the Goals of Civil Justice

Are the goals of civil justice limited to litigation (decision-making in contested matters), or do they also encompass non-contested matters? What is the portion of the work of civil justice in matters such as enforcement, holding of registers (land, company registers), collection of non-contested debt, regulation of future relationships between the parties, etc.? To which extent are the goals of civil justice viewed from the perspective of such tasks of the civil courts?

It is within the scope of the judiciary in Brazil to organize and oversee certain activities which, while having legal connotations, are not encompassed by the legal sphere as such, for example property deeds and debt collection. However, these activities do not qualify as judicial activities though they are monitored and organized by the judicial branch.

Furthermore, it is thought that certain procedures that are carried out before judges require them to perform acts which many are reluctant to qualify as being within the scope of the judiciary. This occurs mainly with proceedings which, in Brazilian civil procedure, are known as 'voluntary judicial proceedings' and in which, according to the majority of legal doctrine, the judge plays a chiefly administrative role, as opposed to those procedures marked by the existence of a conflict of interest.

The concern with the quality of the performance of the judiciary, in these voluntary judicial proceedings, is unequivocal. Proof of this is the attempt to simplify some of the procedures, as was noted with regard to the specific hypotheses of amicable divorce and testament executions, which can be processed without the intervention of a judge and before an extrajudicial registrar/notary.

Finally, it should be noted that in Brazil we have a mechanism (judicial proceedings) very similar to judicial review. Our Supreme Court verifies in a proper kind of action or proceedings, known as *Ação Declaratória de Inconstitucionalidade*, that a statutory law or norm does not violate or contradict the Federal Constitution. Legal writers call this a no-party, no-claim and no-defence lawsuit.

But apart from that, the main and obvious task of civil justice in Brazil is to resolve disputes. It is considered that for the judiciary to play its role (resolving disputes) in an effective way, it has to have three functions:

1. to create or to maintain practical conditions favourable to the effectiveness[17] of a judicial decision, i.e. in order for a judicial decision to be able to generate desirable effects;
2. to state if the claimant has rights (that is, a declaratory function); and
3. to carry out enforcement activities.[18]

---

[17] The main concern of legal authors is to provide a fair trial with fair results (minimal standards related to substantial due process of law) through interpretation of statutory law and creation of new legal mechanisms. Dinamarco, Cândido (2009: vol. 1, chapters 1–5).

[18] José Carlos Barbosa Moreira (2007: 3).says exactly that, also saying that this corresponds to the classifications of the types of lawsuits – cognition, enforcement and urgent measures.

Holding of registers of land or companies are not regarded to be the function of the judiciary in Brazil.

12.4 Brazilian Judiciary Between the Protection of Individual Rights and the Protection of Public Interest

In Brazilian legal doctrine it is stated that the Federal Constitution of 1988 introduced mechanisms that increased the judicialization of politics in Brazil, therefore enabling the judicial branch to exert control over public administration activities. One reaches this conclusion, among other reasons, because of the awarding of greater powers to the judiciary to control the constitutionality of the actions of government bodies/public authorities, the broadening of the scope of class actions and the establishment of the writ of injunction (by means of which the government/authorities are prompted to regulate the safeguarding of constitutional rights and freedom) (Silva 2004: 134–141).

This judicialization of politics, in so far as it interferes with the activities of the government, consequently also generates discussion regarding certain public policies. Moreover, it is also possible to state that the system of civil justice in Brazil takes into consideration public policy, morals, disrespect of the rights of a third party to give the judicial decision its final shape or design *only if the case at hand* (which has to be resolved) can be considered a *hard case*. For example, according to our criteria, hard cases are those which cannot be resolved by the traditional civil law approach.

The traditional civil law approach consists of finding a statutory provision which fits the case at hand. Nevertheless, the complexity of contemporary societies brings before our courts of law cases which cannot be so easily resolved. Judges sometimes have to make a real mixture of elements to support their decisions: statutes, analogy, legal principles.[19] Sometimes it is necessary, and, in my opinion, such conduct could be understood as judicial activism in the best possible sense.

To exemplify:

1. Should maternity leave, awarded to a mother after a baby's birth, also cover cases of adoption if statutory law only refers to the word mother?
2. Should the prisoners of the *Grupo de resistencia antifascista del primero de octubre*, who were on hunger strike and therefore likely to die, have been force-fed?
3. Can artificial insemination by a third party be considered adultery?
4. Does the policy of benign quotas respect the principle of equality?

[19] Our Supreme Court has recently declared, on the basis of the solidarity principle, the unconstitutionality of the enrolment fee for the public universities – public education should be totally public (RE 510378) and also, based on the principle of human dignity, that the handicapped should not pay for public transportation. (ADIN 2.649).

But the expression 'judicial activism'[20] can also refer to the attitude of judges who decide according to their own mind/political ideas/personal convictions, ignoring the law, on the pretext of developing the law. That happens also, but very, very rarely. Judicial activism in this sense to some extent unduly compromises predictability, which is a highly esteemed value in the Brazilian legal system.

One may also ask to what extent civil procedures should reach results that are in line with certain policies (national interest, views of ruling elites or classes, governmental programmes, suppression of illegal activities, reasons of national security, confidentiality obligations, professional privileges, etc.). Procedures[21] should reach results that are in line with certain policies when this is expressly required by statutory law.

What are the issues that the court should (in the context of the goals of civil procedure) determine *ex officio*? The general rule is that in ordinary civil matters the parties decide on the commencement, the end and the scope of proceedings. This rule has a long tradition and is often elevated to a fundamental principle – *Dispositionsmaxime/principe dispositif.*[22] Courts cannot[23] initiate proceedings on their own motion or change their scope. The possibility of *cognitio ex officio* during proceedings is extremely rare in Brazilian law. Judges can determine *ex officio* some procedural matters as for example lack of standing (lack of *legitimatio ad causam* and *ad processum*) or *res judicata*.

As a rule, a judge is limited by the claim[24] presented by the plaintiff, by the terms of the defence[25] and by the evidence brought to the proceedings, which, by the way, can be brought as a result of a judge's request,[26] complementary to the parties' activities.

In Brazil, there are also other actors or bodies, besides the court and the parties that are authorized to intervene in the judicial process. In principle, their role is to assure that the goals of civil justice are being reached. They are basically three: the

---

[20] Legal writers attribute different meanings to the phrase 'judicial activism': a judge who decides *contra legem*, a judge who collaborates with the parties, a judge who innovates, creating law, etc. Lopes (2007: 221).

[21] Naturally, when the judiciary interprets the Federal Constitution, it ends by touching political matters. Inevitably, a judge who is part of our Supreme Court interferes in political themes, for these themes represent the contents of the Federal Constitution. Dinamarco (2009: 467).

[22] According to Brazilian legal writers, the *Dispositionsmaxime* means also that a judge depends on the initiative of the parties to take evidence, i.e. on which facts the parties have alleged. *Iudex secundum alega et probata partium iudicare debet.* Cintra (2009: 64).

[23] The *Dispositionsmaxime* has very few exceptions in Brazilian law, which are in fact not really significant (Barbosa Moreira 2004: 57).

[24] In fact the *petitum* expresses simultaneously the will of claim and what the party expects from the judiciary (Wambier *et al.* 2007: 297).

[25] A judge is limited to the facts brought by the parties but not to the legal aspect. He or she can win on a very different basis as far as the law is concerned (Didier 2008: 290).

[26] This corresponds to a very recent trend in Brazilian law: a judge is considered to have more powers or a stronger power in what concerns the production of evidence. This is considered to be a valid path to reaching real equality between the parties (Bedaque 1994: 72).

Ministério Público (an organ very similar to the French *Ministère Public*), the *amicus curiae* and the *Conselho Nacional de Justiça*.

The *Ministério Público* can intervene in particular circumstances, e.g. when there is a minor involved in the proceedings as a claimant or as a defendant. The members of the *Ministério Público* can even take the initiative of filing a lawsuit (playing the claimant's role) in very special cases described specifically and explicitly by statutory law and in class actions.

The *amicus curiae* has been very recently introduced in Brazilian law. For now, it is established that it can intervene in special situations described by statutory law. But there is a clear trend in the sense that a judge can ask for the intervention of an *amicus curiae* when he or she thinks that this could lead to a better decision.[27]

Some years ago an interesting change took place in Brazil with the creation of the *Conselho Nacional de Justiça* (CNJ). Although it is a body belonging to the judicial branch (cf. art. 92, inciso I, da Constituição Federal), most of its members (a total of 15) emerge from other branches of government. The CNJ has several functions related to the quality control of the judiciary from the point of view of the 'consumer of justice' (cf. art. 103-B, § 4°). In other words, ensuring that the objectives of the activities of the judiciary are attained is one of the aims that motivated the creation and the shaping of the role of this atypical entity.[28] This is a very recent and peculiar situation in the history of Brazilian civil procedure.

The CNJ also has other roles. It is its function to exert administrative, financial and disciplinary control over other bodies of the judiciary. This is one of the reasons why the CNJ can be seen as a link between the judiciary and the society.[29]

The establishment of this body, by the last Constitutional Amendment of 2004, was heavily criticized, mainly because the participation of non-judges could result in the interference of the other branches of government in the judiciary.[30] It was said that the independence of the three branches of government would be compromised. Nevertheless, our Supreme Court does not share this opinion, for judges are not prevented from exercising their activities independently.[31]

Another important issue is the normative power that CNJ attributed to itself. A good example is Resolução 14/2006 that stipulates a limit on the salaries of judges and other civil servants in the judiciary. The CNJ, in the exercise of its regulatory powers, was also highly criticized for establishing a procedure for the trial of the

---

[27] In the *ação declaratória de inconstitucionalidade* n 4451 (which is very similar to the American judicial review), the Supreme Court admitted the Workers' Party as *amicus curiae*. The possible unconstitutionality of the statutes which prohibited any jesting or degrading manifestation towards a candidate running for any political office, or his/her party, was then discussed.

[28] This body controls the judiciary and judges of each and every instance (Dinamarco 2009: 420).

[29] Jorge (2005: 493).

[30] Barroso (2005: 425).

[31] On this subject: ADI 3367, Relator Ministro Cezar Peluso, Tribunal Pleno, julgado em 13/04/2005, publicado em 17/03/2006.

disciplinary breaches of judges, regardless of the provisions on the subject in the individual state regulations.[32]

However, since its establishment 8 years ago, the CNJ has already deterred and punished judges and other members of the judiciary, not only for committing illegal acts, but also for lack of diligence in the handling of lawsuits. It has also intervened to protect institutions that are essential to the exercise of jurisdiction, such as the practice of law, and demanded greater productivity from judicial bodies at various hierarchical levels. Furthermore, the CNJ is known for its stern measures against serious problems such as the overcrowding of prisons, the inclusion of people with disabilities in the judiciary, access to justice and the strategic planning of the judicial branch.[33]

Thus, despite the criticism aimed at its establishment and actions, it seems that the role performed by the CNJ in the improvement of the quality of judicial services rendered to society is a positive one.

12.5 'Material Truth' v. Fair Trial Within a Reasonable Time: The Rise of Interlocutory Relief

One of most delicate issues in Brazilian legal theory concerns the balance between the wish to establish the facts correctly and the need to provide effective protection of rights within an appropriate amount of time. The importance of the search for truth in the proceedings is recognized, but it is also admitted that this search cannot compromise a reasonable duration of proceedings.[34] On the other hand, one cannot state that, in Brazilian civil procedure, there is an absolute and irrevocable choice between either option.[35] In recent decades, perceptible efforts have been made by Brazilian legislators to balance the two needs, that is, to combine speed and accuracy.

In some situations, the legislator favours the timeliness of relief and allows the party to benefit in advance from the effects which would normally only be attained in the final judgment. However, a judicial provision on these terms is an exception and presupposes the fulfilment of some prerequisites, among which is the risk of losses being incurred by the party that claims the rights and the existence of elements that, at least, appear to prove the claimed rights.

---

[32] Welsch (2013: 165).

[33] Garcia (2009: 62).

[34] One of the goals of Brazilian civil procedure is to reach the truth, but certainly it is not the only one, for proceedings cannot last forever (Arruda Alvim 2005: 379).

[35] The various imperative deadlines of Brazilian civil procedure can be considered a device or a method to avoid eternal proceedings (Aragão 1976: 99). To avoid eternal proceedings, there is in Brazilian civil procedure a provision saying that if the defendant does not respond within a certain deadline, facts alleged by the claimant can be considered true by a judge, depending on the context and on certain conditions. It is a technique to speed up proceedings (Dinamarco 2000: 951).

Brazilian law is today generous in remedies based on incomplete cognition[36] (*fumus boni iuris*). That means that a judge can advance the claimant the whole effect (or just part of it) of the final judgment or decision, if there is urgency (*periculum in mora*). Normally, these effects are entirely or partly advanced under the condition of the possibility that the situation returns, in case of loss, to the *status quo ante*. If these prerequisites are not fulfilled, the party must generally wait for the final judgment, based on exhaustive cognition, to then be awarded the claimed rights.

However, upon the enactment of a new bill currently under debate by the legislature, Brazilian civil procedure will undergo significant changes with regard to interlocutory relief. In fact, the new draft bill sets forth, primarily that, regardless of the practical effects obtained from interlocutory relief, there will be no need to file an independent lawsuit for the party to request it. Many other changes will come about as a result.

Once interlocutory relief has been awarded, based on summary cognizance, the defendant is summoned and can challenge it. Should the defendant oppose the relief awarded to the plaintiff, he or she has a period of 30 days (unless otherwise determined by a judge) within which to make a main claim, which will be decided by the judge upon thorough and exhaustive appreciation of the merits. However, if the defendant does not manifest himself or herself, the case will be dismissed and the decision based on summary cognizance will remain in effect for an indeterminate period. It is up to the defendant to stop such effects by filing an action for that purpose. In said action, the judge will analyse the pertinent issues based on a thorough and exhaustive appreciation of the merits, respecting adversary proceedings and the right to be heard (Carneiro 2011: 139). It is said that there will thus be a stabilisation of interlocutory relief in Brazilian civil procedure.

The procedure, briefly described above, is not foreign to the procedural legislation currently in effect in Brazil. There are, in fact, similarities between this procedure and an action on a non-enforceable written instrument, currently governed by items 1102-A to 1102-C, of the Code of Civil Procedure, such as:

1. the rendering of the interlocutory relief decision based on summary cognizance;
2. the possibility of making a decision on the basis of the inactivity of the defendant, producing effects until there is an opposing decision, by means of an independent action filed subsequently by the defendant; and,
3. the absence of *res judicata*, with regard to the interlocutory relief decision, even when it acquires stability due to the inactivity of the defendant.

It is precisely due to such similarities that some envisage an expansion of actions on non-enforceable written instruments in the amendments relating to the abovementioned interlocutory relief (Talamini 2012: 13).

[36] Procedimento monitório. Tucci (1997), *passim*.

12.6 'Hard Cases' v. Mass Processing of Routine Matters: Macro Matters in Special Procedures and Micro System of Special Courts

Some procedures in Brazilian law are, by their very nature and applicability, better suited to the discussion of complex legal issues, which can reflect on the sphere of rights of many members of society. This is noted in procedures aimed at the achievement of the abstract control of constitutionality, as well as those that target the protection of collective rights. Hard cases, which involve the application of general clauses, vague concepts, legal principles or even total absence of explicit regulation by statutory law, are judged and decided taking into consideration all special aspects of the case at hand.

In most cases,[37] a judge is concerned with finding the correct legal solution to resolve a dispute. Of course, when a hard case has to be resolved, the solution is not explicitly described or established by statutory law. It has to be built according to analogy, legal principles or even from a reference to the predominant 'ethos'.

Statutory law indicates or even states that a judge must take into consideration statutory law, analogy, customs and general legal principles when making decisions (LICC – Decreto Lei 4057, 4/set./ 42 now called *Lei de Introdução às Normas do Direito Brasileiro*, art. 4.º). Our Federal Constitution (1988) says: nobody is obliged to do or not to do something, except as a result of the law.

A trend has been noted in the last 30 years: an increase in the number of *hard cases*. In fact, access to justice and the complexities of society brought to the judiciary unique and complex issues, frequently not expressly dealt with by statutory law. Therefore, a judge often has to make decisions based on a mix of elements: statutory law, analogy and legal principles.[38]

Besides that, Brazilian civil procedure has several tools to render practical and easy proceedings involving cases which revolve around the same issues of law.[39] These procedural tools are entirely appropriate to resolve, for example, tax matters.

In 1999 the Small Claims Act (Lei 9099) took effect in Brazil. According to two criteria, the complexity and the value of the claim, some lawsuits are filed before small claims courts. These courts are composed of lay judges, mediators and regular judges. Immediately after that, Act no. 10.259/2001 was passed, creating the so-called

---

[37] To legal writers, examples of equity judgments would be *quantum* of child support, custody of minors, fees and coercive fines fixed in injunctions (Dinamarco 2009: 332).

[38] On the basis of the free initiative principle, our Supreme Court has already decided that the supplier cannot be obliged to sell his products at a price lower than the real price of what he sells (RE 598537). On the other hand, based on the good faith and loyalty principles, our Superior Court of Justice also decided that it can be considered an abuse on the part of an insurance company to try to sign a contract with a client on a totally different basis from what was previously agreed (REsp 1105483).

[39] The Brazilian Code of Civil Procedure authorizes the hearing of appeals which revolve around the same legal issue in a collective way (arts. 543 B and C).

Special Courts[40] within the sphere of the federal justice system. It is currently thought that both acts mentioned make up the legal micro-system of the special courts, defining the specific procedures which they adopt.

There is a heated debate as to whether small claims courts are mandatory or whether they are just a choice to be made by the plaintiff. In addition, it is thought that the informal nature of proceedings before special courts could harm the party's right to defence, especially with regard to the presenting of evidence. For this reason too, it is said that it would not be possible to prohibit parties from filing a claim before another competent legal entity in accordance with the law (Dinamarco 2004: 775).

Yet, there is no real difference in the obligation of a judge to deal with small claims and 'proper' court cases.[41] In Brazil it is considered that refusal to deal with a case which could be seen as not so important, according to some criteria, in the same manner as another admittedly important case is a denial of justice. A petition cannot be refused (and neither can an appeal). There is only one filter, similar to the *Grundsätzlichebedeutung* of German law, applied only to the appeals to Supreme Court of Brazil.

12.7 Final Remarks: Brazilian Civil Justice in an Attempt to Achieve Orientation Towards the Users

Civil justice is all about a delicate balance. However, I would not hesitate to state that the main goal of civil justice is clearly solving problems, *if possible*, with the least amount of effort[42] and expense, and reaching efficient[43] results.[44] Civil justice should be oriented towards its users.

However, civil justice in Brazil is not free. One has to pay to use it. Nevertheless, it is not at all expensive and the amount paid is used within the judiciary itself (e.g. to buy equipment). Besides that, those[45] who really cannot pay for it can have the benefit of gratuity (legal aid). According to the current Brazilian law, a statement declaring poverty or insufficient means signed by the party and his or

[40] *Cortes speciais*, the separate second instance courts that decide appeals against decisions in small claims cases.

[41] Maybe the only visible difference is the major duty of judges to try to settle the parties.

[42] That is why there is very heavy criticism from Brazilian legal writers on the excessive number of appeals of our system that can be at least partly the cause of high costs, excessive duration and the great amount of work for judges (Barbosa Moreira 2003: 105).

[43] The concern with results is obvious for instance in our Small Claims Statute (Art. 59, Act of Law no. 9.099/95) which limits the forms of attack to a judicial decision.

[44] In fact, this is an old and very traditional principle of civil law jurisdictions: the least possible amount of effort should result in satisfactory efficiency (Cintra et al. 2009: 79).

[45] Including small companies, according to STJ, AReg no REsp 1226316/RS, rel. Min. Arnaldo Esteves Lima and Embargos de divergência em REsp 1015372/SP.

her lawyer is enough. Furthermore, Act 9.099 on small claims states that in any case the first instance is free.

In the last 30 years, many alterations have been included in Brazilian law to improve access to justice. It is considered that access to justice deals with the question of how easy or how difficult it is for a potential party to make use of the judicial system. High costs and long duration of proceedings are two factors which render access to justice difficult.

It is undeniable that in Brazil solutions have been devised for this problem: class actions, small claims courts, legal aid (as an exception) and we begin to consider, rightly it seems to me, that ADR also means access to justice. Access to justice must not be understood as an access to public justice. Several tools to stimulate the use of ADR are being conceived.

We cannot deny that there are some characteristics of Brazilian civil justice which are visibly oriented towards solving the problems of the system itself. The goals of civil justice in Brazil are to a large extent oriented or defined by the needs of the system itself and its professional actors, the courts, judges and lawyers. They usually propose various legislative changes and amendments to the Federal Constitution through their professional organizations (Association of Judges, Bar Association, etc.). It is true, we have to admit, that the needs of lawyers or judges do not always correspond to a benefit for those whose rights (legal situation) are at stake. But there are of course others oriented towards the users. Sometimes there is a coincidence between what judges, lawyers and other actors in the judicial scenario and the users want. And, if the result is a judiciary with better performance, everybody is happy.

References

Antonio Carlos de Araújo Cintra, Ada Pellegrini Grinover, Cândido Rangel Dinamarco (2009) Teoria Geral do Processo, 25th ed. Malheiros, São Paulo

Barbosa Moreira JC (1991) Ações Coletivas na Constituição Federal de 1988. Revista de Processo 61 (Jan to Mar). Revista dos Tribunais, São Paulo

Barbosa Moreira JC (1998) Notas sobre alguns aspectos do processo (civil e penal) nos países anglo-saxônicos. Revista de Processo, pp 92–96

Barbosa Moreira JC (2003) Breve notícia sobre a reforma do processo civil alemão. Revista de Processo, pp 107–111

Barbosa Moreira JC (2004) Reformas processuais e poderes do juiz. In: Temas de direito processual, 8.ª série. Saraiva, São Paulo

Barroso LR (2005) Constitucionalidade e legitimidade da criação do Conselho Nacional de Justiça. In: Reforma do Judiciário: primeiras reflexões sobre a emenda constitucional 45/2004. Revista dos Tribunais, São Paulo

Bastos CR (1981) A tutela dos interesses difusos no direito constitucional brasileiro. In: REPRO. 23. RT, São Paulo

Benjamim H (1995) A insurreição da aldeia global contra o processo civil clássico. Apontamentos sobre a opressão e a libertação judiciais do meio ambiente e do consumidor. In: Milaré E (ed) Ação civil pública lei 7.347/85 – Reminiscências e reflexões após dez anos de aplicação. RT, São Paulo

Carneiro AG (2011) O novo Código de Processo Civil: breve análise do projeto revisado no Senado. Revista de Processo 194 (Apr. 2011)
Cassales LD (1996) Ação Civil Pública. In: Revista da Ajufe 48 (Jan–Feb 1996). São Paulo
da Silva Dinamarco P (2001) Ação civil pública. Saraiva, São Paulo
de Aragão EM (1976) Comentários ao Código de Processo Civil. 2. Forense, Rio de Janeiro
de Araújo Cintra AC (2009) Teoria geral do processo, 25th edn. Malheiros, São Paulo
de Arruda Alvim JM (2005) Manual de direito processual civil. 9. Revista dos Tribunais 2, São Paulo
de Barros Leonel R (2002) Manual do processo coletivo. Revista dos Tribunais, São Paulo
de Camargo Mancuso R (1987) O município enquanto co-legitimado para a tutela de interesses difusos. In: Revista de Processo 48 (Oct–Dec 1987). RT, São Paulo
de Camargo Mancuso R (2004) Ação civil pública, 9th edn. Revista dos Tribunais, São Paulo
de Carvalho Rocha JC (1992) Notas sobre a composição do dano ambiental no Brasil e nos Estados Unidos da América. Revista da Procuradoria-Geral da República 1 (Oct–Dec 1992). RT, São Paulo
de Castro Lopes ME (2007) Ativismo judicial e ônus da prova no processo civil. Revista do Instituto dos Advogados de São Paulo, pp 19–224
Didier F Jr (2008) Curso de direito processual civil, 10th edn. Podivum, Salvador
Dinamarco C (2000) Fundamentos e alcance do efeito da revelia. In: Fundamentos do processo civil moderno, 3rd edn. Malheiros, São Paulo
Dinamarco C (2004) Instituições de direito processual civil, 4th edn. Malheiros, São Paulo
Dinamarco C (2009) Instituições de direito processual civil, 6th edn. Malheiros, São Paulo
dos Santos Bedaque JR (1994) Direito e processo: influência do direito material sobre o processo 2. Revista dos Tribunais, São Paulo
Figueiredo LV (1988) Direitos difusos na Constituição de 1988. Revista de Direito Público 88 (Oct–Dec 1988). RT, São Paulo
Garcia RB (2009) O poder judiciário e as políticas públicas no Brasil: análise doutrinária e evolução casuística. Revista dos Tribunais (Jan/2009) 879
Gidi A (1995) Coisa julgada e litispendência em ações coletivas. Saraiva, São Paulo
Gomes Junior LM (2008) Curso de Direito Processual Civil Coletivo, 2nd edn. SRS Editora, São Paulo
Grinover AP (1984) A problemática dos interesses difusos. In: A tutela dos interesses difusos. Max Limonad, São Paulo
Grinover AP (1986) Ações Coletivas para a Tutela do Meio Ambiente e dos Consumidores – a Lei 7.347, de 24.7.85. Revista de Processo 11(44) (Oct to Dec 1986). Revista dos Tribunais, São Paulo
Grinover AP (2002) Ações Coletivas ibero-americanas: novas questões sobre a legitimação e a coisa julgada. Revista Forense 361. São Paulo: Forense
Grinover AP (2005) Código Brasileiro de Defesa do Consumidor: comentado pelos autores do anteprojeto, 8th edn. Forense Universitária, Rio de Janeiro
Jorge MH (2005) O Conselho Nacional de Justiça e o controle externo administrativo, financeiro e disciplinar do Poder Judiciário: violação do pacto federativo. In: Reforma do Judiciário: primeiras reflexões sobre a emenda constitucional 45/2004. Revista dos Tribunais, São Paulo
Lenza P (2003) Teoria geral da ação civil pública. Revista dos Tribunais, São Paulo
Martins SG (2009) Súmula vinculante. Revista de Processo 172 (jun 2009):313
Mazzilli HN (2011) A defesa dos interesses difusos em juízo meio ambiente, consumidor, patrimônio cultural, patrimônio público e outros interesses, 24th edn. Saraiva, São Paulo
Moreira JCB (2007) O novo processo civil brasileiro, 25th edn. Forense, Rio de Janeiro
Prade P (1987) Conceito de interesses difusos, 2nd edn. RT, São Paulo
Shimura SS (2005) Súmula vinculante. In: Reforma do Judiciário: primeiras reflexões sobre a emenda constitucional 45/2004. Revista dos Tribunais, São Paulo
Silva CA (2004) O processo civil como estratégia de poder: reflexo da judicialização da política no Brasil. Renovar, Rio de Janeiro
Talamini E (2012) Tutela de urgência no projeto de novo Código de Processo Civil: a estabilização da medida urgente e a 'monitorização' do processo civil brasileiro. Revista de Processo 209 (Jul/2012)

Tucci JRC (1997) Tempo e processo. Revista dos Tribunais, São Paulo

Venturi E (2007) Processo civil coletivo. Malheiros, São Paulo

Wambier LR, Wambier TAA, Medina JMG (2005) Repercussão geral e súmula vinculante: relevantes novidades trazidas pela EC 45/2004. In: Reforma do Judiciário: primeiras reflexões sobre a emenda constitucional 45/2004. Revista dos Tribunais, São Paulo

Wambier LR et al (2007) Curso avançado de processo civil, 9th edn. Revista dos Tribunais 1, São Paulo

Watanabe K (2005) Código Brasileiro de Defesa do Consumidor: comentado pelos autores do anteprojeto, 8th edn. Forense Universitária, Rio de Janeiro

Welsch GM (2013) O poder normativo do CNJ: possibilidade de criação, modificação e restrição de direitos fundamentais. Revista de Processo 218 (Apr/2013)

Zavascki TA (1997) Reforma do sistema processual civil brasileiro e a reclassificação da tutela jurisdicional. Revista de Processo, pp 88–175

About the Authors

Inge Lorange Backer Professor of Law at the University of Oslo (Norway). Former assistant judge at district court. Former Director General and head of the Legislation Department of the Norwegian Ministry of Justice. Former Chair of the European Committee of Legal Co-operation (CDCJ, Council of Europe, 2002–2004). Honorary Doctorate in Law from Uppsala University (2006).

David Chan Called to the Hong Kong Bar in 2000. Specializes in civil litigation, including personal injuries, landlord and tenant, employment, employees' compensation, commercial law, company law, building management, family law and tort claims. From September 2009 to June 2013, he was a Teaching Fellow at the School of Law of the City University of Hong Kong (Hong Kong, China).

Peter C.H. Chan Teaching Fellow at the School of Law, City University of Hong Kong (Hong Kong, China). Former litigation and regulatory lawyer. Specializes in comparative civil procedure, Chinese civil justice and Chinese legal history.

Gergely Czoboly Lecturer at the Department of Civil Procedure and Legal Sociology at the University of Pécs (Hungary), fellow of the Institute for Legal Studies, Center for Social Sciences, Hungarian Academy of Sciences. Research and teaching in the area of comparative civil procedure and international insolvency law.

Fu Yulin Professor at Peking University School of Law. Specializes in civil procedure, arbitration, evidence, and resolution of civil and commercial disputes in China. Former judge at the Maritime Court and current arbitrator in CIETAC and BAC. Member of the expert group of the draft of the CPL of China 2012. Member of the International Association of Procedural Law (IAPL).

Aleš Galič Associate Professor at the University of Ljubljana, Faculty of Law, and a legal advisor to the Constitutional Court of Slovenia. His major interests in teaching and research are Civil Procedure, International and European Civil Procedure, Arbitration and Alternative Dispute Resolution. Member of the International Association of Procedural Law (IAPL).

A. Uzelac (ed.), *Goals of Civil Justice and Civil Procedure in Contemporary Judicial Systems*, Ius Gentium: Comparative Perspectives on Law and Justice 34,
DOI 10.1007/978-3-319-03443-0,

Miklos Kengyel Chair of the Department of Civil Procedure and Legal Sociology at the University of Pecs (Hungary). Part-time Professor of Comparative Civil Procedure at Andrassy Gyula University in Budapest. Former Dean and Rector. Research and teaching in the area of European, international and comparative civil procedure, evidence and legal culture. Member of the Council of the International Association of Procedural Law (IAPL).

Christian Koller Post-doctoral researcher and Lecturer at the University of Vienna, Department for Civil Procedure. Specializes in international commercial arbitration and litigation, civil procedure, international insolvency law, conflict of laws and comparative law. Acting Co-Chair of the Young Austrian Arbitration Practitioners.

Richard Marcus Horace O. Coil Chair in Litigation at California's Hastings College of Law, San Francisco. Co-author of leading American casebooks on complex litigation and civil procedure, and author of discovery volumes of the leading US treatise on federal practice and procedure. Associate Reporter of the Advisory Committee on Civil rules of the US Judicial Conference. Principal author of the draft of the rules for electronic discovery adopted for US federal courts in 2006, and revisions of the US federal court class action rule in 2003. Member of the Council of the International Association of Procedural Law (IAPL).

Dmitry Heroldovich Nokhrin Advisor to the vice-chairman of the Constitutional Court of the Russian Federation. Graduated from Khabarovsk State Academy of Economics and Law in 2003. Post-graduate studies from 2003 to 2006 at Lomonosov Moscow State University, completed with presentation of a dissertation on compulsory mechanisms in civil procedure. Former consultant at the Law Department of the Russian Federal Assembly (Duma).

Elisabetta Silvestri Associate Professor of Civil Procedure and Comparative Civil Procedure at the University of Pavia, Italy. Graduated from University of Pavia; LL.M. received from Cornell Law School. Visiting scholar at Yale Law School and London School of Economics. Co-director of the Public and Private Justice seminar at the Inter-University Centre Dubrovnik.

Alan Uzelac Professor of Law at the University of Zagreb (Croatia), where he teaches comparative civil procedure, organization of judiciary and alternative dispute resolution. Founding member of the European Commission for the Efficiency of Justice (CEPEJ) in Strasbourg. Co-director of the Public and Private Justice seminar at the Inter-University Centre Dubrovnik. Member of the Council of the International Association of Procedural Law (IAPL).

C.H. (Remco) van Rhee Chair of European Legal History and Comparative Civil Procedure, Maastricht University, the Netherlands. Director of the research program 'Foundations and Principles of Civil Procedure in Europe' of the Ius Commune Research School. Co-director of the Public and Private Justice seminar at the Inter-University Centre Dubrovnik. Member of the Council of the International Association of Procedural Law (IAPL).

Teresa Arruda Alvim Wambier Professor of Civil Procedure at the Catholic University of São Paulo (Brazil). Part-time Professor at the Universidade Paranaense (Brazil). General reporter (appointed by the Senate) of a Bill for a New Civil Procedural Code, which is currently in the Legislative. Practicing lawyer, member of the Bar. President of the Brazilian Institute of Procedural Law (IBDP). Vice President of the Instituto Ibero-Americano de Direito Processual (IIDP). Member of the Council of the International Association of Procedural Law (IAPL).

CPSIA information can be obtained at www.ICGtesting.com
Printed in the USA
LVOW10*1621240114

370837LV00001B/122/P

9 783319 034423